HOW TO OPEN A CHESS GAME

HOW TO OPEN A CHESS GAME

by

Larry Evans
Svetozar Gligoric
Vlastimil Hort
Paul Keres
Bent Larsen
Tigran Petrosian
Lajos Portisch

SIDNEY FRIED, Publisher

BURT HOCHBERG, Editor-in-Chief

R.H.M. Press

a division of R.H.M. Associates of Delaware, Inc.
417 Northern Boulevard, Great Neck, N.Y. 11021

R.H.M. Press
a division of R.H.M. Associates of Delaware, Inc.
417 Northern Boulevard, Great Neck, N.Y. 11021

Library of Congress Catalog Card No: 74-17848

ISBN 0-89058-003-0

Printed in the United States of America

Table of Contents

Acknowledgments

The editor wishes to express his gratitude to the following persons who assisted in the preparation of this book:

Mr. Frank Krcmar, who translated the Hort chapter;

Mr. Endre Boer, who translated the Portisch chapter;

Mr. Hanon Russell, who translated the Petrosian chapter;

Mr. George Mirijanian, who translated the Keres chapter;

Mr. Chris Reid, whose editing and proofreading skills were invaluable;

Mr. Scott Knoke, who contributed long and unusual hours of his time to solve many difficult technical problems.

Symbols

Chess writers use annotative symbols in different ways to mean different things. Context is often the only way to determine the writer's exact intention; for example, an exclamation mark may be used to denote a good move, a surprising move, a new move in a known variation, a good psychological choice, etc.

Some publishers, aiming at a universal system of symbols to give their publications international appeal by avoiding written language completely, use so many symbols that learning them is as difficult as learning a new language (and languages, after all, are nothing more than sets of symbols).

Believing both in the expressive and communicative power of words, and in simplicity regarding symbols, we use only the following ones:

! A good move, better than the alternatives.

!! An excellent, beautiful, or hard-to-find move.

? A poor move.

?? A very poor move; a blunder.

!? A risky move worth trying.

?! A dubious, risky move.

Publisher's Foreword

This remarkable book—HOW TO OPEN A CHESS GAME—had its origin in our first chess book—SAN ANTONIO '72. We had thrown a party for the leading grandmasters at the San Antonio International Tournament and all of us were sitting around in a comfortable circle involved in "chess talk" when this writer interjected an idea. How would it be, we suggested, if each of you leading grandmasters wrote down your thoughts about how a serious chess amateur might best approach the problem of, very simply, "opening" a chess game? What objectives were worth seeking? What should be avoided? Were there some simplified and promising approaches which would carry the player more safely towards the middle game without being quickly crushed by immediately superior strategy on the part of his opponent?

In other words, we asked the grandmasters—if you had carte blanche to write a chapter on "How to Open a Chess Game," just what would you put into it?

Luckily for us, and now for you, the reader, considering the excellence in chess which will spread before you in the pages to come, each grandmaster present was greatly intrigued by the challenge presented in the above questions and agreed to do a chapter as suggested. The result, after *much* work, is in your hands.

There is a postscript here. Present at our San Antonio party was a young grandmaster who disclaimed the idea that he was ready to put his writing alongside such chess-olympian names as Petrosian, Keres, Gligoric, Larsen, Portisch, Hort and Evans. His name was Anatoly Karpov, and many times in the next year we berated ourselves for not insisting more strongly that he should venture a contribution to the book.

But we made up for it in the Nice Olympiad in 1974 when we had the pleasure of speaking to *many* top grandmasters, and after numbers of individual and then collective discussions, there was born the concept of THE R.H.M. SURVEY OF CURRENT CHESS OPENINGS. The chess luminaries who shine in this project are given in the description in the back of the book—it is a most impressive list of Contributing Editors—and we are most happy to report that they include not only the Anatoly Karpov we missed in San Antonio, but also that bright star in the chess firmament, Viktor Korchnoi.

Please be sure to carefully read the description of THE R.H.M. SURVEY OF CURRENT CHESS OPENINGS which follows the last chapter in this book. This new survey will, we feel certain, prove of immeasurable help to all chess players in attaining rapid forward progress in the quality of their play.

We take this opportunity to thank you for your interest in R.H.M. chess publications.

Sidney Fried
Publisher

HOW TO OPEN A CHESS GAME

Introduction

by Larry Evans

From the Horse's Mouth

As the only American grandmaster among the authors of this book, I was asked tc comment on the contributions of my colleagues. Since each chapter is filtered through a different personality, this is a uniquely valuable but somewhat unusual book of instruction. My task is to help you use it most effectively.

When the seven of us (among others) took part in the great international tournament in San Antonio 1972, R.H.M.'s publisher Sidney Fried and editor-in-chief Burt Hochberg prevailed on us to do a book about openings unlike any ever done before. Their idea was to enable the student to see how seven leading grandmasters individually approach this phase of the game. They did not want just columns of analysis—deadwood to memorize—but an insight into chess philosophy. They wanted to provide the chess public with the distilled experience of the world's leading players—how they learned the openings, what they learned, how they developed their attitudes, their styles.

What emerged were the answers to these questions, and many more: How is it possible to be creative despite reams of existing opening literature? What does a grandmaster think about when he sits down at the board? How does he prepare for each contest? What guides his selection of the next move? When should a principle be violated?

Apart from my own chapter on basic opening principles, which lays the groundwork for the discussions that follow, each grandmaster wrote as he pleased. None was given a specific topic or assignment. The result is a remarkable group portrait, as varied, rich and fascinating as the game which binds us together despite the distance separating us.

If there is one common thread, it is this: think for yourself, accept nothing on faith, avoid playing by rote. Each position is new even if you have seen it thousands of times. A chess master is practical, flexible. He learned how the chess pieces work by tinkering with every master game he could find and taking it apart move by move, just as all beginners do. In the end he developed a protective hide, a routine to find good moves quickly. And a style.

What fascinated me as I read the manuscript was how we all developed distinct styles despite our adherence essentially to the same chess principles. Given any position at random and asked to find the best move, there would be little disagreement. Yet our games are as different as our fingerprints. While some are as loathe to trade a Bishop for a Knight as a Cadillac for a Chevrolet, others are prepared to do so without hesitation. While Petrosian concentrates on snuffing out his opponent's counterchances, Larsen is intent on augmenting his own dynamic potential. There are many ways to play chess!

The chapters have been arranged for smooth reading. My work is addressed to the beginner, Keres's to the more advanced player. Start anywhere, go backward or forward. You will find much to inform, much to provoke. When you finish you will play the opening with new vigor and precision, regardless of your present strength.

CHAPTER 1

Larry Evans (USA): "The opening—roughly the first dozen moves —is a fight for space, time, and force."

A player who understands basic principles and applies them consistently will rarely be slaughtered in the opening. Time, space and material are the basic building blocks. The chess master manipulates these elements like a chemist; the chess board is his laboratory. Advantages in time and space seem to evaporate, while material advantages are durable and manifest themselves decisively as the endgame approaches. In general, the whole process of chess technique consists of converting the less durable into the more durable advantage.

In the opening, White strives for the initiative and Black for equality. The modern master makes almost no attempt to win rapidly against a strong opponent but is content to accumulate small advantages which, hopefully, can be exploited in the middlegame.

Gambits pose the conflict between time and force in pure form. White sacrifices a pawn or two in the opening for a quick attack. Black can clutch this material for dear life or return it prudently at an opportune moment. The resulting simplification generally resolves the tension and neutralizes White's attack. This is why gambits have all but disappeared from modern master play, to be replaced by slow positional maneuvering.

Positional judgment can be acquired by practice and the study of master games. An effective way of replaying these games is to cover up the next move and try to predict it. This may prove frustrating at first, but eventually you will develop a real feeling for tactical and strategical considerations.

CHAPTER 2

Svetozar Gligoric (Yugoslavia): "The art of treating the opening stage of the game correctly and without error is basically the art of using time efficiently."

The best way to understand a principle is to watch it in action. It is difficult to apply the right principle in the heat of battle, especially when it conflicts with another principle. When is a violation of principle acceptable and when is it not?

We acquire positional judgment by studying master games. Accordingly, Gligoric analyzes deeply and in plain language eight battles which are decided essentially in the opening. He turns his penetrating gaze on the fight for time, the center, space, material, and Bobby Fischer's "secret weapon"—the fight for the initiative, an unrelenting search for the sharpest continuation, allowing the opponent no respite.

"Each move is a treasure, to be spent only in the most useful way," says Gligoric. If there are rules, there are exceptions, and we are scarcely surprised when he describes a move as "another useful loss of time" and then explains why. No less instructive is his discussion on limiting the opponent's potential.

CHAPTER 3

Vlastimil Hort (Czechoslovakia): "I may say that the production of a *constant and uninterrupted* series of really best moves borders on, or is even beyond, the limits of human capabilities."

The theory of the opening is constantly evolving, even though games separated by a great span in time may have much in common. The principles of sound opening play are constant and were set forth in Nimzovich's *My System,* a book that deeply influenced every generation since its publication in 1925.

To Hort, "the guiding principle of the struggle on the chess board is the fight for the initiative" which in turn "provokes the strongest resistance on the part of the opponent," resulting in the perpetual quest for the best move by both. But is it possible to sustain such an exhausting pace in each and every game? Between two equal grandmasters entering the same tournament, Hort prefers the practical chances of the rested one who relies on intuition to the one who spends himself in the opening on the search for the best move. Although it is axiomatic that best play on both sides leads to a draw, a decisive result is more likely when two opponents search for the best move.

A player with a well-developed feeling for position can enjoy great success by specializing in very few openings. Hort argues, in agreement with Botvinnik, that "memorization of variations could be even worse than playing in a tournament without looking in the books at all." To verify this, I recall the discomfiture of a noted American master who shrugged off a loss by saying that he "crisscrossed columns."

To supplement his theoretical discussion, Hort examines eight of his games (including two that he lost). He concludes with a detailed analysis of an unorthodox opening (1 P-Q4 N-KB3 2 B-N5) and some cogent thoughts on the Caro-Kann, Sicilian and Ruy Lopez.

CHAPTER 4

Lajos Portisch (Hungary): "Your only task in the opening is to reach a playable middlegame."

Each player must develop his own opening repertoire and not merely ape the "fashion designers." Unless you are a professional with unlimited time for study, it is better for you to specialize in a few openings characterized by simplicity and economy. Portisch proceeds to show how his own chess matured despite some "unusual but simple" openings he has used in his career.

The Exchange Variation of the Ruy Lopez (1 P-K4 P-K4 2 N-KB3 N-QB3 3 B-N5 P-QR3 4 B×N) offers White safety and can be played for a lifetime. After analyzing alternatives for Black on the third move, Portisch moves on to an extended study of the "solid" French Defense (1 P-K4 P-K3). He then recommends a closed system against the Sicilian (1 P-K4 P-QB4 2 N-QB3), an exchange against the Caro-Kann (1 P-K4 P-QB3 2 P-Q4 P-Q4 3 P×P), and "the most secure way" of combatting the Pirc Defense.

Turning to the closed openings, he advises a simple system where the first four White moves consist of 1 N-KB3, 2 P-KN3, 3 B-N2 and 4 O-O, known as the Barcza System or the King's Indian Attack. He concludes the study of the closed systems with concrete analysis of the King's Indian, English, Queen's Gambit Declined and Nimzo-Indian Defense.

"The purpose of my discussion has been to demonstrate ways in which the major well-analyzed variations can be avoided, if we choose to study on our own."

CHAPTER 5

Tigran Petrosian (USSR): "Even the most distinguished players have in their careers experienced severe disappointments due to ignorance of the best lines or suspension of their own common sense."

The former World Champion cites some amusing disasters from his own career to illustrate how he lost blind faith in the printed chess word. "Oh, those exclamation points!" he cries. "How they erode the innocent soul of the amateur, removing all hope of allowing him to examine another player's ideas critically!"

A game is an organic whole, and to disjoint the opening from the middlegame is, in effect, "to separate the head from the body." In addition, it is important to penetrate the opponent's thoughts. Petrosian advocates subtle psychological warfare: "Occasionally an opening is used against an opponent who is known to favor it himself. The idea is to force him to fight against his own weapons, when he will have to face not only real dangers but very often imaginary ones as well."

Petrosian reveals how he prepared a defense against Fischer in their 1971 match by studying Fischer's pet variations as "carefully as a field engineer with a mine detector." Indeed, their first four games gave Fischer quite a fright. Petrosian is one of the most original and mystifying players in the history of chess. He rarely plays for an attack, often retreating his pieces and nibbling at enemy terrain. Then: crunch!

Finally, Petrosian the Boa-Constrictor turns his penetrating power of analysis on the glorious pin with B-KN5 in various settings, culminating in the Petrosian Variation with which he scored such resounding successes against the King's Indian (1 P-Q4 N-KB3 2 P-QB4 P-KN3 3 N-QB3 B-N2 4 P-K4 P-Q3 5 B-K2 O-O 6 N-B3 P-K4 7 P-Q5 QN-Q2 8 B-N5). Stay particularly alert when Petrosian advises you that "the next part of the game is rather boring, consisting mainly of positional maneuvering."

CHAPTER 6

Bent Larsen (Denmark): "I don't often play a move I know how to refute."

Larsen's brash approach to the openings is avowedly subjective. He wants to win. To Petrosian a draw is winning half a point; to Larsen it is losing half a point.

Winning entails the taking of calculated risks. Larsen plays the player as well as the board and is willing to accept unclear double-edged positions as long as he feels comfortable with them. "I have never believed, or 'felt,' that the King's Indian is a correct defense for Black, but I have often liked playing it . . . Some openings I consider absolutely correct, but I do not like to play them."

Constant experimentation is the keynote—provided one has Larsen's self-confidence and strength. His desire to surprise his opponents requires a wide opening repertoire. They never quite know whether they are up against inspiration or perspiration. He tells an anecdote about Ivkov preparing for their match by studying Bird's Opening, which Larsen had often played in the past. Finally, exasperated when Larsen did not play it in the match, Ivkov later used it himself rather than have all his work go to waste.

Larsen knows that an eccentric reputation comes in handy when he plays rock-solid chess against someone who is expecting a museum variation at any moment. He cannily confesses that a grandmaster who essays an ancient opening in only three games is considered a leading "expert" in that opening.

He advises the talented amateur to specialize in openings not often played in top-level chess. Knowing the ideas behind the openings is not enough when you face an opponent who knows the ideas *and* a lot of variations. So he concludes his lively discussion with a proposed repertoire for a reasonably aggressive player.

CHAPTER 7

Paul Keres (Estonia): "I will try to show how a well-known variation is taken apart, subjected to thorough examination of its principles, and, as far as possible, enriched with new ideas."

Keres lets us peer into the secret kitchen of a grandmaster and shows us how his home cooking fares against Fischer and the world's leading players. He traces the Keres Variation of the Ruy Lopez (1 P-K4 P-K4 2 N-KB3 N-QB3 3 B-N5 P-QR3 4 B-R4 N-B3 5 O-O B-K2 6 R-K1 P-QN4 7 B-N3 P-Q3 8 P-B3 O-O 9 P-KR3 N-QR4 10 B-B2 P-B4 11 P-Q4 N-Q2) through qualified success, unqualified setback, encouragement, and, finally, success.

This kind of critical creative work, of course, requires a certain minimum playing strength. Keres demonstrates how a grandmaster's vital juices flow until a variation is absorbed, tenderized, improved. His next example is the sharp Siesta Variation of the Ruy Lopez (1 P-K4 P-K4 2 N-KB3 3 B-N5 P-QR3 4 B-R4 P-Q3 5 P-B3 P-B4), introduced by Capablanca. The Cuban "had an especially fine feeling for the openings," Keres tells us, "and therefore one must seriously consider his recommendations." Clearly, Keres respects the ideas of others.

Keres concludes his discussion with how to prepare for a specific, stubborn opponent who clings to a pet variation despite all setbacks. He cites an instructive example against Benko, who had just lost a game. Keres figured Benko would try it again, anticipated Benko's improvement, and found an antidote beforehand.

Playing chess is not all beer and skittles. "There are many grandmasters with different opening repertoires and methods of game preparation, but they will all agree that in today's master tournaments you can hardly count on success without good preparation."

Glossary

by Larry Evans and Burt Hochberg

Note: the following is a list of words that have special meaning in chess. The definitions do not take into account "normal" English usages outside of chess. Certain terms expected to be understood by anyone reading this book have been omitted, such as checkmate, stalemate, pin, etc., which can be found in any general manual on the game.

ACTIVE: Of a move or line of play more aggressive than many of the alternatives.

ADVANTAGE: Superiority because of more advanced development, greater control of space, more material, etc.

ANALYSIS: The process of determining by deliberate study, either during a game or at home, the best moves in a variation or position. Also, the result of such a process.

ANNOTATION: Critical analysis of moves played and their alternatives.

ATTACK: A concentration of force aimed at a specific objective; for example, the enemy King. Also, a simple threat to capture an enemy man.

BACKWARD PAWN: A pawn which has lagged behind and has no support from friendly pawns. Usually a weakness.

BIND: A stranglehold or grip exerted by one side, resulting from a spatial advantage.

BISHOP PAIR: An advantage for the player who has both Bishops, compared with his opponent who has Bishop and Knight or two Knights. The Bishop pair is particularly strong in uncrowded positions, because open lines enhance the mobility of the Bishops.

BLOCKADE: A term popularized by Aron Nimzovich (1886-1935). It refers to a defensive strategy aimed at preventing the advance of an enemy pawn, especially a passed pawn, by stationing a piece directly in front of it.

BLUNDER: A bad mistake stemming from oversight, miscalculation, or violation of principle.

BOOK: The overall body of published theory. A book player is one who relies on published analysis rather than on his own resources. See THEORY.

BREAK: A freeing move or maneuver, usually involving the advance of a pawn.

BREAKTHROUGH: Usually a pawn move (or moves) to clear lines and penetrate enemy terrain.

BRILLIANCY: A beautiful game or combination that contains a surprising, ingenious, intentional, correct, and successful sacrifice.

CENTER: The four squares known as K4, K5, Q4, Q5. Loosely defined, the sixteen squares in the middle of the board.

CENTRALIZE: To place the pieces and pawns so that they exert maximum influence on or at the center.

CLASSICAL: A school or style of play which extols direct occupation of the center and a systematic, sometimes dogmatic, approach to problems of strategy.

CLOSED GAME: A type of position characterized by few exchanges and a dense or interlocked pawn structure. Closed openings are those reached after any other first move than 1 P-K4.

COMBINATION: A series of moves of a definite tactical nature, having elements of surprise and inspiration, and usually involving one or more sacrifices, designed to improve one's position.

COMPENSATION: An approximately equivalent advantage in one element (such as material) to balance the opponent's advantage in another (such as time or space). Also, equivalence within the same element; as, three pawns are compensation for a Knight.

CONNECTED PASSED PAWNS: Two or more passed pawns of the same color on adjacent files.

CONTROL: Domination by one player of an important square, or group of squares (such as the center), or a file.

COUNTERPLAY: The possibility for the defending side to undertake aggressive action on his own, usually by opening another front. When a player is said to have counterplay, the implication is usually that his overall chances are roughly equal to his opponent's.

CRAMP: A disadvantage in space characterized by lack of mobility. Especially, a sort of traffic jam in which one's pieces get in each other's way. Dr. Siegbert Tarrasch (1862-1934) wrote: "The cramped position bears the germs of defeat."

CRITICAL POSITION: That point in a theoretically important line, usually in the opening and more or less forced from the preceding moves, the evaluation of which determines whether that previous sequence favors White or Black. Also, any decisive turning point in a game.

DEFENSE: A move or series of moves designed to meet enemy threats or attacks, whether immediate or long range. Also, used in names of openings when the characteristic positions are determined largely by Black.

DEVELOPMENT: The process of increasing the mobility of the pieces by moving them from their original squares.

DOUBLED PAWNS: Two pawns of the same color lined up on the same file as a result of a capture.

EDGE: A small advantage. Also, the four outside rows of squares on the chess board.

ELO RATING: A number which indicates a player's strength at a given time relative to other rated players. A rating rises and falls according to the player's tournament and match performance. Named for Professor Arpad E. Elo, who developed the rating formula.

ENDGAME: The final phase of a game, characterized by strategies peculiar to that phase, such as pawn promotion, stalemate, zugzwang, "the opposition," etc., and a relative sparsity of material, especially pieces.

EN PASSANT: "In passing." A French term for a certain pawn capture: a pawn, which on its first move advances two squares and passes an enemy pawn on an adjacent file that has advanced to its fifth rank, may be captured by that enemy pawn as if the first pawn had moved only one square. This optional capture may be made only on the first opportunity, else the right in that instance is forfeited. In chess notation, abbreviated e.p.

EN PRISE: "In take." A French term to describe a piece or pawn that is unprotected and exposed to capture.

EQUALITY: A situation in which neither side has any overall advantage.

EXCHANGE: A trade or swap which does not profit either side from the point of view of simple arithmetic. Not to be confused with "THE EXCHANGE" (see below).

EXCHANGE, THE: A term expressing the difference in value between a Rook and an enemy Bishop or Knight. Gaining a Rook for your own Bishop or Knight is called "winning the Exchange."

FIANCHETTO: An Italian word meaning "on the flank." In chess, it refers to the development of a Bishop on KN2 or QN2. Pronounced fyanKETto.

FIDE: An acronym for Federation Internationale des Echecs, the world chess federation.

FILE: A row of eight vertical squares.

FORCE: A general term for all the pieces and pawns; material. One of the major elements of chess.

FORCED: A move or series of moves necessary to avoid disadvantage.

FRONTIER LINE: An imaginary division in the middle of the board which separates the two armies.

GAMBIT: A voluntary sacrifice, usually of a pawn, in the opening; made in the expectation of gaining an attack, increasing the initiative, or obtaining an advantage in development.

GENERAL PRINCIPLES: Words of wisdom expressing fundamental truths or doctrines to serve as guideposts in selecting a move.

GRANDMASTER: The highest title

(except for World Champion) conferred by FIDE. The full title is International Grandmaster. It is awarded to players who meet established performance standards. A lower title is International Master. Either title, once earned, cannot be withdrawn.

GRANDMASTER DRAW: A term, usually derogatory, to describe a quick draw without fight. By extension, such a game between any players.

HANGING: A colloquial term for an unprotected piece or pawn exposed to capture. See EN PRISE.

HANGING PAWNS: Two adjacent friendly pawns on their fourth rank, separated from other friendly pawns and subject to frontal attack on one or two half-open files.

HOLD: To defend successfully.

HOLE: An important square that cannot be defended by pawns, and which can usually be exploited by the opponent in the opening or middlegame.

HYPERMODERN: A school or style which asserts—in opposition to classical precepts—that indirect or long-distance control of the center, especially from the flanks, is more effective in the long run than direct occupation.

INITIATIVE: An advantage in time and space which places the opponent on the defensive. White, because he moves first, has the initiative at the start.

INNOVATION: A new move in an established variation or opening, frequently in a critical position.

INTUITION: The faculty for choosing a move or plan on the basis of experience, feel, and common sense, as opposed to detailed analysis.

ISOLATED PAWN: A pawn with no friendly pawns on either adjacent file.

KINGSIDE: That half of the board comprising the four files originally occupied by the King, King Bishop, King Knight, and King Rook.

LIQUIDATION: Nimzovich's term for a series of exchanges to neutralize an opponent's bid to gain an advantage, especially an attack. Also, a series of exchanges to end the middlegame and enter a more easily won (or drawn) endgame.

LUFT: "Air." A German word which in chess means an escape hatch for a castled King, created by moving one or more of the pawns in front of the castled position.

MAJOR PIECES: The Queens and Rooks. Sometimes called heavy pieces.

MANEUVER: Any series of quiet moves with a specific aim; a redeployment.

MASTER: A general term for a strong player. Also, a national title awarded to a player who has reached a specified Elo rating. Such titles are not permanent but may be lost when the player's rating falls below the required level. In the U.S., a player becomes a master when he reaches a rating of 2200.

MATE: Short for checkmate.

MATERIAL: The forces, or any part of the forces except the King.

MATING ATTACK: A strong concentration of forces specifically directed at the enemy King and expected to end in forced checkmate.

MIDDLEGAME: That phase of the game sandwiched between the opening and the endgame, during which both completely developed sides struggle for advantage.

MINOR PIECES: The Bishops and Knights. Sometimes called light pieces.

MINORITY ATTACK: A maneuver involving two or more pawns (the minority) used as battering rams to weaken an opposing bulwark of three or more pawns (the majority).

MOBILITY: Freedom of movement for the forces.

OCCUPATION: The direct posting of a piece or pawn on a square. Sometimes, temporary or permanent control of a file or rank.

OPEN: When not referring to a type of position (see OPEN GAME) or a file (see OPEN FILE), this term refers to a type of tournament in which any player may compete upon payment of an entry fee. *Chess Life & Review*, the monthly publication of the U.S. Chess Federation (see USCF), lists hundreds of such tournaments held in all parts of the country.

OPEN FILE: A vertical row of eight squares unoccupied by pawns; a highway effectively used by Rooks.

OPEN GAME: A term describing an opening in which both White and Black play P-K4 on their first move. Also, a type of position characterized by lack of crowding, free movement by the pieces, and the possibility of sudden attack.

OPENING: The beginning of a game (usually through the first dozen moves, often more), during which the main objectives for both sides are: quick and effective development of all the forces; occupation or control of as much of the center as possible; establishment of a safe position for the King (usually accomplished by castling)—all for the purpose of increasing one's initiative or attaining some other advantage while preventing the opponent from doing the same. Also, the term is used to describe the clearing of a file; as, "opening a file for the Rooks."

OPENINGS: Established sequences of moves leading to known characteristic positions. Named after players who invented or popularized them, or after places where they were developed or introduced, or for a feature of the play itself.

OPPOSITE-COLOR BISHOPS: A situation in which each player has only one of his Bishops, each of a different color so that the Bishops cannot come in contact.

OVEREXTENDED: Said of a player's position that has weaknesses due to his ambitious but unsuccessful attack.

OVERPROTECTION: Nimzovich's term for supplying a valuable strongpoint with more protection than is immediately needed to safeguard it.

PASSIVE: Used to describe a move that does not help in fighting for the initiative; inactive. Also, a position devoid of counterplay and activity.

PASSED PAWN: A pawn that has passed all enemy pawns capable of capturing it or otherwise stopping its progress to the eighth rank.

PAWN CENTER: The center occupied by pawns, usually those of one player.

PAWN CHAIN: Two or more friendly pawns linked diagonally.

PAWN ISLAND: A group of pawns of the same color separated from other friendly pawns. The more islands there are, the harder each of them is to defend.

PAWN STRUCTURE: The more-or-less fixed overall position of the pawns; the pawn skeleton.

POISONED PAWN: A pawn that is dangerous to snatch (particularly the QNP). Also, any pawn offered as bait in a trap.

POSITIONAL: Describing a move, a maneuver or a style of play which is subtle rather than overtly aggressive.

POST MORTEM: "After death." A Latin term borrowed from medicine. It describes a session by the players and kibitzers after a game to examine the moves played and their alternatives. Sometimes a way for a player to soothe his ego after a loss by proving that he could have won or drawn.

PREMATURE: Said of a move, a maneuver or an attack that is insufficiently prepared.

PREPARED VARIATION: An opening variation, prepared in secret and designed for use against a specific opponent or in a specific tournament.

PROBLEM CHILD: A reference to Black's Queen Bishop, which is often unable to develop freely, particularly in the French Defense and the Queen's Gambit.

PROMOTION: Making a new Queen when a pawn reaches its eighth rank. Also called "queening." See UNDERPROMOTION.

PROTECTED PASSED PAWN: A passed pawn that is protected by a friendly pawn.

QUEENSIDE: That half of the board comprising the four files originally occupied by the Queen, Queen Bishop, Queen Knight, and Queen Rook.

QUIET MOVE: A move that is neither

a capture, a check, nor a direct threat.

RANK: A row of eight horizontal squares.

RATING: See ELO RATING.

REFUTATION: A demonstrable method of proving a flaw in a game, a variation or an analysis.

RESIGNS: Surrenders a game without waiting to be checkmated.

RISK: A characteristic of a move, maneuver, combination or style that aims for advantage while carrying the danger of disadvantage. To a great extent, how much risk a player is willing to take determines his style. In annotations and written analysis, a risky move is accompanied by the symbol "!?" if the writer feels the risk is reasonable despite safer alternatives, or by "?!" if he feels the risk is dubious or too speculative.

ROMANTIC: Said of a player or a style of play characterized by headlong attack, considerable risk, love of brilliance and sacrifice, and dislike of defense.

SACRIFICE: The voluntary offer of material for the purpose of gaining a larger advantage; usually part of a combination.

SEMI-OPEN GAME: The type of position resulting when White plays 1 P-K4 and Black replies with any move other than 1 . . . P-K4.

SHARP: Said of a move that boldly attempts to seize the initiative, involving commitment and bridge-burning. Of a position, one in which such moves are likely. Of a player, one whose style is characterized by such moves.

SHOT: A suddenly strong move, often unexpected by the opponent. Colloquial.

SIMPLIFY: To relieve pressure, reduce complications, or neutralize an enemy attack by exchanging pieces.

SOUND: Safe and solid.

SPACE: One of the elements of chess. The overall area bounded by the four sides of the chess board. Especially, the territory controlled and occupied by each player's forces.

SPECULATIVE: Risky and not clear. Usually said of a sacrifice the outcome of which could not be calculated.

STRATEGY: A long-range master plan. The main idea behind a player's moves, guiding his thinking during the game.

STYLE: A player's preferred and habitual manner of choosing moves and plans to reach the kinds of positions he likes to play.

SWINDLE: A clever trap conceived in desperation, intended to rob the opponent of a well-earned victory.

SYMMETRY: The identical alignment of both armies, such as the original starting position.

TACTICS: Immediate schemes, traps and threats deemed necessary for executing a strategical plan. Combinations are tactical, though their objectives may be strategical or positional.

TEMPO: A Latin word meaning time. The term has been adopted into common chess usage, so the English plural "tempos" is preferred. In chess, a tempo is the unit of relative time represented by one move. For example, a pawn may advance two squares on its first move; if it takes two moves to advance those two squares, a tempo has been lost.

THEORY: The distillation of practical experience in published form. Colloquially, "the book."

THREAT: An attempt to gain an advantage, usually by inflicting some immediate injury on the opponent's position.

TIME: A basic element of chess in all its phases; referring to the relative speed at which the forces enter the struggle in the opening, the rate at which an attack is pursued and defended against in the middlegame, the rapidity of a passed pawn's advance versus the opponent's efforts to stop it, etc. Also, thinking time as measured by special clocks. In professional tournaments, each player usually has two and half hours in which to make 40 moves. See TIME CONTROL, TIME PRESSURE.

TIME CONTROL: The point in actual time by which the 40th move (or whatever number is being used in a particular competition) must be completed. If a player fails to complete the required number of moves in the allotted time, he loses the game by forfeit.

TIME PRESSURE: That period of a game when a player (often both players) has very little left of his allotted time to make the remainder of his moves. Time pressure becomes a factor in the game usually around the 30th move (often earlier) and features moves made in great haste, leading to mistakes and miscalculations.

TRANSITIONS: The phases of the game when the opening merges into the middlegame, and the middlegame into the endgame.

TRANSPOSITION: A sequence of moves which leads to the same position as a different sequence. For example, the French Defense can be reached by the normal sequence 1 P-K4 P-K3 2 P-Q4 P-Q4, or "by transposition" 1 P-Q4 P-K3 2 P-K4 P-Q4.

TRAP: An inducement to a careless opponent to make an error, usually by offering bait.

UNCLEAR: See CLEAR.

UNDERPROMOTION: Making a Rook, Knight or Bishop (instead of a Queen) when a pawn reaches the eighth rank.

UNSOUND: See SOUND.

USCF: The initials of the United States Chess Federation, 479 Broadway, Newburgh, New York 12550.

VARIATION: A line of play, especially in the opening. Also, any sequence of moves, usually alternatives to the line of play actually used.

WEAKNESS: A square (or a pawn occupying that square) that is a natural target for enemy attack because it is difficult or impossible to defend.

WILD: Extremely unclear and risky; desperately speculative; too sharp.

ZUGZWANG: "Compulsion to move." A German term which refers to that unwelcome predicament when a player damages his position because he must move.

ZWISCHENZUG: "In-between move." A German term to describe a move played instead of an apparently forced one. Often an unexpected finesse.

CHAPTER 1

Basic Chess Strategy

by Larry Evans

Chess is easy to learn, fun to play, difficult to master. By following these guidelines you should be able to conduct an intelligent game against anyone!

General Principles

1. Always play to dominate the middle of the board. Occupy, attack, or watch the center; the sides and corners are lifeless.
2. Develop *all* your men fast, not just one or two. The opening is a race for rapid and continuous development. The aim of development is to connect the Rooks so that they can occupy central posts for the middlegame and seize open files.
3. Castle early. This brings the King to safety and a Rook into play. Conversely, try to prevent your opponent from castling—if possible, without sacrificing material.
4. Don't sacrifice material unless you see a way to get it back or to force checkmate.
5. Don't lose time by moving the same piece twice.
6. Make few pawn moves, only enough to free your pieces.
7. Develop Knights before Bishops.
8. Avoid early Queen adventures. Develop minor pieces (Knights and Bishops) before major pieces (Queen and Rooks).
9. Avoid giving useless checks.
10. Assume that your opponent will find the right moves, and don't play for crude traps except in desperation.

It's not important to memorize detailed opening variations. Concentrate on applying sound general principles and you will rarely go wrong. Develop rapidly, castle early, centralize your pieces. The idea is not to trick your opponent, but to keep on strengthening your position.

According to Bobby Fischer, four ingredients are essential to success at chess:

1. **Concentrate.** Just one slip can cost the game. Chess requires total concentration. Many players use only a fraction of their energy. Keep your mind completely on the game. Play to win. Nobody's interested in excuses when you lose.

2. **Think ahead.** Distrust your first instinct in selecting a move. Sit on your hands. To avoid disaster, each time your opponent moves STOP and ask yourself: "What's the threat?" Don't move until you understand the position. Remember, it's absolutely essential for your

development as a chess player to adhere to the rule of "touch-move"—once you touch a piece you must move it. Give no quarter and ask for none!

3. **Learn from your losses.** Record your games, including the offhand ones, and study them later to try to find your mistakes—if you don't already know what they were. You are not likely to lose two games the same way, and you will also retain a permanent record of your progress.

4. **Study.** Play over recent games of masters in books and magazines. Combine this study with actual play against strong opponents. Spend as much spare time at the game as you can.

The opening—roughly the first dozen moves—is a fight for space, time and force. These three elements are like earth, air and water. Understanding these key concepts will help you to start the game with a harmonious plan.

Space

The chess board consists of 64 squares. It would seem that a square is a square is a square. But some squares are more equal than others.

Every move in the opening should have some bearing on the central squares. Work toward the middle! This principle is called "centralization."

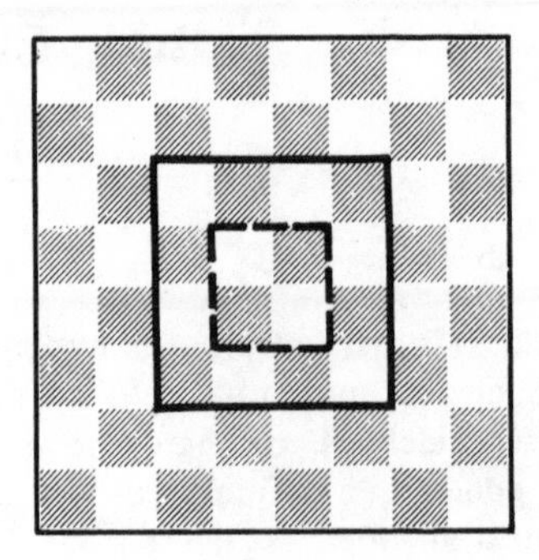

The Center

The center contains 16 squares within the bold outline in the diagram, with four critical squares at the core. You can control the center directly by occupying it (classical school) or indirectly from the wings (hypermodern school). Most good players combine both strategies.

Every move you make is related to every other. If one piece is badly posted, your whole game is bad.

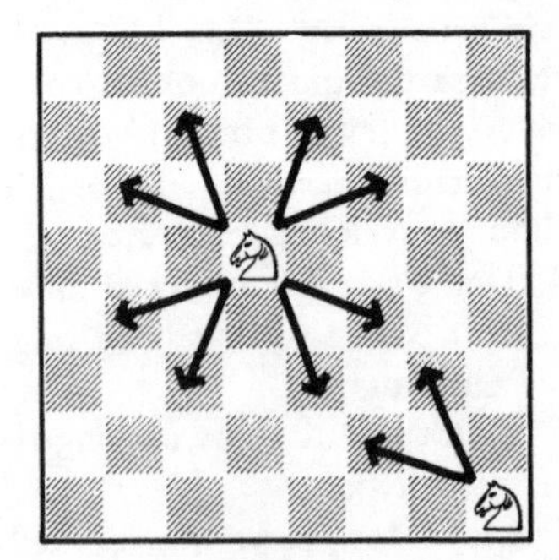

Mobility

THE PLAYER WHO CONTROLS MORE SPACE ENJOYS SUPERIOR MOBILITY FOR HIS PIECES. When pieces occupy the center, they radiate greater mobility. They are more efficient. In the diagram above, compare the Knight on the central square Q5, striking at eight squares, with its counterpart on KR1, striking at only two squares. The centralized Knight is *four times more powerful.*

Units increase in mobility as they approach the center. The more the mobility of a unit is restricted, the less powerful it becomes.

The idea of the opening is to bring all the minor pieces (Knights and Bishops) toward the center, increasing their mobility. There is a natural (though imaginary) dividing line between the two armies, a moat at the fourth rank, which should be approached with all due speed.

Bring your men up to the frontier line, but be wary of crossing into enemy territory. Any invasion must be carefully prepared. The advanced troops must be maintained by steady lines of communication, a flow of supplies and reinforcements. Napoleon's army stranded in the Russian campaign has its chess counterpart in premature invasion.

Consider this sequence in the Sicilian Defense:

White	**Black**
1 P-K4	......

The most common first move, this bold thrust frees two pieces (Queen and Bishop) and immediately occupies a crucial central square.

1	**P-QB4**

This puts pressure on the center but frees only one piece—the Queen. Instead of squaring off in the center of the ring (with 1 ... P-K4), Black prefers a more flexible formation.

2 N-KB3	......

The most active post for the Knight, this also prepares rapid Kingside castling (White must evacuate the Knight and Bishop before he may castle).

2	**N-QB3**

This brings more pressure to bear against White's Q4 square and develops a new piece, adhering to the rule of posting Knights before Bishops.

3 P-KN3	......

Preparing a flank development (fianchetto) of the Bishop on KN2, where it can exert indirect pressure on the center.

3	**N-B3**

Developing another piece toward the center and threatening to capture the KP.

4 P-K5?	......

Black purposely provoked this premature advance in order to lure the pawn across the frontier line (better is 4 P-Q3). White figures he "gains time" by forcing Black's Knight to move a second time, but he has succeeded only in weakening his own KP.

4 ...... N-KN5!

This violates the principle of not moving the same piece twice in the opening, but Black can hardly ignore the threat of P×N. Black's justification in crossing the frontier line is the double attack on White's unstable KP.

5 P-Q4 ......

Coming to the defense of the beleaguered KP. No better is 5 Q-K2 Q-B2!, attacking the KP for the third time while it is only defended twice.

5 ...... P×P

By undermining the support of the KP, Black again threatens to capture it on the next move. A mistake would be 5 ... N×QP? 6 N×N P×N 7 Q×N, snaring a piece.

6 B-KB4 ......

Now White thinks he is sitting pretty: his KP is amply defended and he threatens P-KR3 (driving the upstart Knight back) followed by N×P regaining the pawn.

6 ...... KN×KP!

This looks impossible! The KP is attacked twice and defended twice. Doesn't this capture just lose a piece? Do you see what Black has in mind as a follow-up?

7 N×N ......

There is nothing better, as otherwise White remains a couple of pawns behind without any compensation.

7 ...... N×N
8 B×N ......

Apparently coming out a piece ahead. A dreadful mistake, however, is 8 Q×P?? N-B6ch! (a fork) followed by N×Q next.

8 ...... Q-R4ch!

The point. This double attack on the King and Bishop regains the piece that Black sacrificed on move 6.

9 N-Q2 ......

White can also interpose with 9 P-B3 or 9 Q-Q2, but Black still makes the same reply.

9 ...... Q×Bch

Now, no matter what White does (10 B-K2 P-KN3 11 O-O B-N2) Black remains two pawns up with a winning game.

At the turn of the century Dr. Tarrasch observed: "The cramped position bears the germs of defeat." When the pieces are herded like cattle it is a sure sign that a player has done something wrong. Consider this variation of the Nimzo-Indian Defense:

White	Black
1 **P-Q4**	......

This excellent move occupies a key central square and frees two units: the Queen and Bishop.

2 ...... N-KB3

Black does not yet want to commit himself by moving any pawns, so he places a Knight on a natural post and awaits further developments.

2 P-QB4 ......

Trying to stake a claim on the center by fortifying the pressure against White's Q5. Strictly speaking, this second pawn thrust does not contribute to piece development (getting the pieces off the back row), but it does hurl another spear at the center.

2 ...... P-K3

A modest move which frees the King Bishop. As a general rule, each side moves just enough pawns to free the pieces behind them.

3 N-QB3 ......

This Knight goes to its most effective post and intensifies the pressure against the center. Note that 3 N-Q2 is bad (it blocks the Bishop and Queen) while 3 N-QR3 violates the centralization principle.

3 ...... B-N5

The characteristic move of the Nimzo-Indian Defense. By pinning the Knight, Black prevents White from expanding in the center with 4 P-K4 (which simply loses material to 4 ... N×P).

4 P-K3 ......

This move has the slight drawback of hemming in the QB. On the other hand, it frees the KB and paves the way for rapid castling.

4 ...... P-QN3

Preparing a fianchetto (flank development) of the QB. On QN2 the Bishop can keep a weather eye on the center from the wing (a hypermodern concept).

5 N-K2 ......

The idea behind this is to play P-QR3 and recapture with the Knight should Black reply with ... B×Nch. White wants to avoid doubled pawns. More natural and straightforward is 5 B-Q3 followed by N-B3 and O-O.

5 ...... B-N2

As advertised. The Bishop's scope has been increased on this diagonal.

6 P-QR3 ......

To break the pin. This is known as "putting the question to the Bishop." Black must now meet the threat of P×B.

6 ...... B-K2

To save his skin. The worst retreat would be 6 . . . B-R4? 7 P-QN4 trapping the Bishop. A simpler solution, however, is 6 . . . B×Nch 7 N×B P-Q4, immediately challenging White's center. But Black does not want to exchange a Bishop for a Knight (giving up the Bishop pair) and considers this retreat the lesser evil.

7 P-Q5! ......

Crossing the frontier line! This powerful advance restricts the mobility of Black's fianchettoed Bishop (makes it "bite on granite" in Nimzovich's words). White must be absolutely certain that there is no risk in such an advance and that he can reinforce the extended pawn, if necessary.

7 ...... O-O

Black sees that he cannot win any material since 7 . . . P×P 8 P×P N×P? 9 N×N B×N 10 Q×B nets White a piece. So he brings his King to safety before launching any further counteraction.

8 P-K4 ......

Creating a wedge and increasing the stability of the advanced center pawns. Note that White has just opened the diagonal for his QB.

8 ...... P-Q3

Trying for some elbow room. A mistake is 8 . . . P-B3? 9 P-Q6! winning Black's Bishop.

9 P-KN3 ......

White prepares to fianchetto his Bishop on KN2 and indirectly support the outpost on Q5.

9 ...... P-K4

Black abandons all hope of assailing the central wedge. White keeps the advantage against 9 . . . P-B3 by 10 P×KP P×P 11 N-Q4 B-B1 12 B-R3! P-K4 13 B×B Q×B 14 N-B5. So Black prefers to close the lines.

10 B-N2 ......

This quiet developing move enables White to castle next. Not every move must contain a devastating threat. Position play is the art of accumulating small advantages until they explode in a winning combination.

10 ...... QN-Q2

Developing a Knight toward the center. Unfortunately, Black is reduced to passive moves.

11 O-O ......

Having secured a complete strategical victory in the center, White is ready to face the middlegame with confidence.

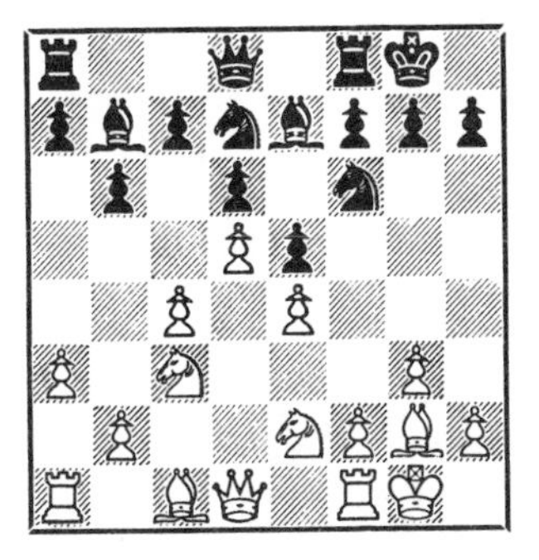

Black is horribly cramped

If you cannot see at a glance that White's position is freer, there is a foolproof way to count space. How many squares does each side control or occupy beyond the frontier line? Black strikes at Q5 and KB5 (with his KP) and K5 and KN5 (with his Knight), for a total of four. White occupies Q5 with a pawn and strikes at K6 and QB6 with the same unit, hits QN5 twice (with QBP and QN), hits KB5 (with the KP), and strikes at KN5 and KR6 with the QB, for a grand total of eight. Thus, White has an advantage in space by eight squares to four.

Time

The first question a good player asks when he looks at a position is: "Whose move is it?" Time is so vital that if a player with only mediocre ability were allowed to move twice in a row, at his option, just once in every game, he could become World Champion! The right to move is precious.

The main thing to aim for in the opening is *rapid and continuous development*. Bring your pieces out as fast as possible toward the center. Never move the same piece twice, unless you must. Useless, unnecessary and over-cautious moves are all wastes of time. Shun them.

Develop Knights before Bishops. The best square for a Knight is usually KB3 and/or QB3, whereas the course of the game often determines the most effective posts for the Bishops. So wait and see.

Don't bring your Queen out too early since the enemy can generally gain time by taking potshots at her majesty. A simple example arises in the Center Game: **1 P-K4 P-K4 2 P-Q4 P×P 3 Q×P N-QB3.** Black has gained a tempo. White is forced to move the Queen again to prevent Black from capturing it with the Knight (Q-QR4 is probably best). Black then brings out another piece.

A common failing of the beginner is that he makes premature threats and then gnaws his nails hoping his opponent will overlook the right defense. This is shabby chess. When a cheap trap works, it only speaks poorly for the loser. If you really want to improve, always assume your opponent will find the best reply, and plan accordingly.

Consider this position arising

from **1 P-K4 P-K4 2 B-B4 B-B4 3 Q-R5!?** aiming for the simplistic Scholar's Mate.

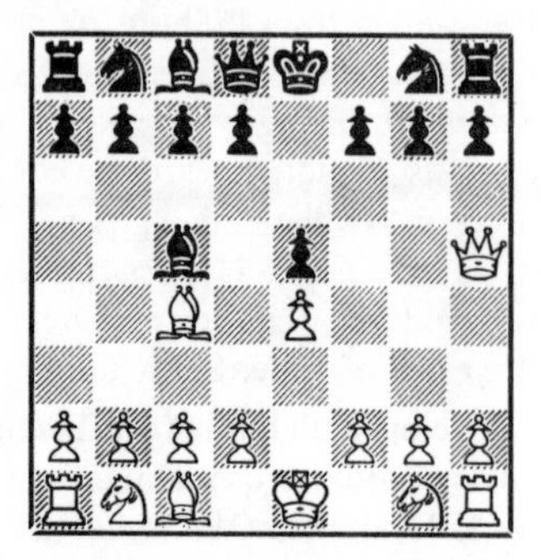

What should Black play?

Superficially, White's Queen sortie looks difficult to meet: it creates a double threat of Q×BP mate or Q×KPch, and it might even succeed against an inexperienced opponent. But it violates the principle which states that minor pieces (Knights and Bishops) should be developed before major pieces (Queen and Rooks).

Is there some way to punish White for his rashness? What form should this punishment take?

First things first. Black must defend against the immediate threat with **3 . . . Q-K2!** Now **4 N-KB3** looks good, because it develops a fresh piece and renews the attack against the KP, which Black guards modestly with **4 . . . P-Q3** (incidentally releasing the diagonal for the QB) **5 O-O N-KB3!** This is the punishment. Black gains a "free" developing move by harrying the misplaced White Queen. On 6 Q-R4 N-B3, Black already has at least an equal game.

This may not sound like much. But consider that White has a definite advantage at the beginning by virtue of having the first move: he has first crack at occupying and controlling the center. Black must be content with a passive role since one false step is fatal. With correct defense Black can neutralize White's serve after long and patient maneuvering. We call this "equality." When White lost a tempo with his Queen, as above, he also lost his heritage—the initiative. It is true that the better player will win with either color, but it takes longer with Black.

The purpose of the opening is NOT to checkmate in a handful of moves. In fact, premature attacks usually boomerang against proper defense.

Just keep bringing your pieces out and have patience. The ideal of development is to clear the first rank of all units except Kings and Rooks, then connect Rooks by castling. The following position, from Fleischer-Evans, U.S. Open Championship 1949, illustrates this vital principle.

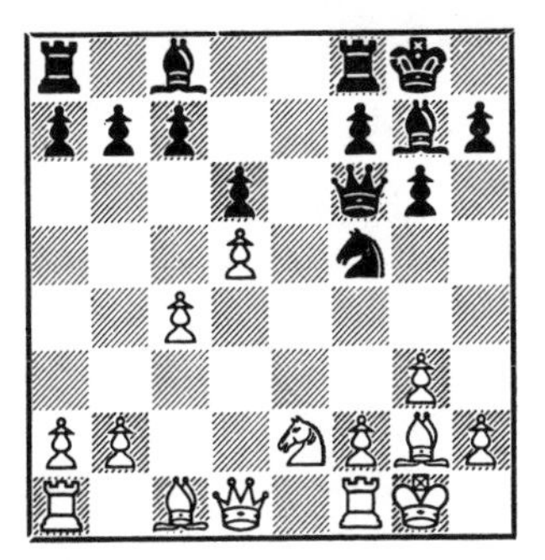

What should Black play?

White	**Black**
1	**B-Q2!**

Black takes advantage of the lull to develop the QB, even if only to such a modest square as Q2. This frees the QR, thus accomplishing the connection between the two Rooks on the back rank. When Rooks are connected in this fashion, it generally heralds the end of the opening and the beginning of the middlegame.

It is true that Q2 is not a very potent square for Black's Bishop, but it's the only square available. Don't argue with necessity. Have faith that development will pay off.

2 Q-N3? ......

White is also striving to connect his Rooks, but he has a problem: the QB cannot move immediately without dropping the QNP. Therefore a better try is 2 N-B3 in order to shield that weakness so that the QB can move.

2 ...... **QR-K1!**

Seizing open files maximizes the power of the Rook. In addition, Black gains time by attacking the undefended Knight.

3 Q-Q1? ......

This only loses more time. Again, 3 N-B3 is to be preferred.

3 ...... **R-K2!**

Preparing to double Rooks on the open file, doubly desirable.

4 N-B3 ......

Finally White gets the right idea, but in the meantime Black has gained three moves! Compare this position with the original diagram, when White could have made this move immediately.

4 ...... **KR-K1**

The logical follow-up.

5 B-Q2 ......

At last White gets this Bishop out, but he has still not connected his Rooks—the Queen is in the way.

5 ...... **P-KR4**

Black has no way to penetrate and makes an aggressive gesture, possibly anticipating a Kingside attack.

6 R-K1 ......

Challenging Black's control of the open King file before it becomes too dominating.

6 ...... R×Rch
7 B×R N-Q5

Black has a clear advantage in space and his pieces are posted actively, but he does not yet have a decisive continuation.

8 N-K4 ......

White attacks the Queen not because he expects Black to overlook it, but because he wants to make a square available at QB3 for his QB and repulse the upstart Black Knight.

8 ...... Q-B4

Threatening 9 ... R×N 10 B×R Q×B, winning two pieces for a Rook. Of course, White cannot permit this.

9 P-B3 ......

To maintain the Knight on K4.

9 ...... Q-K4

Threatening ... P-KB4 dislodging White's Knight.

10 B-B3 ......

Actually threatening to win a piece with P-B4.

10 ...... P-KB4

Setting up a counterthreat against White's Knight.

11 P-B4 ......

Repulsing the Queen. Black must drop everything else and stave off this threat.

11 ...... Q-K2

11 ... Q×N 12 B×Q R×B does not give Black enough material compensation for the Queen, so this retreat is "forced." We speak of a move as forced when all the alternatives are demonstrably weak.

12 B×N ......

White is temporarily a piece ahead.

12 ...... P×N

Black has an obligation to restore material equality.

13 B×B? ......

White has defended well after a shaky start, but now he begins to buckle under the pressure. Of course, bad would be 13 B×RP?? P-N3! followed by ... R-R1 trapping the Bishop. But after 13 B-K3!, blockading the KP, Black would have great difficulty making any headway. 13 ... B×P would be answered by 14 R-N1 (attacking the Bishop) 14 ... B-N2 15 R×P regaining the pawn advantageously.

13 ...... Q×B

Threatening to capture the QNP.

14 Q-Q2 ......

White is in dire straits. If 14 Q-K2 B-N5! 15 Q-Q2 P-K6 leads to a variation similar to the actual game (notice how handy 5 ... P-KR4 came in).

14 ...... **P-K6**

This passed pawn is extremely dangerous because there is no enemy pawn to stop it from queening —it must be stopped by heavy pieces.

15 Q-B3 ......

White is hoping that an exchange of Queens will ease the pressure, but he must ruin his pawn formation to reach an endgame.

15 ...... **Q×Q**
16 P×Q ......

Doubled pawns are undesirable because they lose mobility and mutual protection by being stacked up on the same file.

16 ...... **B-B4**

The threat is ... B-Q6, picking off a pawn.

17 R-K1 ......

White would like to save the pawn with 17 B-B1, but this is refuted by 17 ... P-K7!, winning a piece.

17 ...... **B-Q6**

White still gets no relief from 18 B-B1 because of 18 ... P-K7 19 B-N2 B×P, etc.

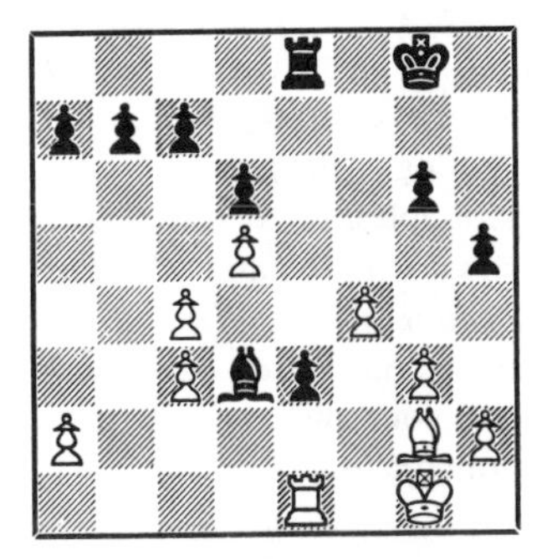

Black wins a pawn

The rest is a matter of technique. Just for the record, the remaining moves were: 18 P-QR3 B×P 19 B-B3 K-N2 20 P-R3 K-B3 21 K-N2 K-B4 (the King is a fighting piece in the endgame—use it) 22 P-KR4 R-K2 23 K-N1 P-QN4 24 K-N2 K-Q1 25 K-N1 K-B3 26 K-N2 K-B2 27 K-N1 K-K1 28 K-N2 K-Q1 29 K-N1 K-B1 30 P-N4 P×P 31 B×Pch K-N2 32 B-K6 K-N3 33 R×P B×P, and White soon resigned.

With skillful play an early advantage can be maintained right through to the ending. The player who mobilizes all his forces faster than the opponent secures an advantage in time and space. Often this is decisive if it can be transformed into a mating attack or material gain.

Force

"When right opposes right, force decides."

The basic principle of force is that *material superiority is decisive when all other things are equal.* Capablanca put it this way: "The winning of a pawn among good players of even strength often means the winning of the game."

The simplest method of determining who is winning and who is losing is to *count pieces.* Without resorting to any elaborate system, pair off each of your men against each of your opponent's.

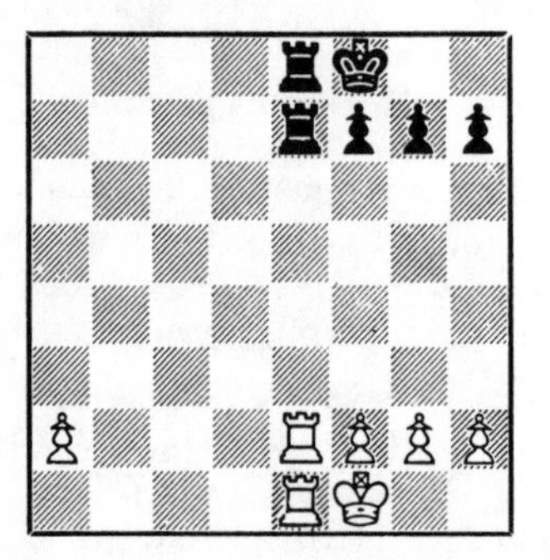

Who's winning: White or Black?

A simple count shows that White is a pawn ahead. If it were his move, the quickest win is to exchange pieces: 1 R×R R×R 2 R×R K×R 3 K-K2 followed by centralizing the King and pushing the passed QRP. If it is Black's move, his best chance to draw is to keep at least one Rook on the board after 1 ... R×R 2 R×R R-R1.

THE PLAYER WHO IS AHEAD IN MATERIAL SHOULD TRADE AS MANY PIECES AS POSSIBLE. THE PLAYER WHO IS BEHIND SHOULD TRY TO AVOID EXCHANGES. Proportionately, 16 to 15 is not a very great advantage. But if you keep swapping, eventually you will reach 2 to 1, and that's overwhelming. It is essential at all times not to fall behind in material.

Most games are lost as a result of oversights. Leaving pieces unprotected is far and away the greatest error committed by beginners. Even masters are not immune from these obvious blunders. Never make a move without considering your opponent's threats. If you find that your opponent's move contains a threat, you must do something about it immediately.

When you post a piece on a good square, don't try to leave it there forever. Your strategy depends to a great extent on how your opponent handles his side of the board. Be flexible. Abandon a plan the instant you see it has no chance of succeeding, and find another one.

In the course of a game you will be called upon to make and to meet threats. Give, take, and roll with the punches!

A threat is not an end in itself. Don't make a threat just for the sake of making a threat—unless you see nothing better to do. The purpose of a threat is to gain an advantage. It should leave your position better off than it was before. But often the psychological problem is greatest for the defender when there are no threats!

Let us examine a typical "threat" after **1 P-K4 P-K4 2 N-KB3.**

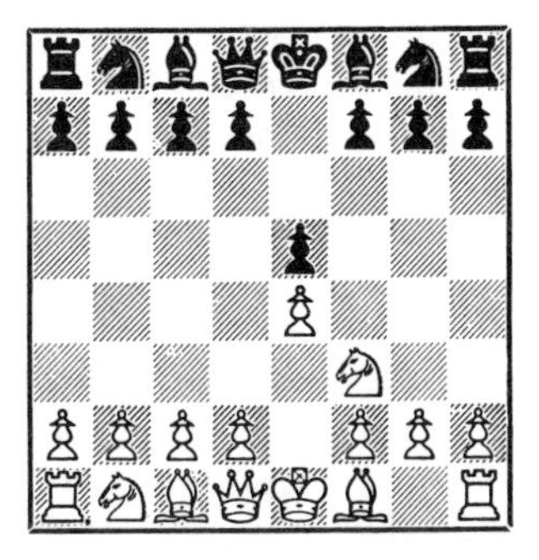

Black's KP is threatened

White attacks the KP as a by-product of developing his Knight, not because he expects to win the pawn.

2 . . . N-QB3 is the best reply. This natural developing move guards the KP and brings out a Knight in the process without interfering with the mobility of the other men. 2 . . . P-Q3 would also meet the threat, but it has the drawback of hemming in the KB.

But suppose, for the sake of argument, that Black completely ignores the threat and plays **2 . . . P-KR3,** a move which has no bearing on development or the center. How does White go about exploiting it? Simply by carrying out his threat: **3 N×P!** Now Black must try to get his pawn back or remain behind in material without any compensation. So the game might continue: **3 . . . Q-K2 4 P-Q4 P-Q3 5 N-KB3 Q×Pch 6 B-K2.**

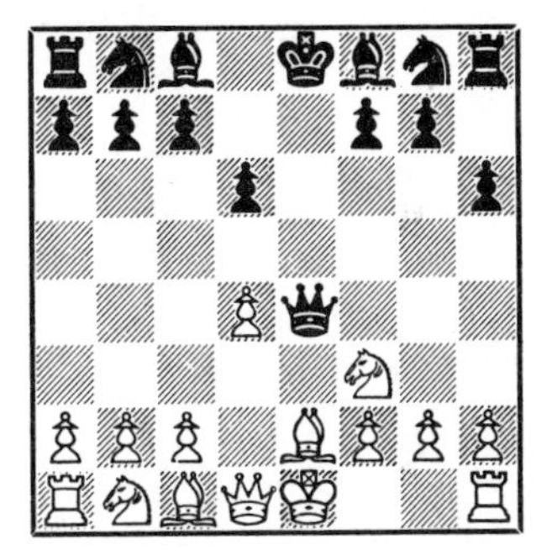

Black has regained his pawn—but at what a cost! Even though it is Black's move, White has a fantastic lead in development. The only piece Black has out is the Queen, and it's located on a terrible square—due to get "kicked" when White brings his other Knight to its normal developing post on QB3. White has two minor pieces developed and his King is ready to castle in one move.

2 . . . P-KR3? has resulted in several lost tempos for Black. As so often happens, one bad move leads to another. In a game between masters, Black's position already would be considered hopeless!

Everyone knows that superior force wins, except when . . . Your chess career will be filled with these exceptions. Judging a position requires much more than asking whose move it is and counting pieces. Particular attention must be paid to the quality of the pawn structure. Consider this endgame from Smyslov-Evans, Helsinki Olympic 1952, a painful lesson for the strict materialist.

Black moves

Black is a pawn ahead, but the extra pawn is tripled. The reason doubled or tripled pawns are bad, especially in the ending, is that they cannot be mobilized. In effect, the tripled pawns count as one, and Black is in reality a pawn down! The game continued:

White	Black
1	**P-B5**

Black must cough up. If this pawn could not advance, Black would have a draw by stalemate.

2 P×P	**P-B4**
3 K-B6	**P-B3**

Again forced. If 3 . . . K-R2 4 K-B7 K-R3 5 P-N8=Q is decisive.

4 K-Q6!	......

Black was hoping for a stalemate after 4 K-N6.

4	**K×P**
5 K-K6	**Resigns**

White lunches on the pawns at his leisure. If 5 . . . K-B2 6 K×P/4 K-Q2 7 K ×P K-K1 8 K-N5, etc.

Before you learn the openings it is important to master these elementary endgames. What good is a material plus if you don't know what to do with it? As Purdy observed: "Pawn endings are to chess what putting is to golf." In order to appreciate the advantage of a Rook or Queen, remove all the pieces from the board and see how long it takes to mate the lone enemy King. (See *Basic Chess Endings,* by Reuben Fine.)

Another troublesome situation to evaluate is the gambit. A gambit is the voluntary sacrifice of material (usually a pawn) to seize an early initiative. The gambiteer banks on rapid development and superior mobility to score an early victory, or to regain the material with interest. But it stands to reason that if his opponent has made no error, such optimism is unfounded.

Returning to an earlier example in the Center Game: **1 P-K4 P-K4 2 P-Q4 P×P,** White can avoid the loss of time which ensues after 3 Q×P N-QB3 by continuing with the further offer of a pawn via **3 P-QB3!?**

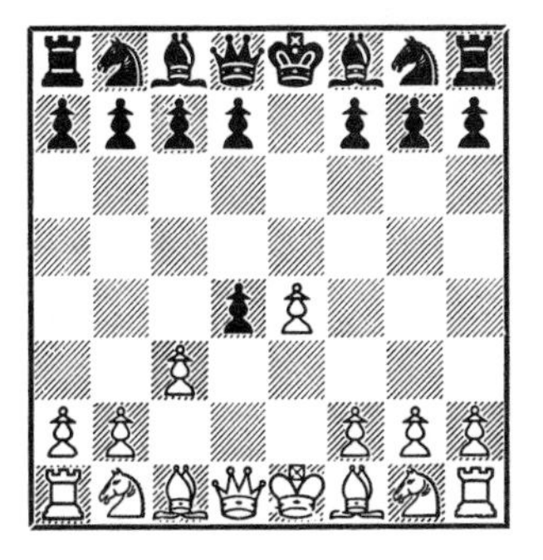

This gambit can prove very dangerous against an inexperienced opponent. White's intention is to acquire a broad center with P×P next. Black can either decline the gambit or accept it. There's an old adage that the best way to refute a gambit is to accept it; and I also advise students always to snatch material—if they can do it and live.

Black gets a satisfactory position by declining with 3 . . . P-Q4 (less effective is 3 . . . P-Q6 4 B×P, allowing White to recapture the pawn while developing a piece) 4 KP×P Q×P 5 P×P N-QB3 6 N-KB3 B-KN5 (notice how Black systematically exploits White's isolated QP by undermining the pieces that defend it) 7 B-K2 O-O-O (hasty is 7 . . . B×N? 8 B×B Q×QP?? 9 B×Nch P×B 10 Q×Q, winning Black's Queen) 8 N-B3 (gaining a tempo) 8 . . . Q-QR4 and Black has lasting pressure against White's central pawn, although material is even after 9 B-K3.

3 . . . P×P 4 N×P (in the Danish Gambit, 4 B-QB4!? P×P 5 B×P, White offers a second pawn, whereupon Black can doggedly cling to his extra material with 5 . . . P-QB3 or return it with 5 . . . P-Q4 to force simplifications and ease the pressure) leads to double-edged play.

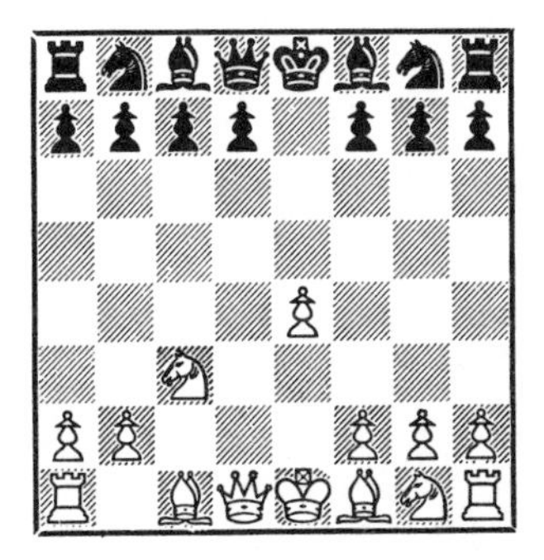

White is a pawn down, but he already has a Knight out, a pawn in the center, and open diagonals for both of his Bishops (we call this "compensation"). Time is more important than force *in the opening.* But if Black can survive the attack and consolidate, his reward is a winning ending. Dr. Tarrasch put it: "Before the ending the gods have placed the middlegame." An attacking player would prefer White, a defending player would prefer Black. Objectively speaking, Black has the better long-range chances. Each exchange brings him closer to victory. White must justify his sacrifices quickly before the day of reckoning. (Consult the opening manuals for possible continuations after 4 . . . B-N5 or 4 . . . P-Q3.)

CHAPTER 2

The Elements of Opening Strategy

by Svetozar Gligoric

The Fight for Time

Since you are reading this book, it is safe to assume that you like to play chess. And you probably want to play better than you do now.

It will be well for you to remember, therefore, that the chess board is a battlefield where two armies fight. These armies, though made of wood, nevertheless behave in many ways like real flesh-and-blood armies. The sooner a general can bring his forces into battle, the better his chances for victory. This illustrates one of the most important factors in the chess opening—the factor of *TIME*.

When we speak of time we are not referring to the minutes and hours used for thinking about your moves. This kind of time will play a role, however, when you become a tournament player and have to submit to the rigorous discipline of the chess clock. World Champion Robert ("Bobby") Fischer never allows himself to become short of thinking time. He believes that when players hurry their moves, making all kinds of mistakes, they are not even playing chess! It is a mistake to spend so much time thinking in the early stages of the game that there is not enough time later to find the best moves. Great players like Reshevsky and Korchnoi are well known for their ability to play quite well in "time pressure," but this is not to be recommended to everyone; even those who have that ability frequently find it deteriorates as they grow older.

There is another meaning of time that is peculiar to chess, and it is this definition we refer to when speaking of the function of time in the opening. This kind of time is measured in moves rather than minutes. (We use the term "tempo" to describe the unit of time represented by one move.) In the opening we are concerned with the rate at which the chess pieces enter the fight. The efficient use of time in the opening requires generally that each move should be used to develop a new piece. So it is necessary to try to avoid moving the same piece more than once in the opening. Your playing strength will depend to a large extent on how efficiently you are able to use this kind of time. If you can learn to use it with very great accuracy you could become an even better player than many masters and grandmasters! There are very few players in the world who are really supreme in that respect. The problem is that it is easy to explain a principle and it may be easy to understand it, but it is very difficult to make that principle work perfectly in practice. For the question will always arise, complicated by the many thousands of possible positions, some differing only slightly: In which order should the pieces be developed, and where? There are usually several alternatives, but probably there is only one that is best.

But preaching will not take us very far—the moment has come to start learning from practical examples.

Moscow 1935
CARO-KANN DEFENSE

White	Black
M. Botvinnik	**R. Spielmann**

1 P-QB4 ......

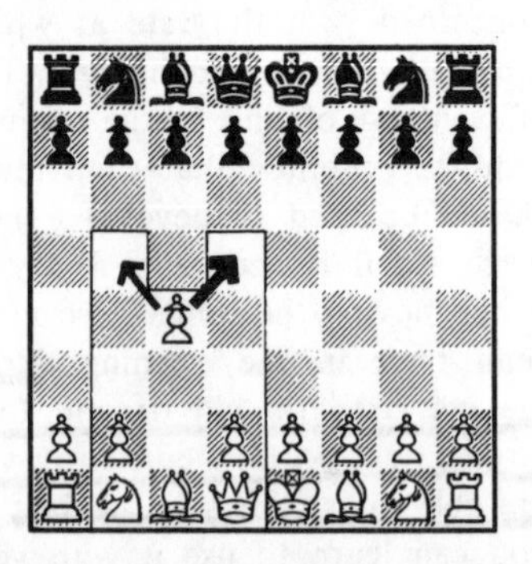

The pawn advances two squares instead of only one. This is already an example of the efficient use of time: why should it take a pawn two moves to reach the 4th rank when it can get there in one?

This move is also motivated by another important factor in chess: *control of space*. The move denies Black important maneuvering room, as can be seen in the diagram above, where White's area of control is marked.

Of special significance is the pressure White exerts on the central square Q5 (note the thicker arrow). *The most important area on the chess board is the center.* Only from the center can the pieces exercise their maximum activity and cover the greatest possible number of squares. This is why 1 P-QB4 is just as good as 1 P-Q4 or 1 P-K4, although the latter move is most popular with beginners (and not only beginners) because it opens lines for the development of the King Bishop and the Queen at the same time.

Since 1 P-QB4 was played to exert pressure on Q5, the next few developing moves for White are comfortable and easy to understand: he will increase the pressure on Q5 and, in general, develop new pieces while directing their power towards the center.

1 ...... P-QB3

Black would like to play P-Q4 but he cannot easily do it at once, for after 1 ... P-Q4 2 P×P Q×P 3 N-QB3, White increases his advantage in development.

Of course, Black has many other moves at his disposal here. He may play 1 . . . P-K3 with the intention of supporting a later . . . P-Q4 (similar to our game), or he can play 1 . . . P-K4 with the idea of capturing more space, or he may try to maintain symmetry with 1 . . . P-QB4. He can start his fight for center control by developing a piece with 1 . . . N-KB3 or preparing to develop a piece with 1 . . . P-KN3—but sooner or later he will have to engage his central pawns in the struggle.

2 P-K4 . . . . . .

White insists on controlling Q5. Another possibility is 2 P-Q4 P-Q4, transposing into the Slav Defense of the Queen's Gambit (for which the usual order of moves is 1 P-Q4 P-Q4 2 P-QB4 P-QB3).

We have mentioned the advantages of the initial pawn moves. But because pawns can never retreat, the advance of a pawn leaves in its wake potentially weak squares, or "holes." Holes are squares that cannot be defended by pawns and are therefore attractive targets for the opponent's pieces; the defense of such squares against occupation or exploitation by enemy pieces often ties up your own pieces, which should be put to better use elsewhere.

In the above diagram, the heavier crosses indicate the holes in White's position. Because of White's second move, these squares can no longer be protected by the King pawn. The light crosses mark squares that are not yet weak but will become weak if the QRP or the KNP later advance.

Nevertheless, an attempt by Black to exploit the weakness of White's Q4 with 2 . . . P-K4 (2 . . . P-QB4? is an obvious loss of time) would fail, because White would eliminate the weakness and gain control of more space by playing 3 N-KB3 and 4 P-Q4.

2 . . . . . . **P-Q4**
3 KP×P . . . . . .

Of the two advanced White pawns, the KP is undefended; therefore it is advisable to exchange it to avoid losing time defending it later.

3 . . . . . . **P×P**
4 P-Q4 . . . . . .

This position is characteristic of the Panov Attack in the Caro-Kann Defense, for which a more usual order of moves is 1 P-K4 P-QB3 2 P-Q4 P-Q4 3 P×P P×P 4 P-QB4.

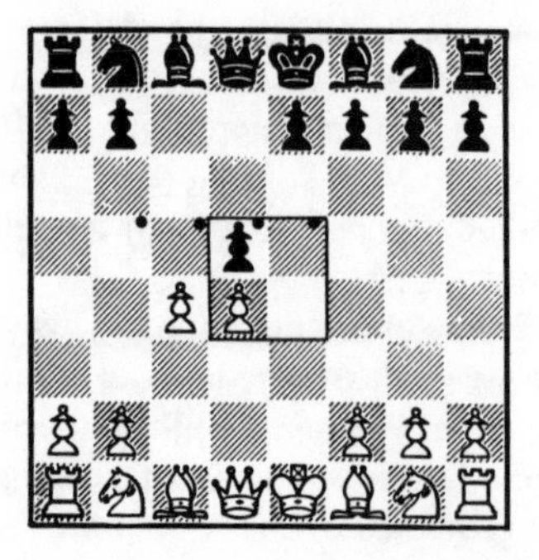

Strictly speaking, pawn moves in the opening are not developing moves; but they are useful to obtain space and are often necessary to enable the pieces to be developed. White's last move is both useful and necessary, as it completes his influence over the row of squares marked by dots in the above diagram. Particularly important are the potential outpost on K5 and the positional pressure exerted on Q5, the two squares in Black's half of the vital central area outlined in the diagram.

Although White's fourth move looks very much like a positional necessity, it was possible to play first 4 P×P. Black then would not reply 4 ... Q×P? because of 5 N-QB3 which, by forcing the Queen to move again, would increase White's advantage in time and the lead in development he already has by virtue of having the first move. Instead, Black would reply 4 ... N-KB3 with good prospects of recapturing the QP later and building a blockade in front of White's isolated central pawn.

Note the term "isolated pawn." After 4 P×P the White Queen pawn (on Q2) is isolated because White's QBP and KP, the two pawns adjacent to it, are gone and there are no other pawns to protect it. Such a situation would arise after either 4 P×P or 4 P-Q4 P×P; but there is an important difference between these two alternatives. We know that after four moves White has used four tempos; but now it is time to learn how to count tempos in a more subtle way. This knowledge is indispensable for the accurate handling of the opening; to ignore this most significant detail is to disregard one of the basic tenets of opening theory. The point here is that if 4 P×P it is White who spends a move on the pawn exchange, but if 4 P-Q4 P×P 5 B×P it is Black who spends the move. So here we have two positions with similar characteristics, but in the second one White's development is slightly improved. Sometimes this may be of great importance. The central pawn, though isolated, gives White more space and therefore the possibility of more activity for his pieces. But if he is too slow bringing them into the battle, Black will have time to direct his pieces against White's isolated pawn and turn it from a strength into a weakness in White's position.

4	**N-KB3**
5 N-QB3	......

These "natural" moves could be described as follows: Black develops another piece and strengthens the key square Q4; White also develops and increases his pressure on the Black Queen pawn.

5 ...... N-B3

A safer but more passive method of adding support to Q4 is 5 ... P-K3 6 N-B3 B-K2, a position that could also be reached by transposition from the Queen's Gambit if, after 1 P-Q4 P-Q4 2 P-QB4 P-K3 3 N-QB3 P-QB4 4 P-K3 N-KB3 5 N-B3, Black somewhat prematurely agrees to open White's King file and Queen Bishop's diagonal by 5 ... BP×P 6 KP×P, with prospects for a White initiative.

6 B-N5 ......

An energetic move which develops the Bishop and attacks the Knight that supports Black's center.

6 ...... Q-N3?

This move was recommended at the time by Czech master Rejfir and was known to Botvinnik. In fact, he spent only twenty minutes on the entire game, merely confirming the accuracy of his home analysis on which he had spent many hours of hard work. This approach is typical of modern chess competition, where thorough preparation is required.

The early development of the White Queen Bishop has weakened White's Queenside (most of the time, Lasker's rule of developing Knights before Bishops is a valuable guide in the opening) and Black is anxious to exploit this weakness. But Black's move is bad and the cause of his defeat because he starts a premature attack with the Queen alone, instead of normally developing his other pieces.

Obviously, Spielmann did not like 6 ... P×P 7 P-Q5 N-K4 8 Q-Q4 N-Q6ch 9 B×N P×B 10 N-B3! and White has a lead in development (Botvinnik-Flohr, match 1933).

7 P×P Q×NP

Other moves would increase White's lead in development: 7 ... KN×P 8 N×N Q-R4ch 9 N-B3 Q×B 10 N-B3, or 7 ... QN×P 8 KN-K2 N×N 9 KB×N. They were therefore unattractive to Black.

8 R-B1! ......

Although it develops a new piece and protects the White Queen Knight, this move was a surprise for Grandmaster Spielmann, who was expecting a continuation (then recently published in the press) in which, although White wins material after 8 N-R4 Q-N5ch 9 B-Q2 Q×P 10 P×N N-K5 11 B-K3 Q-N5ch 12 K-K2 P×P!, Black would have the attack he was hoping for.

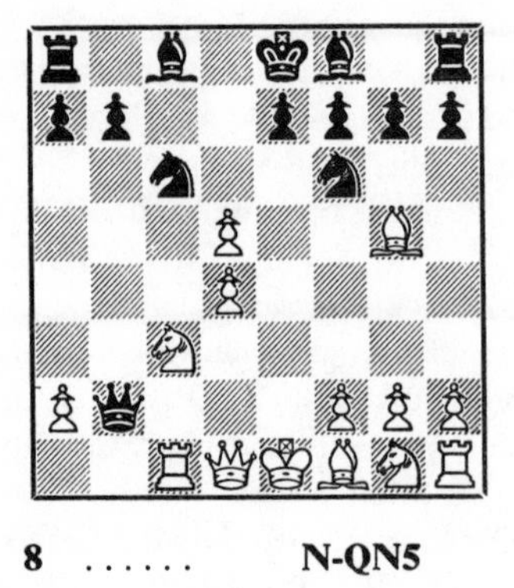

8 ...... N-QN5

Black had no good move for his Knight:

1) 8 ... N-QN1 9 N-R4 Q-N5ch 10 B-Q2;

2) 8 ... N-QR4 9 Q-R4ch;

3) 8 ... N-Q1 9 B×N KP×B 10 B-N5ch B-Q2 11 R-B2 Q-N5 12 Q-K2ch! B-K2 13 B×Bch K×B 14 Q-N4ch with a decisive advantage.

9 N-R4 ......

The end is near; Black can save his wayward Queen only at the cost of a piece.

9 ...... Q×RP
10 B-QB4 ......

It is always a pleasure to develop with a gain of time.

10 ...... B-N5
11 N-KB3 B×N
12 P×B Resigns

After 12 ... Q-R6 13 R-B3 he would have to give a piece away by 13 ... N-B7ch.

Beginners have a tendency to make early excursions with the Queen in the opening for the sake of cheap threats, but here, as some consolation, it was done by a grandmaster. The punishment was instructive in its swiftness.

Although every rule has its exception, the reader who knows the relative strengths of the pieces could easily conclude from the previous example that the general recommendation should be to develop gradually, starting with the pieces of lesser value and spending each move on the development of another piece. This sounds simple, but it is not quite so easy when one considers certain specific opening problems. It must not be forgotten that the time factor does not lose its importance once your pieces have been mobilized—it continues to play a vital role throughout the game in both attack and defense. Let us look at another game:

Belgrade 1946
RUY LOPEZ

White	**Black**
S. Gligoric	**P. Bidev**

1 P-K4 ......

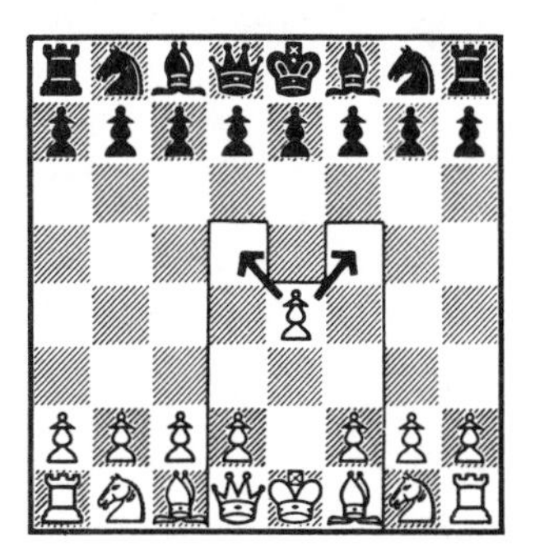

The area of White's influence, outlined in the above diagram, is different from that in the first game. Even the very first move determines the character of the future course of the game.

1 ...... P-K4

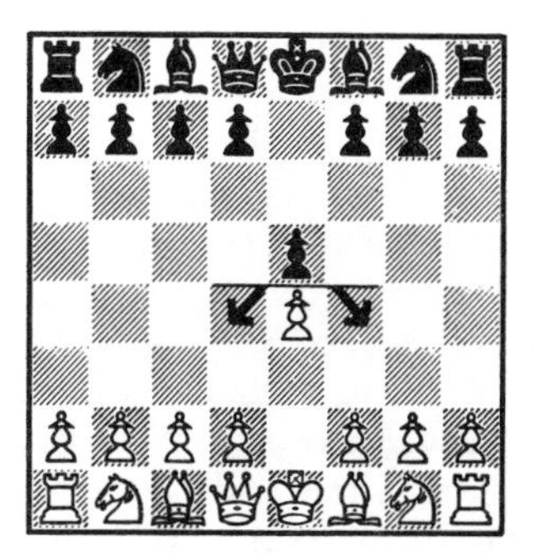

The classical reply. Black puts a "stop-sign" in front of the enemy forces at the line marked in the diagram, and tries to keep an equivalent area of space under his control. This will not be easy, for White moves next and will put pressure on Black's key square K4 (White's K5) with his pieces. Black's main positional task will be to reinforce this key central point as an obstacle to White's further progress.

2 N-KB3 ......

The Knight enters the action and attacks Black's most important pawn.

2 ...... N-QB3

Develops a piece and defends the pawn at the same time.

3 B-N5 ......

The most effective way to fight for superiority in the center. This developing move, which attacks the piece defending the Black King pawn, defines the Ruy Lopez.

3 ...... P-QR3

This move is possible because the White King pawn is still undefended.

4 B-R4 ......

The continuation 4 B×N QP×B 5 N×P Q-Q5 followed by 6 ... Q×KPch is not dangerous for Black. But playable is 4 B×N QP×B 5 O-O, creating a real threat to the Black King pawn and hoping for an advantage in the endgame because of White's effective pawn majority on the Kingside after an eventual P-Q4.

But White does not yet believe that obtaining the more favorable pawn formation is quite worth giving up the advantage of the two Bishops. To see why, place a Bishop and a Knight at the center of an empty chess board. From there the Knight will attack eight squares, but the Bishop thirteen. In practice, though, the two pieces are about equal in strength: if the position is fairly closed, with pawns blocking the diagonals, the Knight may be superior to a Bishop obstructed by the pawns.

But the combined strength of pieces working together can alter their normal relative values. It is a rare exception when two Bishops together are not superior to two Knights, for the Bishops cooperatively cover both the light and dark squares at long distances and nothing can escape their long glance. This is why White wishes to preserve his two Bishops, especially while Black still has his.

We have seen that, although the pieces have certain known values relative to each other, the actual worth of a piece at a given moment in a game can be to some extent determined by the characteristics of the position. It is said, for example, that the Queen is about equal to two Rooks in strength. Nevertheless, the Queen will be able to fight two powerful Rooks much better if each side also has a minor piece (a Knight or a Bishop), for the Queen needs a helper—even if only a pawn—to produce mating threats around the opponent's King (which, of course, is the object of the game, a far more important one, ultimately, than the mere capture of material). This is an example of how the effectiveness of the pieces can be increased by coordinating their activities.

4 ...... N-B3

This move is played for the same reasons as White's second move. Black does not want to chase the White Bishop to a better diagonal prematurely by 4 ... P-QN4 5 B-N3, where the Bishop would control the central square Q5 and attack Black's well-known weakness—the KBP—so early in the game. Moreover, 4 ... P-QN4 is another pawn move and does nothing to advance Black's development.

If at QN3 White's Bishop is on a better diagonal than when placed at QN5, one may ask why the Ruy Lopez is a better opening than the Giuoco Piano, in which White places his King Bishop on that "better" diagonal at once. Well, in that opening, after 1 P-K4 P-K4 2 N-KB3 N-QB3 3 B-B4 B-B4 4 P-B3 N-B3 5 P-Q4 P×P 6 P×P B-N5ch 7 B-Q2 B×Bch 8 QN×B P-Q4!, Black equalizes easily, as White has no time to keep his advantage in the center with 9 P-K5 because his Bishop is attacked. In the Ruy Lopez this central counterstroke by Black does not work so easily. Note this peculiarity of Bishops: they prefer to work from unexposed squares in the opening!

5 O-O B-K2

After 5 ... N×P 6 P-Q4 (6 R-K1, though playable, offers less) White will recapture the pawn with the better game. The move played gives some needed protection to the King and prepares for castling.

6 R-K1 P-QN4

This move is now advisable, for Black was in danger of losing a pawn since the White King pawn is now protected (6 ... O-O? 7 B×N QP×B 8 N×P!).

7 B-N3 ......

In spite of the explanation after Black's fourth move, the student might still have some doubts about White's procedure which has allowed Black to gain space on the Queenside "for free": Black's two pawn moves on the Queenside were not a waste of time because the White Bishop has had to move the same number of times. Well, first of all, the conditions at the center of the board count the most in the opening; what happens away from the center matters less. Second, any advanced pawn, although it controls forward space, is exposed and there fore a potential weakness to be attacked, giving the enemy a chance to open a file for his own use. For example, with the Black pawn on K4, White would like to be able to play either P-Q4 or P-KB4; and with the White pawn on K4 Black would be happy to strike in the same way if he could. But chess is a game based on reason and logic; it does not allow such radical moves without sufficient preparation, and preparation takes time and makes the struggle more complex.

In the same way, the Black QNP here becomes a target for an eventual P-QR4 by White. White has obtained the option of opening the QR file when it suits him, and Black has the additional worry of protecting his exposed QNP (its protection by the Black QBP is temporarily blocked by the Black Queen Knight). True, Black has freed the developing square QN2 for his Bishop, but it is not clear that this Bishop is posted better there than on its original diagonal, where it can defend KB4 (the hole created by Black's very first move!) from occupation by a White Knight, or perhaps support the QNP from Q2.

7 ...... O-O
8 P-B3 ......

The pieces will not have good attacking prospects without a strong center. Therefore, it is more effective to prepare P-Q4 than to develop the Queen Knight at once to QB3.

8 ...... P-Q3
9 P-KR3 ......

Another useful "loss of time," this move is played to prepare P-Q4. After an immediate 9 P-Q4 B-N5 (the move prepared by 8 . . . P-Q3) the pin on the White Knight would be unpleasant and White's QP would come under increasing pressure.

9 . . . . . . B-N2

More frequently played continuations are the classical 9 . . . N-QR4, or 9 . . . N-N1 and 10 . . . QN-Q2 to connect the Queenside pawns, or 9 . . . P-R3 and 10 . . . R-K1 to strengthen the K4 bastion.

10 P-Q3 . . . . . .

This move is intended to restrict the activity of the Black Queen Bishop by keeping its diagonal closed; but more energetic and stronger is 10 P-Q4, wasting no time starting the vital center action.

10	. . . . . .	**N-Q2**
11	**QN-Q2**	**N-B4**
12	**B-B2**	. . . . . .

A very good recommendation by Philidor (1726-1795) was to place the pieces behind the pawns, which to him represented the "soul" of chess. (Philidor's great discovery was that the arrangement of pawns had a fundamental influence on the character of the game.) Although his pieces have been driven back, White's position is more flexible and better. The student should understand that pieces are not at all dead when placed behind pawns, although they seem to lose in scope. They continue to radiate power and they can contribute significantly to the strength of advanced pawns. For instance, here White is better prepared to strike in the center with P-Q4; as long as there are White pieces to occupy the squares Q5 and KB5 which are controlled by the White KP, there is great potential energy stored in the White King Bishop and King Rook. White pieces placed on Q5 or KB5 can be captured by Black, true, but only at the cost of increasing the power of White's Bishop and Rook. For the same reason, Black cannot strike back with . . . P-Q4 without taking the risk of releasing the energy of the White pieces.

A good illustration of what is meant by the "radiation" of a piece's power is the 16th game of the Fischer-Spassky World Championship Match in Reykjavik 1972: 1 P-K4 P-K4 2 N-KB3 N-QB3 3 B-N5 P-QR3 4 B×N QP×B 5 O-O P-B3 6 P-Q4 B-KN5 7 P×P Q×Q 8 R×Q P×P 9 R-Q3 B-Q3 10 QN-Q2 N-B3 11 N-B4 N×P 12 N/4×P B×N/6 13 N×B O-O 14 B-K3 P-QN4 15 P-B4; now Black played 15 . . . QR-N1! and after 16 R-QB1 P×P 17 R-Q4 KR-K1 18 N-Q2 N×N 19 R×N R-K5 20 P-KN3 B-K4 21 R/1-B2 K-B2 22 K-N2 the energy of the Black Queen Rook was released by the sudden tactical shot 22 . . . R×P! Or take another example from a game Suetin-Gligoric, Havana 1969, where after 1 P-K4 P-K4 2 N-KB3 N-QB3 3 B-N5 P-QR3 4 B-R4 N-B3 5 O-O B-K2 6 R-K1 P-QN4 7 B-N3 P-Q3 8 P-B3 O-O 9 P-QR3!? N-Q2 10 P-Q4 B-B3 11 B-K3, Black disclosed White's hidden weakness on the QN file by 11 . . . R-N1! and after 12 QN-Q2 N-N3 13 R-QB1 B-N5 14 P-Q5? N-R4 15 B-R2 N/4-B5! White was not able to exchange pieces advantageously and had to concede to his opponent the advantage of the Bishop pair (see the note after White's fourth move).

12 . . . . . . P-Q4?

Safer was 12 . . . B-B3 to strengthen Black's hold on the center. The premature text move will cause Black's defeat because he has wasted time. Let us just count tempos: to make this break in the center Black has spent two moves on the Knight maneuver, removing that piece from the defense of the Kingside, and another tempo in playing this pawn to Q4 in two moves instead of one. Even if White repays part of the debt in tempos by moving his own QP twice, his Queen Knight will enter the fight with a gain of time and that will give our equation a plus on White's side.

13 P×P Q×P
14 N-B1 QR-Q1

15 N-K3 . . . . . .

Already we can see the drawbacks of Black's 12th move. After the text, White's initiative is quickly converted into a blistering attack against the Black King.

15 . . . . . . Q-Q2
16 P-Q4! . . . . . .

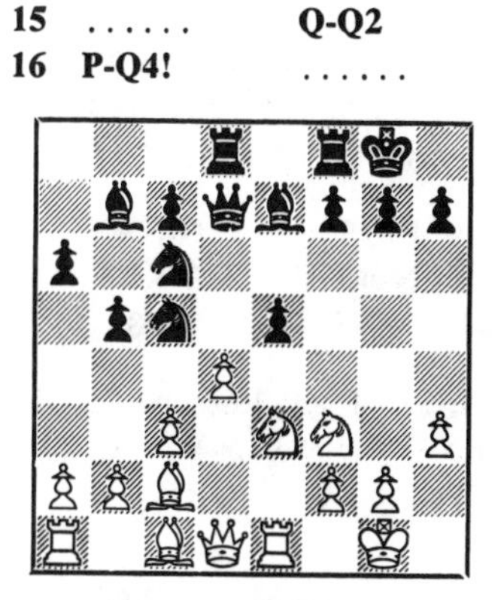

You will remember our earlier discussion of the radiation of the power of White's pieces from behind his pawns. Suddenly these pieces come powerfully into play in the attack against the enemy King, a result of Black's premature 12th move.

16 . . . . . . P×P

Because 16 . . . P-K5? loses a pawn after 17 N-Q2.

17 P×P Q-B1

The pawn was taboo: 17 . . . N×P 18 N×N Q×N 19 Q×Q R×Q 20 N-B5, and White wins material.

18 B-Q2! . . . . . .

Since 18 B×Pch K×B 19 Q-B2ch P-N3 20 P×N is refuted by 20 ... N-N5, when Black has some counterplay for the pawn.

18 ...... N-R5

It is a sad necessity that both Black Knights will have to stray from the defense of the Kingside, for 18 ... N×P? 19 N×N R×N is not playable because of 20 N-B5.

19 P-Q5 N-N1
20 N-B5 B-KB3
21 N-N5 P-N3

21 ... R×P loses by force: 22 Q-R5 P-R3 23 N-R7! Q-Q1 24 N×Pch P×N 25 Q×P.

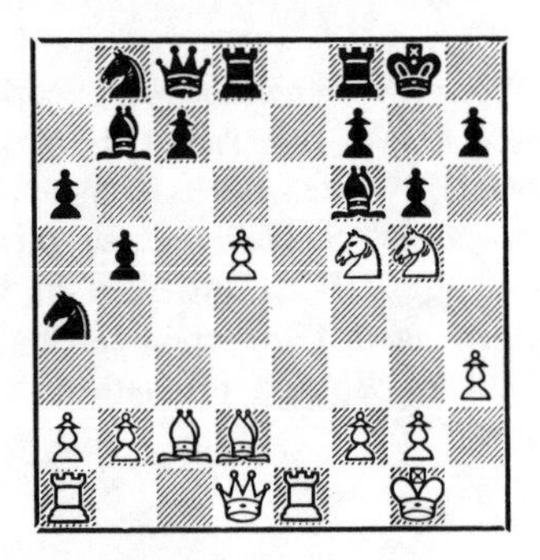

22 N×RP! ......

White starts to strip the pawn cover from the abandoned King.

22 ...... K×N
23 N-K7 ......

Getting the Knight out of the way of White's King Bishop.

23 ...... B×N
24 Q-R5ch K-N1

24 ... K-N2 25 Q-R6ch would amount to the same thing.

25 B×P P×B
26 Q×Pch K-R1
27 R×B Resigns

Black is unable to avoid mate.

The Fight for the Center

We have seen that fighting for time means fighting for development. But this has to be combined with fighting for the center, for without good control of the small central area (by either pawns or pieces) the developed pieces will remain ineffective as they will not have sufficient scope for activity. In the previous game, Black neglected the time factor by making a premature break in the center; in the next game Black is guilty of neglecting control of the center.

Venice 1971
BUDAPEST GAMBIT

White	Black
S. Gligoric	**H. Westerinen**

1 P-Q4 N-KB3
2 P-QB4 P-K4

The term "gambit" implies a pawn sacrifice—either temporary or permanent—in the opening to obtain some compensating advantage, such as more power in the center or better development with chances for attack. A gambit may be sound or unsound, the final judgment depending on whether the advantage gained is demonstrated to have been worth the sacrificed material. The Queen's Gambit, for example, is sound because White obtains a strong grip on the center and is even able to regain his sacrificed pawn (assuming Black accepts it in the first place). But the gambit used in this game belongs to the unsound group: it produces only an inferiority in the center for Black, who vainly hopes for some tactical chances in compensation for this positional inferiority.

3 P×P N-N5

Note that it is the already developed piece that fights for the recapture of the material, evidence that this system of play for Black is dubious.

4 B-B4 N-QB3

Playable is 4 . . . P-KN4, but after 5 B-Q2!, intending B-B3, Black would remain with a weakened Kingside (the advanced KNP would be a target, as we have seen).

5 N-KB3 B-N5ch
6 N-B3 ......

This is more active than the cautious 6 QN-Q2.

6 ...... Q-K2
7 Q-Q5! ......

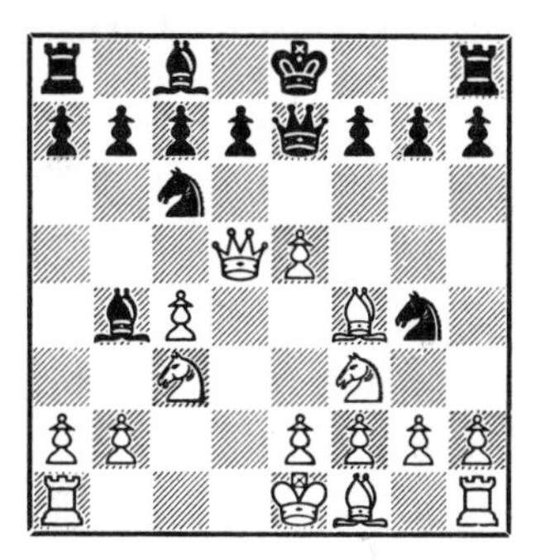

White is ready to give back a pawn, but not the one on K5 which has a cramping effect on Black's position.

7 ...... B×Nch
8 P×B Q-R6

Black would have to agree to the permanent loss of a pawn by 8 . . . P-B3 if he wishes to get his King Knight back to KB3.

9 R-B1 ......

Naturally, White would not be satisfied with the repetition of moves 9 Q-Q2 Q-K2 10 Q-Q5 Q-R6.

9 ...... Q×P

The sacrifice of a pawn after 9 . . . P-B3 10 P×P N×P/3 11 Q-Q2 P-Q3 12 N-Q4 O-O 13 P-B3! would not give Black sufficient counterplay, but the recapture of the pawn as played gives White the opportunity to obtain a very strong initiative.

10 P-R3 N-R3
11 P-K4! ......

White takes the whole range of central squares under powerful control and leaves the Black pieces without good play. The exchange of his strong Bishop for the passive Black King Knight (11 B×N) for the sake of spoiling Black's Kingside pawn formation is not a worthwhile transaction.

11	......	**N-KN1**

White's strength in the center forces the Black pieces to dance around helplessly.

12	**P-B5!**	......

This frees an active square for his King Bishop.

12	......	**Q-R6**

There was no joy for Black in the endgame 12 ... Q×Q 13 P×Q N-R4 14 N-Q4 with the threat of N-N5.

13	**B-B4**	**N-Q1**
14	**B-K3**	......

A useful prophylactic move which removes the Bishop from its exposed square and protects the pawn at QB5.

14	......	**N-K2**
15	**Q-Q1**	**P-QN3**
16	**O-O**	......

Notice that White is anxious to complete his development and thus increase his advantage.

16	......	**P×P**
17	**Q-Q3**	......

The immediate threat is 18 R-R1 Q-N7 19 KR-N1.

17	......	**Q-R4**
18	**R-N1**	......

Taking the retreat square N3 from the Black Queen and thus forcing Black to weaken his Q3 square to provide a new retreat.

18	......	**P-QB3**
19	**R-R1**	**Q-B2**
20	**B×P**	......

Black is strategically lost; the rest is just an execution.

20	......	**N-K3**
21	**B-Q6**	**Q-Q1**
22	**N-Q4**	......

Black's Bishop has no future, and that alone is enough to make his position hopeless. The move played clears the way for the advance of White's KBP.

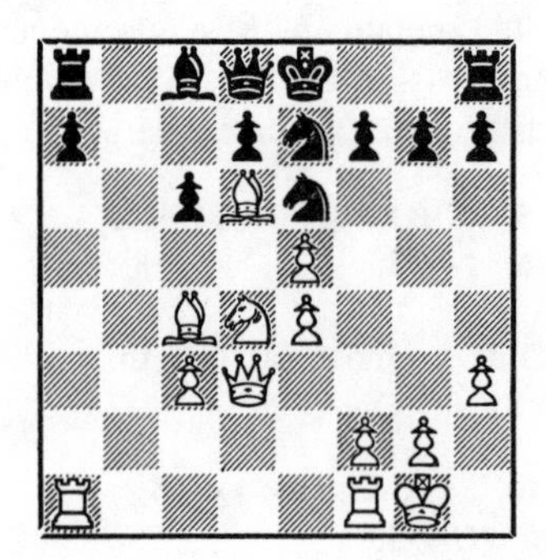

22	......	**N-N3**
23	**N×N**	......

This removes the only active Black piece, which is always the simplest method in a winning position. The alternative was 23 N-B5.

23	......	**QP×N**
24	**P-B4**	**P-B3**
25	**Q-K3**	**P-QR4**
26	**Q-B5**	**B-Q2**
27	**P-B5**	**Resigns**

On 27 . . . KP×P 28 P-K6, White wins.

Now, for a change, let us look at a sound gambit, where White temporarily offers a pawn for a good purpose—superiority in the center.

Busum 1969
QUEEN'S GAMBIT ACCEPTED

White	**Black**
S. Gligoric	**T. Ghitescu**

1	**P-Q4**	**P-Q4**
2	**P-QB4**	......

White attacks the Black Queen pawn; this pawn controls White's central square K4 and hinders the advance of the White forces.

2	......	**P×P**

Black may also enter the Queen's Gambit Declined by supporting his Queen pawn with either 2 . . . P-K3 or 2 . . . P-QB3.

3	**N-KB3**	......

First White secures domination of K5, for he has time to recapture the pawn later. It would seem quite natural to take the opportunity presented by Black's second move to play 3 P-K4, but this move is less common because of the simplifying answer 3 . . . P-K4. However, after 4 N-KB3 (not 4 P×P Q×Qch 5 K×Q B-K3 and Black will develop more comfortably) 4 . . . P×P 5 Q×P White still may count on some advantage in the endgame.

3	......	**N-KB3**

Black develops and prevents P-K4.

4	**P-K3**	......

The safest way to recapture the pawn. The more ambitious 4 N-B3 P-QR3! could complicate that task.

4	......	**B-N5**

The alternative is 4 . . . P-K3 and 5 . . . P-B4, attacking White's central stronghold.

5	**B×P**	**P-K3**
6	**P-KR3**	**B-R4**
7	**N-B3**	......

White prefers solid development to the sharp continuation 7 Q-N3 B×N 8 P×B QN-Q2 9 Q×P P-B4, when Black would have good counterplay for the pawn.

7	......	**QN-Q2**
8	**B-K2**	......

This move violates the rule of not moving the same piece twice in the opening, but, as we have pointed out, there is no rule without exceptions. Trying to obtain the full pawn center with 8 P-K4 would not work out well because of the simplifying 8 . . . B×N 9 Q×B N-N3, attacking the Bishop and the Queen pawn simultaneously. The move played removes the Bishop from its exposed square and gets rid of the pin on the King Knight, which is essential for White's control of the center, for Black aims to free his game with . . . P-K4 after sufficient preparation.

8 . . . . . . B-N3

But this is a waste of time, for Black will not be successful in keeping K5 under his supervision for long. It was better to complete the development of his Kingside. But he should be careful not to do this by 8 . . . B-Q3 9 O-O O-O because of 10 N-QN5! P-K4 11 P×P N×P 12 N×B! with a positional advantage.

9	**O-O**	**B-K2**
10	**N-KR4!**	**O-O**
11	**N×B**	**RP×N**
12	**P-K4**	. . . . . .

With his 10th move White achieved two advantages: the full pawn center and the Bishop pair.

12 . . . . . . P-B3

Black decides on passive, stubborn tactics which, nevertheless, are not very promising. However, the active 12 . . . P-B4 would be met by the unpleasant 13 P-K5.

13 B-K3 . . . . . .

White is in no hurry to begin an attack and calmly improves the position of his pieces under the protection of his powerful center.

13 . . . . . . P-R4

Here we have the same situation as in the previous game: White has a firm grip on the center, and Black is obliged merely to mark time.

14	**R-B1**	**Q-N1**
15	**P-R3**	**R-Q1**
16	**Q-B2**	**R-QB1**
17	**KR-Q1**	**P-QN4**

Having no suitable plan at his disposal, Black loses patience and tries to get some space—if nothing else—on the wing, but this maneuver only weakens his position.

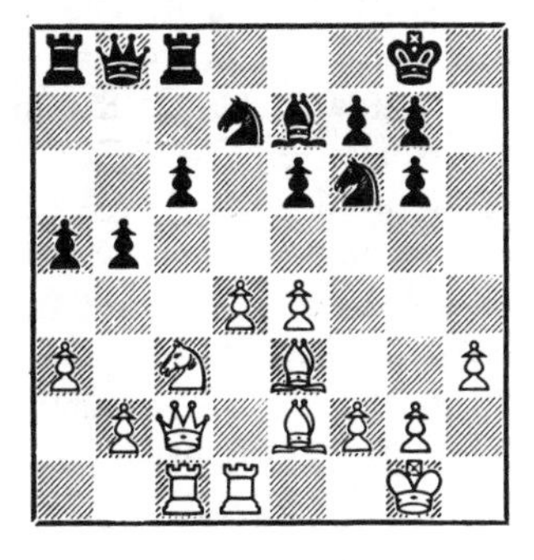

18 P-K5 N-K1

The point of White's pawn advance is that the natural 18 ... N-Q4 is answered by 19 N×N KP×N (not 19 ... BP×N because the QNP needs protection—remember our discussion of the weakness of advanced pawns!) 20 B-N4 Q-N2 21 P-K6, destroying Black's King-side.

19 N-K4 ......

The point of White's previous move is this centralization of his Knight, which is now ready to take part in the attack against the enemy King and simultaneously oversee the hole at QB5.

19 ...... N-N3
20 B-N5! B-B1

This Bishop is needed to protect the weak dark squares in Black's camp, particularly QB4 and KN4.

21 P-KR4! ......

Remember our lesson about exposed pawns. Here Black's doubled KNP is the target that White will use to open the KR file on which he will build up mating threats.

21 ...... N-Q4
22 Q-Q3 ......

Because White controls more space, he has no difficulty in transferring his Queen to the opposite side for the attack.

22 ...... Q-N2
23 Q-R3 Q-Q2
24 P-R5 ......

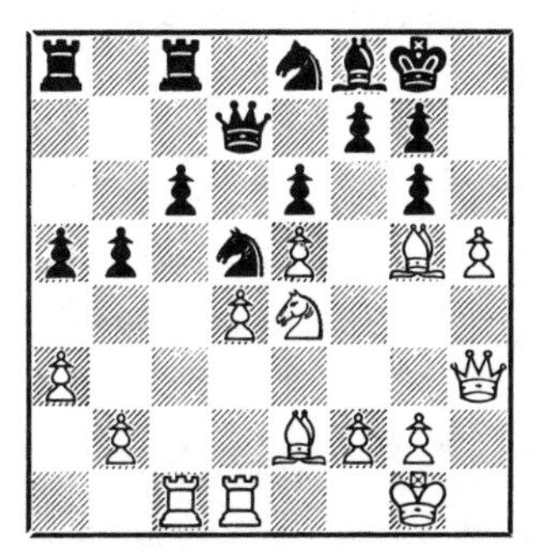

This is White's reward for having more power in the center: by just quiet means he has reached a winning position.

24 ...... P×P
25 B×RP Q-R2
26 B-N4 P-QB4
27 B-Q2! Resigns

The threat of 28 N-N5, which has long been in the air, is now irresistible. Black cannot meet it with

27 . . . B-K2 because of 28 B×KP!

In the last two games we have seen what child's play it was to win when White had a great superiority in the center. But sometimes overwhelming power in the center is not needed; just the control of more space than the opponent may decide the issue, as Fischer shows in the next game.

Buenos Aires 1970

PETROFF DEFENSE

White	**Black**
R. Fischer	**F. Gheorghiu**

1 P-K4 P-K4
2 N-KB3 N-KB3

There are several openings in which Black may try this solid method of repeating White's moves, but chess would be a dull game indeed if Black could maintain this symmetry for very long.

3 N×P P-Q3

Black would lose material after 3 . . . N×P? 4 Q-K2, so first he drives the Knight back.

4 N-KB3 N×P

Now 5 Q-K2 would be answered by 5 . . . Q-K2.

5 P-Q4 B-K2

A more active continuation might appear to be 5 . . . P-Q4 6 B-Q3 B-Q3 7 O-O O-O, but this would give White the initiative after 8 P-B4 and 9 N-B3, undermining the advanced Black Knight. This is a good example of how time may be gained by attacking units that support an exposed enemy piece.

It is interesting that White could have had a similar position, but with his Knight still at K5, with the variation 3 P-Q4 N×P 4 B-Q3 P-Q4 5 N×P!, but after 3 P-Q4 Black has the simplifying alternative 3 . . . P×P 4 P-K5 N-K5 5 Q×P P-Q4 6 P×P e.p. N×QP.

6 B-Q3 N-KB3

This modest move is an idea of Petrosian's, who likes to play positions "without weaknesses."

7 P-KR3! . . . . . .

This costs a tempo, true, but what would be the use of White's greater mobility if Black were permitted to develop his Queen Bishop to an active position at KN5?

7 . . . . . . O-O
8 O-O R-K1

In the 5th game of the Fischer-Petrosian match, Buenos Aires 1971, White had the upper hand after 8 . . . P-B3 9 R-K1 QN-Q2 10 B-KB4 R-K1 11 P-B4 N-B1 12 N-B3 P-QR3.

9 P-B4 N-B3
10 N-B3 P-KR3

This preventive move is necessary, although it pays back Black's debt in time, for 10 ... B-B1 11 B-N5 could be unpleasant.

11	**R-K1**	**B-B1**
12	**R×R**	**Q×R**

With his timely 11th move White has succeeded in exchanging the active Black Rook with no waste of time.

13	**B-B4**	**B-Q2**
14	**Q-Q2**	**Q-B1**

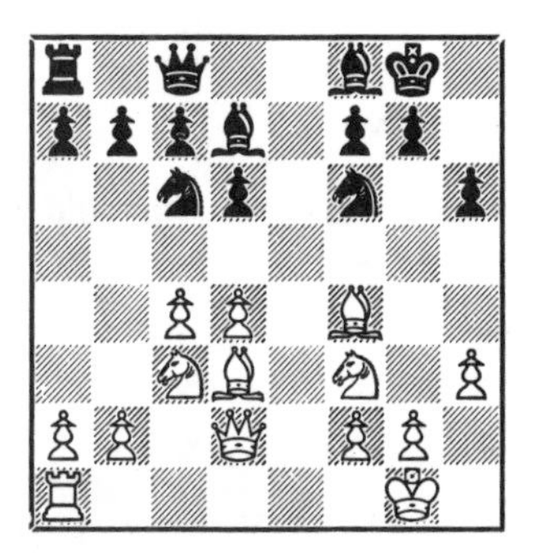

The practical consequence of his cramped position is that Black finds it difficult to bring his Queen Rook into play. Now he hopes to free his game with 15 ... B-B4, but White does not allow it.

15	**P-Q5!**	**N-QN5**
16	**N-K4!**	**N×N**
17	**B×N**	**N-R3**
18	**N-Q4**	......

By clever maneuvering based on the simultaneous attack on both Black Knights, White has reduced the number of pieces that defend the Black King and has prevented the vital freeing move ... B-KB4.

18	......	**N-B4**
19	**B-B2**	**P-QR4**

The well-placed Black Knight looks good, but it merely fans the air and cannot join in the defense of the Kingside.

20	**R-K1**	**Q-Q1**
21	**R-K3!**	......

This is a good illustration of the practical meaning of greater space: White has the third rank for the aggressive operations of his Rook, and two clean diagonals for his attack against the Black King.

21	......	**P-QN3**

This loss of tempo will seal Black's fate, but he did not like 21 ... Q-B3 22 R-R3 P-QN3 23 P-QN4 N-N2 24 N-N3.

22	**R-KN3**	**K-R1**

Necessary to prevent 23 B×RP.

23	**N-B3!**	......

We have stressed the importance of control of the center. One major advantage belonging to the player who has a greater share of center control than his opponent is that he is able to centralize his pieces to increase their mobility and hence their power. Here, the centralized Knight retreats to give its place to the Queen, which will now be able to exercise its maximum potential.

23 ...... Q-K2

23 ... Q-B3 would be met by 24 B-K3 and 25 B-Q4 with the irresistible threat of 26 Q×KRP. Now Black can meet 24 B-K3 with 24 ... N-K5, but ...

24 Q-Q4 ......

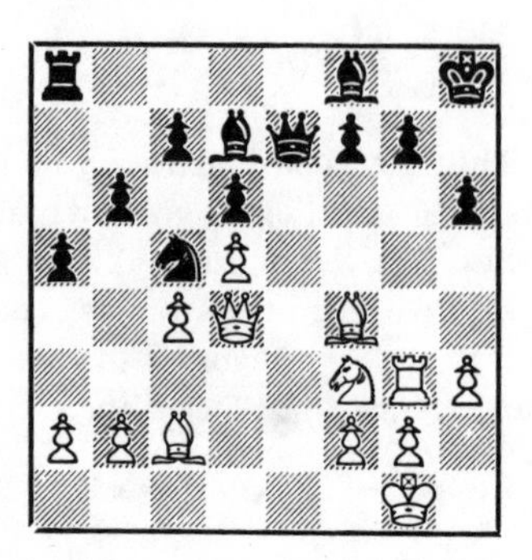

What is Black to do against 25 B×RP? If 24 ... P-KB3, the light squares around his King would be disastrously weakened (25 N-R4).

24 ...... Q-B3

This is a necessary but unpleasant choice. White's attack will now be converted into a superior endgame where Black's Kingside pawns will be hopelessly weak and ultimately doomed.

25 Q×Q P×Q
26 N-Q4 ......

The Knight prepares to make good use of the now-permanent base at KB5.

26 ...... R-K1
27 R-K3 R-N1

Black desperately tries his only counterchance by preparing to open the QN file.

28 P-QN3 P-N4
29 P×P B×NP
30 N-B5 ......

Material loss is no longer to be avoided.

30 ...... B-Q2
31 N×RP R-N5
32 R-N3 ......

White threatens two different mates.

32 ...... B×N
33 B×B N-K5
34 B-N7ch K-R2

34 ... K-N1 35 B×N R×B 36 B×Pch would only prolong Black's agony.

35 P-B3 Resigns

The Knight cannot be saved.

Bobby Fischer's Secret Weapon

Chess is a game that requires the utmost accuracy and precision. Sometimes one side, though standing no worse in space or center control, finds itself desperate to regain the balance lost in the opening. We return our attention now to that element in chess that World Champion Robert Fischer, whether playing

Black or White, understands better than anyone else: the element of time.

In the game that follows, the "secret weapon" he employs to reach the first goal in the opening—the initiative—is his absolute accuracy in the employment of time and his colossal ability to notice and exploit even the smallest error in that respect by his opponent. The loser of this game is no less than a former world champion and a great chess thinker who often uses his extraordinary creative gifts in the avoidance of known lines of play. He does so here, but this time obtains an unsatisfactory position.

Palma de Majorca 1970
ENGLISH OPENING

White	**Black**
V. Smyslov	**R. Fischer**

1	**P-QB4**	**P-KN3**
2	**N-QB3**	**B-N2**
3	**P-KN3**	......

The network of Fischer's roads toward a good game is very dense. On 3 N-B3 he might have tried 3 ... P-QB4 4 P-Q4 P×P 5 N×P N-QB3, as he did against Naranja in the same tournament, when suddenly White did not know what to do about his Knight in the center (6 N×N NP×N would only strengthen Black's center) and so he played the modest 6 P-K3, relieving Black of any worries in the opening.

3	......	**P-QB4**
4	**B-N2**	**N-QB3**
5	**P-N3**	......

Smyslov favors the double fianchetto (the wing development in which the Bishop is posted on the long diagonal, often the most active place for it) at this unusual moment instead of the recognized variation 5 P-K3 P-K3 6 KN-K2 KN-K2 7 O-O O-O 8 P-Q4 P×P 9 N×P P-Q4 10 P×P N×P 11 R-K1! In Petrosian-Fischer, second round of the match USSR vs. World (Belgrade 1970), there occurred 5 N-B3 P-K3! (Fischer remarked here: "Now it is Black who is playing for the center") 6 O-O KN-K2 7 P-Q3 O-O 8 B-Q2 P-Q4 9 P-QR3 P-N3 10 R-N1 B-N2 11 P-QN4 BP×P 12 RP×P P×P 13 P×P R-B1! and here also Fischer had the upper hand, attacking White's "hanging pawns" on the Queenside. White had spent too much time on his wing maneuvers.

5	......	**P-K3!**

We may repeat here that it is Black who is now playing for the center.

6	**B-N2**	**KN-K2**
7	**N-R4**	......

As with White's 5th, this move has a special meaning. In an earlier Smyslov-Fischer game (Buenos Aires 1970), White played 7 N-B3. If we interpolate here 7 N-B3 O-O and then try 8 N-QR4, as played in that game, Black makes White's Queen Bishop a futile piece by 8 . . . P-K4! since 9 N×BP P-K5! 10 B×B P×N would cost White material.

The game mentioned above illustrates another goal of opening strategy, that of limiting the opponent's potential. One of the best means of achieving this is, as we have learned: *concentrating power in the center.*

7 . . . . . . B×B
8 N×B O-O

White has accomplished his objective—the trade of black-bound Bishops—but, it should be noted, at a loss of time. Getting used to counting tempos precisely, we can see that after the exchange of Bishops it was Black's turn to move and that White will have to spend another move to bring his Queen Knight back into play. That slight loss of time is enough to hand the initiative over to Black!

9 P-K3 . . . . . .

After the time lost by White with his 7th move, this one is a luxury he cannot afford. White is playing for positional gain when he should be rushing to catch up in development to be able to hold the balance. 9 N-B3 is indicated.

9 . . . . . . P-Q4
10 P×P . . . . . .

10 N-K2 P-Q5 could be unpleasant because of White's stray Queen Knight.

10 . . . . . . N×P

The text creates pressure along the Queen file and is therefore far better than 10 . . . P×P.

11 N-K2 P-N3!
12 P-Q4 . . . . . .

White considers that because of 12 . . . B-R3 this is the last chance to free his game. But he will always be one move late in consolidating his position. Since his development is backward, the passive 12 O-O B-R3 13 P-Q3 is better than the text, which opens files and diagonals that Black, being further developed, is in a better position to use.

12 . . . . . . B-R3
13 P×P . . . . . .

This capture costs White another tempo. But it is hard to blame him at this point: 13 N-QB4 P-QN4 is not an attractive alternative.

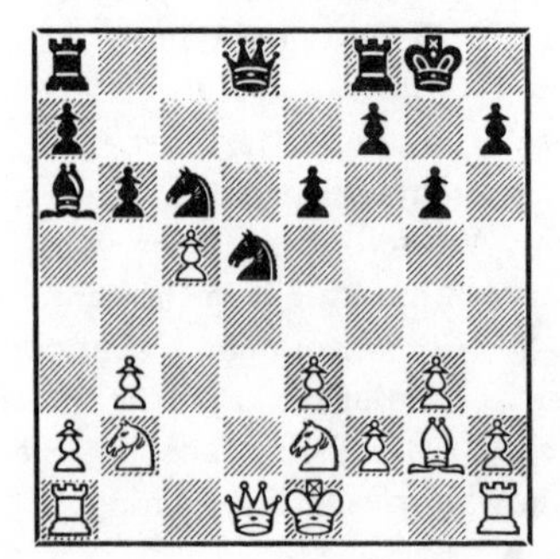

13	......	**Q-B3!**
14	**N-QB4**	**N-B6!**

The point is that White will be unable to castle and will have to lose more time connecting his Rooks.

15	**N×N**	......

It is obvious that on 15 Q-B1 N×N 16 K×N, Black counts on time rather than material for his superiority, and develops an irresistible attack by 16 ... QR-B1! 17 P×P N-K4.

15	......	**Q×Nch**
16	**K-B1**	**KR-Q1**

Black employs simple and efficient mathematics to bring new forces into play in minimum time.

17	**Q-B1**	**B×Nch**
18	**P×B**	**Q-Q6ch**
19	**K-N1**	**QR-B1**

One phase of the game has been concluded. At the cheap cost of one pawn, Black dominates the open central files while White is playing without the use of one of his Rooks.

20	**P×P**	......

White's best hope lies in reducing the material on the board and giving back the extra pawn in a more simplified position.

20	......	**P×P**
21	**Q-N2**	......

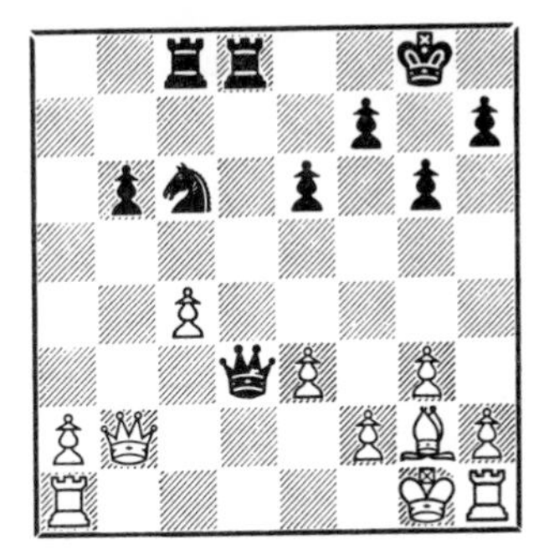

White activates the Queen and removes it from its exposed position on the QB file. Further trading by 21 B×N serves no useful purpose as then Black's heavy artillery penetrates rapidly with disastrous effect.

21	......	**N-R4**
22	**P-KR4**	......

White tries to bring his King Rook into play. 22 Q×P N×P 23 Q-N3 Q-Q7 would be almost suicide, considering the many threats against White's King.

22	......	**N×P**
23	**Q-B6**	**Q-B4!**

Fischer made this move without hesitation, which illustrates the efficiency of his technique. White's only active piece will be traded off. Black has no illusions about continuing the King hunt and instead goes for an increased advantage in the endgame after the Queens have been exchanged. Also, there was some threat of 24 P-R5.

24	**Q×Q**	**NP×Q!**

This removes the White Rook pawn's target, and now Black's more centralized pawn chain limits the possibilities of White's Bishop.

25 P-R5 ......

White aims to activate his King Rook on the fourth rank. 25 K-R2 R-Q7 26 KR-KB1 N-K4 27 K-N1 R/1-B7 28 P-R4 N-N5 is even worse for White.

25 ...... **R-Q7**
26 R-QB1 ......

White offers to return a pawn, trying to salvage the game by this pin and an ensuing simplification by B-B1, etc. But Black's reply kills even this hope.

26 ...... **R-B4!**

Now the pin is futile, and this Rook move will lead to the creation of a terrible passed pawn which decides the game.

27 R-R4 **N-K4**
28 R×R ......

This exchange is unpleasant but forced—otherwise Black gets both Rooks on the seventh rank and wins material.

28 ...... **P×R**
29 R-R4 ......

At last this Rook gets into the fight, but unfortunately it is in front of White's passed pawn. Black's passed pawn, well supported by his pieces, will advance much too fast.

29 ...... **P-QB5**
30 P-R6 **K-B1**
31 R-R8ch ......

Here 31 P-B4 N-N5 32 R×P fails because of 32 ... R×Bch.

31 ...... **K-K2**
32 R-QB8 ......

Black's pawn must be stopped, and it's now or never.

32 ...... **R×RP**
33 B-B1 ......

33 P-B4 still doesn't work, for the reason given after White's 31st move.

33 ...... **R-B7**
34 K-N2 ......

White has no useful move and must stand by while Black wins material.

34 ...... **N-N5**
35 K-N1 ......

Played to avoid the worst with 35 . . . N×Pch. Now the White Kingside pawns are ripe to fall, and Black sells his passed pawn for that rich harvest.

35	......	**R×P**
36	**B×P**	**R-B6**
37	**K-N2**	**R×P**
38	**R-KR8**	**N×P**
39	**R×P**	**N-N5**
40	**B-N5**	**R-N6**
41	**B-B6**	......

The momentum of the game keeps White playing even though he is two pawns down.

41	......	**R-N7ch**
42	**K-N1**	**N-K4**
43	**B-R8**	**R-N1**

If Black wants to exchange Rooks, he can do it by 44 . . . N-N3 and 45 . . . R-KR1.

44	**B-R1**	......

White resigned without waiting to see his opponent's reply.

By now the reader should be trained well enough to realize that each move is a treasure, to be spent only in the most useful way. Otherwise, punishment at the opponent's hands may be expected. Of the moves available to each player in the opening, only a few need be devoted to the aim of efficient gain of space and control of the center to create the necessary conditions for maximum activity of the pieces. The other moves in the opening stage should be used to move all the pieces into conflict with the enemy in the minimum time. This is why we repeat the advice to learn to count tempos. *The art of treating the opening stage of the game correctly and without error is basically the art of using time efficiently.*

If a player at a given moment feels obliged to move a developed piece a second time to correct its position, there may be something wrong with his opening strategy. An exception is when that piece, by moving again, performs the new task of delivering a serious positional or other threat to the opponent, forcing him to spend an equal amount of time on the defense but without simultaneously improving his development. The following game is a very fine illustration of this idea.

Match, Buenos Aires 1971
SICILIAN DEFENSE

White	**Black**
R. Fischer	**T. Petrosian**

1	**P-K4**	**P-QB4**

This move defines the Sicilian Defense. In most of the games discussed in this chapter, the contestants have focused their attention in the opening on the same central area of the chess board; but this game is different. With his very first move White has declared his intention to capture space on the Kingside, while Black, with his, seeks to gain space on the opposite wing. The following diagram illustrates this. Black's first move also indicates his dissatisfaction merely with inert resistance to pressure, and his desire, after neutralizing the center, to strike back on his own account. Thus this opening is to be considered less a defense than a counterattack.

With his first move Black prevents White from dominating the center with pawns, and when White eventually plays P-Q4 Black will exchange his pawn of lesser importance for White's center pawn. (It is a general rule that center pawns—KP and QP—have greater value than flank pawns.) Black's positional gain is counterbalanced by the fact that White's first move contributes better to development than Black's move, for Black will later have to make an extra pawn move to open diagonals for both of his Bishops.

2	**N-KB3**	**P-K3**
3	**P-Q4**	**P×P**
4	**N×P**	......

The pawn exchange has diminished Black's pressure on White's Q4, and has opened the Queen file for White's heavy pieces and the QB file for Black's. Emanuel Lasker (1868-1941) summed it up: "All in all, the Sicilian opening is full of tension."

4	......	**P-QR3**

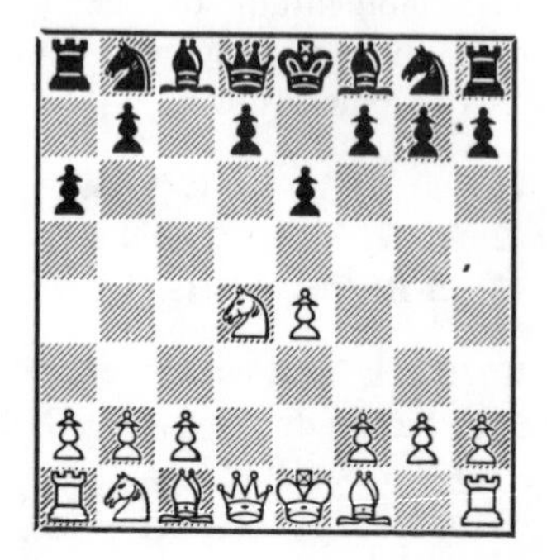

This move, invented by Louis Paulsen (1833-91), has in this century become a part of the modern positional approach, which is to limit the scope of the opponent's pieces (it controls Black's QN4) and to prepare a more extensive capture of space on the Queenside by ... P-QN4. The hole at Black's Q3 created by his second move needs protection from a White Knight which could have come to QN5 to attack it.

Dr. Siegbert Tarrasch (1862-1934), known for his rigid chess principles, emphatically claimed that Black's 1 . . . P-QB4 does "nothing" for the proper development of the pieces. (The reader will remember that pawn moves, strictly speaking, are not developing moves.) Tarrasch said of the Sicilian that though the Black pawns in the center will outnumber the White ones, the latter's attacking chances should prevail because he has better development and more space. If that exaggerated judgment was ever true after 1 . . . P-QB4, it should be even more so after the further "waste of time" with 4 . . . P-QR3.

But let us follow Fischer's game instead of drawing premature conclusions.

5 B-Q3 . . . . . .

This move develops a piece and protects the undefended KP. It is more flexible than 5 N-QB3, for it leaves the White QBP the option of advancing to strengthen White's grip on the center.

5 . . . . . . **N-QB3**
6 N×N **NP×N**

Black's strengthened pawn center is now going to be weighed against White's better development. For with his 6th move White has saved a tempo, and now it is his turn again to do something to advance the mobilization of his forces.

7 O-O **P-Q4**

All this was played by Petrosian in rapid-transit style, for he had good experience with this line in his world championship match with Spassky.

8 P-QB4! . . . . . .

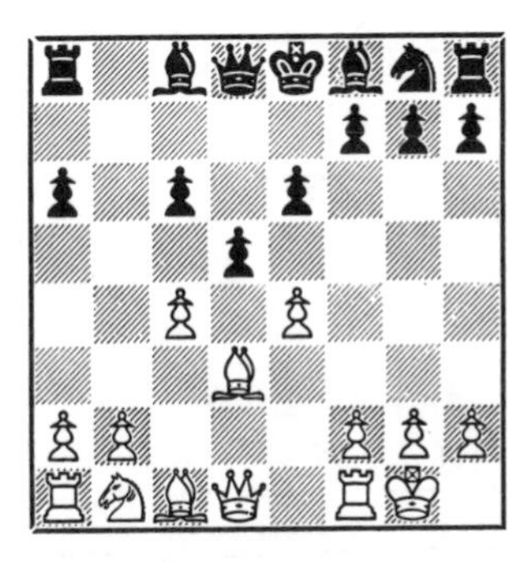

This is the only correct treatment of the position (Spassky had played 8 N-Q2). The text move neutralizes Black's superiority in the center and opens lines there, thus increasing the effectiveness of White's advantage in development.

8 . . . . . . **N-B3**

Black, being behind in development, would prefer to keep the position closed, but he has no time for 8 . . . P-Q5 because of the cramping 9 P-K5! Also, exchanging pawns here would lead to an unfavorable ending with three pawn "islands" on Black's side against two on White's. By "islands" we mean disconnected pawn groups; the more there are the harder each of them is to defend.

9 BP×P **BP×P**

10 P×P P×P

Black decides against the more attractive 10 . . . N×P because of the unpleasant 11 B-K4. But now Black has the three pawn islands.

11 N-B3 B-K2
12 Q-R4ch! . . . . . .

Just in time. Petrosian, who had thought for only five minutes up to this point, took 24 minutes for his reply. White's move, which prepares the centralization of the Queen, disrupts the harmony of Black's position because none of the Black pieces would be posted well at Q2.

12 . . . . . . Q-Q2

On the alternative 12 . . . B-Q2 13 Q-Q4 B-K3 (notice that Black did not pick up a tempo with his 12th move because his isolated QP needs defense) 14 B-KB4 O-O 15 KR-K1 White has much the better of it.

13 R-K1! . . . . . .

Remember well this lesson in simple mathematics! Each move develops a new piece. White is right to prefer this safe continuation to the dubious hunt of material with 13 B-QN5 P×B 14 Q×R O-O 15 Q-R5 P-Q5! 16 N×P B-N2, when Black would have strong counterplay.

13 . . . . . . Q×Q

Black is forced to help his opponent! This exchange moves the White Knight towards the strong outpost at QB5, contributing to his advantage, but Black had no other way to close the King file.

14 N×Q B-K3
15 B-K3 O-O

15 . . . N-Q2 would protect the hole at QB4 better, but it would give White a vital tempo to take control of the QB file with 16 QR-B1.

16 B-QB5! . . . . . .

White removes the defender of the weak dark squares in his opponent's camp.

16 . . . . . . KR-K1
17 B×B R×B
18 P-QN4! . . . . . .

This nails the Black Rook pawn to the weak QR3 square and activates White's pawn majority on the Queenside.

18 ...... K-B1
19 N-B5 B-B1

Black is doomed to passivity. 19 ... P-QR4 20 P-N5 would give White a strong passed pawn.

20 P-B3 ......

This opens the road to the center for the White King and takes a couple of squares away from the Black Knight.

20 ...... R/2-R2

Black's choice was a difficult one, made after half an hour of thought. 20 ... R×Rch 21 R×R N-Q2 22 N-N3 or 22 R-QB1 looks hopeless. The move played gives addditional protection to the QRP and prepares the activation of the Black Bishop.

21 R-K5! ......

He maintains the pressure and ties down the Black Knight to the defense of the Queen pawn.

21 ...... B-Q2

Threatening ... B-N4.

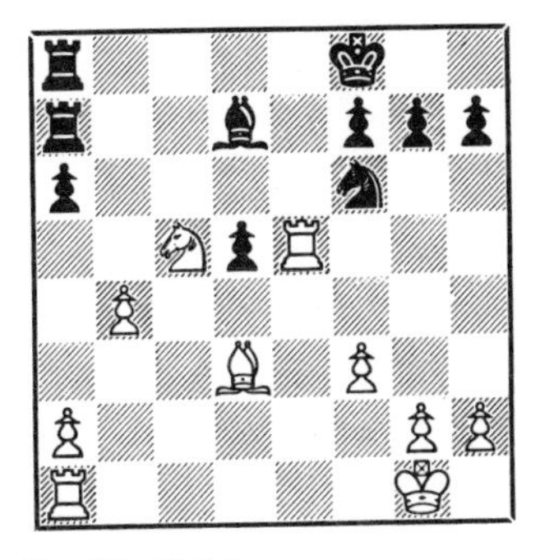

22 N×Bch! ......

Played instantly and without prejudice in favor of his proud Knight as against the Black Bishop, which was defending several weak spots in Black's position. The important point is that White next takes the QB file, where Black has become more vulnerable after the disappearance of his Bishop. 22 P-QR4 was also playable, but less effective.

22 ...... R×N
23 R-QB1 R-Q3

Played to free the other Rook from the defense of the QRP.

24 R-B7 N-Q2

Hoping at least to cut the communications between the White pieces. 24 ... R-K1 25 R×Rch N×R 26 R-R7 would have cost a pawn.

25 R-K2 P-N3
26 K-B2 P-KR4

Black is almost in a kind of zugzwang. 26 . . . R-K1 27 R×Rch K×R 28 R-R7 R-N3 29 P-QR3 N-N1 30 K-K3, or 26 . . . R-N1 27 P-QR3 R/1-N3 28 R-R7 could not help much, either.

27 P-B4 **P-R5**

Not knowing what to do that may be of any use, Black only creates another weakness.

28 K-B3 . . . . . .

White threatens 29 K-N4.

28 . . . . . . **P-B4**
29 K-K3! **P-Q5ch**

Otherwise, 30 K-Q4 would follow. Black is forced to expose himself more and more.

30 K-Q2 **N-N3**
31 R/2-K7 **N-Q4**
32 R-B7ch **K-K1**
33 R-QN7 **N×BP**

33 . . . R-N3 34 R×R N×R 35 R-KN7 K-B1 36 R×P N-Q4 37 B-B4 is equally hopeless for Black.

34 B-B4! **Resigns**

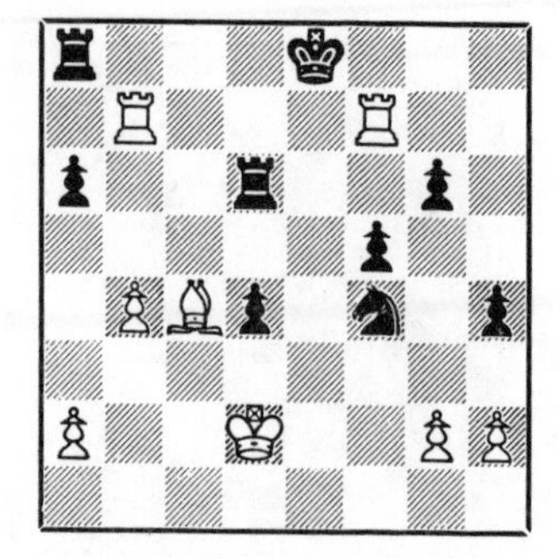

He is helpless against the threat of R-N7. For example, 34 . . . P-N4 35 R-N7 R-KB3 36 R-KN8ch R-B1 37 B-B7ch and wins. Or here 35 . . . N-N3 36 B-B7ch followed by R-KN8ch also leads to mate.

If we look for the cause of Black's defeat in this game, we realize that the character of the opening placed the positionally ambitious Black on sensitive ground, and after falling behind in development with his fourth and fifth moves his real trouble began. When White destroyed Black's superiority in the center with his eighth move, Black's compensation for White's rapid mobilization disappeared too. Then we saw the finest example of how to count tempos and exploit them.

Knights, Bishops, Rooks, Queen

By now the student has had plenty of opportunities to learn how to save time in the opening. This knowledge has to be combined with an understanding of where the pieces are best placed and, of course, with an appreciation of the order in which the pieces should enter the play. Very often there are exceptions, which the reader has already seen in the above games, but the order usually recommended is: Knights, Bishops, Rooks (castling on either side usually mobilizes the Rooks) and, finally, the strongest piece, the Queen. The following game is a clear illustration of this.

Lugano Olympiad 1968
NIMZO-INDIAN DEFENSE

White	**Black**
S. Gligoric	**L. Portisch**

1 P-Q4 N-KB3

The center can be controlled by pawns, as we have seen, but also by pieces. In this case the Knight development prevents White from playing 2 P-K4.

2 P-QB4 ......

An attempt to create a full pawn center with 2 N-QB3 would fail on 2 ... P-Q4, and the White QBF would be blocked from participation in the fight for the center. So White makes this precautionary move first, which puts pressure on Q5 and increases White's space on the Queenside.

2 ...... P-K3
3 N-QB3 B-N5

Black develops his Kingside quickly and with this pin again prevents P-K4. In this defense, invented by Nimzovich, the great master of the blockade, Knights often have exceptional usefulness and become superior to Bishops, whose power is greatest in open positions.

4 P-K3 ......

White does as much as he is allowed. He is ready for B-Q3 now, continuing the fight for the central square K4. He would prefer to be able to play P-K4 at once, of course, but the text is not a waste of time and gives needed support to the central pawn on Q4.

4 ...... O-O
5 B-Q3 P-B4

Sooner or later pawns have to take part in the contest for the center. White's hoped-for P-K4 will not be possible now because the KP is needed to defend the QP due to Black's threat to undermine it with ... BP×P.

6 N-B3 ......

It is normal for the Knight to prefer this developing square to K2, from where it would attack only one of the central squares instead of two (Q4 and K5). On KB3 the Knight also helps to protect the possibly sensitive point KR2 and other squares around the King when White castles on the Kingside.

The King Knight should go to K2 when the nature of the position requires the White KBP to remain free to advance. If 6 P-QR3 B×Nch 7 P×B White achieves the Bishop pair and a certain strengthening of the center, but after 7 ... N-B3 8 N-K2 P-QN3 9 P-K4 N-K1! 10 B-K3 P-Q3 11 O-O B-R3 Black has blocked the weak doubled pawns, and on 12 P-B4 he blocks the Kingside too with 12 ... P-B4!; so here again the Black Knights would be stronger than the White Bishops.

6	......	**P-Q4**
7	**O-O**	**QP×P**
8	**B×P**	**P×P**

Black hopes to exploit the weakness of the isolated White QP later, but this pawn, as we know, will give the White pieces greater freedom of movement.

9	**P×P**	**P-QN3**

This opens the best diagonal for the Black Queen Bishop, where it will exercise firm control over the blockading square Q4.

10	**B-KN5**	**B-N2**
11	**R-K1**	**QN-Q2**

The Knight, though not very actively placed here, lends needed support to its pinned colleague which defends the Kingside.

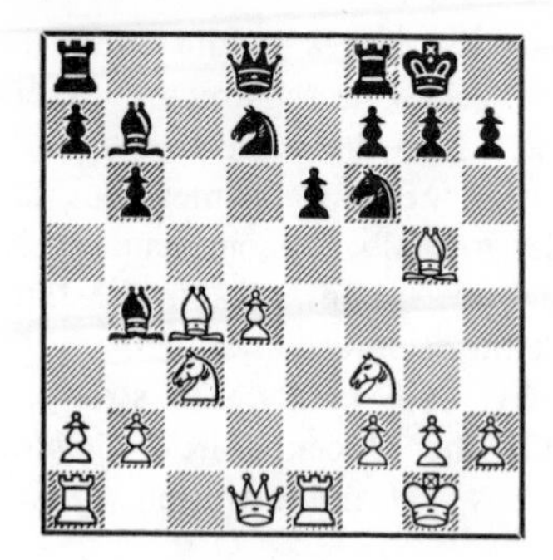

12	**B-Q3**	......

Superficially, this move is not in accordance with the advice that a piece should move only once in the opening. Yet it is a very good move. White was not ready to play P-Q5, and there was the threat of 12 ... B×N 13 P×B Q-B2 and 14 ... N-K5. With the text, White removes the Bishop from the exposed file, where it does nothing, and puts it on a more active diagonal where it aims at the enemy King.

12	......	**R-B1**
13	**R-QB1**	**R-K1**
14	**Q-K2!**	......

The Queen develops last. The bright side of the isolated White QP is not only the advantage in space it provides, but the notable characteristic of such positions in that the Black Queen has no equally good developing square.

14	......	**B×N**

Black could not logically proceed

with 14 . . . N-B1 because of the unpleasant 15 B-N5 (15 . . . B-B3 16 B-QR6). So he decides to give his opponent the Bishop pair and strengthen his opponent's pawn center in order to close the QB file and secure the comfortable QB2 square for his Queen, hoping to exert pressure on White's "hanging pawns" in the center.

15 P×B **Q-B2**
16 P-B4 **Q-B3**

There was no danger of 16 . . . N-N5 because of 17 P-KR3! B×N 18 Q×B Q-R7ch 19 K-B1, and the Black pieces would be on the wrong side of the board, while White would have the winning threat of B-KB4.

17 P-KR3 **QR-Q1**

17 . . . P-K4 fails on 18 B×N.

18 QR-Q1 . . . . . .

White calmly maintains the pressure.

18 . . . . . . **N-B1**
19 Q-K5! . . . . . .

Black displays no effective plan, so White seizes the opportunity to maneuver his Queen toward the Kingside.

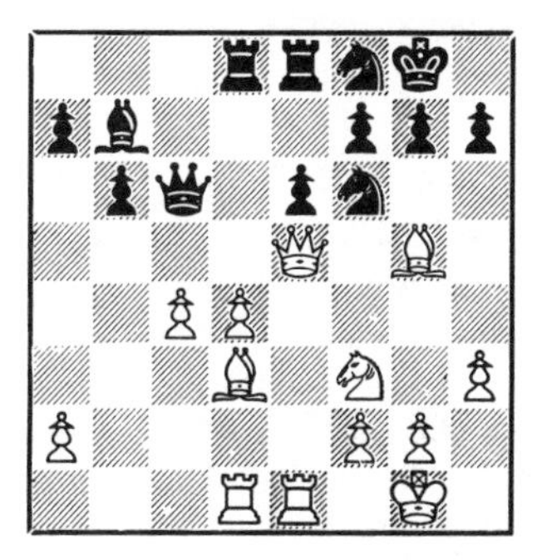

19 . . . . . . **N/3-Q2**

Trying something different.

20 Q-N3 **R-R1**

Not 20 . . . R-B1 21 B-K4 Q-B2 22 B-B4.

21 P-KR4 . . . . . .

Sooner or later the march of this pawn will force Black to weaken the pawn structure on his Kingside.

21 . . . . . . **K-R1**

Black tries in vain to keep his pawn structure intact.

22 B-QB1 **P-B3**

The weakening process begins. Black could not wait for 23 B-N2 and 24 P-Q5.

23 P-R5 **P-KR3**

Now the Black King's position is full of holes, but he could not stand 24 P-R6 creating great danger on the long diagonal with the Black

King Bishop gone.

24 P-Q5! ......

A thematic break in this kind of position. Black cannot answer 24 ... P×P because of 25 N-Q4 and 26 N-B5.

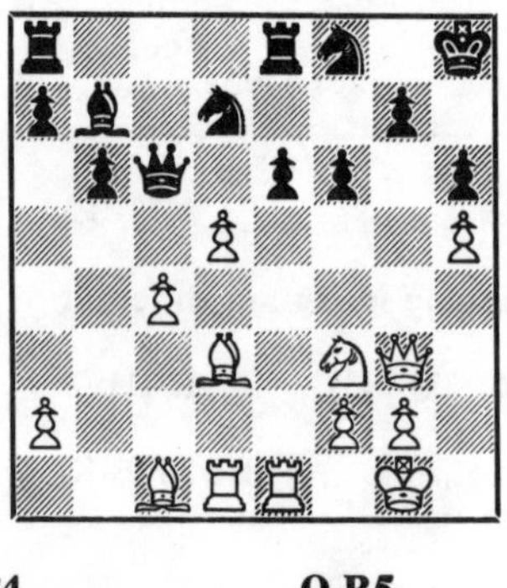

24	**Q-R5**
25 N-Q4	**N-B4**
26 P×P	......

White reduces the number of defending pawns.

26	**N/4×P**
27 B-B2!	......

Chasing the Queen far from the endangered Black Kingside.

27 ...... **Q×RP**

Black had no attractive alternative: 27 ... Q-Q2 28 N×N (if 28 B-B5 Q×N with chances for defense) 28 ... R×N 29 R×Q R×Rch 30 K-R2 N×R 31 Q-Q3! N-B1 (or 31 ... B-K5 32 Q-Q2) 32 B-R3 K-N1 (or 32 ... B-K5 33 Q-Q2, winning material) 33 B×N K×B 34 Q-R7, destroying the Black Kingside pawns; or 27 ... Q×BP 28 B-N3 Q×N 29 R×Q N×R 30 R×R R×R 31 Q-B7!, retaining the material advantage.

28 R×N! **R×R**

A mating attack would follow 28 ... N×R 29 N×N R×N 30 Q-N6.

29 N×R	**N×N**
30 Q-Q3	**N-B1**
31 B-R3	**P-B4**
32 Q-QB3!	**Resigns**

There was a chance of meeting the threat of 33 R-R1 with 32 ... N-K3!, and if 33 R-R1 N-B5!; but White intended to play 33 B-N2 Q-R4 34 Q-K3! with a winning position, for there are two diagonals open for White's irresistible attack.

CHAPTER 3

Theory and Practice

by Vlastimil Hort

I: Learning the Principles

"The opening" in chess refers to that phase of the game during which the forces of both sides are mobilized to encounter each other in the middlegame. This definition is affirmed in every book on the opening.

Opening theory is continually developing. Nevertheless, every writer who has undertaken to summarize theoretical chess knowledge has been obliged to base his teachings on the experience and prevailing opinion of the particular historical stage of chess development in which he wrote. In addition, each author's philosophy is arrived at through examination of individual and varying points of view, some of them contrary to his own. A theoretician may come up with a new idea that changes the evaluation of a whole variation for several years to come, another may question the evaluation, and a third may attempt to rehabilitate the original opinion . . . The chain may be endless.

At the beginning of this century, chess theory was still only in diapers. Yet today, when the body of theory accessible to every enthusiast has grown to vast proportions, it is still possible to compare games separated by a great span of time and to find in them much in common.

Vienna 1910
CARO-KANN DEFENSE

	Reti	Tartakower
1	P-K4	P-QB3
2	P-Q4	P-Q4
3	N-QB3	P×P
4	N×P	N-B3
5	Q-Q3	P-K4
6	P×P	Q-R4ch
7	B-Q2	Q×KP
8	O-O-O	N×N??

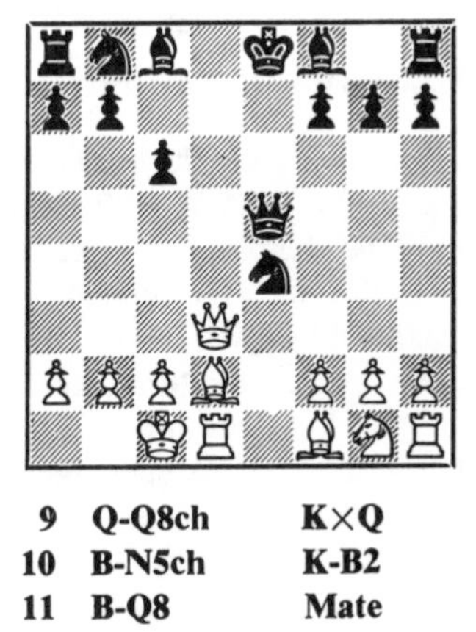

9	Q-Q8ch	K×Q
10	B-N5ch	K-B2
11	B-Q8	Mate

Forty years later, the following game was played.

Sochi 1950
CENTER GAME

	Bronstein	**Amateur**
1	**P-K4**	**P-K4**
2	**P-Q4**	**P×P**
3	**Q×P**	**N-QB3**
4	**Q-R4**	**N-B3**
5	**N-QB3**	**P-Q4**
6	**B-KN5**	**P×P**
7	**N×P**	**Q-K2**
8	**O-O-O**	**Q×N??**

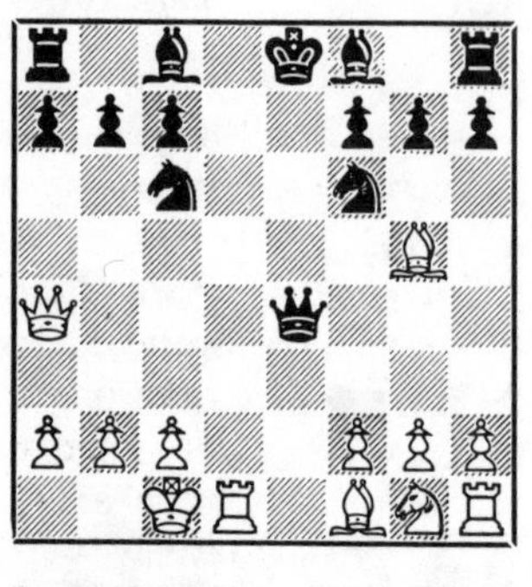

9 R-Q8ch!! Resigns

Black cannot avoid the loss of material after 9 . . . K×R 10 B×Nch.

Surely the similarity of these two games is obvious, even though they are separated by forty years and the experience of many thousands of master games. In both cases, Black made a mistake in the opening and was immediately punished.

How is one to avoid mistakes in the opening and overcome its problems? A thorough understanding of the basic principles of sound opening play is the first step in becoming competent in this phase of the game.

My System, a book the student will find very instructive, was written by Grandmaster Aron Nimzovich in 1925. In his first chapter Nimzovich summarizes the principles of sound opening play in seven axioms. These are worth close examination.

1) Development is understood to be the strategic advance of the troops toward the frontier line. (The frontier line is Nimzovich's term for the boundary between the fourth and fifth ranks.) "To have brought out one, two, or three pieces does not mean that we are developed," Nimzovich continues. "A democratic spirit should inspire the period of development; for instance, it would be undemocratic to issue a pass to one soldier only and let him go on a long trip while the others stay home and get bored. No, instead let each soldier make one move only, and dig himself in."

2) "A pawn move must not in itself be regarded as a developing move, but merely as an aid to development. The attacking force of pawns is small compared with that of pieces, so we should give priority to developing our pieces rather than advancing our pawns. As an aid to development, however, we should build a pawn center to prevent our developed pieces from being driven back by enemy pawns." (The center is defined as the four squares that enclose the midpoint of the board· K4 and Q4 on both sides.)

The following example shows how

piece development without a supporting pawn center can be ruinous. (White gave odds by playing without his Queen Rook and with his QRP on R3.)

GIUOCO PIANO

	Nimzovich	Amateur
1	P-K4	P-K4
2	N-KB3	N-QB3
3	B-B4	B-B4
4	P-B3	N-B3
5	P-Q4	P×P
6	P×P	B-N3
7	P-Q5	N-K2
8	P-K5	N-K5
9	P-Q6	P×P
10	P×P	N×BP
11	Q-N3	N×R
12	B×Pch	K-B1
13	B-N5	Resigns

Obviously, Black had no understanding of the above principle.

3) "To be ahead in development is the ideal to be aimed for." Nimzovich illustrates this by analogy: "If I were running a race with someone, it would not be wise to waste valuable time picking my nose. But if I could induce my opponent to waste time by some similar action, I should then get an advantage in development over him." In practical terms, we force our opponent to lose time when we make a developing move that simultaneously attacks one of his pieces which he has already moved. For example, in the Center Counter Opening, after 1 P-K4 P-Q4 2 P×P Q×P 3 N-QB3, the Black Queen must lose time retreating while White continues his development.

4) "Exchange with resulting gain of tempo. This principle was already illustrated by the above example. Another is the following fairly common mistake by Black: 1 P-Q4 P-Q4 2 P-QB4 N-KB3? 3 P×P, and if now 3 . . . Q×P 4 N-QB3, or if 3 . . . N×P 4 P-K4. In both cases, White has already reached his goal: to be ahead in development."

5) "Liquidation, with consequent development or disembarrassment. When a merchant sees that his business is not succeeding, he does well to liquidate it and invest the proceeds in a more promising venture. Instead, however, our merchant may try to find refuge in another dubious transaction: he may borrow money from one source to pay his debt to another, and continue this chain until finally he is able to pay no more. Translated into chess terms, this means that when your opponent threatens to impede your development, you must look for a radical cure rather than waste time with palliative measures."

Nimzovich uses the following example to illustrate the principle of liquidation:

1	P-K4	P-K4
2	N-KB3	N-QB3
3	P-Q4	P-Q4?!
4	P×QP	Q×P
5	N-B3	B-QN5!

6	**B-Q2**	**B×N**
7	**B×B**	**N-B3**

By exchanging his Bishop for a Knight, Black has relieved the tension in the center and is in no way behind in development. To better illustrate his point, Nimzovich notes the questionable move 3 . . . P-Q4?! and indicates that 4 B-QN5 would secure a small advantage for White, although Black should be able to nullify this with correct play.

This concept of liquidation does not appear in the work of any other authority, so let us illustrate it further with another example.

The Danish Gambit is characterized by the moves:

1	**P-K4**	**P-K4**
2	**P-Q4**	**P×P**
3	**P-QB3**	**P×P**
4	**B-QB4**	**P×P**
5	**B×P**	. . . . . .

White has sacrificed two pawns to get an advantage in development. Now Black has two alternatives: he can try to hold on to his material advantage, which may require a desperate defense, or he can liquidate:

5	. . . . . .	**P-Q4!**
6	**B×QP**	**N-KB3**
7	**B×Pch**	**K×B**
8	**Q×Q**	**B-N5ch**
9	**Q-Q2**	**B×Qch**
10	**N×B**	. . . . . .

Note that White's advantage in development completely evaporated through liquidation as the endgame approached.

The significance of this can be clearly seen in another variation of the Danish Gambit (by transposition from the Goring Gambit) that has become popular recently:

1	**P-K4**	**P-K4**
2	**N-KB3**	**N-QB3**
3	**P-Q4**	**P×P**
4	**P-B3**	**P-Q4**
5	**KP×P**	**Q×P**
6	**P×P**	**B-N5**
7	**B-K2**	**B-N5ch**
8	**N-B3**	**B×KN!**
9	**B×B**	**Q-B5**

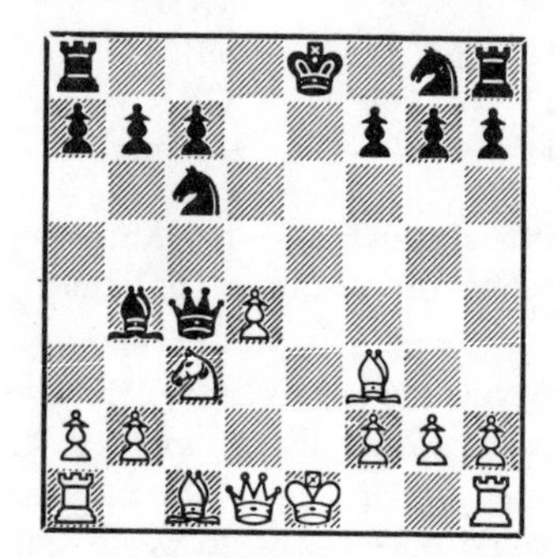

Black has relieved the tension in the center, prevented White from castling, and now threatens the Queen pawn. White has no better move than 10 Q-N3, and the position is about equal.

6) The pawn center must be mobile. "As we have seen, a mobile pawn center is a deadly weapon of attack because it threatens to advance and drive back the enemy pieces. In such cases the question is whether the attacked piece will be driven to an inferior post with loss of tempo, or whether it will be driven to a better post, which would be a tempo well spent."

A good example of this idea from modern tournament practice is Alekhine's Defense:

1	**P-K4**	**N-KB3**
2	**P-K5**	**N-Q4**
3	**P-QB4**	**N-N3**
4	**P-Q4**	**P-Q3**

Black has already moved his Knight three times; but proof that White's advanced center is an advantage, or that it is just the opposite, must await the further development of the theory of this opening. Alekhine himself remarked: "Sometimes it is to our advantage to attack the pawn center, rather than defend it."

7) **"There is no time for pawn hunting in the opening, except for center pawns.** Because the mobilization of the forces is by far the most important operation in the opening, the spectacle of a less experienced player eagerly chasing pawns before completing his development seems comical to anyone who knows this principle. Even an amateur who is highly logical and intelligent in his other undertakings may play this way." Nimzovich compares a young player eager to collect pawns in the opening to a six-year-old playing the stock market.

Let us see how this principle works in practical play. The following game shows clearly that winning a pawn in the opening costs too much time, and the logical punishment is a fatal neglect of development.

Ostend 1905
GIUOCO PIANO

	Marshall	Burn
1	**P-K4**	**P-K4**
2	**N-KB3**	**N-QB3**
3	**B-B4**	**B-B4**
4	**P-B3**	**N-B3**
5	**P-Q4**	**P×P**
6	**P×P**	**B-N5ch**
7	**K-B1**	**N×KP?**
8	**P-Q5**	**N-K2**
9	**Q-Q4**	**N-KB3**
10	**B-KN5**	**N-N3**
11	**N/1-Q2**	**P-KR3**
12	**R-K1ch**	**K-B1**
13	**B-Q3**	**B-K2**
14	**B/3×N**	**RP×B**
15	**N-K5!**	**P×B**
16	**N×NPch**	**K-B2**
17	**R×Bch**	**K×N**
18	**Q-Q3ch**	**K-R3**
19	**P-KR4**	**P-N5**
20	**P-R5**	**N×RP**
21	**Q-B5**	**Resigns**

Of course, 21 ... P-KN3 does not hold because of 22 R×Nch P×R 23 Q-B6 mate.

A bright beginner may conclude after studying Nimzovich's seven axioms that opening problems are rather simple. But his own experience will prove that the opposite is true. Let us not forget that even today the problem of pawn hunting in the opening is still a matter of theoretical dispute. In the Fischer-Spassky World Championship Match, Reykjavik 1972, Fischer as Black twice captured the "poisoned" QNP offered by White in the Najdorf Variation of the Sicilian Defense. Fischer won the first game in that line, but in the second his opening strategy was completely ruined, and he did not play the line again. One may well imagine the hours of sweat a player puts into the preparation of a pawn sacrifice in the opening!

When teaching opening theory, one must of course take into consideration the age of the student and his level of comprehension. The age at which chess can be learned is becoming lower all the time. But how do you lecture children of 8 or 10, who are eager to play and win and are not at all interested in Nimzovich's theories? Yet, obviously, from that generation future world champions will emerge.

The late Emil Richter, who was twice champion of Czechoslovakia, used to tell us when we were little, having our chocolate milk and cookies: "Never forget that each piece must have a lot of air!" So we tried to give the Bishops open diagonals and the Rooks open files. I remember very clearly a schoolteacher, fond of chess, who after 1 P-K4 P-K4 gently scolded the move 2 Q-R5?? with these words: "Do you have a little sister at home?" "Yes, I do." "And does your mother let her go out alone in the evening?" When I shook my head, he turned the conversation back to chess: "Well, you should not let the Queen go out alone, either."

Undoubtedly it is an advantage to start learning chess at an early age. The renowned Czech pedagogue Jan Amos Komensky (1592-1670) expressed this principle for educating the young: "Through play, knowledge." Young students, by playing many quick offhand games, develop an intuitive feeling for position which may develop into a very rare mastery (as, for instance, that of Capablanca and Reshevsky). Young players have the great advantage of acquiring good habits early, and of course their tournament experience will be longer until they reach their most productive age at maturity (usually about 30).

But the child of 8 or 10 absorbs formal instruction in specific chess ideas only with difficulty (even the idea of checkmate is too abstract). Players of that age are usually content with the acquisition of a material advantage and are not ready to comprehend the positional nuances of the game. Since the principles of the opening cannot be understood without at least some grasp of general positional ideas, how well such youngsters play the opening depends almost entirely on their native talent.

When chess is taken up at a later age (15 to 18), the approach is entirely different. Rules and principles are already familiar, and, assuming a certain level of intelligence, this knowledge may be applied in practical play. What the beginner of 8 or 10 will absorb through practice (and often through painful defeats), the older beginner must learn through conscious study and deliberate analysis of his own games, for which the aid of a good teacher or guide is almost indispensable.

When and how to start is an eternal problem facing theoreticians. However, it is never too late to begin the study of chess; we have the example of Botvinnik, who, despite a relatively late start, reached the highest pinnacle of chess art.

In fact, the older beginner has an advantage in being ready to understand the opening principles of the late Soviet Grandmaster Alexei Suetin. It is extremely interesting to compare Nimzovich's *My System* with Suetin's *Chess Handbook for the Advanced.* In general, the two authors agree, but Suetin is more specific. He offers four main elements of opening play, followed by thirteen axioms.

A) The fight for control of the center.

B) The striving for the quickest and most active development.

C) The creation of conditions that permit early castling.

D) The formation of an advantageous pawn structure.

Every beginner (and indeed all players) should know the following axioms from memory:

1) Take advantage of every tempo. The major pieces (i.e. Rooks and Queen) should not be brought into the game too early, for they could easily be attacked by enemy units of lesser value, resulting in retreat and loss of time.

2) Do not make pawn moves without careful planning.

3) Begin the game with a center pawn, and develop the minor pieces so that they influence the center.

4) Develop flexibly! Too much detail in planning the opening is not advisable.

5) Develop harmoniously! Play with *all* your pieces and do not concentrate your attention on only one flank.

6) Do not make aimless moves. Each move must be part of a definite plan.

7) Do not be too eager for material gain. The fight for time is much more important than the search for material, especially in open positions.

8) A weakening of your own pawns may be accepted only if it is compensated by a more active placement of your pieces.

9) With the help of your pawns, try to get an advantage in space and weaken your opponent's pawn position.

10) Do not obstruct your pawns by grouping your pieces directly in front of them; pawns and pieces must work together.

11) During the first few moves, pay special attention to the vulnerable KB2 square on both sides.

12) Remember that the poor placement of even a single piece may destroy the coordination of the other pieces.

13) With White, exploit the advantage of having the first move and try to gain the initiative. With Black, try to organize counterplay.

These thirteen points may remind the reader of a manufacturer's instructions for washing fabric! However, these concisely-stated principles are the distilled experience of many generations of players.

The last point is worth particular attention, for, though it contains much wisdom, it is not always applied in current tournament practice. Unfortunately, we belong to a time when White usually tries to gain only a minimal advantage, because to try for more entails the taking of risks. Black, having no sure method of developing counterplay without risk, usually tries to simplify the position to minimize White's attacking possibilities. The game thus proceeds toward an endgame in which neither side has real winning chances.

How long is the opening? The question is really academic, but it is interesting that chess writers differ in their opinions. Lisitsin believes 10 to 20 moves constitute the opening, Levenfish thinks the number should be 13 to 15, Sokolsky says 10 to 15. Lipnitsky claims the correct figure is 8 to 15, but he stresses that the transitions from opening to middlegame and from middlegame to endgame should be thought of as gradual.

Lipnitsky is most thorough in his discussion of transitional, or critical, positions, i.e. those which arise after the mobilization of the pieces has been accomplished. It is his opinion that such positions are subject to exactly the same kind of specific variation-analysis as positions at earlier stages of the opening. Though this assertion seems reasonable and sound, it does not meet the test of provability. The obligation of proof is the yardstick that must be applied to all theories. In this case, as long as transitional, critical, positions provoke differing judgments among players and theoreticians, and as long as such positions cannot be relied on to produce consistent results, Lipnitsky's theory cannot be trusted. The possibility of error on the part of a player or theoretician, and the fact that applied technique and theoretical analysis have yet to attain perfection, mean that such theories will remain only theories, not accepted principles.

The initial position of the 32 pieces and their first moves have been shown capable of a certain standardization; the opening is therefore subject to concrete, specific, analysis. Because of this, one simply *must* analyze the opening; not to do so is obviously foolhardy. Other phases of the game, particularly the middlegame where imagination and fantasy are given free rein, are less capable of definitive analysis.

But even in the opening, analysis is not the end of the story. Inevitably there follows the well-known process of refutation, research, new analysis, testing, rehabilitation. . .

To take the initiative; to create an active strategic plan; to hinder the opponent's plans: how incredibly easy it all sounds! But how thorny is the path to chess mastery!

II: Methods of Study

As the beginner gradually advances, he eventually reaches a point when he wonders: "What now?" By this time he knows the rules and principles of the opening fairly well, but he confronts the problem of how to improve further. Let us again consult the experts. In his book *The Chess Basics,* G. Rokhlin quotes former World Champion Botvinnik on his method of preparation for a tournament:

I begin my preparations with a review of the chess literature that I have not previously seen. This is necessary to acquaint myself with interesting new games. I make notes on the problems that interest me. I pay particular attention to the games of my rivals in the forthcoming competition. I analyze the peculiarities of their play and learn all their favorite variations; this knowledge comes in very handy when I am later preparing for a game with one of them. Then I study those opening lines that I intend to play during the contest. But I must point out that a player cannot and should not play all the openings known to theory. For one tournament, three or four opening systems prepared for White and three or four for Black are quite sufficient. But all these systems must be prepared extremely well. Unless a master has several opening systems thoroughly prepared, he cannot count on success. Note too that it is highly disadvantageous to play only one opening. For one thing, the opponents will be well prepared for it; for another, one's horizons will be too narrow and he will in some situations find himself "swimming."

As marginal comments on the whole question of the opening, incomplete though they are, we may accept these opinions: Yuri Averbakh says that concrete analysis of your own games to find the causes of success or failure, combined with serious work on the opening with the help of an instructor, is the most useful method of choosing effective opening systems. The late V. Simagin assures us that the best way to build an opening repertoire is through correspondence chess, because it is possible to check actual variations without risk. Finally, prominent Soviet Grandmaster Viktor Korchnoi, speaking of his own tournament preparation (quoted in Rokhlin's book), says:

> **I try to play in a strictly classical style. I avoid moves which do not conform to the requirements of the position. I like tactical intricacies only when it is necessary to undergo a complex and difficult defense, in contrast to Tal, who often provokes tactical clashes for purely esthetic reasons. I am not an adherent of the modern preciseness in the handling of the opening.**

The reader will not have to be told what Korchnoi refers to in his final comment.

From all this we can see that insufficient understanding of opening problems, or lack of thorough preparation in a particular system must be extremely disadvantageous for the lower-ranked player, while for the master such shortcomings will cause at the very least the expenditure of extra time for thought, and a consequent feeling of insecurity during the game.

As a result of the spread of chess and the recognition of its social value among various levels of society, a great many amateurs have emerged who are increasingly interested in the problems of the opening. The importance of a scientific approach, of objective and systematic preparation, first recognized by Botvinnik, became equally clear to his rivals. The masters of today, and even the amateurs, are fully acquainted with this approach and take it for granted.

Bulletins and publications about all the major tournaments, and theoretical analysis of all important games, are available to the entire chess world. The only advantage today's master may hope for must come from the quality of his preparation. Success can come only from the knowledge and talent of the one who does the analysis, how hard he works, how much time he spends on critical positions.

Theoretically, a group analyzing together would seem to have an advantage over a solitary master. But considering that in chess it is two individuals who are pitted against each other, it would be nearly impossible to create a coherent group on a level high enough to benefit the individual for whom they toil. Moreover, the activities of such a group may be hampered by individual interests.

The only valid measure of one's ability to play chess is his results.

And results are now charted on the so-called Elo rating scale. Obviously, since the individual player is alone responsible for the improvement of his own rating, he alone can perfect his preparation. There are several ways to do this: he may improve his physical and psychological training; he may study endgames; he may, suspecting weaknesses in his opening play, try other opening systems and attempt to find more suitable ones. The possibilities are endless. Again, the choice of method and the nature of the preparation must be left to the individual. He must even decide whether to work alone or with a trainer; in the latter case, the trainer will of course learn all the player's secrets.

In a sense, the individual pursues a long course in self-knowledge. Eventually he reaches a certain point, usually coinciding with his period of greatest success, at which a sense of self-confidence appears. He then will have achieved a style suited to his own character and temperament; in other words, he will have completed his self-portrait as a chess player.

The "Best" Move

The overall guiding principle of the struggle on the chess board is the fight for the initiative through the most efficient coordination of the pieces and pawns. This must be one's aim from the very first moves. It is in pursuance of this aim that one normally tries to find the "best" move. Capablanca warned of the coming "draw-death" of chess because, in his opinion, the best players would always find the best moves in any situation and therefore it would soon be impossible to defeat any of them. Our discussion, however, is on a more practical and limited plane.

How can we define the "best" move so that we can recognize it? One approach is this: the "best" move is that which promotes the most efficient coordination of the forces and which therefore develops the initiative to the greatest degree. Such a move is bound to be the result of highly intense thought and a synthesis of logic, fantasy, imagination, memory, attention, will, and emotion—in other words, the mastery of all these qualities and their best application.

From this we can see that the attempt to find the "best" move makes very great demands on the player. In fact, I may say that the production of a *constant and uninterrupted* series of really best moves borders on, or is even beyond, the limits of human capabilities, considering the complicated nature of modern chess. This production of best moves would have to reflect the clearest comprehension of the quintessence of chess creativity, to a degree which I hold to be unattainable today.

Furthermore, this relentless pursuit of the initiative naturally provokes the strongest resistance on the part of the opponent. He is himself forced to find the best moves, even if only one exists. Here one may apply the metaphor of a boomerang. For example, certain game situations may be compared to a foot race in which one runner exerts himself mightily and takes an early lead, only to find later that this has spurred his competitors to greater efforts. And, as the leader tires, perhaps discouraged by the stiff competition, he drops back and is overtaken. The boomerang effect also operates in chess, especially to the disadvantage of the player who, despite natural talent and thorough preparation, lacks an extremely strong and enduring will to win. Seeking "best" moves, therefore, may not be good enough. Believers in the best-move theory would succeed consistently on the international rating scale only if they could produce best moves throughout not only one game from beginning to end, but a whole tournament.

Bronstein, a Soviet grandmaster who dislikes draws as much as any player ever did, suggests that a mutual search for best moves by two rivals leads less often to draws than to an "exchange of points." (He has also made the proposal, incidentally, that a draw, instead of awarding a half a point to each player, should give the player with greater material a greater share of the point. This idea would have a profound effect on the conduct of the entire game because certain materially unbalanced endgames known to be drawn could no longer be confidently approached by the materially weaker side.)

But from what was said above in connection with the boomerang theory, it should be easier (and, for me, preferable) to defend against a player who constantly searches for the best move than to seek deeply hidden reserves of initiative for oneself.

Top professional players do make conscious efforts to find and play the strongest moves. But often they follow their intuition, though this can be risky. In certain situations, in fact, a master may deliberately avoid playing what looks like the "best" move because he cannot analyze the consequences of each possible reply to sufficient depth, or because the positions reached in his calculations are unclear, or even because he knows that the "best" move is exactly what the opponent is expecting.

Now we approach the root of the problem: in actual practice, is finding the "best" move worth the extraordinary effort? How many tournaments can a player endure under such an exhausting strain in game after game, from first move to last?

Let us examine, for instance, a

typical contemporary tournament which includes two players of approximately the same Elo rating. Grandmaster A plays all his games from beginning to end according to the best-move theory. Grandmaster B arrives at the board more rested. He plays White without undue ambition and with Black he meets each problem as it arises. It has been my experience that Grandmaster B will more often finish a tournament ahead of Grandmaster A, despite the fact that the latter has made a much greater effort both before and during each game, and has produced games of higher objective quality.

Considering the implications of this, the reader may not entirely agree. But perhaps in that case he should try to appreciate the differences between amateur and professional approaches to chess. A full discussion of these differences is beyond the scope of this chapter, but it may be said that the experienced professional relies more, and more successfully, on his *feeling for position.*

The Feeling for Position

Insufficient variety in one's opening repertoire can cause a certain monotony in one's play. Botvinnik warned against this in his remarks quoted earlier. Still, it is possible to enjoy tournament successes even with a single opening, but only if the player has a well-developed feeling for position. This feeling becomes refined and more reliable by the constant repetition of the same opening (but not the same variation!).

A player with a reliable feeling for position can generally win against an opponent who has spent several hours preparing for the game, analyzing critical positions and trying in vain to master them through the study of variations. We do not have to look far to find a player with such positional feeling. I don't wonder that Wolfgang Uhlmann of East Germany has not yet tired of the French Defense: why should he give it up when he continues to achieve positive results with it? The kind of rewards one looks for again depends on the player. Each individual must decide whether the success he desires is best achieved through the painstaking examination of variations, or whether a beautiful esthetic experience is more satisfying.

The meaning of "feeling for position" was clearly understood by M. Tchigorin, whose remarks about the opening are pertinent:

> **In almost every opening it is possible to find moves that are in no way inferior to the theoretical ones. The game of chess is much richer than we can imagine on the basis of existing theory, which tends to keep the game within certain boundaries.**

This belief is supported by those who create their own ideas in their play. But again we can see the gulf that separates the professional from the amateur: the professional has a much more reliable feeling for position and he therefore makes fewer mistakes.

Even so, I have seen the strongest players suffer catastrophic defeats because of poor opening play. Sometimes it happens to me. The explanation for this is extremely complicated, but there seem to be three main causes for such failures:

A) The variation or the critical position was appraised incorrectly by the player during his home preparation; the variation itself may need improvement in this case.

B) The critical position was appraised correctly, but the player made mistakes during play; in this case, his positional feeling deceived him and the problem is not with the variation.

C) The player took an intuitive approach to the opening which was too experimental, and so began the real battle with a bad position. In other words, his opponent took advantage of the fact that the bounds of correctness had been exceeded.

Let us take a closer look at this last situation, for your own approach to the opening may be similar. Lasker, the great psychologist of the chess squares, said:

The player who wishes to know how to think for himself must avoid all that is dead in chess. He must also avoid all shaky theories which are based on only a few actual examples but on very many made-up variations. He should not form the habit of playing with weak opponents. Further, such a person should not repeat unsuccessful openings without critical and careful thought. He should not accept without discretion rules applied by others.

Knowing this, would our grandmaster of situation C, who has suffered a fiasco, have the audacity to experiment again? Could he trust his feeling for position?

It is quite possible, if he does, that next time he will win! Sometimes this requires the help of the opponent, who may get into trouble because he is unfamiliar with the position. From my own experience I can say that most highly rated and prominent grandmasters have found themselves in situation C, since they are players who rely on their feeling for position. In these cases, Bronstein's theory of "exchange of points" is affirmed.

But isn't grandmaster C skating on very thin ice? Yes, but if he has very good nerves and is psychologically alert, why not? Experience based on tournament play clearly shows that the art of chess flourishes when the bounds of correctness are being stretched.

Even after all that has been said, the advanced player will again ask: "How should I study the opening?" And again, you may be reminded of that manufacturer's directions for washing his product:

It is very dangerous to learn a variation by memorization because you are then relying on someone else's experiences and opinions. This can only have a negative effect on your entire development as a player.

Remember that all theoretical variations are grounded in general strategic and tactical principles, the understanding of which is absolutely essential.

It is also important for a player to consider his own likes and dislikes, his strengths and weaknesses. One player might think: "The critical positions I aim for are those that allow the greatest activity for my pieces even at the cost of material sacrifice, because I like to attack and I'm good at it." Another could say: "My orientation in unclear positions is not good, and therefore those I like best are crystal clear and have an obvious strategic character." And so on.

We opened this section by peeking into Botvinnik's kitchen. His approach to the opening, brought to amateur level, should be helpful to many. But whatever method of study you choose, Botvinnik's comment in the introduction of Panov's *A Course in the Opening,* is valuable:

It makes no sense simply to memorize variations. The best way to study opening theory is to apply theory to tournament practice. Memorization of variations could be even worse than playing in a tournament without looking in the books at all.

Practical Considerations

I will give here eight examples from my own play to supplement the perhaps too-theoretical preceding material. They have been chosen to demonstrate how a mistake or a poor strategical plan in the opening led to ultimate defeat.

Example 1:

Wijk aan Zee 1969

QUEEN'S GAMBIT DECLINED

	Hort	Platonov
1	P-QB4	N-KB3
2	N-QB3	P-K3
3	N-B3	P-Q4
4	P-Q4	P-B4
5	BP×P	N×P
6	P-K4	N×N
7	P×N	P×P
8	P×P	B-N5ch
9	B-Q2	B×Bch
10	Q×B	O-O
11	B-B4	N-B3
12	O-O	Q-R4?
13	Q-K2!	Q-R4
14	QR-N1	P-QN3
15	KR-B1	B-N2

16	**B-R6**	**B×B**
17	**Q×B**	**Q-R4**

18	**Q-N7!**	**N-N5**
19	**N-K5**	**N×P**
20	**R-B7**	**QR-N1**
21	**Q-B6**	**QR-Q1**
22	**P-R3!**	**R×P?**
23	**N×P**	**Q-QB4**
24	**Q×Q**	**P×Q**
25	**R/1-N7**	**Resigns**

Discussion

a) Black lost too much time with the moves Q-R4-KR4. As a result, White gained pressure along the QB file and then, by centralizing all the pieces, pressure also against KB7.

b) The Black Knight on QR7 was completely cut off from action, and even the better move 22 ... QR6 (instead of 22 ... R×P) was not good enough because of 23 Q-B4 with the threat of 24 R-R1, and Black's situation would still be critical. Even 22 ... Q-Q7 would not help because of 23 N-B3! Q-Q6 24 Q-B2 with a decisive advantage for White.

c) The playability of the whole variation for Black depends a great deal on the evaluation of Fischer's 8 ... N-B3 9 B-B4 P-QN4 (as he played in the 9th game of the match against Spassky in Reykjavik 1972), and on the evaluation of the better 12 ... P-QN3! instead of 12 ... Q-R4.

Example 2:

Skopje Olympiad 1972

PIRC DEFENSE

	Hort	**Donner**
1	**P-K4**	**P-Q3**
2	**P-Q4**	**N-KB3**
3	**N-QB3**	**P-KN3**
4	**P-B4**	**B-N2**
5	**N-B3**	**O-O**
6	**B-Q3**	**N-B3**
7	**P-K5**	**P×P**
8	**QP×P**	**N-Q4**
9	**B-Q2**	**N×N?!**
10	**B×N**	**B-B4?!**
11	**B×B**	**Q×Qch**
12	**R×Q**	**P×B**
13	**R-Q7**	**QR-B1**
14	**P-KR3**	**P-B3?**

15	**P-K6!**	**KR-Q1**

16	R×R	N×R
17	N-Q4!	B-B1
18	P-QN4!	P-B4
19	P×P	R×P
20	K-Q2	R-Q4
21	K-B1	P-KR4
22	P-KR4	B-R3
23	P-N3	K-B1
24	R-Q1	K-K1
25	P-R4	B-B1
26	R-Q3	R-Q3
27	R-K3	R-R3
28	P-R5	N-B3
29	N×N	R×N
30	K-N2	K-Q1
31	K-N3	R-Q3
32	B-N4	R-Q8
33	R-Q3ch	R×Rch
34	P×R	K-B2
35	K-B4	P-R3
36	B-B5	K-Q1
37	B-N6ch	K-B1
38	P-Q4	K-N1
39	P-Q5	B-R3
40	B-B5	B-B1
41	B-Q4	K-B2
42	K-B5	Resigns

Black is in zugzwang (42 ... B-R3 43 P-Q6ch P×Pch 44 K-Q5 and wins).

Discussion

a) Black's error lay first of all in the superficiality of his opening play. Possibly he thought he would obtain a quick draw through the exchange of pieces. This shows that rushing towards the endgame is not correct strategy when even small errors occur.

b) Instead of 9 ... N×N?!, Parma's suggestion 9 ... N/3-N5 10 B-K4 N-N3 is strongly recommended.

c) 14 ... P-B3? was a serious positional error and resulted in an inferior position. Black would have obtained better play after 14 ... KR-Q1 15 R×Rch R×R 16 P-KN4.

d) After White's 15th move Black was strategically lost as his Bishop was confined to the very short diagonal KB1-KR3.

Example 3:

Athens 1969

QUEEN'S GAMBIT ACCEPTED

	Hort	Huebner
1	P-Q4	N-KB3
2	N-KB3	P-Q4
3	P-B4	P×P
4	P-K3	B-N5
5	B×P	P-K3
6	P-KR3	B-R4
7	N-B3	QN-Q2!?
8	O-O	B-Q3
9	P-K4	P-K4
10	B-K3	O-O
11	R-K1	P-QR3?!
12	P-QR4	B-QN5?!
13	P-N4!?	B-N3
14	B-KN5!	P-R3
15	B-R4	P×P
16	Q×P	B-QB4

17	**Q-Q1!**	**N-N3**
18	**B-QN3**	**B-N5**
19	**N-K5**	**K-R1**
20	**P-R5**	**Q×Q**
21	**KR×Q**	**N-B1**
22	**B×N**	**P×B**
23	**N-Q7**	**R-Q1**
24	**N×P**	**R×Rch**
25	**R×R**	**N-K2**
26	**P-B4**	**K-N2**
27	**P-K5**	**N-B3**
28	**P-B5**	**B×N**
29	**NP×B**	**N×KP**
30	**N-Q7!**	**N-B6ch**
31	**K-B2**	**N-N4**
32	**P×B**	**P×P**
33	**N-B5**	**N×Pch**
34	**K-N3**	**N-N4**
35	**R-Q7ch**	**K-B3**
36	**R×P**	**K-K4**
37	**N-Q3ch**	**K-Q3**
38	**R×P**	**R-KB1**
39	**B-B4**	**N-K5ch**
40	**K-N2**	**N×P**
41	**R-N6ch**	**Resigns**

Discussion

a) Black's opening strategy was very interesting. Instead of the theoretical 7 . . . P-QR3 and later . . . N-B3, he tried the seldom-seen 7 . . . QN-Q2!? But later he did not pay sufficient attention to the center and his game drifted from its strategic concept.

b) Better than 11 . . . P-QR3?! is 11 . . . P-B3, with the idea of developing the Queen naturally to QB2. The move 12 . . . B-QN5?! was based on the tactical possibility 13 P-N4 B-N3 14 P×P? N/3×KP 15 Q-N3 B×N 16 P×B N/2-B4, with a good game for Black.

c) White avoided the error 17 Q-Q2? N-K4!; by correctly retreating the Queen to Q1 White confirmed his advantage.

d) The obvious drawback of Black's plan of placing his King Bishop on QN5 was that its repeated moves cost too much time.

e) By taking advantage of the uncomfortable position of Black's Bishop on KN3, White won a pawn. After 23 N-Q7 his position was won.

Example 4:

Vinkovci 1968

KING'S INDIAN DEFENSE

	Hort	**Bertok**
1	**P-Q4**	**N-KB3**
2	**P-QB4**	**P-KN3**
3	**N-QB3**	**B-N2**
4	**P-K4**	**P-Q3**
5	**N-B3**	**O-O**
6	**B-K2**	**P-K4**
7	**B-K3**	**QN-Q2**
8	**O-O**	**P-QR4?**
9	**Q-B2**	**N-N5**
10	**B-N5**	**P-KB3**

11	B-R4	P-KN4?!
12	B-N3	N-R3
13	N-N5!	N-B2
14	QR-Q1	R-K1?

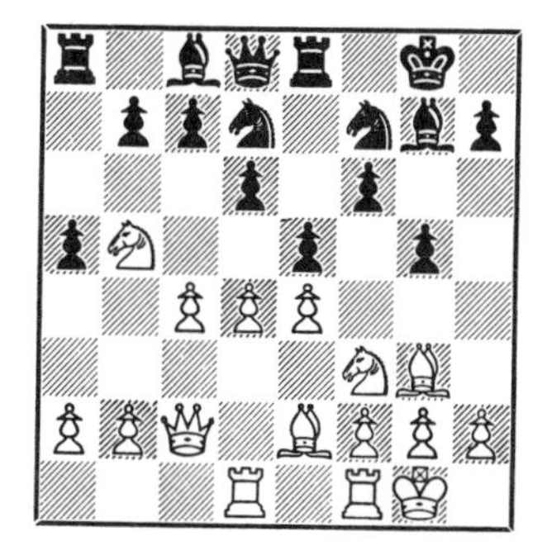

15	P-B5!	QP×P
16	P×KP!	P×P
17	B-QB4	P-R5
18	N×NP	Q×N
19	N×P	Q-Q1
20	N×QR	Q-R4
21	P-B4	N-B1
22	P-B5	B-R3
23	Q-K2	Resigns

Discussion

a) Black made a serious opening mistake with 8 . . . P-QR4? This pawn move was unnecessary as long as the center had not been closed. Furthermore, the QN4 square was weakened, where White later stationed a Knight.

b) 11 . . . P-KN4 was also weak and confirmed the principle that one cannot play successfully on both flanks simultaneously.

c) Black's final mistake in an already bad position was 14 . . . R-K1? White took systematic advantage of this with 15 P-B5!, opening his Queen file and his QR2-KN8 diagonal. This led to material loss for Black, and eventually cost him the game.

Example 5:

Wijk aan Zee 1972

CARO-KANN DEFENSE

	Hort	Pomar
1	P-K4	P-QB3
2	P-Q3	P-Q4
3	N-Q2	P×P?!
4	P×P	N-B3
5	KN-B3	B-N5
6	P-KR3	B×N
7	Q×B	QN-Q2
8	B-K2	P-K3?!
9	O-O	Q-B2
10	P-QR4	R-Q1
11	N-B4	P-QN4?

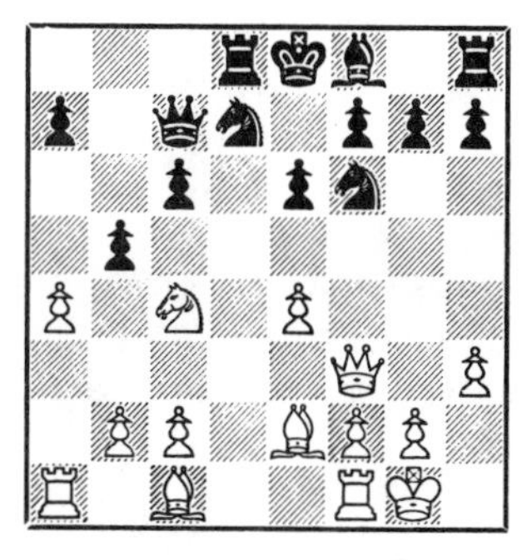

12	P×P	P×P
13	B-B4!	Q-B3
14	N-R5	Q-N3
15	P-B4!	P×P
16	N×P	Q-N5
17	KR-Q1	B-B4
18	B-B7	R-QB1
19	B-Q6	P-K4

20	R×P	R-Q1
21	R-B7	B×B
22	N×Bch	K-K2
23	B-N5	KR-N1
24	N-B5ch	K-K1
25	Q-Q3	Resigns

Black could not avoid losing a piece.

Discussion

a) Black made several mistakes in the opening. 3... P×P?! was premature and, in view of Black's following exchange of Bishop for Knight, opened the position unnecessarily for White's Bishop pair.

b) 8 ... P-K3?! relinquished space. Better would be 8 ... P-K4.

c) Black's premature opening of the Queenside with 11 ... P-QN4?, coupled with his lagging Kingside development, gave White the chance for the clever B-B4! two moves later. Black could not play to win a piece by 13 ... P-K4, since after 14 N×P N×N 15 B×Pch N/3-Q2 16 Q-KN3 P-B3 17 KR-Q1 White would gain a strong attack and full compensation for his sacrificed piece.

d) White correctly took advantage of Black's predicament with 15 P-B4!, which allowed him to gain control of the key Q6 square and keep Black's King in the center.

Example 6:

Lugano 1968

ENGLISH OPENING

	Hort	Unzicker
1	N-KB3	N-KB3
2	P-KN3	P-KN3
3	B-N2	B-N2
4	P-B4	P-B4
5	P-Q4	P×P
6	N×P	O-O
7	N-QB3	N-B3
8	O-O	N×N
9	Q×N	P-Q3
10	Q-Q3	B-B4?!
11	P-K4	B-K3
12	B-Q2	P-QR3
13	P-N3	N-Q2?!
14	Q-K2!	N-B4
15	QR-B1	B-Q2?
16	KR-Q1	R-B1
17	B-K3	Q-K1
18	N-Q5	B-QB3

19	P-K5!	N-K3
20	P×P	P×P
21	Q-Q2	P-B3
22	R-K1	Q-B2
23	R-K2	KR-K1
24	QR-K1	B-B1
25	Q-N2	B-N2

26	**B-Q2!**	**Resigns**

Discussion

a) Black actually helped White create a strong center and neglected to counter on the Queenside with the standard moves . . . R-QN1 and . . . P-QN4. His plan of transferring the Knight to QB4 after 10 . . . B-B4 was not good; and the loss of time for the retreat of the Black Queen Bishop—10 . . . B-B4?!, 11 . . . B-K3, 15 . . . B-Q2? and 18 . . . B-QB3—was very serious.

b) Instead of 18 . . . B-QB3, which led to the weakening of Black's pawn structure, correct was 18 . . . B-K3.

c) Although White had systematically increased his pressure and stood much better in the final position, Black's resignation seemed premature.

Example 7:

Moscow 1971

QUEEN'S GAMBIT DECLINED

	Hort	**R. Byrne**
1	**P-Q4**	**N-KB3**
2	**P-QB4**	**P-K3**
3	**N-QB3**	**P-Q4**
4	**N-B3**	**B-K2**
5	**B-N5**	**QN-Q2**
6	**P-K3**	**O-O**
7	**R-B1**	**P-QR3**
8	**P×P**	**P×P**
9	**B-Q3**	**P-B3**
10	**Q-B2**	**R-K1**
11	**O-O**	**N-B1**
12	**N-K5?!**	**N-N5!**
13	**B×B**	**Q×B**
14	**N-B3?!**	**N-N3**
15	**P-KR3**	**N-B3**
16	**N-QR4**	**N-K5**
17	**N-N6**	**R-N1**
18	**B×N**	**P×B**
19	**N-Q2**	**. . . . . .**

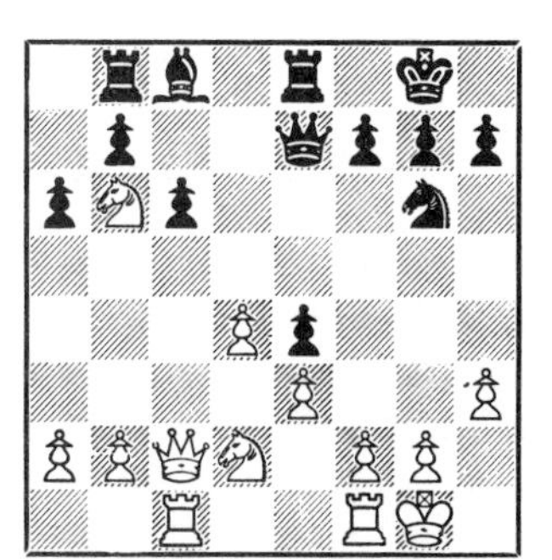

19	**. . . . . .**	**N-R5!**
20	**Q-B5**	**Q-B3**
21	**K-R2?**	**B-B4!**
22	**QR-K1?**	**QR-Q1**
23	**P-B4**	**P×P e.p.**
24	**N×P**	**B-Q6**
25	**R-B2**	**B-K5**
26	**Q-N4**	**B×N**
27	**P×B**	**R×KP!**
28	**R×R**	**Q-B5ch**
29	**K-N1**	**Q×R**
30	**Q-B3**	**Q-B5!**
31	**P-Q5**	**Q-N6ch**
32	**K-B1**	**Q×Pch**
33	**K-K2**	**P×P**
34	**Q-B7**	**R-K1ch**
35	**K-Q2**	**Q-K3**
	Resigns	

Discussion

a) The premature 12 N-K5?! lost time because the Knight could not be maintained on K5.

b) White evaluated the position incorrectly when he played 14 N-B3?! It was necessary to play 14 N×N with the aim of breaking up the position. Black's initiative on the Kingside was the primary characteristic of the position.

c) White underestimated his opponent's attacking chances on the Kingside. Otherwise he would have continued 21 N×B instead of 21 K-R2?; his Knight on N6 was too far away from the main battle.

d) 22 QR-K1? clearly was a losing move. Correct was 22 P-B4, which would have left White in an inferior but still playable position.

e) Black took advantage of his opponent's inaccuracies, which resulted from playing too mechanically. Black's Bishop maneuvers 24 .. B-Q6 and 25 . . . B-K5 set White up for the final attack.

Example 8:

Bamberg 1972

SICILIAN DEFENSE

	Huebner	**Hort**
1	**P-K4**	**P-QB4**
2	**N-KB3**	**P-K3**
3	**P-Q4**	**P×P**
4	**N×P**	**N-QB3**
5	**N-QB3**	**P-Q3**
6	**B-K3**	**N-B3**
7	**B-QB4**	**B-K2**
8	**Q-K2**	**P-QR3**
9	**O-O-O**	**Q-B2**
10	**B-N3**	**P-QN4?**
11	**N×N!**	**Q×N**
12	**B-Q4**	**B-N2?!**
13	**KR-K1**	**R-QB1?!**
14	**P-B4**	**O-O**
15	**N-Q5!**	**Q-K1**
16	**N×Nch**	**P×N**
17	**P-B5**	**P-K4**
18	**Q-R5**	**K-R1**
19	**R-Q3**	**R-KN1**
20	**B×BP**	**Q-B1**
21	**B×R**	**Q×B**
22	**B-B3**	**P-Q4**
23	**R-N3**	**Q-K1**
24	**Q×Qch**	**R×Q**
25	**P×P**	**B×P**
26	**R×P**	**Resigns**

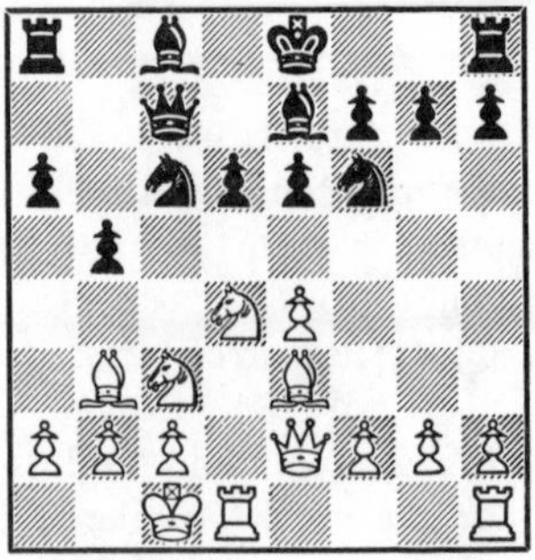

Discussion

a) Black made an instructive theoretical mistake in the opening with 10 . . . P-QN4?; he should have played 10 . . . O-O. The text move gave Black a very difficult position, if indeed not already lost.

b) Because of various tactical threats after the exchange on his QB6, White had the strong attack N-Q5 which later decided the game.

c) Instead of 13 . . . R-QB1?!

Black should have continued with 13 . . . P-K4 which, however, would still give White better play since it would concede to him permanent control of his Q5 square.

d) The final attack after 15 N-Q5! was very powerful. White played the ending instructively.

III: For the Advanced Player: Notes on 1 P-Q4 N-KB3 2 B-N5?!!

After **1 P-Q4 N-KB3,** the move **2 B-N5?!!** is in line with the most modern tournament tactic of trying to surprise one's opponent and force him to think for himself. Since it occurs so rarely in tournament practice, it places the opponent in virtually unexplored territory. The Bishop move is much better known and more thoroughly analyzed when played on White's 3rd move (after 1 P-Q4 P-Q4 2 N-QB3 N-KB3); however, in that variation White avoids the exchange of his Bishop for Black's Knight.

The aim of 2 B-N5?!! is not to transpose into the Queen's Gambit or one of the Indian systems; White simply wants to exchange his Bishop for the Knight and weaken Black's pawn structure. The psychological value of a move depends, of course, on choosing the right game and the right opponent. This move is probably not appropriate against a player who is well versed in the Indian defenses. In an unfamiliar position such a player will use his well-developed intuitive feeling to guide his play, especially since it is beyond his (or anyone's) power to calculate definitively critical positions in sharp variations. The reader will not be far from the truth if he sees an analogy with the Exchange Variation of the Ruy Lopez (4 B×N), which in its time caused Black great problems.

Black has five more or less satisfactory replies to 2 B-N5. The moves 2 . . . P-B4 and 2 . . . N-K5 lead to very sharp play, while 2 . . . P-Q4, 2 . . . P-KN3 and 2 . . . P-K3 are more positional continuations. In addition, 2 . . . P-QN3 has been tried recently.

A: 2 . . . . . . P-B4!?

This is the continuation recommended by theory.

3	**B×N**	**NP×B**
4	**P-Q5**	. . . . . .

Not good is 4 P×P, trying to transpose into a position similar to the Queen's Gambit Accepted with colors reversed, because Black can avoid this by 4 . . . N-R3.

4	. . . . . .	**Q-N3**

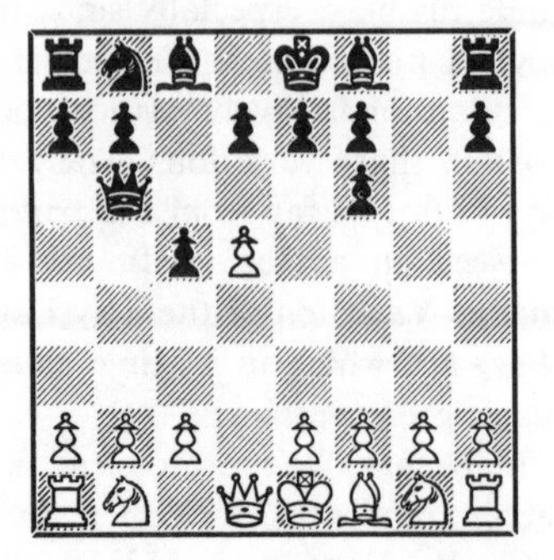

In two of my games (Hort-Hartston, Hastings 1972/73, and Hort-Ribli, Las Palmas 1973), White continued:

5 N-Q2 ......

The pawn sacrifice gives White some advantage in development, and he looks forward to further gain of time as the Black Queen will be pushed about.

5 ...... **Q×P**
6 P-K3 **P-B4**
7 R-N1 ......

The suggestion of V. Jansa is also worth considering: 7 N-R3 B-N2 8 R-QN1 Q-B3 9 N-KB4 with a promising game for White. On the other hand, 7 B-B4? proved to be a poor idea in the Hort-Ribli game: 7 ... B-N2 8 R-N1 Q-B3 9 N-K2 (9 Q-B3? P-Q3 10 N-K2 N-Q2 gives Black the better game) 9 ... P-Q3 10 N-KN3 N-Q2 11 B-N5 R-QN1! 12 Q-R5 P-KB5 13 N-B5 (better is 13 N/2-K4 Q-N3 14 P×P, although the position would still be unclear) 13 ... P-QR3! 14 N-K4 Q-N3 15 B-Q3 N-K4 16 Q×Q RP×Q 17 N×Bch K-B1 18 P×P N×Bch 19 P×N P-QN4!, and Black has a winning position. The move 7 **B-B4?** senselessly abandoned the idea of exerting pressure against Black's pawn on KB4.

The Hort-Hartston game continued:

7 ...... **Q-B3**
8 B-Q3!? **B-R3!?**

Black was probably afraid of 8 ... P-Q3 because of 9 Q-B3, or 9 Q-R5 Q-N3 10 Q-B3, which also results in an unclear position.

After **9 N-K2 P-Q3 10 N-KN3 P-KB5 11 N-R5 Q-R5 12 N×P B×N 13 P×B Q×P/4 14 O-O K-Q1 15 R-K1,** it seems that White has enough for the sacrificed pawn and, indeed, in this game White had the initiative for a long time. The question remains, of course, whether either side could have improved his play up to this point; future tournament practice should provide the answer.

From the position of the last diagram, in Alburt-Savon, Baku 1972, White did not want to give up the pawn by 5 N-Q2.

5 Q-B1 **B-N2**

Boleslavsky recommends 5 ... B-R3 6 P-K3 P-B4 and evaluates the position as good for Black.

6 P-QB3 ......

Here, according to Boleslavsky, White should play 6 N-QR3!?

6	**......**	**P-K3**
7	**P-K4**	**P-B4**
8	**N-QR3**	**O-O**
9	**N-B4**	**Q-Q1!**

An unknown position has been reached. Black's position looks better, as the White Queenside seems too compromised. 5 Q-B1 may be too passive; further tournament tests are needed.

B: 2 ...... N-K5!?

Here White can continue in either of two ways.

B1: 3 B-R4 ......

This proved to be a good choice in Balashov-Furman, Moscow 1969. Furman's reaction was the natural one.

3 ...... P-QB4!?

The most logical move, as 3 ... P-Q4? leads to the gambit 4 P-KB3 N-KB3 5 P-K4! with an extra tempo for White.

4	**P-KB3**	**P-KN4!?**
5	**P×N**	**P×B**
6	**P-K3!**	**......**

Supporting the center with a pawn this way is best. After 6 N-QB3? Black gained a clear advantage in the correspondence game Kunz-Moiseev, 1970, when White lost control of the black squares in the center after 6 ... P×P! 7 Q×P R-N1 8 P-K5 N-B3 9 Q-K4 Q-R4 10 N-B3 P-Q3 11 O-O-O B-K3 12 P×P O-O-O.

After 6 P-K3, two moves have been tried.

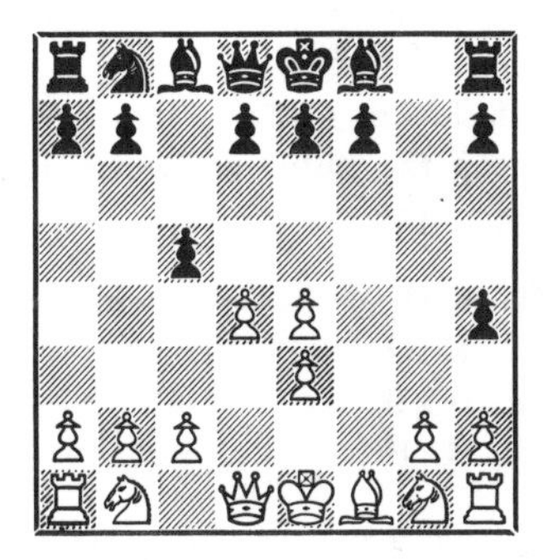

B1a: 6 ...... Q-N3?!

This was the continuation in Balashov-Furman. White now sacrifices a pawn for the initiative and an extremely tense situation arises.

7 N-KB3 Q×P

After 7 ... B-R3, White gets an advantage by means of 8 N-B3! P-K3 9 K-B2.

8 QN-Q2 Q-B6

The best move in a problematic situation. 8 ... B-R3? 9 QR-N1 Q×RP (if 9 ... Q-R6 10 R-N3) 10 B-B4 Q-R4 11 R-N5 Q-B2 12 B×Pch would give Black a much worse position.

9 B-Q3 B-R3

According to Petrosian, Black could have headed for the ending by 9 . . . P-B5 10 B×P Q×Pch 11 Q-K2 Q×Qch 12 K×Q, although he evaluates the resulting position as in White's favor, probably because of the variation 12 . . . N-B3 13 P-B3 P-R6 14 N-N5 P×P 15 B×Pch K-Q1 16 KR-KN1.

Balashov now offers another pawn to keep the initiative, which Furman accepts.

10	**O-O**	**B×Pch**
11	**K-R1**	**B×N!**
12	**N×B**	**N-B3**
13	**R×P**	. . . . . .

Furman has been defending well, but this surprising move costs him his composure. Now either 13 . . . K-Q1!? or 13 . . . P-R6 14 NP×P P×P would lead to an extremely sharp game with chances for both sides. Furman, however, overlooks the threatened mate by the Bishop.

13	. . . . . .	**P-KR4?**
14	**P-K5!?**	**Q×QP**

An unfortunate necessity, for if 14 . . . K×R 15 Q-B3ch K-K1 16 B-N6ch wins, or if 15 . . . K-N2 16 R-KB1 gives White a decisive attack.

As the game goes, White instructively increases his initiative.

15	**N-B3**	**Q-K6**
16	**B-N6**	**K-Q1**
17	**Q-KB1**	**Q-R3**
18	**B-K4**	. . . . . .

Black's position is under strong pressure. He cannot play, for instance, 18 . . . R-B1, because 19 P-K6! P×P 20 N-K5 wins.

After **18 . . . K-K1 19 N×P Q-K3 20 B-B5 Q-Q4 21 R-Q1 Q×RP 22 P-K6,** White had a decisive advantage. The game is quite interesting, but it is unconvincing theoretically because of Black's error on his 13th move.

Returning to the previous diagram, Szabo-Florian, Hungary 1971, continued:

B1b: 6 . . . . . . **B-R3!?**

Black gained a decisive advantage in this game, which took an unusual course: **7 B-B4?! P-K3 8 Q-K2 Q-N4 9 N-QB3 N-B3 10 P-Q5 N-K4 11 N-B3 N×Nch 12 P×N Q×KP 13 Q×Q B×Q 14 K-K2 B-B5 15 QR-KN1 P-QR3 16 P-R4 P-KR4 17 P-R5 B-B2 18 R-N5 B×QRP 19 P-Q6 B-Q1.** But there are many unanswered questions. Florian recommends 8 Q-B3 instead of 8 Q-K2, giving the variation 8 . . . P×P?! 9 P×P B-B8? 10 Q-B3 with advantage to White. But instead of the questionable Bishop maneuver, Black has the better possibility 8 . . . Q-N4, with the same idea as in the game, and also 8 . . . N-B3 and 8 . . . Q-N3 deserve serious consideration. However, White may be able to improve earlier; Petrosian suggests 7 K-B2!? (instead of 7 B-B4?!), with a good game for White. This whole variation certainly deserves testing.

Furthermore, instead of 9 ... N-B3, it seems that Black can gain the advantage by 9 ... Q×KP 10 Q×Q B×Q 11 N-N5 K-Q1! Szabo obviously played inexactly against 9 ... N-B3 even later; for instance, he could have tried 16 R-N4, and if 16 ... B-B2?! 17 P-R4 with an unclear position. However, Black can retreat his Bishop to a better square with 16 ... B-K4 and will keep a small advantage.

B2:

1	**P-Q4**	**N-KB3**
2	**B-N5**	**N-K5**
3	**B-B4**	**P-Q4**

This leads to a much quieter game. The text is the most natural reaction, for 3 ... P-QB4?! 4 K-KB3 N-KB3 5 P-Q5 leads to the Benoni system with an advantage for White.

4	**P-KB3**	**N-KB3**
5	**P-K4**	......

This continuation was seen in the games Jansa-Pavlov, Bucharest 1971, Jansa-Malich, Zinnowitz 1971, and Jansa-Balcerowski, Smokovec 1971.

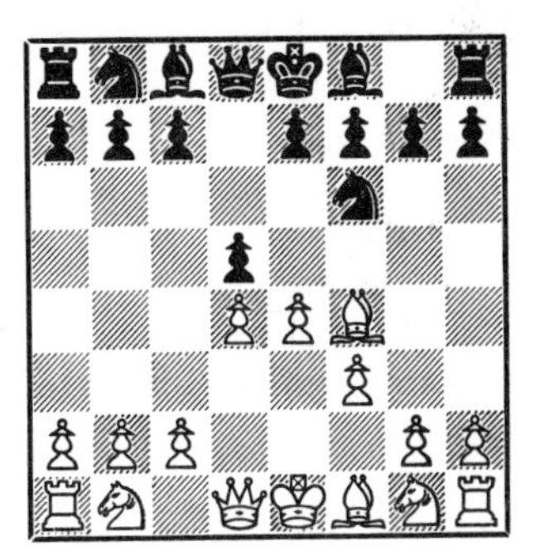

Jansa-Pavlov entered gambit waters early:

5	......	**P×P?!**
6	**N-B3**	**B-B4**
7	**P×P**	**N×P**
8	**Q-B3!?**	......

A similar position can be reached via the Blackmar-Diemer Gambit, but White in the present game is a tempo ahead.

8	......	**N×N**

8 ... Q×P is not good because of 9 N-N5, winning.

9	**P×N**	**Q-B1**

This is best, but White has an active game for his pawn.

10	**B-B4**	**N-Q2**

The quiet 10 ... P-K3 deserves preference over this Knight maneuver. White's superior piece coordination triumphs now.

11 N-K2 N-B3 12 B-K5 P-B3 13 O-O B-K3 14 B×B Q×B 15 N-B4

Q-B5 16 QR-N1 O-O-O 17 R-N4 Q-R3 18 P-B4! N-Q2 19 N-Q3 P-B3 20 B-N3 P-K4 21 P-B5. White has won a pawn and has a decisive advantage. Black's 5 . . . P×P?! is not recommended.

In Jansa-Malich (see previous diagram) Black chose a more modest continuation:

5	**. . . . . .**	**P-K3**
6	**N-B3?!**	. . . . . .

To be considered is 6 P-K5, with a position similar to the French Defense.

6	**. . . . . .**	**B-N5?!**
7	**P-QR3**	**B×Nch**
8	**P×B**	**P-B4**
9	**B×N!**	**R×B**
10	**P-K5**	**N-N1?!**

Better is 10 . . . N-Q2 followed by . . . Q-R4 and the transfer of the Knight to QB5.

After **11 P-KB4 Q-R4 12 Q-Q2 N-K2 13 N-B3 B-Q2 14 B-Q3 B-N4 15 O-O,** White had a minimal advantage.

In Jansa-Balcerowski (from the diagram), Black attacked the center at once.

5	**. . . . . .**	**P-B4!?**

White applied the same idea as in the previous game.

6	**B×N!?**	**R×B**
7	**P-K5**	**N-Q2**
8	**P-B3**	. . . . . .

The game took an interesting course: **8 . . . Q-N3 9 Q-Q2 P-K3 10 P-KB4 P×P?! 11 P×P Q-N5 12 N-QB3 N-N3 13 B-Q3 B-Q2 14 KN-K2 N-B5 15 B×N Q×B 16 O-O B-N5 17 P-QR3,** and White had a minimal advantage. Despite this, Black's 5 . . . P-B4!? seems the most logical continuation because, instead of 10 . . . P×P?!, he has the interesting plan 10 . . . R-R1 followed by N-N1-B3. But White does not have to go in for that original and ingenious exchange on QN8; instead, he can transpose into French-type positions by 6 P-K5 N-Q2 7 P-B3, followed by B-K3.

C: 1	**P-Q4**	**N-KB3**
2	**B-N5**	**P-Q4**

After this the soundest continuation is:

3	**B×N**	**KP×B**
4	**P-K3**	. . . . . .

In Gurgenidze-Kholmov, USSR 1972, White chose 4 N-Q2, but after 4 . . . P-KB4 5 P-K3 B-K3 6 N-K2 N-Q2 7 N-KB4 N-B3 8 P-B4 P-B3 9 B-Q3 B-N5, he did not accomplish much. It is clearly better for White to delay the development of his Queen Knight.

In two games Zoltan Ribli applied himself to the problem of the most efficient development for Black in this line.

Jansa-Ribli, Bucharest 1971:

4	......	**B-K3**
5	**B-Q3**	**P-QB4?!**
6	**P-QB3**	......

The immediate 6 P×P is worth consideration.

6	......	**N-Q2**
7	**N-Q2**	**P-B4**
8	**Q-B3**	**P-KN3**
9	**N-K2**	**P-QB5**
10	**B-B2**	**B-Q3?**

In this complex position, Black could have taken advantage of his opponent's indecisiveness with regard to QB5 by employing the standard maneuver 10 ... N-B3! with ... N-K5 to follow. Now the Black Knight wil not get to K5, and White obtains a small advantage.

11 B-R4 R-QN1 12 B×Nch Q×B 13 N-B4 Q-B3 14 P-KR4 P-QN4 15 P-R3 P-KR4 16 Q-N3 K-Q2 17 N-B3 Q-B2 18 O-O KR-N1 19 N-K5ch! B×N 20 P×B Q×P 21 KR-Q1, and White had more than enough for the pawn. Black can do nothing but mark time.

Hort-Ribli, Budapest 1973 (from the last diagram):

4	......	**P-B3**
5	**B-Q3**	**B-Q3**
6	**Q-B3**	**Q-N3**

This attempt by Black to get active play on the Queenside seems logical. But Black here plays too ambitiously.

7	**P-QN3**	**P-QR4?!**
8	**P-QR3!**	**B-K3**
9	**N-K2**	**P-QB4?!**
10	**N/1-B3**	......

White already stands better.

10 ... P×P 11 N/2×P N-B3 12 N×P Q-B4 13 N×B P×N 14 N-B4 P-KN4 15 N-K2 K-K2 16 P-KR4 P-R3 17 Q-K4 P-B4 P-B4 18 Q-QB4 Q-K4 19 N-Q4 QR-QB1 20 N×Nch R×N 21 Q-Q4, and, in exchange for his sacrificed pawn Black has at best some drawing chances.

Critically important for the whole variation is the game Hort-Ree, Wijk aan Zee 1971, where Black successfully tried a new plan. From the last diagram:

4	......	**P-B3**
5	**B-Q3**	**Q-N3**
6	**P-QN3**	**B-K3!**
7	**Q-B3**	**N-Q2**

Black prepares to castle on the Queenside, which certainly deserves serious attention. More passive plans for Black, which include castling Kingside, give White a comfortable game. For instance, the game Jansa-Ostojic, Vrnjacka Banja 1973 (continue from the previous diagram), proceeded much like the Exchange Variation of the Queen's Gambit, where Black developed his King Bishop at once: 4 . . . B-K2?! But after 5 B-Q3 O-O 6 Q-B3 P-B3 7 N-K2 R-K1 8 N-Q2 N-Q2, he received an unpleasant surprise: 9 P-KN4!? N-B1 10 O-O-O B-K3 11 P-KR4 R-B1?! 12 K-N1 Q-Q2 13 QR-N1 (13 KR-N1 is better) 13 . . . P-QN3 14 P-N5 P-KB4 15 N-KB4 P-B4 16 P×P P×P 17 P-B4 P×P 18 N×P, and White had a permanent advantage.

Instead of the text move, Hort-Kozma, Bratislava 1973, continued with the strategically dubious 7 . . . P-QB4?!, and after 8 P-B3 N-B3 9 N-K2 P×P 10 KP×P B-Q3 11 N-Q2, White, with prospects for active Queenside play, stood better.

When White omits Q-B3 in this system, his opening is generally ineffective. However, this Queen move may not be necessary. Another idea for White that seems worth trying is an immediate Queenside advance. After **1 P-Q4 N-KB3 2 B-N5 P-Q4 3 B×N KP×B,** in Gurgenidze-Tseshkovsky, Kislovodsk 1972, White, instead of the weaker 4 N-Q2 which he played against Kholmov (cited earlier), chose **4 P-K3 P-B3 5 P-QB4!? P×P 6 B×P B-Q3 7 N-Q2 O-O 8 Q-B2 P-KB4 9 N-K2 P-KN3 10 P-KR4 N-Q2 11 P-R5 N-B3 12 P×P P×P 13 P-B3,** with a very sharp game.

D:	**1**	**P-Q4**	**N-KB3**
	2	**B-N5**	**P-KN3**

This move is rarely played. If Black later attempts to obtain a grip on the center, positions strategically similar to those arising after 2 . . . P-Q4 may arise.

An interesting theoretical duel in Jansa-Pribyl led to an unclear game but probably with better prospects for White: **3 B×N P×B 4 P-K3 P-KB4 5 B-Q3 P-Q4 6 Q-B3 P-QB3 7 N-K2 N-Q2 8 P-B4!? P×P 9 B×QBP N-N3 10 B-N3 P-QR4 11 P-QR3 P-R5 12 B-R2 B-N2 13 QN-B3 Q-K2 14 P-R4 B-K3 15 B×B P×B 16 P-R5.** In this position Black played too optimistically; after **16 . . . P-K4?! 17 QP×P B×P 18 O-O-O N-B5 19 N-Q4!** he was faced with the problem of where to put his King, as 19 . . . O-O-O could be answered by 20 N×QBP P×N 21 Q×QBPch Q-B2 22 Q-R8ch Q-N1 23 Q-R6ch and wins. The game quickly turned to White's advantage after **19 . . . R-R3? 20 P×P P×P 21 N×KBP!,** and Black had to resign in a few moves.

Black's opening problems were solved in an original way in the game Jansa-Marjanovic, Vrnjacka Banja 1973: **3 B×N P×B 4 P-K3**

B-N2 5 B-Q3 P-KB4 6 Q-B3 N-B3!? 7 P-B3 P-QN3 8 N-K2 B-N2 9 Q-N3 O-O 10 P-KR4?! After the game White decided he should have tried a different plan, giving preference to 10 N-Q2 followed by Q-B4, P-KR3 and P-KN4. The game continued: **10 . . . P-KR4 11 N-Q2 N-K2 12 N-KB4 N-Q4 13 N×N B×N 14 O-O-O P-R4 15 K-N1.** Neither player had any advantage and the game was soon drawn. Black's plan in this game is certainly worth further testing in tournament play.

E: 1	**P-Q4**	**N-KB3**
2	**B-N5**	**P-K3**

After 3 N-QB3 P-Q4 4 P-K4, a normal French Defense is reached. But if Black wants the two-Bishop advantage at any price, a position may be obtained after 3 N-QB3 P-KR3 4 B×N Q×B 5 P-K4 in which White has an advantage in space and in development. The continuation 2 . . . P-K3 has few supporters, and there is only one game in the literature. Hort-Mista (Luhacovice 1973): 3 P-K4 B-K2 4 N-QB3 P-KR3 5 B-R4!? (5 B×N B×B 6 P-K5!?) 5 . . . N×P 6 B×B N×N 7 B×Q (7 Q-N4? K×B! with Black better) 7 . . . N×Q 8 B×P N×NP 9 B-Q6 (White has an advantage in development in exchange for his sacrificed pawn) 9 . . . N-B3 (9 . . . P-QN3? 10 R-N1! N-R5 11 R-N4 N-B6 12 R-B4 and White wins) 10 N-B3 P-QN3 11 P-QR4 N-R4 12 N-Q2 N-N2 13 B-N4 P-Q4 14 B-B3 N-B5 15 N×N P×N 16 B×P. After a series of almost forced moves, White has regained the pawn and has the advantage of the two Bishops.

F: 1	**P-Q4**	**N-KB3**
2	**B-N5**	**P-QN3**

This hypermodern idea was tried in Jansa-Keene, Amsterdam 1973. With quiet play White gained an advantage after **3 B×N KP×B 4 P-K3 B-N2 5 N-Q2 P-N3 6 KN-B3 P-KB4 7 P-B3 B-N2 8 B-Q3 O-O 9 O-O P-Q3 10 P-QR4 N-Q2?! 11 P-R5 N-B3 12 Q-R4 Q-K2 13 P-R6.** Instead of playing 10 . . . N-Q2?!, Black should have stopped the advance of White's QRP by 10 . . . P-QR4!?, but it looks like White would have the advantage anyway.

IV: Notes on Some Theoretical Variations
Caro-Kann Defense

A game Pribyl-Kholmov began with **1 P-K4 P-QB3 2 P-Q3 P-Q4 3 N-Q2 P-KN3 4 KN-B3 B-N2 5 P-KN3.** This is the well-known closed variation of the Caro-Kann. Now, instead of following the usual plan of holding the center with 5 . . . P-K4 and . . . N-Q2, Kholmov played **5 . . . P×P 6 P×P** followed by the new move **6 . . . P-N3!?**

The idea behind this move is based on the fact that White's King Bishop cannot control both his KB1-QR6 and KR1-QR8 diagonals. Black's position would be quite satisfactory after 7 B-N2 B-QR3 8 P-B4 P-K4!. White therefore chose **7 B-B4!?**, and there followed **7 . . . N-B3 8 Q-K2 O-O 9 O-O P-QR4 10 P-QR4 Q-B2.**

In this complex position White did not dare try 11 P-K5!? and decided first to protect his weak light squares with **11 K-N2.** Now Kholmov could have equalized with 11 . . . P-K4!?, but he chose instead to retain attacking possibilities on the long diagonal; after **11 . . . N-R3 12 P-K5 N-Q4 13 N-N3 Q-Q2 14 R-K1 N/3-B2,** the position was difficult to evaluate, and later Black's play on the long diagonal was counterbalanced by White's superior control of space. Kholmov's idea is worth further testing and certainly deserves the attention of theoreticians.

Sicilian Defense

After **1 P-K4 P-QB4 2 N-KB3 P-K3 3 P-Q4 P×P 4 N×P N-KB3 5 N-QB3 P-Q3,** Keres's continuation **6 P-KN4!?** has given Black many difficult moments. Perhaps in fear of 7 P-N5 and the subsequent N/4-N5, Black in recent years has avoided 6 . . . N-B3 in favor of either 6 . . . B-K2 or 6 . . . P-KR3. But **6 . . . N-B3** was played in the very interesting recent game Plachetka-Hort, Luhacovice 1973. After **7 P-N5 N-Q2 8 N/4-N5 N-N3. 9 B-KB4,** Black played **9 . . . N-K4!?,** whereupon White tried to destroy his position immediately with **10 Q-R5!?,** with several threats. Black cannot play 10 . . . P-N3 because of 11 Q-R3, and the pressure on Black's Q3 will be intolerable. Black's defense is clearly difficult, but **10 . . . B-Q2** leads to a critical position whose ultimate evaluation must depend on future games.

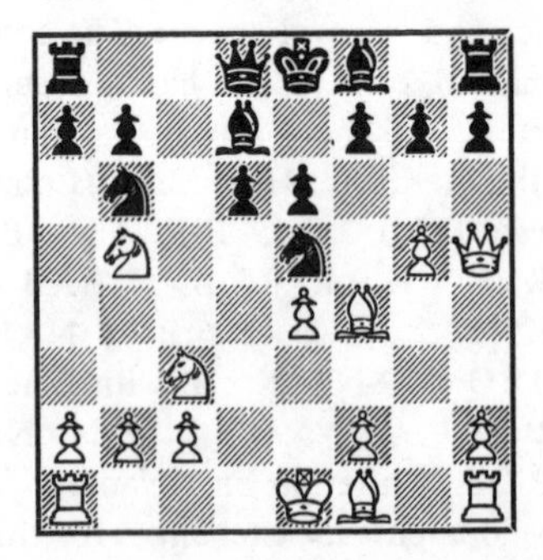

The logical follow-up to White's last move is **11 B×N!? P×B** (not P-N3? because of 12 B×QP, winning) **12 P-N6 P-QR3 13 P×Pch.** It is interesting to note that Ivkov, who played this line with Black later in 1973 against Szabo at Hilversum, evaluates this position as advantageous for White. That game is given below.

Plachetka-Hort continued: **13 . . . K-K2 14 N-R3 Q-B2 15 O-O-O P-N3 16 Q-R4ch K×P 17 N-B4! N×N 18 B×N B-K2 19 Q-N4 QR-Q1 20 B-N3 B-QB1 21 P-KR4 P-KR4 22 Q-N3,** reaching an unclear position in which Black must weigh each move with extreme care. If he can survive White's Kingside attack, his strategy will be vindicated. After **22 . . . R×Rch 23 R×R B-B3** (23 . . . B-B1 is better) **24 N-K2 B-N2 25 K-B1 B-R3,** it seemed that White had not achieved anything concrete.

The Szabo-Ivkov game mentioned above followed the same course until move 19, when, instead of 19 Q-N4, White retreated his Queen with **19 Q-N3!?** to avoid the loss of a tempo if Black plays . . . P-KR4. The game continuation was similar to Plachetka-Hort: **19 . . . QR-Q1 20 B-N3 B-QB1 21 P-KR4 R×Rch 22 N×R R-Q1 23 P-R5 P-KN4 24 N-K3 P-R3 25 Q-N4 K-B3.** Here, according to Ivkov, White had a considerable advantage. Szabo's 19 Q-N3!? is definitely an improvement, but something should be said about the whole variation by Sicilian specialists, who are often seen defending even more suspicious positions than this one. Perhaps someone will attempt the variation again some day.

Ruy Lopez

In the so-called Archangelsk Variation, **1 P-K4 P-K4 2 N-KB3 N-QB3 3 B-N5 P-QR3 4 B-R4 N-B3 5 O-O P-QN4 6 B-N3 B-N2,** White has several available continuations. The moves 7 R-K1 and 7 P-Q4 are chosen most often, but for some reason 7 P-B3!?, which imposes the greatest burden on Black, is generally avoided. It is true that in several games Black obtained easy draws against this move. Another reason for the avoidance of 7 P-B3 may be that no one wants to give up the KP without good advance preparation. Still, it seems that this move can give Black quite a headache.

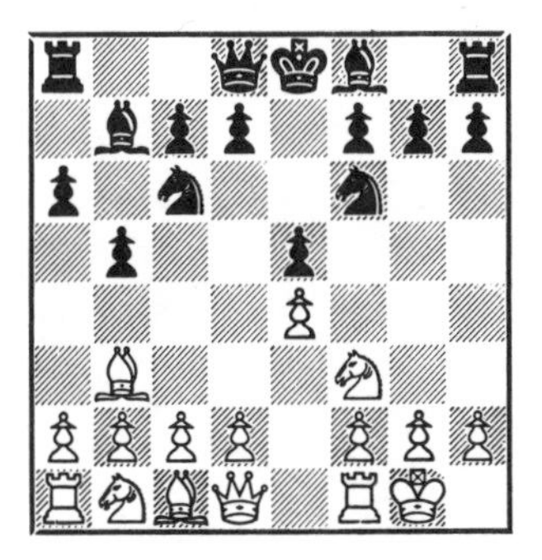

After **7 P-B3!? N×P?!,** the most logical continuation is **8 P-Q4!?** Lutikov played 8 R-K1 in a game against Planinc, but after 8 . . . N-B4 9 B-Q5 B-K2 10 N×P N×N 11 B×B N/K-Q6!, Black at least equalized.

The critical question for Black is how to meet 8 P-Q4. His weakest reply seems to be 8 . . . P×P because of 9 R-K1 P-Q4 10 N-N5!, and he cannot cope with the unpleasant threats of 11 R×Nch! and 11 P-B3. Even after 8 . . . P-Q4?!, which is better than 8 . . . P×P, White continues quietly with 9 P×P N-R4 10 B-B2, transposing into an advantageous variation of the Open Defense of the Ruy Lopez in which the deployment of Black's QB on N2 and Knight on QR4 seems very suspicious. Better for Black seems **8 . . . N-R4 9 B-B2 P-Q3,** which leads to an unclear position after 10 R-K1 P-KB4. But White can play 10 Q-K2 and his position seems to be superior.

CHAPTER 4

Developing an Opening Repertoire

by Lajos Portisch

General Considerations

The opening is perhaps the most difficult part of the chess game. Endgames and certain positions in the middlegame can usually be analyzed satisfactorily, but we can never be safe from improvements prepared against our favorite opening lines. Few opening variations have been appraised with finality. Some, which from time to time may disappear from tournament practice, remain alive for theoretical research. The proverb "seek and you shall find" is true in chess. No opening or defense can be laid to rest. The Ruy Lopez, for example, though now so popular it is regarded as almost obligatory for White after the first two moves, may in time be replaced by the fashion of the 19th century, the Giuoco Piano, or by some sort of gambit popular then.

Fashions do not change only in dressmaking. In chess, though, it is the best grandmasters who are the "fashion designers." As their games circulate around the globe, less-qualified opponents may prepare variations with which to refute the grandmasters' ideas. Does this pose a threat to the ordinary player? Well, good chess players are not so easily persuaded to yield any advantage; their own research along ever newer paths never ceases, even if their "latest fashion" is no more than a surprise move—an "improvement."

The crowd mimics its heroes. This is a natural tendency, but there is no need for such mimicry. It is illogical for one who has not earned his master title to ape the complicated opening variations played by, say, a world champion. After all, while the opening is indeed important in chess, it is still only one part of the game; victory can be found as well in the middlegame or endgame. *Your only task in the opening is to reach a playable middlegame.* (Taking advantage of a good middlegame position requires instruction that is beyond the intentions of this book.)

What is our task, then? How should we lay the foundations of our opening repertoire?

It is hard to come up with a single answer to satisfy every player. Individuals will have different objectives in the opening, as well as different playing strengths. Nevertheless, to all players I can recommend the following: *simplicity and economy.* These are the characteristics of the opening systems of many great masters. They do not strain unduly for advantages in the opening; they would just as soon move on to the next stage of the game, hoping their skill will overcome the opponent in the middlegame or endgame. Not even the greatest players, however, can afford to play the openings indiscriminately.

A solid opening repertoire fosters self-confidence. You should not worry that an opponent may be prepared for your opening. If you are well versed in your repertoire, the antidote to a sudden surprise can be found over the board—unless you indulge in wild openings or use dubious variations that can be refuted by a single sharp move. Let it also not be forgotten that the most complicated variations demand huge amounts of time for home analysis, time available only to professional chess players. With Black, for example, your knowledge of the Najdorf Variation of the Sicilian Defense may be deficient because you could not have read all of the many technical articles on this variation; therefore, a slightly more passive defense would be an appropriate choice for the student.

I will discuss here only openings and defenses that in my opinion offer simplicity and economy. Let me remind the reader that every grandmaster was once a beginner, and even beginners must play openings. Simplicity is obviously a necessity. I will try to show how my own play matured despite some unusual but simple openings I used at various times in my career. With all the books on openings available to the student, my advice can be only a small pointer, and, in the framework of my discussion, my choices are selective. But I sincerely hope that most readers, perhaps even the best-informed, will find useful information here.

Kingside Openings

Many players regard **1 P-K4 P-K4** as the sharpest opening. This judgment is correct if we consider only gambits arising from these moves; however, such gambits are out of fashion and are rarely encountered. I do not recommend them as effective weapons in serious play. Beginners and young players, however, should not ignore the classical gambits, for the principles of opening play—rapid development, control of the center, King safety—can be learned quickly from them. Of course, it is inadvisable and unnecessary to simply parrot memorized variations. Instead, try to absorb the fighting spirit of the great past masters of gambits, and polish your fighting skill by replaying their games *in full,* not merely the openings. I recommend the use of gambits in practice games. While your immediate results may not be satisfactory, it would be pointless to win games now at the expense of future improvement. Practice for the sake of learning will pay large dividends.

For White: The Ruy Lopez Exchange Variation

One opening that promises White safe play after 1 P-K4 P-K4, and can be played for a lifetime if you so decide, is the Ruy Lopez. Simple variations of the Ruy Lopez are safe to use in tournament games, leaving gambits only for practice and social occasions.

What is the essential idea of the Ruy Lopez?

	White	Black
1	P-K4	P-K4
2	N-KB3	N-QB3
3	B-N5	P-QR3

White develops two minor pieces, attacks Black's central KP, and prepares to castle. Black's KP seems to be threatened, but the threat does not become real for a few moves. More than one of my opponents in simultaneous exhibitions have overlooked the threat to this important pawn: 4 B-R4 N-B3 5 O-O B-K2 6 R-K1 O-O? 7 B×N and 8 N×P.

Why can't White win Black's KP immediately? After 4 B×N QP×B 5 N×P Q-Q5! White must retreat the Knight; Black then captures the pawn on White's K4 and the open position promises excellent chances for Black to exploit the advantage of his two Bishops. (In this open position in the Exchange Variation of the Ruy Lopez, the Bishop pair is stronger than White's Knight and Bishop, and is an important ace in Black's hand.) Lately, after 3 . . . P-QR3 White often exchanges on Black's QB3 but, of course, he does not then capture Black's KP.

The Exchange Variation promises simpler play than 4 B-R4, 5 O-O and 6 R-K1, followed by P-B3 and P-Q4 (we cannot realistically expect Black to allow his KP to be won), and excludes large numbers of complex variations in which Black may have chances to direct the course of the game. The main variations of the Ruy Lopez are very complicated and we need not suffer through them here; many have been analyzed in detail for some twenty moves! Let us leave such variations to the grandmasters; when you reach master strength there will be time enough to learn them.

Not only has the Exchange Varition far fewer variations to study, it has no less prestige and soundness than other lines, as proven by the fact that it is often used today by such grandmasters as Fischer and Mecking, and in the past by Emanuel Lasker, to name but a few.

4 B×N QP×B

There are now two main branches: the classical 5 P-Q4 (or 5 N-B3 and 6 P-Q4); and the modern 5 O-O.

By 5 P-Q4 White aims to eliminate Black's central pawn and gain a 4-3 pawn majority on the Kingside, while Black's Queenside pawn majority is theoretically worthless because of his doubled, and therefore weaker, pawns.

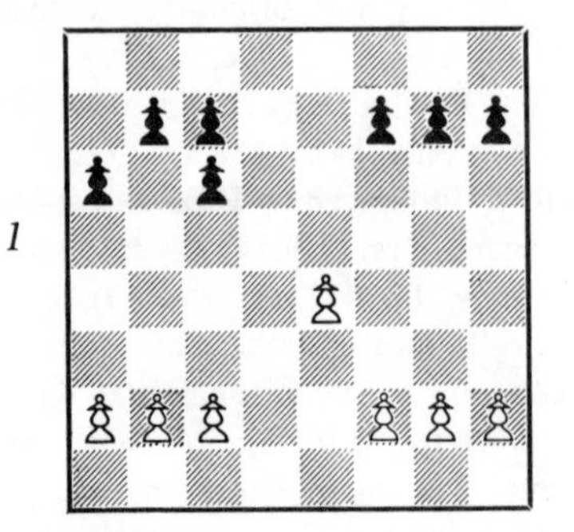

1

The diagram shows the characteristic pawn structure after 5 P-Q4 P×P 6 Q×P (or 6 N×P). If only the Kings were now added to the picture, Black would hardly be able to save the endgame because White could easily get a passed pawn on the Kingside while Black could not do the same on the Queenside. Thus, the final outcome of the game can be determined by the pawn structure after only a few moves of the opening! In order to reach the desired endgame as just described, White must endeavor to exchange pieces; Black, to avoid it, must seek opportunities for counterplay in the middlegame. Experience teaches us that Black's two Bishops are sufficient compensation for his weakened pawn structure, and that White cannot automatically expect to achieve his goal against correct Black play.

This is the reasoning behind Black's 3 . . . P-QR3. If he thought that 4 B×N would lead him into a dangerous endgame, he obviously could not play such a third move. In the analysis that follows I will not, discuss alternatives to 3 . . . P-QR3, since it is fully playable, in my opinion.

Among White's continuations on the fifth move, the older classical methods with the early P-Q4 pose no particular problems for Black. The modern method, however, is more dangerous:

5 O-O! . . . . . .

In the last ten years this move has all but superseded 5 P-Q4 and 5 N-B3. After 5 O-O White threatens to win Black's KP and Black must now decide how to meet this real threat. It is not yet possible to state with assurance which of Black's five main choices is best: 5 . . . B-KN5, 5 . . . P-B3, 5 . . . Q-Q3, 5 . . . Q-K2, 5 . . . N-K2?!

The natural 5 O-O used to be considered inferior because of 5 . . . B-KN5, after which the obvious 6 P-KR3 P-KR4 (with 6 . . . B×N Black gives up his advantage of the two Bishops, his compensation for the doubled pawns) seemed to give Black dangerous attacking chances. But modern tournament play indicates that his attack comes to naught and that White, with precise play, can maintain his small advantage.

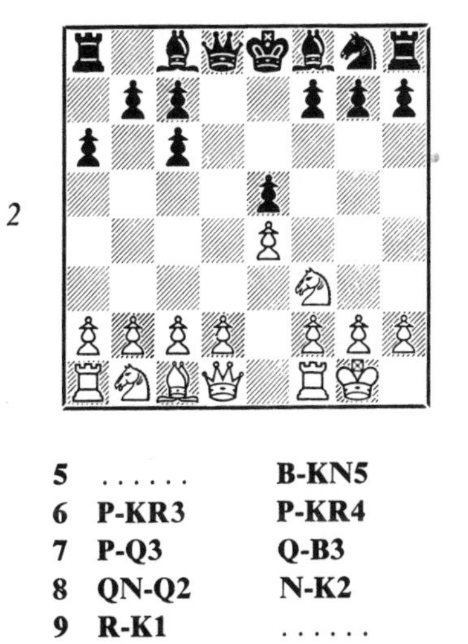

2

5	......	**B-KN5**
6	**P-KR3**	**P-KR4**
7	**P-Q3**	**Q-B3**
8	**QN-Q2**	**N-K2**
9	**R-K1**	......

The Black Bishop cannot be captured, of course, for then Black would launch a dangerous attack on the opened KR file.

9	......	**N-N3**
10	**P-Q4!**	**B-Q3**
11	**P×B**	......

Now this is possible, thanks to White's preparatory moves.

11	......	**RP×P**
12	**N-R2**	**R×N**
13	**Q×P**	**Q-R5**
14	**Q×Q**	**R×Q**
15	**N-B3**	......

And White has the better endgame.

Black gets more complicated play after (continue from *Diagram 2*):

5	......	**P-B3**
6	**P-Q4**	......

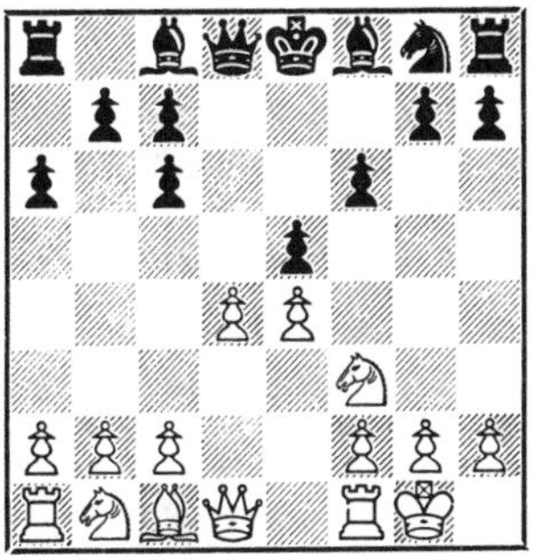

3

Black may now choose 6 . . . P×P or 6 . . . B-KN5.

6	......	**P×P**
7	**N×P**	......

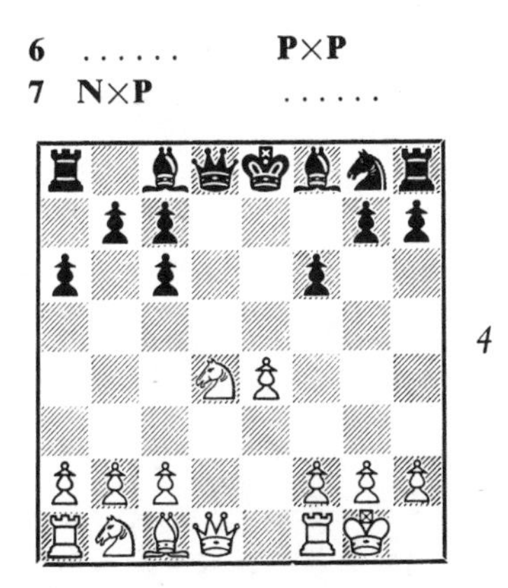

4

White gets no advantage by 7 Q×P, exchanging Queens. In a well-known game with the text move (Fischer-Portisch, Havana 1966), Black forced the exchange of Queens, but at the cost of time:

7	......	**P-QB4**
8	**N-N3**	**Q×Q**
9	**R×Q**	**B-Q3**

9 . . . B-Q2 10 N-B3 O-O-O 11

B-B4 P-B5 12 N-R5 P-QN4 13 N-Q5 B-KN5 14 P-KB3 B-B4ch 15 K-B1 B-R4 16 N-B6 R-Q2 17 N×QBP! gave White a decisive advantage (Ribli-Medina, Wijk aan Zee 1972). Black could have defended better with 11 ... B-K3, but White had the advantage anyway.

10 N-R5! P-QN4?

In Bagirov-Keres, Team Championship 1967, Black played 10 ... N-R3 11 B×N P×B 12 N-B4 B-K2 and soon equalized. That continuation cannot be recommended, however, as in this case the two Bishops do not compensate for Black's many weaknesses. That Black was able to draw the game was due to the fact that his name was Keres, not to the qualities of his position.

11 P-QB4! N-K2
12 B-K3 P-B4

Hoping for a counterattack.

13 N-B3 P-B5 14 P-K5! B×P 15 B×QBP B×N 16 P×B N-N3 17 N-B6 B-K3 18 P×P P×P 19 N-R7! QR-N1 20 KR-N1. Black cannot avoid the loss of material.

We can question Black's 10th move here, but even if there is a better move, the plan of exchanging Queens in this way has no solid foundation.

Black can do better by emphasizing rapid development. Continuing from *Diagram 4*, an obvious answer to 7 N×P is·

7 ...... B-Q3

If White cooperates by now playing only normal developing moves, Black can solve his problems with ... N-K2 and ... O-O. But White can interfere with this plan by the unpleasant:

8 Q-R5ch P-N3
9 Q-B3 ......

9 Q-R4 is weaker because the Queen is poorly placed after 9 ... P-KR4!

9 ... B×Pch 10 K×B Q×N 11 R-Q1 Q-B5 12 B-B4 Q-B2 13 Q-QN3! Q×Q 14 RP×Q B-K3 15 B×P. White's potential exploitation of the weak dark squares offers him a lasting advantage (Hecht-Gligoric, Teesside 1972).

In the position of *Diagram 4*, Black does better with:

7 ...... N-K2!

This eliminates the dangers of White's Q-R5ch. I surprised Hort with this move at Skopje 1968; the Czech grandmaster failed to find the correct answer and fell behind after **8 N-QB3 N-N3 9 P-B4? P-QB4!** (This is the right time for this move) **10 N-B3 Q×Q 11 R×Q B-N5 12 K-B2 B-Q3 13 N-Q5 O-O-O 14 P-B5 N-K4 15 B-B4 KR-K1.**

White should not play P-KB4 in the Exchange Variation of the Ruy Lopez (as Hort did on his 9th move) because it weakens his K4. After 7 ... N-K2 White should try 8 B-K3

N-N3 9 N-Q2, aiming at possible occupation of KB5 with the Knight. This line of play needs further testing and analysis.

Black can play 6 . . . B-KN5 (instead of 6 . . . P×P), maintaining control of his K4 and forcing White to make a decision. This may be called the Main Variation of this system.

White can choose to play for the endgame with 7 P×P, or he can sustain the center tension with 7 P-B3. After 1 P-K4 P-K4 2 N-KB3 N-QB3 3 B-N5 P-QR3 4 B×N QP×B 5 O-O P-B3 6 P-Q4, we have the position of *Diagram 3.*

6	**. . . . . .**	**B-KN5**
7	**P×P**	**Q×Q**
8	**R×Q**	**P×P**

8 . . . B×N? 9 P×B P×P 10 B-K3 B-Q3 11 N-Q2 N-K2 12 N-B4 is favorable for White because Black's isolated KP is more of a liability than White's doubled KBP (Fischer-Rubinetti, Buenos Aires 1970).

9	**R-Q3**	**B-Q3**

9 . . . B×N used to be played and White's usual recapture was with the Rook. But against Tringov at Varna 1972, young Hungarian grandmaster Adorjan who is a specialist in this line, played 10 P×B! and after 10 . . . N-B3 11 N-Q2 P-QN4 12 P-QR4 B-Q3 13 N-N3 O-O 14 N-R5 P-B4 15 P-QB4 he gained the advantage, as did Fischer in the game cited above.

10	**QN-Q2**	**N-B3**
11	**N-B4**	**N×P**

This exchange is probably advantageous for White. Black has better chances for equality with 11 . . . O-O! 12 KN×P B-K7! 13 R-K3 B×QN 14 N×B B-B4 15 R-K1 QR-K1 16 B-K3 B×B 17 R×B R×P (Ribli-Matanovic, European Team Championship, Bath 1973), or 15 R-K2 QR-K1 16 B-K3 R×P! (Stean-Geller, same tournament). Black drew both games and in the second one he even had the better endgame later.

After 11 . . . N×P White can capture the KP with 12 N/4×P B×KN 13 N×B O-O, as in the 16th game of the Fischer-Spassky World Championship Match in 1972, where Black had a satisfactory game. Far stronger is:

12	**N/3×P**	**B-K3**
13	**P-KB3**	**B×KN**
14	**N×B**	**N-B4**

Or 14 . . . N-B3 15 B-N5 O-O 16 B×N! P×B 17 N-Q7 R-B2 18 N-B5, with endgame advantage (Bronstein-Lengyel, Moscow 1971).

15 R-K3 O-O-O 16 R-K1 B-B4? (Here 16 . . . KR-K1 is necessary; however, White would still be better off) **17 B-K3 R-Q4 18 B×N! R×B 19 P-QB4** (The Black Rook is forced out of play. The ensuing moves are especially instructive, so we shall follow the game to its end) **19 . . .**

R-K1 20 P-B4 P-QR4 21 P-KN4 B-N3 22 P-KR4 R-Q1 23 P-N3 P-N4 24 P-R5 B-K1 25 P-R4 P×BP 26 P×P R-Q5 27 K-R2 P-N3 28 P×P P×P 29 QR-Q1!, Black resigns. After the forced exchange of Rooks by 29 . . . R×R 30 R×R P-N4 31 K-N3 P×Pch 32 K×P, Black is in zugzwang and cannot avoid the loss of material (Adorjan-Eley, Teesside 1973). White's careful exploitation of Black's pawn weaknesses yielded decisive advantages. This game was played after the European Team Championship (mentioned earlier); it is possible that Adorjan also had an improvement ready against Geller's move 11 . . . O-O.

White can aim for steady control of the center, beginning with the position of *Diagram 3*:

6	. . . . . .	**B-KN5**
7	**P-B3**	**B-Q3**
8	**B-K3**	. . . . . .

The immediate 8 QN-Q2 would have locked in the Bishop.

8	. . . . . .	**N-K2**

8 . . . N-R3?! is interesting.

9	**QN-Q2**	. . . . . .

At this point it is difficult to recommend a specific plan for Black. White's plan is clear: he will exchange on K5 and try for P-QB4-B5. Black may try to meet this by seeking counterplay with a Knight stationed on KB5.

It is difficult for White to decide whether or not to interpose P-KR3 B-R4. True, this will hinder Black's plan to maneuver his Knight to KB5 via KN3, but P-KR3 may turn out to be a weakening of White's King position. The Black Bishop, moreover, will be well placed on KB2, so White may not wish to force it there.

One example of the type of play in this line is Mecking-Unzicker, Lugano 1968:

9 . . . Q-B1 (9 . . . Q-Q2 is possible, but then the Bishop must return to K3 after 10 P-KR3 because of the pitfall 10 . . . B-R4? 11 N×P! B×Q 12 N×Q and White wins a pawn. Also to be considered is 9 . . . N-N3) **10 N-B4 O-O 11 P×P B×P** (If 11 . . . P×P 12 Q-N3! is strong) **12 QN×B P×N 13 Q-N3ch B-K3 14 Q-N4! N-N3 15 N-N5 P-QR4 16 Q-R4 P-R3 17 N×B Q×N 18 Q-N3!** Again, White has the better endgame.

As we mentioned, there are other tries for Black besides 5 . . . B-KN5 and 5 . . . P-B3. Of the others, perhaps **5 . . . Q-Q3** is most acceptable for Black. (1 P-K4 P-K4 2 N-KB3 N-QB3 3 B-N5 P-QR3 4 B×N QP×B 5 O-O, reaching the position of *Diagram 2*):

5	. . . . . .	**Q-Q3**

The obvious purpose of 5 . . . Q-Q3 is simply to castle on the Queenside after 6 . . . B-Q2 or 6

. . . B-N5. The disadvantage of the move is that White will later gain an important tempo with N-QB4. White cannot try to win the tempo at once with 6 N-R3 because of 6 . . . P-QN4!, but after castling Queenside Black will not want to risk such a weakening move with the QNP.

White does best to answer 5 . . . Q-Q3 with **6 P-Q3** followed by 7 QN-Q2, or 7 B-K3 and then 8 QN-Q2. Less effective for White is 6 P-Q4: the exchange 6 . . . P×P 7 Q×P Q×Q is advantageous for Black despite his loss of a tempo, while 7 N×P leads to sharp play because of the open Queen file, as demonstrated in the game Andersson-Portisch (Las Palmas 1972): **6 P-Q4 P×P 7 N×P B-Q2 8 N-QB3 O-O-O 9 B-K3 N-R3 10 P-KR3 P-KN4!?**

The idea of **5 . . . Q-K2** (from *Diagram 2*) is similar to that of 5 . . . Q-Q3. Smyslov won decisively against Gheorghiu with this move at the 1973 Interzonal in Petropolis, but White's play was too passive. White's best plan against the developing move 5 . . . Q-Q3 (6 P-Q3) is not so good against 5 . . . Q-K2, and vice versa: against 5 . . . Q-K2, the moves 6 P-Q3 and 6 P-QN3 have no meaning; but White should try for an advantage with 6 P-Q4 because after 6 . . . P×P he can recapture safely with his Queen. In chess your plans must always be flexible!

Lastly, and most interesting (see *Diagram 2*), there is:

5	. . . . . .	**N-K2**
6	**N×P**	**Q-Q5**
7	**Q-R5**	. . . . . .

Although after the obvious 7 N-KB3 Q×KP 8 R-K1 Q-N3 9 N-K5 Q-B3 Black successfully castled Queenside in Ree-Keres, Amsterdam 1971, this continuation is not quite safe either.

7	. . . . . .	**P-KN3**
8	**Q-N5**	**B-N2**
9	**N-Q3**	**P-KB4!?**
10	**P-K5!**	**P-B4**
11	**P-QN3!**	. . . . . .

This complicates matters greatly. Black can hardly capture White's Rook because after 12 N-B3 and 13 B-N2 he would have to give up his Queen. In general, two Rooks are of greater value than a Queen, but when there are many minor pieces on the board this evaluation must remain open.

For Black: The Modern Steinitz

If Black wishes to answer **1 P-K4** with 1 . . . P-K4, he must take into account a number of possible gambits, the Giuoco Piano, perhaps the Two Knights Defense and the Three Knights Game. When facing such openings it is important to select effective but uncomplicated defenses. These openings are thoroughly analyzed in books on theory and, in the present state of the art, present no real difficulties for Black.

But what should you do when facing the Ruy Lopez? Moves other than 3 . . . P-QR3 have little to recommend them, but even after that move you may have to deal not only with the Exchange Variation but with other lines, including particularly the Main Variation: 4 B-R4 N-B3 5 O-O B-K2 6 R-K1 P-QN4 7 B-N3 P-Q3 8 P-B3 O-O 9 P-KR3, with P-Q4 to follow. Just as White is able to avoid this line, so is Black if he chooses to: all he has to do is play some move other than 4 . . . N-B3.

We will consider **1 P-K4 P-K4 2 N-KB3 N-QB3 3 B-N5 P-QR3 4 B-R4 P-Q3,** the Modern Steinitz Defense. The old Steinitz Defense with 3 . . . P-Q3 was popular during the 19th century; if it interests you, I advise the sequence 3 . . . N-B3 4 O-O P-Q3. The Modern Steinitz, with its interpolated 3 . . . P-QR3, prevents White's dangerous Queen-side castling and is more effective in neutralizing the pressure on Black's KP. Even those faithful to the old Steinitz Defense can do no harm to themselves by reviewing the modern system.

After 4 B-R4 P-Q3, White has three main choices: 5 B×Nch, 5 P-B3, and 5 O-O, though the latter two may be combined. After 5 P-Q4 P-QN4 6 B-N3 N×P 7 N×N P×N 8 B-Q5 (but not 8 Q×P? P-QB4 9 Q-Q5 B-K3 10 Q-B6ch B-Q2 11 Q-Q5 P-B5, trapping the Bishop) 8 . . . R-N1 9 Q×P N-B3 10 B-B6ch B-Q2, Black gets comfortable play.

5	**B×Nch**	**P×B**
6	**P-Q4**	. . . . . .

Black can now hold the center with 6 . . . P-B3; but let us consider a move Keres has been playing in recent years.

6	. . . . . .	**P×P**
7	**N×P**	. . . . . .

An obvious move, though 7 Q×P! may be better because it maintains the threat of P-K5, which is often effective against the developing move . . . N-KB3. For this reason, against Mecking in the 1973 Interzonal in Petropolis, Keres (Black) developed his Knight to KN3 via K2 and secured equality.

7	. . . . . .	**P-QB4!**
8	**N-K2**	. . . . . .

White would do better to play 8 N-KB3.

8	. . . . . .	**N-B3**
9	**QN-B3**	. . . . . .

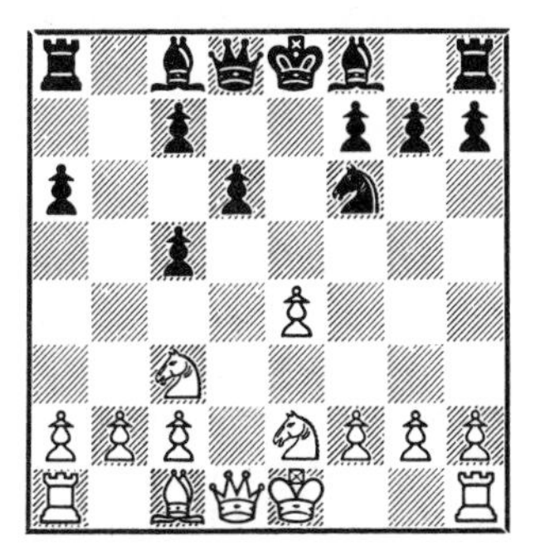

9 . . . B-K2 10 O-O O-O 11 N-N3 R-K1 12 P-N3 B-B1 13 B-N2 R-N1 14 R-K1 P-B3 15 P-K5 P×P 16 R×P Q×Qch 17 N×Q B-K3 18 R-K1 N-Q4 19 N-K3 QR-Q1 20 N/N3-B1 N-N3 21 B-B3 N-Q4 22 B-N2 P-B3 23 N-B4 N-N5 24 N/1-K3 B-B2 25 P-QR3 N-Q4 26 P-R3 R-N1 27 B-B1 N-B5 28 B-Q2 N-K3! 29 B-B3 N-Q5 (Jimenez-Keres, Marianske Lazne 1965). Black's maneuvers—the way he counterbalanced his pawn weaknesses by coordinated piece play and eventually took control—deserve close study. (The order of moves given is a slight transposition of Jimenez-Keres; Black exchanged on Q5 only after 4 . . . P-Q3 5 O-O B-K2 6 B×Nch P×B 7 P-Q4.)

From the position of *Diagram 5*, Black can develop his King Bishop more effectively:

9 . . . B-N2 10 N-N3 P-N3! 11 O-O B-N2 12 R-K1 O-O 13 B-B4 R-K1 14 Q-Q2 N-N5 15 P-KR3 N-K4 16 P-N3 N-B3 17 QR-Q1 N-Q5. Black has the better game (Daskalov-Keres, Tallinn 1971).

In the Modern Steinitz Defense Black need not fear 5 B×Nch as he may in the Exchange Variation. His only problems occur when White builds a pawn center with 5 P-B3 B-Q2 (I will not discuss here the gambit line 5 . . . P-B4, which I cannot recommend) 6 O-O, or 6 P-Q4 and then O-O.

After 1 P-K4 P-K4 2 N-KB3 N-QB3 3 B-N5 P-QR3 4 B-R4 P-Q3, White can immediately play:

5 O-O **B-Q2!**

The sharp variation 5 . . . B-N5?! is recommended only for practice games.

6 P-Q4 **N-B3**

The pawn sacrifice cannot be accepted, for after 6 . . . P-QN4 7 B-N3 N×P 8 N×N P×N 9 P-QB3! White would have too great a lead in development.

7 P-B3 

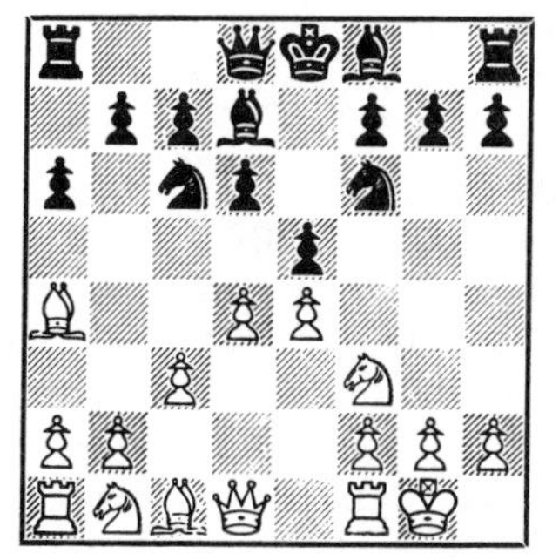

6

7	......	**B-K2**
8	**QN-Q2**	**O-O**
9	**R-K1**	**R-K1!**
10	**P-KR3**	......

Black gets good play for the pawn after 10 B×N B×B 11 P×P P×P 12 N×P B×P 13 N×P K×N 14 N×B Q×Q 15 N-N5ch K-N1 16 R×Q B-B4.

10 ... B-KB1 11 B-B2 P-KN3 (Also worth considering is 11 ... P-R3, with ... P-QB4 to follow) **12 N-B1 B-N2 13 N-N3 Q-K2 14 B-K3 N-QR4 15 P-N3 P-B4,** with equal play (Djurasevic-Smyslov, 1956).

It can be concluded from this game that Black's position is solid and not easily undermined—his K4 is properly secured. His King Bishop may be fianchettoed in this line, and this wing development can be accelerated. Continuing from *Diagram 6*:

7	......	**Q-K2!?**

An odd move at first glance, but it is logical. The immediate 7 ... P-KN3 runs into the unpleasant 8 B×N! B×B 9 P×P N×P 10 QN-Q2! B-K2 11 N×N B×N 12 P×P Q×P 13 Q×Q P×Q 14 R-K1 B-Q4 15 B-N5, with the better endgame for White (Geller-Zhukhovitsky, USSR Championship 1969). And 7 ... P-QN4 followed by ... P-N3 causes a later weakness of Black's QB4 if White decides to exchange on his K5.

8	**R-K1**	**P-KN3**
9	**QN-Q2**	**B-N2**
10	**N-B1**	......

If 10 P×P QN×P 11 N×N P×N 12 B×Bch N×B 13 N-B3 O-O-O! 14 B-K3 P-KB4! with advantage to Black (Jansa-Keres, Luhacovice 1969).

10 ... O-O 11 N-K3 (11 B-KN5 develops better, but White gets no advantage after 11 ... Q-K1) **11 ... QR-K1! 12 B-B2 P×P 13 N-Q5?** (Very bad, but even after 13 P×P N-QN5 14 B-N1 P-QR4! White has difficulty completing his development) **13 ... N×N 14 P×N N-K4 15 N×P Q-R5!** Black has the advantage (Tatai-Portisch, Las Palmas 1972).

The French Defense

The French is one of the most solid defenses against 1 P-K4. It has the virtues of simplicity and economy, which we recommended at the beginning of this chapter. It also has a drawback: it demands patience. But patience is needed for chess in any case. There are far fewer variations than after 1 P-K4 P-K4, and experimental and unexpected moves can be tried without fear. The French is a "closed" defense, and in closed positions a slight disadvantage may be tolerated. Of course, there are complicated variations in the French Defense, but we can (and should) avoid them. Also, choosing the French Defense means polishing your middlegame, which is always helpful.

It is unthinkable to study the French Defense without examining the games of Nimzovich and Botvinnik. From gambits we can develop tactical skill; from the games of these two chess giants we can learn modern chess strategy.

1	**P-K4**	**P-K3**
2	**P-Q4**	**P-Q4**

We will consider—primarily from Black's viewpoint—White's possible choices 3 N-QB3, 3 N-Q2, and other moves.

3	**N-QB3**	**B-N5**
4	**P-K5**	......

White's fourth move presents a major problem to Black, who must decide at once what kind of game to play. Those who like tactical complexity will choose 4 . . . P-QB4 5 P-QR3 B×Nch 6 P×B N-K2 7 Q-N4! Q-B2! 8 Q×NP R-N1 9 Q×P P×P 10 N-K2 QN-B3 11 P-KB4 B-Q2, a variation that demands considerable study.

As a young master, I developed a system against White's early Queen maneuver by playing my own Queen out first:

4	......	**P-QB4**
5	**P-QR3**	**B×Nch**
6	**P×B**	**Q-R4!?**
7	**B-Q2**	**Q-R5**

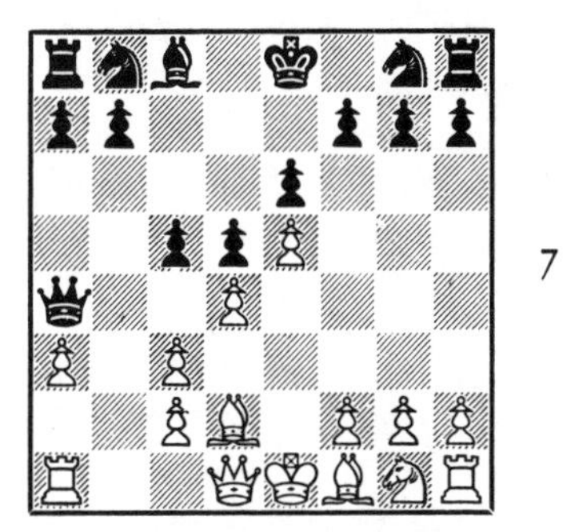

7

Thus White's Queenside is blockaded. Such blockading is the essence of this variation. The Black Queen is ideally posted on QR5, its presence precluding White's often useful developing moves P-QR4 and B-QR3. The only question is: How dangerous will White's initiative on the Kingside be? Well, after 8 Q-N4, the only reasonable reply is 8 . . . P-KN3 (8 . . . K-B1 is not in accordance with Black's plans), but this weakens the dark squares on Black's Kingside. Therefore, Black's early Queen maneuver is not entirely safe: there are disadvantages.

But the first time I tried my new continuation I had complete success.

8	**Q-N4**	**P-KN3**
9	**R-R2**	**N-QB3**
10	**N-B3**	**P-KR3!**
11	**Q-B4**	**P-B5**

Eliminating the possibility of 12 P×P.

12 P-R4 B-Q2 13 N-R2 (Premature) **Q-N4! 14 R-R1 Q-N7 15 R-B1**

Q×RP 16 B-K2 O-O-O 17 O-O White should have tried 17 Q×BP, though 17 ... KN-K2 followed by ... QR-B1 and an eventual ... N-B4 would have to be considered) **17 ... R-B1 18 R-R1 Q-N7! 19 KR-B1 P-B3 20 B-Q1 Q-N3 21 KR-N1 Q-Q1 22 Q-N3 KN-K2 23 B-N4? P-B4 24 B-K2 P-B5! 25 Q-N4 N-B4 26 N-B3 P-KN4! 27 P×P P×P 28 Q×NP Q-K1,** and Black has a decisive advantage (Zsedenyi/Berger-Portisch, Budapest 1956).

Again from *Diagram* 7:

8	**Q-N4**	**P-KN3**
9	**R-B1**	......

If White must lose a pawn anyway, this is more logical than 9 R-R2.

9	......	**N-QB3**
10	**N-B3**	**P-KR3!**
11	**B-Q3**	**P-B5**
12	**B-K2**	**B-Q2**
13	**Q-B4**	**R-R2!**

This is why 10 ... P-KR3 was important, in addition to controling KN4.

14 P-R4 O-O-O 15 O-O Q×RP 16 R-R1 Q-B1 (16 ... Q-K2, to further control KN4, is also to be considered; the point is that after 17 N-R2 Black can play 17 ... R-N2 followed possibly by ... P-KN4)**17 N-R2 P-B4 18 P×P e.p. N×BP 19 B-B3 N-KN1 20 Q-N3 KN-K2 21 B-N4 P-N3.** Difficult play is in prospect, with Black's chances no worse than even (Parma-Portisch, Bled 1961). This game ended in a draw, although I probably could have won.

Since the aggressive Queen move 8 Q-N4 led to the loss of a pawn, in other games my opponents played differently. Continuing from *Diagram* 7:

8	**N-B3**	**N-K2**

There is also 8 ... P-QN3!, preventing White's next maneuver and threatening 9 ... B-R3, a positional exchange maneuver characteristic of the French Defense.

9	**Q-N1!**	**P-B5**

Or 9 ... O-O 10 B-QN5 Q-R4 11 B-Q3 P-B5 12 B-K2 N-Q2 13 O-O N-QB3 14 R-K1 P-B3 15 P×P N×BP 16 Q-N2 N-K5, with equal chances (Uusi-Portisch, Tallinn 1957).

10 P-N3 QN-B3 11 B-N2 B-Q2 12 O-O O-O-O 13 N-N5 QR-B1 14 P-B4 P-B3 15 N-B3 K-N1, and Black has good chances (Dely-Portisch, Balatonfured 1959).

After 1 P-K4 P-K3 2 P-Q4 P-Q4 3 N-QB3 B-N5 4 P-K5, instead of 4 ... P-QB4 Black can get a solid position with:

4	......	**P-QN3**

8 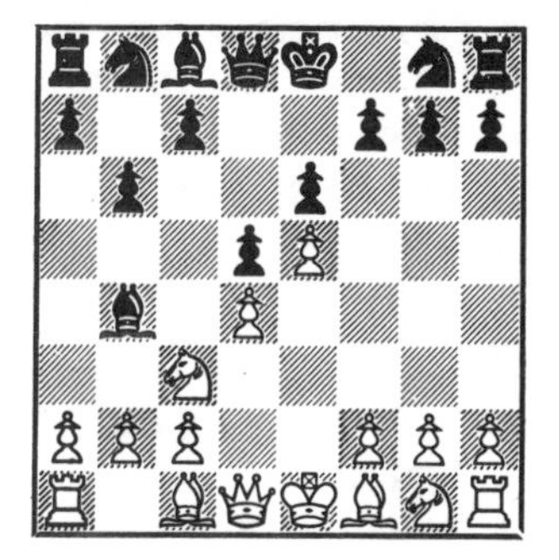

This keeps the position closed, and Black can afford the loss of a tempo.

5 Q-N4 B-B1

5 . . . B-B1 testifies to the flexibility of the French Defense: White's 4 P-K5 has closed the center, achieving one of Black's goals, and Black can keep his King Bishop, which is not needed on QN5. Furthermore, the White Knight on QB3 has no effect against Black's . . . P-QB4, which will be played later to disrupt White's pawn structure. Also, KN4 is not a good post for the White Queen. In the following game, Black exploited this situation (though it is true White did not suspect the trap).

6 B-N5 Q-Q2
7 O-O-O P-KR3
8 B-R4?? . . . . . .

8 B-K3 was necessary, after which Black could have played 8 . . . B-R3, or even 8 . . . B-N2, 9 . . . N-QB3 and 10 . . . O-O-O.

8 . . . . . . P-KN4

Now White realized that 9 B-N3 would lose a piece after 9 . . . P-KR4 (10 Q×NP? B-KR3), so he played **9 B×P P×B 10 K-N1,** continuing the game only out of respect for his teammates (Padevsky-Portisch, Varna Olympiad 1962).

If White does not answer 4 . . . P-QN3 with the Queen move, Black can aim for the exchange maneuver with . . . B-QR3, or even for castling Queenside after . . . Q-Q2, . . . N-QB3 and . . . B-QN2. Even against 5 P-QR3 there is no need to exchange Bishop for Knight—5 . . . B-B1! is better.

Here are a few examples, continuing from *Diagram 8*:

5 N-B3 Q-Q2 6 B-Q3 N-QB3 (Note that 1 P-K4 N-QB3 2 N-QB3 P-K3 3 N-B3 P-Q4 4 P-Q4 B-N5 5 P-K5 Q-Q2 6 B-Q3 P-QN3 reaches the same position, though starting as a Nimzovich Defense!) **7 O-O B-N2 8 N-K2 P-B4 9 N-B4 B-K2 10 P-B3 O-O-O 11 P-KR4 N-R3 12 N-N5 B×N 13 P×B N-B2 14 N-R5 P-KR3! 15 P-N6 N-N4 16 N-B4 N-K5.** Black has the initiative (Foldi-Portisch, Budapest 1957).

5 N-B3 B-B1!? 6 B-K2 N-K2 7 O-O N-N3 8 R-K1 B-K2 9 P-KN3 P-QB4 10 P-KR4 P-KR3 11 B-Q3 N-B1 12 P-R4 P-R3 12 P-QR5? P-B5 14 B-B1 P-QN4, and Black will win White's advanced QRP (Campos-Lopez vs. Petrosian, San Antonio 1972). Black can allow for practically anything in this variation!

5 P-QR3 B-B1 6 P-B4 N-K2 7 B-K3 P-KR4 8 N-B3 Q-Q2 9 B-B2 N-B4 10 B-Q3 B-R3! (Note that Black offers this exchange only after White's Bishop has moved, thereby gaining an important tempo) **11 B×B N×B 12 Q-Q3 N-N1 13 N-K2 P-B4** (Zuidema-Andersson, Wijk aan Zee 1973).

Not everyone with the White pieces willingly accepts the bind after 3 . . . B-N5 and the disruption of his pawn structure that often accompanies it. After 1 P-K4 P-K3 2 P-Q4 P-Q4, many prefer:

3 N-Q2 . . . . . .

Black has three acceptable responses: 3 . . . P-QB4, 3 . . . N-KB3, and 3 . . . N-QB3. I will discuss the latter move in some detail, not only because it was my favorite defense in my youth, but because the others are far more complex (and not necessarily any better).

Usually, **3 . . . P-QB4** leads to an isolated pawn for Black, which many players are unwilling to accept.

Against **3 . . . N-KB3,** I developed a strong position as White in my game against Tal in Oberhausen 1961, and since then almost everyone plays the same line: **4 P-K5 KN-Q2 5 P-KB4 P-QB4 6 P-B3 N-QB3 7 N/2-B3! Q-N3 8 P-KN3! P×P 9 P×P P-B3 10 B-R3 P×P 11 BP×P B-N5ch 12 K-B1 N-B1 13 N-K2 N-N3 14 K-N2 O-O 15 B-N4 B-Q2 16 P-KR4!**, with a clear advantage for White.

After 3 N-Q2, we will analyze the third alternative mentioned above.

3 . . . . . . **N-QB3**
4 KN-B3 **N-B3**
5 P-K5 **N-Q2**
6 N-N3 . . . . . .

The usual White move. There is an interesting alternative, played in Benko-Portisch, Budapest 1956: 6 P-QN3 P-B3 (this is also a good answer to 6 P-B3, and after 7 P×P recapturing with the Queen) 7 B-N2 P×P 8 P×P B-K2 9 P-N3 O-O 10 B-KR3 N-B4 11 O-O P-QR4! 12 Q-K2 P-R5 13 P-R3 P×P 14 P×P Q-K1 15 N-Q4 Q-N3 16 P-B4 N×N 17 B×N P-N3 18 P-QN4 B-R3 19 Q-N4!? B×R 20 R×B Q-Q6 21 N-B3 N-N6 22 Q×KPch R-B2, with enormous complications.

6 . . . . . . **B-K2!**

Studying my earlier games, I concluded that 6 . . . P-B3 is premature against 6 N-N3. Either 7 B-QN5 or the position after 7 B-KB4 P×P 8 P×P, followed by P-B3, B-Q3 and Q-K2, would be reason enough for my conclusion.

7 B-QN5 **O-O**

The interpolation of 7 . . . P-QR4 8 P-QR4 should also be considered.

In the April 1972 issue of the journal of the Moscow Central Chess Club, an interesting pawn sacrifice is suggested: 8 ... N-R2!? 9 B×Nch Q×B 10 N×P P-QN3 11 N-N3 B-R3.

8 O-O **N/3-N1!**

9

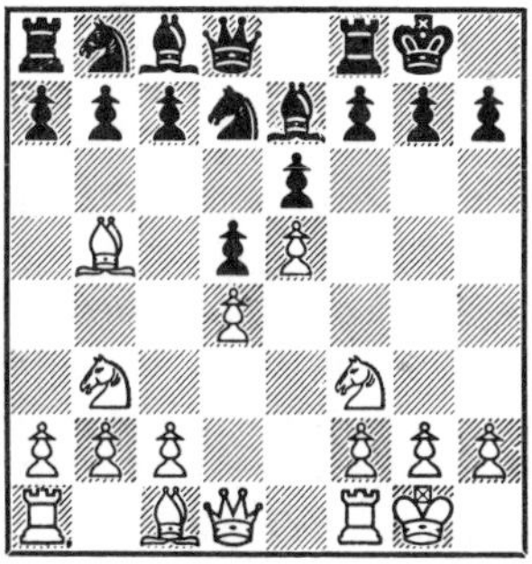

The Knight has served its purpose on B3; its retreat, like the retreat ... B-KB1, is a permitted strategy in the French Defense.

9	**P-B3**	**P-QN3**
10	**N-K1**	**P-QB3**
11	**B-K2**	**B-R3**

The usual maneuver to exchange Bishops.

12	**B×B**	**N×B**
13	**Q-N4**	......

Now Black should have played 13 ... K-R1 with equal chances in the middlegame. Instead, I played **13 ... R-K1? 14 B-R6 B-B1 15 B-N5 B-K2 16 B×B Q×B 17 P-KB4 P-KB4 18 P×P e.p.** (Yanofsky-Portisch, Munich Olympiad 1958), which left Black's K4 weak while White was able to mobilize along the King file.

Starting again from *Diagram 9*:

9 B-Q3 **P-QR4**

As before, 9 ... P-QN3 should also be considered.

10 B-K3 P-R5 11 QN-Q2 P-QB4 12 P-B3 P-R6 13 P-QN3 P×P (Premature) **14 B×P! N-QB3 15 R-K1 N-B4 16 B-B2 P-QN3 17 P-QN4! N-Q2 18 R-N1 Q-B2 19 R-K3 B-N2 20 N-N3 P-N3 21 P-R4!** White has a strong Kingside initiative (Minic-Korchnoi, Zagreb 1970). Although Black lost both games given above, the variation is quite playable, as we have noted.

Among alternatives to 3 N-QB3 and 3 N-Q2, the Exchange Variation 3 P×P (as well as the delayed exchange with 3 N-QB3 B-N5 4 P×P) cannot pose any real problems for Black, who can adjust his play to his blood pressure: he can follow his opponent and castle on the Kingside or he can adopt the sharper Queenside castling in the style of Nimzovich.

Of course, Nimzovich was not right about everything: after all, he preferred 3 P-K5 where, after 3 ... P-QB4 4 P-QB3 N-QB3 5 N-B3 Q-N3, Black already stands very well. True, Nimzovich had in mind variations in which White sacrifices his QP, but today Black has better methods of meeting that sacrifice than those known to Nimzovich's opponents.

Finally, a few words about White's play against the French Defense. Your task will be greatly simplified if on the second move you do not play the usual 2 P-Q4, aiming instead for a position with 2 P-Q3 P-Q4 3 N-Q2, then KN-B3, P-KN3 and B-N2. With this series of moves you direct the play into the King's Indian Attack (discussed later).

Here I will give only one example:

1	**P-K4**	**P-K3**
2	**P-Q3**	**P-Q4**
3	**N-Q2**	**N-KB3**
4	**KN-B3**	**N-B3**

This is considered good for Black. The point is that if 5 P-KN3 Black can develop conveniently with 5 ... P×P 6 P×P P-K4, followed by 7 ... B-QB4. Ljubojevic found a fine move against me in the Petropolis Interzonal, 1973:

5	**P-B3!**	......

Now 5 ... P×P would be premature because the White Bishop could then develop along the open diagonal to QN5. And if 5 ... P-K4 6 P-QN4. I therefore replied:

5	......	**P-QR4**

This should not hurt Black, but it will not help a great deal either.

6	**P-K5**	**N-Q2**
7	**P-Q4**	......

I should now have played 7 ... P-B3 with play similar to a variation beginning 1 P-K4 P-K3 2 P-Q4 P-Q4 3 N-Q2. Instead I played: **7 ... P-QN3 8 P-KR4! B-K2 9 B-N5 N/3-N1 10 N-B1 B-R3 11 B×B R×B** (Even better was 11 ... N×B) **12 Q-Q3,** and White was better.

Other Defense Against 1 P-K4

The Sicilian Defense, 1 ... P-QB4, is perhaps the most fashionable defense today. This fact makes it a very difficult subject for the student. One inaccurate move can lead to loss of the game; in fact many victories by White can be attributed to powerful attacks resulting from inaccurate Black play. In the Sicilian, one must be constantly alert to new theoretical developments and must analyze the latest tournament games. Nowadays it is difficult to find a variation in the Sicilian that does not have extensive published theory. The Dragon and Najdorf Variations, for example, have been analyzed to twenty moves and more; if a player without adequate preparation walks into an analyzed sequence he may lose even to a weaker opponent. Under no circumstances should you handle these variations in serious games unless you are a professional chess player with unlimited time for study.

Toward the end of the 1950s I worked a lot with the Sicilian (until then I occasionally played the variation 2 N-KB3 P-QR3 with Black).

In those days there was no "theory" on the Modern Paulsen Variation, so I liked it. But I can no longer recommend this variation to the beginning or intermediate student because, like the Dragon and the Najdorf, it is very fashionable and has been analyzed to death.

Black has other defenses than the Sicilian to choose from, but as White you cannot avoid it if you are a devotee of 1 P-K4. If you play the main variation with 2 N-KB3 and 3 P-Q4, you will be unable to predict which of many possibilities your opponent will choose. Therefore, I suggest that you consider systems that are simpler to learn or that lead to simplification of the position: the wing gambits with P-QN4 (but of course not everyone likes to sacrifice a pawn); or P-QB3 followed by P-Q4; or variations with B-QN5 (2 N-KB3 N-QB3 3 B-N5, or 2 N-KB3 P-Q3 3 B-N5ch); or systems with P-KN3 (2 N-KB3 P-K3 3 P-Q3 P-Q4 4 QN-Q2 followed by P-KN3) with transposition to the King's Indian Attack.

Among the systems in which P-KN3 is played, best known is the Closed Sicilian (2 N-QB3 and 3 P-KN3), with which Spassky and Smyslov have had many successes.

The strategy of the Closed Sicilian is relatively simple: White can indulge his attacking disposition (indicated by his choice of 1 P-K4), for usually White advances his Kingside pawns effectively in the middlegame. As an example of the type of play you may encounter in the Closed Sicilian, here is a little-known game that is one of my favorites (Portisch-Barcza, Hungarian Championship 1961):

1	**P-K4**	**P-QB4**
2	**N-QB3**	**N-QB3**
3	**P-KN3**	**P-KN3**
4	**B-N2**	**B-N2**
5	**P-Q3**	**P-Q3**
6	**P-B4**	**N-B3**

Probably a better defense is 6 . . . P-K3 and 7 . . . KN-K2, hoping to blunt White's attack against KB4, but the text move has certain advantages.

7	**KN-K2!**	. . . . . .

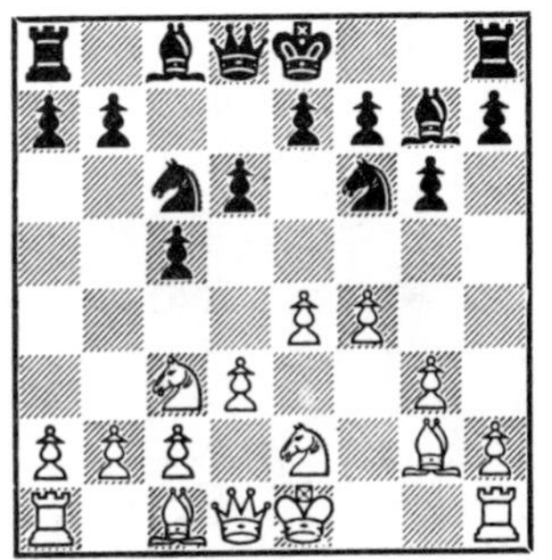

10

In his 1968 match with Geller, Spassky developed this Knight to KB3 and followed with P-KR3 and P-KN4. But the Knight may be better placed eventually on KN3.

7	. . . . . .	**B-Q2**
8	**P-KR3**	**R-QN1**
9	**P-KN4**	**N-Q5**

10	**N-N3**	**B-B3**
11	**O-O**	**O-O**
12	**B-K3**	**N-Q2**
13	**Q-Q2**	**P-K3**
14	**N-Q1!**	......

A typical maneuver to chase the Knight back.

14 ... P-Q4 15 P-B3 N-N4 16 P-QR4 N-B2 17 P-B5! QP×P 18 N×P B×N 19 B×B KP×P 20 P×P Q-R5 21 Q-N2 B-R3 22 B-B2 Q-Q1 23 N-K3 N-B3 24 N-N4! N×N 25 Q×N N-Q4 26 Q-B3 N-B3 27 B×BP N×B 28 P×N R-K1 29 P×P Q-N4ch 30 K-R1 Q×P 31 R-KN1 B-N4 32 R×B, Black resigns.

To avoid the complex variations of the **Caro-Kann Defense,** the Exchange Variation may be played. Against the French Defense, exchanging pawns in the center may be meek, but that is not the case in the Caro-Kann:

1	**P-K4**	**P-QB3**
2	**P-Q4**	**P-Q4**
3	**P×P**	**P×P**
4	**B-Q3**	**N-QB3**
5	**P-QB3**	**N-B3**
6	**B-KB4**	**B-N5**
7	**Q-N3**	**Q-B1**

Or 7 ... N-QR4?! 8 Q-R4ch B-Q2 9 Q-B2 P-K3 10 N-B3 Q-N3 11 P-QR4! R-B1 12 QN-Q2 N-B3 13 Q-N1 N-KR4 14 B-K3 P-KR3 15 N-K5, giving White attacking chances (Fischer-Petrosian, Belgrade 1970).

8 N-Q2 P-K3 9 KN-B3 B-K2 10 O-O O-O 11 N-K5 B-R4 12 Q-B2! B-N3 13 N×B RP×N 14 N-B3, and White has the better chances (Browne-Larsen, San Antonio 1972).

In recent years, the **Pirc-Ufimtsev Defense** has become quite popular. The following is the most secure way to play against it:

1	**P-K4**	**P-Q3**
2	**P-Q4**	**N-KB3**
3	**N-QB3**	**P-KN3**
4	**N-B3**	**B-N2**
5	**B-K2**	**O-O**
6	**O-O**	**B-N5**

If 6 ... P-B3 7 P-KR3 followed by B-K3 and P-QR4, planning to hold Q4 in case Black plays ... P-K4, or White can play B-QB4, exchanging pawns if Black plays ... P-K4.

7	**B-K3**	**N-B3**
8	**Q-Q2!**	......

White's development is excellent; after 8 ... P-K4, either 9 P-Q5 or 9 P×P gives him a slight advantage.

Closed Openings and Defenses

After the most usual first moves in the closed openings—1 P-Q4, 1 P-QB4, 1 N-KB3 (1 P-KN3 often transposes into the English Opening or King's Indian Attack, as does 1 P-QN3)—we must deal with a greater number of defenses than after 1 P-K4. It may be possible, however, to transpose from one line to another unless we insist on 1 P-Q4. The popularity of the closed openings, especially those beginning with 1 N-KB3 and 1 P-QB4, is explained by the fact that their variations do not change as often as in the KP openings. In practice, this means that we do not have to fear prepared innovations that much.

King's Indian Attack

This system, as I mentioned earlier, can develop after 1 P-K4 in the French Defense or the Modern Paulsen Variation of the Sicilian Defense. It is easy to remember the first few moves of this opening, so when beginners ask me for the best way to open a game, I often advise 1 N-KB3, 2 P-KN3, 3 B-N2 and 4 O-O, after which few troubles loom for White. As a player's strength increases, of course, so do the demands on his ability to play the openings. It is necessary, therefore, to develop such skills beyond the mere memorization of a few opening moves.

1	**N-KB3**	**P-Q4**
2	**P-KN3**	**P-QB4**
3	**B-N2**	**N-QB3**
4	**O-O**	......

White can also play 4 P-Q4 and then attack Black's center with P-QB4, but this demands exact play from both sides.

4	......	**P-K3**

4 . . . P-K4, which transposes into the King's Indian Defense with colors reversed and thus an extra tempo for White, need not be discussed here. The characteristic strategy of the King's Indian Defense is appropriate in that case, and the extra tempo makes it stronger than usual.

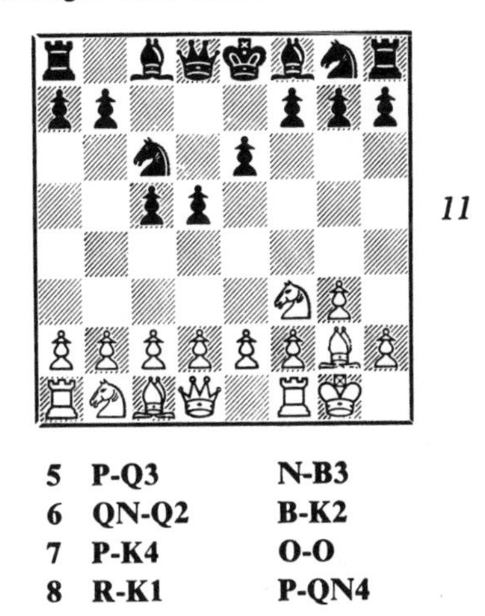

11

5	**P-Q3**	**N-B3**
6	**QN-Q2**	**B-K2**
7	**P-K4**	**O-O**
8	**R-K1**	**P-QN4**

This position can also be reached through the French Defense. Black aims for a quick Queenside initiative, while White attacks on the Kingside.

9	**P-K5**	**N-Q2**
10	**N-B1**	**P-QR4**
11	**P-KR4!**	**P-N5**
12	**B-B4**	**P-R5**

This position is characteristic of the King's Indian Attack.

White is planning P-R5-R6, and Black leaves his Queen on Q1 for the time being to keep control of his KN4. After White plays P-R5,

Black cannot play . . . P-R3 because of the coming sacrifices on the King-side after N/1-R2-N4 and Q-Q2, and, after White's P-R5-R6, Black must play . . . P-N3 when White can continue with B-N5 if the Black Queen moves.

Meanwhile, Black is threatening 13 . . . P-R6 and if 14 P-N3 N-R2 followed by . . . N-N4. Against this threat Fischer found an excellent move.

13	**P-R3!**	**P×P**
14	**P×P**	**N-R4**

If 14 . . . B-R3 15 N-K3 N-Q5 16 P-B4! N-N6 17 P×P! N×R 18 Q×N P×P 19 N×P and White's initiative compensates him for the sacrificed Exchange (Gheorghiu-Uhlmann, Sofia 1967).

15 N-K3 B-R3 16 B-R3 P-Q5 17 N-B1 N-N3 18 N-N5 N-Q4 19 B-Q2 B×N 20 B×B Q-Q2 21 Q-R5 KR-B1 22 N-Q2! N-QB3 23 B-B6! Q-K1 24 N-K4 P-N3 25 Q-N5, and White has a winning position (Fischer-Miagmasuren, Sousse 1967).

This game illustrates the kind of dangers Black faces in this variation. Statistics show that White often wins, so a better defensive system is needed. Continuing from *Diagram 11:*

5	**P-Q3**	**B-Q3!**
6	**QN-Q2**	**KN-K2**
7	**P-K4**	**O-O**

12

Black's development is more harmonious than in the preceding variation. White's P-K5 advance wil not be easy, but even if he succeeds in playing it a later . . . P-B3 should be taken into consideration.

Black now demonstrates how to exploit hesitant play and lack of planning by White.

8	**R-K1**	**B-B2**
9	**P-B3**	. . . . . .

9 P-K5 is not good because of 9 . . . N-N3.

9	. . . . . .	**P-QR4!**
10	**P-QR4**	**P-QN3**
11	**P×P**	. . . . . .

White cannot seem to find a strategy, which eases Black's burden.

11 . . . P×P 12 P-Q4 B-N5 13 P×P P×P 14 N-N3 B-Q3 15 P-R3 B-B4 16 B-K3 Q-N3 17 R-R2 QR-Q1 18 B-KB1 P-R3 19 B-B1 B-K3 20 QN-Q2 P-B5! 21 N-N1 B-B4, and Black's advantage is decisive.

The proper plan for White, again

shown by Fischer (see *Diagram 12*):

8	**N-R4!**	**P-QN3**
9	**P-KB4**	**P×P**
10	**P×P**	**B-R3**
11	**R-K1**	**P-B5**
12	**P-B3**	**N-R4?!**
13	**P-K5**	**B-B4ch**
14	**K-R1**	**N-Q4**
15	**N-K4**	**B-N2**
16	**Q-R5**	**N-K2**
17	**P-KN4!**	**B×N**
18	**B×B**	**P-N3**
19	**Q-R6**	**N-Q4**
20	**P-B5**	......

White has a decisive attack (Fischer-Ivkov, Santa Monica 1966).

Of course, we cannot draw a final conclusion from one game; in this case Black's defense can be improved (for example, 11 ... R-B1 or 12 ... R-B1). The fact remains, however, that in this variation the Fischer type of attack gives Black major problems.

Against the King's Indian Attack with the moves 1 N-KB3 P-Q4, Black often develops his QB to KB4 or KN5. This is not dangerous for White, however, for he will soon be able to play P-K4 after which Black's QB will not be well placed. On P-K4, if Black exchanges pawns White should not consider a later P-K5, as that would only reopen a diagonal for Black's Bishop. In most cases White gains the advantage because Black's Bishop will be locked out of play.

King's Indian Defense

This defense, the reverse of the King's Indian Attack, is perhaps the most economical choice against closed openings. Its great advantage for Black is that whether White opens with 1 P-Q4, 1 P-QB4, or 1 N-KB3, Black may achieve the King's Indian formation after 1 ... N-KB3, 2 ... P-KN3, 3 ... B-N2, and 4 ... O-O, whereas White, if he desires, can vary his opening moves to steer clear of the other modern defenses, such as the Gruenfeld, the Modern Benoni and the Nimzo-Indian. Many players prefer 1 P-QB4 or 1 N-KB3 with White because 1 P-Q4 can be answered in so many ways. We should include the King's Indian Defense in our repertoire of openings.

Our problem is simplified if we employ the King's Indian only against 1 N-KB3, using other preferred defenses against 1 P-Q4 or 1 P-QB4. In this way it is possible to avoid many dangerous variations in the King's Indian, such as the Saemisch Variation and the Four Pawns Attack.

1	**N-KB3**	**N-KB3**
2	**P-KN3**	......

After 2 P-B4 Black can play 2 ... P-B4 with transposition to the Symmetrical Variation of the English Opening (discussed later).

2	......	**P-KN3**

3	**B-N2**	**B-N2**
4	**O-O**	**O-O**
5	**P-Q4**	**P-Q3**
6	**P-B4**	......

Obviously, we can get this position in various ways. Now Black can choose among several methods of defense, but almost all of them are difficult and require extensive theoretical knowledge. To avoid complications as Black, I used to play exclusively a continuation seldom discussed in books on chess theory:

6	......	**P-B3**
7	**N-B3**	**B-N5**

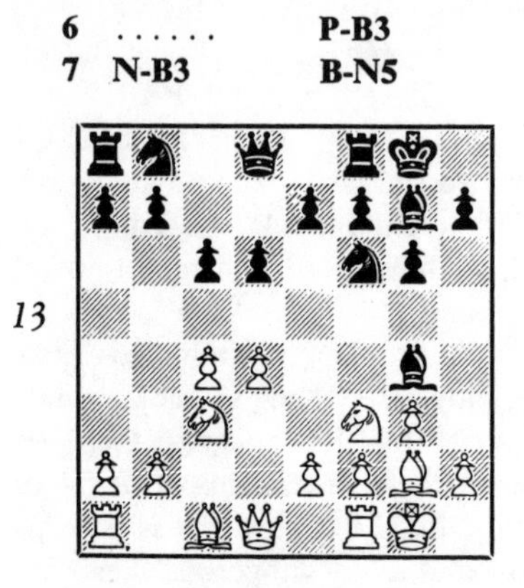

13

Naturally, this is not advanced as an ideal system, but even today it has great advantages: it has no theory of its own, and only very experienced players are able to find the best lines of play. Although one unpleasant loss dampened my enthusiasm for this variation, actually the cause of my defeat was not the opening. Certain opening variations are buried not for objective but for psychological reasons.

My opponents continued play in a number of ways; many could not find the correct 8th move. For example:

8 Q-B2 ......

8 . . . QN-Q2 9 P-KR3 B×N 10 B×B P-K4 11 R-Q1? P×P 12 R×P N-Q4! 13 R-Q1 N×N 14 P×N N-K4 15 B-B4 Q-K2, and Black has the edge (Tokaji-Nagy vs. Portisch, Budapest 1960).

This game demonstrates Black's central theme: after exchanging his Bishop for White's King Knight, White's control of his Q4 is weakened. Another method of exploiting White's weakened Q4 tactically occurred in a training game (continue from *Diagram 13*):

8 B-K3 ......

8 . . . QN-Q2 9 N-K1 N-N3! 10 P-KR3 (10 P-N3 P-K4 is good for Black because after 11 P-Q5 P×P 12 B×N P×B! White cannot recapture on Q5 with a piece because Black exchanges and then plays . . . P-K5) **10 . . . N×P!? 11 P×B N×B 12 P×N N×P** (Black has two pawns for his sacrificed piece, as well as a considerably weakened White Kingside) **13 Q-Q2?** (A mistake; if 13 Q-Q3 P-K4 14 N-B2 Q-N4 15 B-R3 P-KB4 16 B×N Q×B 17 K-N2 P-K5! followed by 18 . . . P-Q4, it is hard to evaluate the chances) **13 . . . P-K4 14 N-Q1 Q-N4 15 P-Q5** (Further weakening the dark squares, but White's position is difficult anyway) **15 ... Q-R4 16 N-KB3 P-K5 17 N-R4 B-K4 18 R-B4 P-KB4! 19 P×P P×P 20 Q-B2 P-N4 21 Q×BP P×N!,** and Black won (Koberl-Portisch, 1960).

It is not advisable for White to try to exploit Black's apparently weak QN2 (continue from *Diagram 13*):

8 Q-N3 ......

8 ... Q-N3 9 R-Q1 QN-Q2 10 P-KR3 B×N 11 P×B? P-K3! 12 P-Q5 (To prevent 12 ... P-Q4) **12 ... KP×P 13 P×P P-B4 14 B-B4 KR-Q1 15 R-K1 P-QR3 16 Q×Q? N×Q 17 R-K7 KN×P 18 R×NP B×N 19 P×B N×B,** and Black has a won endgame (Reilly-Portisch, Madrid 1960).

If White wants to recapture on KB3 with the pawn, it is more accurate to do it this way (continue from *Diagram 13*):

8 P-KR3 ......

8 ... B×N 9 P×B!? P-Q4 10 P-B5 P-K4!? (10 ... QN-Q2 11 P-B4 P-K3, maintaining the closed position, is also good) **11 P×P KN-Q2 12 P-B4 N×BP 13 R-K1 QN-R3 14 P-R3 P-Q5 15 N-K4 N×N 16 B×N Q-Q2 17 P-QN4 QR-Q1 18 P-KR4 P-QB4 19 B-Q3 P-QN4 20 P×P N×P 21 P-R5 R-B1,** leading to sharp play (Busek-Portisch, Budapest 1960).

Black is not hurt if White attempts to keep control of his Q4 as follows (continue from *Diagram 13*):

8 P-KR3 **B×N**
9 B×B ......

9 ... QN-Q2 10 B-N2 P-K4 11 P-K3 N-K1 12 P-N3 P-KB4 13 P×P? P×P 14 Q-B2 P-K5 15 B-N2 N-K4 16 KR-Q1 Q-K2 17 N-K2 N-Q3, and Black gets a good game (Kanko-Portisch, World Student Team Championship, Budapest 1959).

The only weakness in Black's system may be seen in the following continuation (continue from *Diagram 13*):

8 P-K4 ......

Or, similarly, 8 P-KR3 B×N 9 B×B QN-Q2 10 P-K4.

8 ... QN-Q2 9 P-KR3 B×N 10 B×B (10 Q×B is also possible) **10 ... P-K4 11 P-Q5 P-B4**

11 ... P×P? would only open lines on the Queenside to White's advantage. Lacking a white-squared Bishop, Black cannot contemplate a Kingside attack, especially since ... P-KB4, a characteristic advance in the King's Indian, would further weaken his white squares; White could react with P-KR4-R5. Therefore, Black seeks an alternative.

12 B-N4 N-N3 13 P-N3 N-K1 14 Q-B2 (14 P-KR4, mentioned above, would be better) **14 ... P-KR4 15 B-K2 P-R5! 16 B-N4 K-R2!** (Preparing a positional exchange maneuver) **17 P-R4 P-R4 18 R-R2 Q-K2 19 N-Q1 B-R3! 20 B×B K×B 21 N-K3 K-N2 22 N-N2 P×P 23 P×P N-B3,** and Black has a good game (Aaron-Portisch, Stockholm 1962). Later in that game I overlooked a combination and for that reason the whole variation was abandoned; I have not played it since.

English Opening

Among closed openings, the English Opening is even more popular than the King's Indian Attack. Though Black has a large choice of defenses against 1 P-QB4, many variations merely transpose to the Queen's Gambit or the King's Indian Defense. Only 1 P-QB4 P-K4 and 1 P-QB4 P-QB4 have independent variations.

The disadvantage of 1 P-QB4 P-K4 for Black is that White can play the Sicilian Defense with colors reversed and thus a tempo ahead! In view of this extra tempo, Black's early . . . P-Q4, as in analogous systems of the Sicilian Defense, cannot be recommended; moreover, White can even play positions from the Closed Sicilian with advantage.

The Symmetrical Variation, one of the most logical defenses against the English Opening, is far more popular:

1	**P-QB4**	**P-QB4**
2	**N-QB3**	**N-QB3**
3	**P-KN3**	**P-KN3**
4	**B-N2**	**B-N2**

Black can imitate White for a long time without fearing sudden tactical turns, for White's advantage is reduced to a single tempo. (In open games, however, imitation is not advisable.) It is possible to interpolate N-KB3 for both sides, but it is better for White to hold back this move; the purpose of N-KB3 is to prepare P-Q4, but that move is inconsistent with White's characteristic aim in this variation for a quick Queenside initiative. One possibility is 5 N-KB3 N-KB3 6 O-O O-O 7 P-Q4 P-Q3 (or 7 . . . P×P), arriving at the extremely complex Yugoslav Variation of the King's Indian Defense, which we do not deal with here.

More characteristic of the English is 5 P-QR3 followed by R-N1 and P-QN4. Black, if he wishes, can stop this maneuver only by . . . P-QR4, which weakens his own QN4 and is therefore not generally played. However, Black can neutralize White's advantage by making similar moves:

5	**P-QR3**	**P-QR3!**
6	**R-N1**	**R-N1**
7	**P-QN4**	**P×P**
8	**P×P**	**P-QN4**
9	**P×P**	**P×P**

The position is still completely symmetrical, but White's next move force Black to vary.

10	**N-B3**	. . . . . .

14

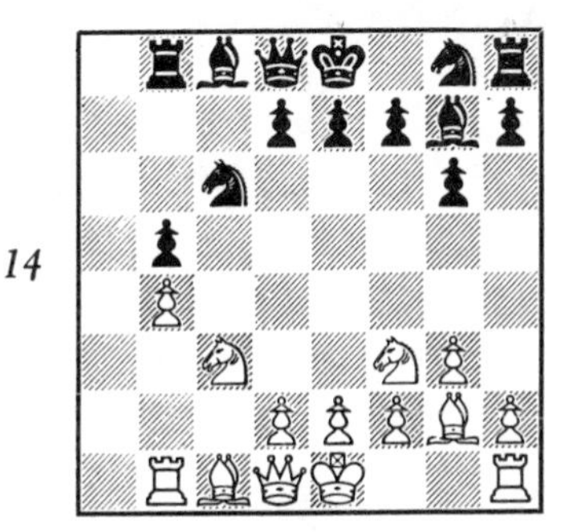

Now Black must decide how to proceed. Continuing the symmetry cannot be carried too far:

10	**......**	**N-B3**
11	**O-O**	**O-O**
12	**P-Q4!**	**N-K1**

The symmetrical 12 ... P-Q4 would emphasize White's tempo-advantage: 13 B-B4 R-N3 14 Q-N3 P-K3 (if 14 ... B-B4 15 R-R1!) 15 KR-B1 B-N2 16 P-K3 P-R3 17 B-K5! K-R2 18 B-B1 N×B 19 N×N with positional advantage for White because of Black's weakness at QB4 (Larsen-Ivkov, Palma de Majorca 1967).

13 B-B4 P-Q3 14 Q-Q2 B-B4 15 P-K4 B-N5 16 P-Q5 B×KN 17 B×B N-K4 18 B-N2 Q-N3 19 Q-K2 N-B5 20 KR-B1 N-B2 21 N-Q1! B-Q5 22 N-K3 B×N 23 B×B N×B 24 R-B6 Q-R2 25 Q×N Q×Q 26 P×Q N-K1 27 R-R1, and White has the advantage in the endgame (Portisch-Barczay, Hungarian Championship 1958).

An alternative is (continue from *Diagram 14*):

10	**......**	**N-R3**
11	**P-K4**	**......**

A strong move, excluding the Black Knight from KB4.

11	**......**	**P-K3**

If 11 ... P-B4 12 P-Q4! P×P 13 N×KP N-B4 14 P-Q5 N/3-Q5 15 N×N N×N 16 P-Q6! N-B4 17 B-N5 B-B3 18 P-N4!, and White has a decisive advantage (Timman-Kostro, Wijk aan Zee 1971).

12 P-Q4 P-Q3 13 B-N5 P-B3 14 B×N! B×B 15 P-Q5 N-K4 16 N-Q4 P×P 17 N/4×P O-O 18 Q×Pch N-B2 19 O-O, and Black's position does not smell of roses (Portisch-Pogats, Budapest 1958).

Perhaps Black's best move is (continue from *Diagram 14*):

10	**......**	**P-K4!**
11	**P-Q4!?**	**......**

White gains nothing by the commonplace 11 P-K4 KN-K2 12 O-O O-O 13 R-K1 P-Q3 14 P-R3 P-R3 15 P-Q3 B-K3 (Reshevsky-Petrosian, Los Angeles 1963). But can the weakness of Black's Q3 be exploited by the sacrifice of White's QP?

11	**......**	**N×QP**
12	**N×N**	**P×N**
13	**N-K4**	**P-Q3**
14	**B-N2**	**Q-N3**
15	**P-K3**	**B-N2**

16	**B×P**	**B×B**
17	**Q×B**	**Q×Q**
18	**P×Q**	**K-Q2**
19	**O-O**	**P-B4**

Black has equalized in this game (Gheorghiu-Jansa, 1970), but the variation needs more research.

Queen's Gambit Declined

Among the closed systems, the classical Queen's Gambit Declined poses some of the gravest problems for Black. White must be prepared to play against it, however, for if Black insists White will be unable to avoid it, even by 1 P-QB4. Here the most common sequence is 1 P-QB4 P-K3 2 N-QB3 (if 2 N-KB3, hoping for the Catalan System with 2 . . . P-Q4 3 P-KN3, Black can play the Queen's Indian with 2 . . . N-KB3 and 3 . . . P-QN3, one of the safest ways to equalize in the closed openings) 2 . . . P-Q4 3 P-Q4.

White faces a large number of possible variations in the Queen's Gambit Declined; for this reason, even such great players as Botvinnik and Reshevsky almost invariably simplified this problem by exchanging on Q5 on the third or fourth move, thereby determining the character of the game at once. In the Exchange Variation, Black has few options for strategical planning and White will determine the type and location of the play.

1	**P-Q4**	**P-Q4**
2	**P-QB4**	**P-K3**
3	**N-QB3**	**N-KB3**
4	**P×P**	**P×P**
5	**B-N5**	**P-B3**
6	**P-K3**	**B-K2**
7	**Q-B2**	**O-O**
8	**B-Q3**	**QN-Q2**
9	**N-B3**	**R-K1**
10	**O-O**	**N-B1**
11	**QR-N1**	**. . . . . .**

15

This is the characteristic position of the Exchange Variation. White's 11th move initiates a plan that should be familiar to everyone who plays this variation: he threatens to attack the Black pawn chain with P-QN4-N5. Because two pawns attack three, this is called a minority attack. Black's Kingside counterplay should be based on occupation of his K5. In my youth I fancied the minority attack as an almost automatic win, and it was my favorite weapon. Experience has since taught me that Black's counterplay is not to be underestimated.

Black can defend in two ways: he can permit White's P-QN4, or he can prevent it temporarily by . . . P-QR4. There is no great difference, for White can carry out his plan in either case.

11 ...... N-K5
12 B×B ......

12 B-KB4! is also worthy of consideration.

12 ...... Q×B
13 P-QN4 P-QR3
14 P-QR4 B-Q2?

Far stronger is 14 ... N-N3!, transposing into the next game.

15 N-K5 P-B3? 16 N×B N/1×N 17 P-N5 RP×P 18 P×P P-KB4 19 P×P P×P 20 N-K2 P-B4? 21 N-B4 Q-Q3 22 N×P! and White won (Portisch-Pacsay, Budapest 1953).

Black has a better move, preventing White's B-KB4 (continue from *Diagram 15*):

11 ...... N-N3!
12 P-QN4 ......

White should play 12 B/5×N!

12 ...... P-QR3
13 P-QR4 ......

13 KR-K1 is not very good, as demonstrated by Zhukhovitsky-Zhidkov, Soviet Spartakiad 1967: 13 ... N-K5 14 B×B Q×B 15 B×N P×B 16 N-Q2 P-KB4 17 P-B3 P×P 18 N×P B-K3 19 P-QR4 QR-B1, with a good game for Black.

13 ...... N-K5
14 B×B Q×B
15 KR-B1? ......

Unnecessarily cautious. 15 P-N5! RP×P 16 P×P B-N5 17 B×N! is similar to the next game.

15 ... B-N5 16 N-K1 N-R5! 17 B×N P×B 18 N-K2 QR-Q1 19 N-N3 R-Q4! 20 Q-R2 B-K3 21 Q-K2 R-KN4! 22 R-B5 B-Q4. Black obtained a dangerous attack with a later ... P-KR4 (Portisch-Barczay, Gyor 1954).

Again (continue from *Diagram 15*):

11 ...... P-QR4
12 P-QR3 N-K5
13 B×B Q×B
14 P-QN4 P×P
15 P×P N-N3
16 P-N5 B-N5
17 B×N ......

17 N-Q2? is an instructive error: 17 ... N×N/7 18 Q×N N-R5! Against the threat of either 19 ... B-B6 or 19 ... B-R6, White could find nothing better than 19 P-B3 Q×Pch 20 Q×Q R×Q 21 P×B R×B, and Black won a pawn (Taimanov-Nezhmedtinov, 21st Soviet Championship 1954).

17 ...... P×B
18 N-Q2 B-B4

18 ... P-KB4!? may be better.

19 P×P P×P
20 N-K2 ......

White has a positional advantage (Averbakh-Konstantinopolsky, Moscow 1956).

White's minority attack can be accelerated if, instead of playing 11 QR-N1, he exchanges his QB for the Black Knight at once; the exchange also relieves the pressure against White's K4.

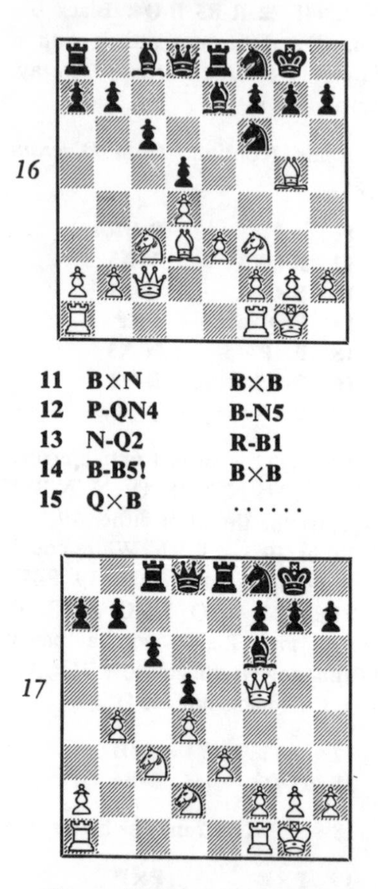

16

11	**B×N**	**B×B**
12	**P-QN4**	**B-N5**
13	**N-Q2**	**R-B1**
14	**B-B5!**	**B×B**
15	**Q×B**	......

17

The exchange of Black's Knight on KB3 is a recurrent theme in this variation. White's two Knights can be most helpful in a Queenside attack.

15 ...... N-K3

16 QR-N1 P-KN3 17 Q-Q3 B-N2 18 N-R4 P-N3 19 KR-Q1 Q-Q2 20 N-QB3 KR-Q1 21 N-B3 P-KB4 22 N-K2 Q-Q3 23 P-N3 P-KR3 24 P-KR4 R-B2 25 N-B4! N-B1 26 P-N5 Q-K2 27 P×P R×P 28 KR-QB1, with advantage for White (Bagirov-Klovan, 31st Soviet Championship 1963/64). This game shows how by correct play White weakens Black's Q4.

In Reshevsky-Miagmasuren (Sousse 1967), White achieved his aim again (continue from *Diagram 17*):

15 ...... P-KN3

16 Q-Q3 Q-Q3 17 KR-N1 B-N2 18 P-QR4 N-Q2 19 R-R2 R-K3 20 R-B2 QR-K1 21 N-N3! N-B3 22 P-R3 P-N3 23 N-B1 B-R3 24 N/1-K2 N-R4 25 P-N5!

It is obvious in the last two games that Black cannot accomplish much by waiting tactics: he must look for counterplay. This can be developed on the Kingside by placing the King Bishop on Black's QN1-KR7 diagonal (continue from *Diagram 17*):

15 ...... B-K2

16 QR-N1 P-QR3 17 P-QR4 B-Q3 18 R-N3 R-K3 19 KR-N1 R-B3 20 Q-Q3 R-R3 21 P-B4 P-KN4! (Euwe-Guimard, New York 1951). White's play could be improved, of course; his Rook maneuvers seem too slow.

Black's problem with developing

his QB in the Queen's Gambit Declined is a theme that recurs in the Exchange Variation. For this reason, Black has often played the following variation, which aims to exchange that troublesome piece:

1	**P-Q4**	**P-Q4**
2	**P-QB4**	**P-K3**
3	**N-QB3**	**B-K2**

It is not dangerous for Black to exchange his Queen Bishop, especially if White plays routinely, for example: 4 N-B3 N-KB3 5 P×P P×P 6 Q-B2 P-B3 7 B-N5 P-KN3! 8 P-K3 B-KB4 9 B-Q3 B×B. In this case the Exchange Variation is harmless to Black.

Botvinnik's system, hindering the development of Black's QB, may be the best: on 3 . . . B-K2 the former World Champion would immediately exchange on Q5. Often he played:

4	**P×P**	**P×P**
5	**B-B4**	**P-QB3**
6	**P-K3**	**B-KB4**
7	**P-KN4!?**	**B-K3**

If 7 . . . B-N3 there follows the unpleasant 8 P-KR4! B×P 9 Q-N3 P-N3 10 N-B3 and 11 N-K5.

8	**P-KR3**	. . . . . .

An interesting feature of this variation is White's 7 P-KN4, the object of which is not to attack but to gain positional advantages. White will not castle Queenside, but will "castle" by K-B1-N2.

Black's most logical continuation is:

8	. . . . . .	**N-KB3**

If 8 . . . B-Q3 9 KN-K2! is strong.

9	**N-B3**	**O-O**
10	**B-Q3**	**P-B4**
11	**K-B1!**	**N-B3**
12	**K-N2**	**P×P**
13	**KN×P**	**N×N**

White will control Q4 advantageously after 13 . . . B-Q3 14 B×B Q×B 15 N/3-K2 (Geller-Spassky, Moscow 1967).

14	**P×N**	. . . . . .

Although White won this game (the 14th game of the Botvinnik-Petrosian World Championship Match, 1963), we can regard the position as about even. Of course, the variation needs further research: White may consider other ways to develop, for example 10 B-N2! (instead of 10 B-Q3), making it complicated for Black to seek counterplay with . . . P-QB4 because of the resulting weakness of his QP.

Nimzo-Indian Defense

This is one of the most popular defenses to 1 P-Q4. The Nimzo-Indian is very logical, but, like the Sicilian and the Ruy Lopez, it is burdened by too many variations and too much analysis.

1	**P-Q4**	**N-KB3**
2	**P-QB4**	**P-K3**
3	**N-QB3**	**B-N5**
4	**P-K3**	......

This move of Rubinstein's causes Black the most problems. He must immediately decide which road to take and, if he is unwilling to play a variation that has been analyzed twenty moves deep, his choices are limited. When I was a candidate-master I developed a sequence of moves (under the influence of Nimzovich) which is now a major variation. Fischer used it with good results against Spassky in the 1972 World Championship Match.

Let us first look at a game that had a great effect on me during my learning years, and on which I based my variation:

18

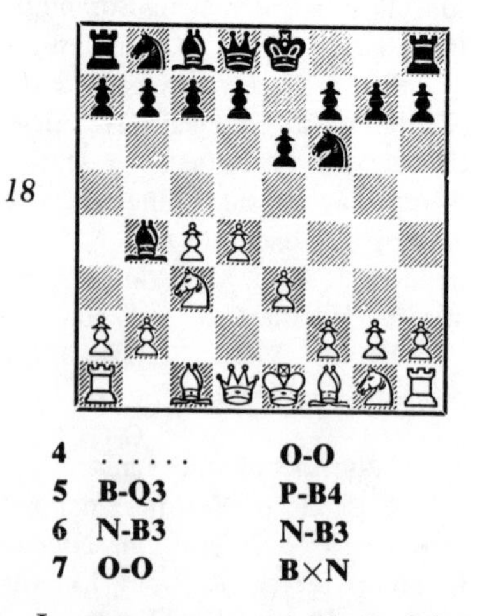

4	......	**O-O**
5	**B-Q3**	**P-B4**
6	**N-B3**	**N-B3**
7	**O-O**	**B×N**

In many games as Black, Nimzovich captured on White's QB3 without being forced to, thus exemplifying a main strategy in the Nimzo-Indian: doubling White's pawns on the QB file and making them weak, particularly the one on QB4.

8	**P×B**	**P-Q3**
9	**N-Q2**	**P-QN3**
10	**N-N3**	**P-K4**
11	**P-B4?**	......

White's aimless development only helps Black construct a blockade—another characteristic of this defense—which in time will relegate the White Bishops to frustrated inaction.

11 . . . P-K5 12 B-K2 Q-Q2! (A typically deep Nimzovich move) **13 P-KR3 N-K2 14 Q-K1 P-KR4! 15 B-Q2 Q-B4! 16 K-R2 Q-R2! 17 P-QR4 N-B4 18 P-N3 P-R4.** Later, Black prepared the opening of King-side files with . . . P-KN4 and won with a beautiful attack (Johner-Nimzovich, Dresden 1926). Black's sequence of moves was not entirely correct, however. White could have played 7 P-Q5! instead of the routine 7 O-O, because 7 . . . P×P 8 P×P N×P 9 B×Pch K×B 10 Q×N is advantageous for him.

We can draw two important conclusions from this game: Black castled too early, and his Knight on QB3 should retreat to K2 rather than advance to QR4 as is customary in many variations in which Black attacks the White QBP. The correct sequence is (continue from *Diagram 18*):

4	......	**P-B4**
5	**B-Q3**	**N-B3**
6	**N-B3**	**B×Nch**
7	**P×B**	**P-Q3**

19

White has two possible plans: he can play P-Q5, or he can try to control Q4 as in the preceding game, but in better circumstances.

8	**O-O**	**P-K4**
9	**P-Q5**	**N-K2!**

And not 9 ... N-QR4.

10	**N-Q2**	**B-B4!?**
11	**B×B?**	......

11 P-K4 was necessary.

11 ... N×B 12 P-K4 N-K2 13 P-B4 P×P 14 R×P N-N3 15 R-B5 O-O, and Black has the advantage (Papai-Portisch, Veszprem 1954).

Now suppose White plays (continue from *Diagram 19*):

8	**P-K4**	**P-K4**
9	**P-Q5**	**N-K2**

White has several continuations. One is:

10	**O-O**	**P-KR3!**

After 10 ... O-O 11 N-R4! Black still must play 11 ... P-KR3, as in a similar position from the 5th Spassky-Fischer World Championship Match game, but then White should not hurry to play P-B4 (as Spassky did). He is better off with 12 P-N3, to which Black can hardly reply ... P-KN4 because of his early castling. Trying 11 ... N-K1 (instead of 11 ... P-KR3) with the threat of ... P-B4 is not very good: White stands better after 12 N-B5! N×N 13 P×N Q-B3 14 Q-B3 (Haggquist-Portisch, World Student Team Championship, Reykjavik 1972).

11	**N-K1**	**P-KN4!?**

20

After the passive 11 ... Q-B2 12 N-B2 B-Q2 13 N-K3 O-O-O 14 P-B3 P-KN4 15 R-N1 K-N1 16 B-B2 N-R4 17 B-R4! B-B1 18 R-B2 N-N2 19 KR-N2 K-R1 20 Q-N3 QR-B1 21 B-B6! N×B 22 P×N Q×P 23 N-Q5 N-K3 24 Q-R3 K-N1 25 R-N5, White obtained a decisive attack in Shashin-Novikov, Leningrad 1972.

I first used this plan playing Black against Bisguier in the 1961 tournament at Bled. Clearly, Black should prepare to castle on the Queenside. Unaccountably, I played differently.

12	**P-B3**	**N-R4(?)**

13 P-N3 N-N2 14 N-N2 B-R6 15 R-N1 Q-Q2 16 R-B2 B×N 17 R×B N-N3 18 Q-N3 QR-N1 19 Q-N5 K-K2 20 KR-N2 Q-B1 21 Q-R4, and I got into a very difficult position.

Correct play for Black is (continue from *Diagram 20*):

12	**N-B2**	**B-N5!?**
13	**P-B3**	**B-Q2**
14	**N-K3**	**Q-B2**

Of course, it is not necessary to play . . . B-N5 to force White to play P-B3—he will play it anyway. Better is an early . . . N-N3, since KB4 need not be protected.

In Bokor-Szabo (Budapest 1972), White continued weakly: 15 N-B5? N×N 16 P×N O-O-O 17 B-Q2 QR-N1 18 Q-B2 P-KR4! 19 QR-K1 P-R5! and White has fallen behind. Necessary was 15 R-N1 O-O-O 16 B-B2!, as in Shashin-Novikov above. The variation needs further analysis.

Let us return to *Diagram 19*:

8	**P-K4**	**P-K4**
9	**P-Q5**	**N-K2**

Now, instead of 10 O-O we will consider:

10	**N-R4!?**	**P-KR3**

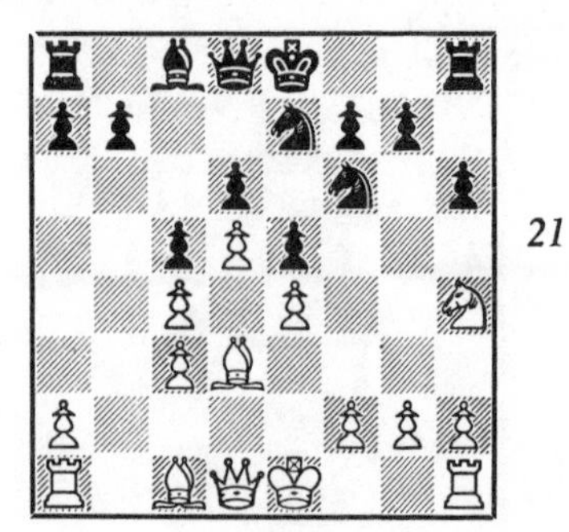

21

10 . . . N-N3 is weak: after 11 N-B5! B×N 12 P×B N-K2 13 B-N5 Q-R4 14 Q-Q2, White's position is better (Ravn-Portisch, Reykjavik 1957).

Here White may choose from several plans:

11	**P-N3**	**P-KN4**
12	**N-N2**	**Q-R4**
13	**Q-N3?!**	. . . . . .

Better is 13 B-Q2 B-N5! (otherwise 14 N-K3 followed by Q-B3 is unpleasant) 14 P-B3 B-Q2.

13 . . . B-R6 14 O-O O-O-O 15 R-N1 Q-B2 16 P-B3 K-N1 17 R-B2 KR-N1 18 N-K3 B-B1, with chances for both sides (Najdorf-Huebner, Wijk aan Zee 1971).

Continuing from *Diagram 21*:

11	**P-B3**	**Q-R4**
12	**Q-B2**	**P-KN4**
13	**N-B5**	**N×N!**

In many games the Bishop makes this capture, but the Knight move is more logical.

14 P×N B-Q2 15 P-KR4 P-N5 16 P×P? N×NP 17 B-K2 KR-N1 18 B×N? R×B 19 B×P B×P! 20 Q×B Q×Pch 21 K-B2 Q-N7ch 22 K-K3 R×NP, White resigned (Donner-Portisch, Skopje Olympiad 1972).

Again from *Diagram 21*:

11	**P-B4!?**	**N-N3!**
12	**N×N**	**P×N**
13	**O-O**	......

In the 5th game of the 1972 World Championship Match, Spassky committed a serious positional error against Fischer with 13 P×P?, and in the resulting closed position his Bishops became ineffective.

13 . . . O-O 14 P-B5 P×P 15 P×P P-K5 16 B-K2 Q-K2 17 B-K3 B-Q2 18 Q-K1 N-R2 19 P-N4 N-N4 20 Q-N3, with complicated play (Gligoric-Mecking, San Antonio 1972).

Because of his possession of the pair of Bishops, White should keep the tension in the center, avoiding P-Q5. He can do this in several ways. Again returning to *Diagram 19*:

8	**O-O**	**P-K4**
9	**N-Q2**	**O-O**

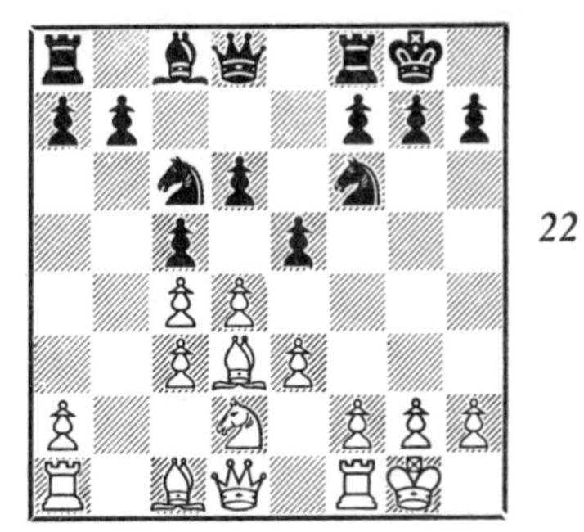

22

Accepting the pawn sacrifice is dangerous because the White Bishops will be too powerful on the open diagonals.

10	**R-K1**	**R-K1**

11 P-B3 KP×P 12 QP×P P×P 13 P-K4 N-Q2 14 N-N3 P-QR4 15 P-QR4 N-B4, and Black has good play (Florian-Portisch, Gyor 1954).

Continuing from *Diagram 22*:

10	**N-N3**	**P-K5**

11 B-K2 Q-K2 12 P-QR4 B-B4 13 K-R1 P-KN4!? 14 P-B4 P-N5 15 P-Q5 N-Q1 16 B-Q2 K-R1 17 B-K1 R-KN1 18 B-R4 R-N3 19 P-R5 Q-Q2 20 N-Q2 N-N1 21 K-N1 P-B3 22 Q-B2 R-R3 23 B-N3 Q-K1, with chances for both sides (Forintos-Portisch, Budapest 1955).

Again from *Diagram 22*:

10	**N-N3**	**P-QN3**

11 B-Q2 N-K2? (Prematurely giving up control of the center) **12 P-K4 N-N3 13 P-B4! P×BP 14 B×P N×B 15 R×N,** and White has the advantage (Portisch-Huguet, Las Palmas 1972).

Again after 7 . . . P-Q3 (see *Diagram 19*), an interesting development occurred in Taimanov-Portisch, Budapest 1959:

8	**O-O**	**P-K4**
9	**N-N5**	**O-O**
10	**P-B4!?**	. . . . . .

An open KB file would help White, so Black avoids opening it. **10 . . . KP×QP 11 BP×P P-KR3 12 N-B3 R-K1 13 P-Q5 N-QN5 14 B-N1 P-QN4!? 15 P-QR3 N-R3 16 R-K1 P×P 17 P-K4 N-B2 18 P-QR4 R-N1,** and Black has a fair game.

Finally, White can try to keep the center fluid this way (continue from *Diagram 19*):

8	**P-K4**	**P-K4**
9	**P-KR3**	. . . . . .

But this will not give him any advantage. Moiseev-Portisch (Amsterdam 1967) continued:

9 . . . P-KR3 10 O-O O-O 11 Q-K2 N-Q2 12 B-K3 R-K1 13 P-Q5 (Now White has nothing better than closing the center, just what Black wants him to do) **13 . . . N-K2 14 P-N3 P-B4! 15 P×P N-KB3 16 N-R4 P-K5 17 B-B2 N×BP 18 N×N B×N,** and Black stands better.

In spite of these examples, we cannot draw a final conclusion about this variation, for White can try other moves. But by now we know how Black is to find the proper answer, whatever White plays. One virtue of the early . . . B×N system, compared with other variations, is that relatively little importance can be attached to which specific sequence of moves is chosen. We do not have to play according to the book move by move—we need only keep the underlying strategic ideas in mind.

If White does not wish to enter the variations explained above, he can avoid them after 1 P-Q4 N-KB3 2 P-QB3 P-K3 by 3 P-KN3 or 3 N-KB3. The former generally leads into the Catalan Opening, and the latter (after 3 . . . P-QN3) to the Queen's Indian Defense, which is popular and easy to learn but has the disadvantage that Black gets an easy game—most Queen's Indians end in draws. For this reason, one should choose a variation of the Nimzo-Indian which, though less fashionable, offers Black fewer choices.

The Leningrad System against the Nimzo-Indian Defense was for a long time my favorite:

1	**P-Q4**	**N-KB3**
2	**P-QB4**	**P-K3**
3	**N-QB3**	**B-N5**
4	**B-N5**	. . . . . .

The following moves are fairly obvious:

4	. . . . . .	**P-KR3**
5	**B-R4**	**P-B4**

6 P-Q5 ......

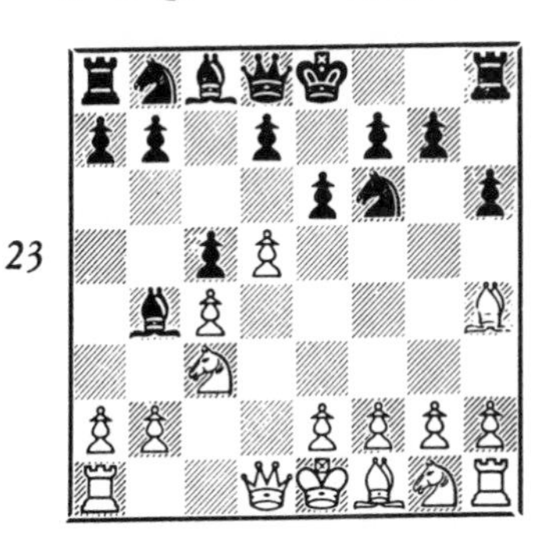

23

There are three main lines here: an early ... P-K4; exchanging pawns with ... P×P; and the ... P-QN4 gambit. First:

6 ...... B×Nch
7 P×B P-K4
8 P-K3 ......

I have never played 8 P-Q6!? If Black fears this continuation, he should play 6 ... P-Q3 and only after 7 P-K3 should he play 7 ... B×Nch 8 P×B P-K4.

8 ...... P-Q3
9 Q-B2 ......

9 N-B3 Q-K2 10 N-Q2 creates no problems for Black: 10 ... P-KN4 11 B-N3 B-B4! 12 P-KR4 R-N1 13 P×P P×P 14 Q-N3 N-K5 gave Black comfortable play in Portisch-O'Kelly, Madrid 1960.

Donner's plan, against which I had to defend, also deserves attention: 9 P-B3 Q-K2 10 P-K4 QN-Q2 11 N-K2 N-B1 12 B-B2 N-N3 (12 ... P-KN4 followed by ... N-N3 is more effective) 13 N-N3 N-B5? 14 B-K3 N-R2 15 P-KR4! N-B1 16 Q-Q2 N/1-N3 17 P-R5 Q-N4 18 K-B2 N-K2 19 N-K2 P-B4 20 P-N3 P×P 21 P×N Q-B3 22 P/3×P with decisive advantage for White; Black got little in exchange for his piece (Donner-Portisch, Madrid 1960).

The two above examples show some of the advantages of this variation for White. He can play it without studying many sub-variations, just keeping in mind that, fundamentally, the struggle is over control of White's K4.

9 ...... QN-Q2
10 B-Q3 Q-K2
11 P-B3 ......

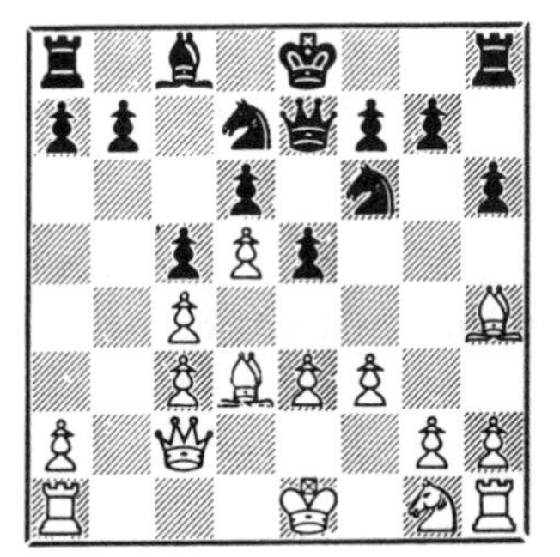

24

A tough positional fight in the middlegame developed in Keres-O'Kelly, Budapest 1952, after:

11 ...... P-KN4

12 B-N3 N-R4 13 N-K2 QN-B3 14 QR-N1 N-N2 15 B-B2 P-KR4 16 P-KR4 P-N5 17 P-K4.

After 11 ... P-KN4 I have experimented with 12 B-B2, trying to accelerate the N-K2-N3 maneuver. The disadvantage of that move is that after Black sacrifices with . . . P-K5!, his control of his K4 gives him dangerous counterplay. A successful game for White was Portisch-Domotor, Zalaegerszeg 1954 (continue from *Diagram 24*):

11	. . . . . .	**P-KN4**
12	**B-B2**	**N-R4**

13 N-K2 QN-B3 14 P-N4! N-N2 15 P-KR4 KR-N1 16 P×P P×P 17 N-N3 K-Q1 18 O-O-O K-B2 19 R-R6 B-Q2 20 QR-R1 QR-K1 21 N-K4 N×N 22 B×N Q-Q1 23 B-N3 QR-B1 24 B-R7! R-R1 25 R×P!! P-B3 (If 25 . . . K×R 26 B×Pch K×B 27 R-R6 followed by Q-K4 mate or Q-R2 mate) **26 P-B4 K×R 27 P×Pch P×P** (The reader can convince himself that there is no way to resist White's attack) **28 B×Pch K-K2 29 P-Q6ch K-K3 30 R-R6ch,** and White won easily.

Black's second choice after 6 P-Q5 is (continue from *Diagram 23*):

6	. . . . . .	**P×P**
7	**P×P**	**P-Q3**
8	**P-K3**	**QN-Q2**
9	**B-Q3**	. . . . . .

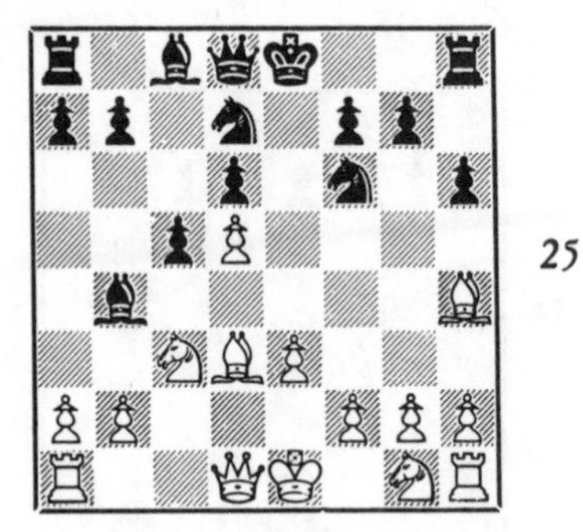

25

9 B-QN5 is also interesting, preventing Black from winning the QP: 9 . . . Q-R4?! 10 B×Nch N×B 11 N-K2 N-K4 12 O-O B-B4 13 P-K4 B-Q2 14 P-B4! N-N5 15 R-B3 P-KN4 16 B-K1 P-B5 17 P-KR3 Q-N3ch 18 K-R1 P-KR4 19 P×P O-O-O 20 P-QN3! QR-B1 21 P-KR4 N-K4 22 R-B6 Q-K6 23 B-B2 Q-Q6 24 P×P, and White won substantial material (Portisch-Barcza, Nagykanizsa 1954.

9	. . . . . .	**Q-R4**
10	**N-K2**	**N×P**
11	**O-O**	**B×N**
12	**P×B!**	. . . . . .

12 N×B N×N 13 P×N O-O! 14 B-K2 N-K4! 15 Q×P N-N3 16 B-N3 B-K3 is less accurate (Portisch-Eliskases, Munich Olympiad 1958).

After the text move, Black cannot castle because after 12 . . . O-O 13 B-B2! N×BP 14 N×N Q×N 15 R-B1, Black's QP cannot be defended and his King is threatened. White's initiative would be worth the sacrificed pawn.

Therefore, in Portisch-Donner, Madrid 1960, Black took the second pawn, too: 12 . . . N×BP 13 N×N Q×N 14 B-K2 O-O 15 Q×P P-QR3 16 KR-Q1 R-K1 17 QR-B1, but White still has satisfactory compensation.

We have observed that pawn-grabbing can be dangerous for Black (continue from *Diagram 25*):

9 . . . . . . O-O

This is better for Black than 9 . . . Q-R4.

10 N-K2 N-K4

This maneuver is aimed at breaking the pin.

11 O-O N-N3 12 B-N3 N-R4 (Unnecessary; 12 . . . P-R3 should be considered) **13 P-B4! N×B 14 N×N B×N 15 P×B P-B4 16 Q-B2 N-R5 17 QR-K1 Q-B2 18 Q-K2 B-Q2 19 Q-R5 P-B5 20 B-N1 Q-Q1 21 P-K4,** and White's position is better (Portisch-Ulvestad, Malaga 1964).

Finally, after 6 P-Q5 there is the dangerous gambit variation (continue from *Diagram 23*):

6 . . . . . . P-QN4!?

In Spassky-Tal, Tallinn 1973, White's capture of the pawn gave Black a good game: 7 QP×P BP×P 8 P×P P-Q4 9 P-K3 O-O 10 N-B3 Q-R4! 11 B×N R×B 12 Q-Q2 P-R3!

But the best counter to the pawn offer is a counter-sacrifice:

7 P-K4! . . . . . .

I have often played this. The critical position appears after:

7 . . . . . . P-N4
8 B-N3 N×KP
9 Q-B3! . . . . . .

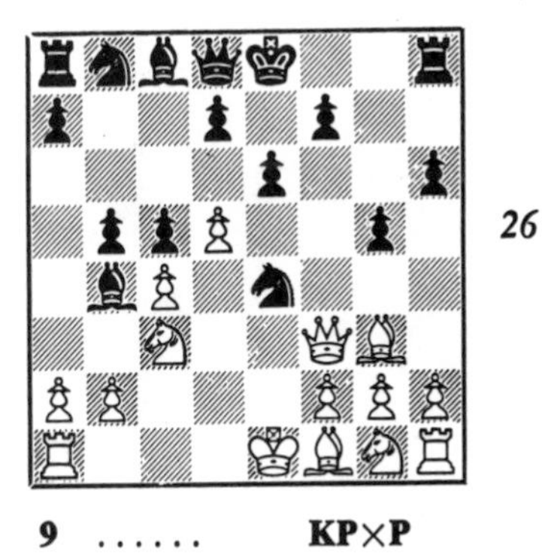

26

9 . . . . . . KP×P

10 O-O-O! B×N 11 R×P! Q-K2 12 P×B N×B 13 Q×N P-Q3, and now, instead of the passive 14 B-K2 N-Q2 15 B-B3 QR-N1 (Portisch-Barcza, Hungarian Championship 1957), a better move is 14 B-Q3!, giving White good chances (. . . Q-K8ch is harmless). Naturally, the complications have to be analyzed further.

But Black does not have to enter complications. Thus, in Portisch-Darga, Bled 1961, Black played (in the position of *Diagram 26*):

9 . . . . . . B×N

10 P×B KP×P 11 P×QP O-O

12 B-Q3 P-B4 13 B×N/4 P×B 14 Q-K3 Q-B3 15 P-KR4 P-KN5 16 N-K2 P-Q3 17 O-O, but White would have maintained the better game with 17 B-B4 and 18 Q-N3.

Possibilities for further study abound, not only in this line, but in the whole Leningrad System (4 B-N5). In fact, the purpose of my discussion has been to demonstrate ways in which the major well-analyzed variations can be avoided, if we choose to study on our own.

It is to be hoped that my discussion provides a direction; I urge the reader to do his own analysis in the development of an opening repertoire.

CHAPTER 5

Questions of Opening Theory

by Tigran Petrosian

I: Blind Faith Versus Analysis

It is certainly no secret that the best and probably the only road to mastery in chess is profound study of the games played by chess masters. The beginning of the game, the opening, is no exception.

How does one begin a game? What is opening theory and how can it be learned? Today these are not merely abstract questions for one who wants to achieve success in chess. Long ago, the chess master did not concern himself very much with the details of opening play, placing his hopes instead in his general playing skill. Today, however, books and periodicals devoted to opening play are published throughout the world, and the latest findings in opening theory are followed avidly by amateurs and professionals alike. Although these publications have become indispensable to some, it must be emphasized that the study of opening theory should not displace the study of general strategy and the perfecting of tactical ability.

In addition to discussing theory, I would like to share with you some of the fortunes and failures which have accompanied my chess career. Do not be surprised to see here not only opening variations but also complete games. This is only natural; to study opening variations without reference to the strategic concepts that develop from them in the middlegame is, in effect, to separate the head from the body. To determine that one part of a game is the opening and another the middlegame is of minor importance.

Much of the following analysis is accompanied by ordinary prose. But in some places words have been replaced by symbols which, like amulets from a witch's bag, have the power to consume the living spirit of chess. The notorious "! !" can never approximate the human emotions which accompany an "excellent move" or a "great idea."

For those who have decided to take up chess seriously or even professionally, it is important to examine systematically the games played in various competitions. This allows the student to keep his finger constantly on the pulse of chess, to maintain a working familiarity with the ideas of masters and theoreticians. These ideas must then be subjected to his own detailed analysis, which may lead to the discovery of new ideas and variations, even if they are not immediately applicable in practice.

A striking example of keeping a new ideas secret until the arrival of the right opportunity to use it is the famous game Averbakh-Estrin, 33rd Soviet Championship Semi-finals, 1964. The game begins with one of the sharpest and most interesting variations of the Queen's Gambit, a system of counterattack known as the Vienna Variation.

QUEEN'S GAMBIT DECLINED

	Averbakh	Estrin
1	P-Q4	P-Q4
2	P-QB4	P-K3
3	N-QB3	N-KB3
4	N-B3	B-N5
5	B-N5	P×P
6	P-K4	P-B4
7	B×P	......

Avoiding the complications which are the heart of the Vienna Variation: 7 P-K5 P×P 8 Q-R4ch N-B3 9 O-O-O B-Q2. Averbakh chooses a quieter route which promises him a small but solid advantage.

7	......	P×P
8	N×P	......

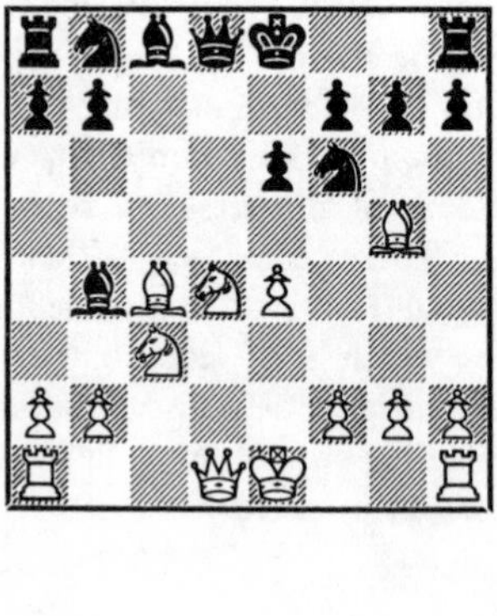

Until this game, Ragozin's move 8 ... Q-B2, which he first employed in 1946, had withstood the test of time; the basic variation was 9 Q-R4ch N-B3 10 N×N B×Nch 11 P×B B-Q2!, with a fairly good position for Black. In 1946, Averbakh, then a young master, found an interesting idea which refutes Black's play. But he kept his secret hidden for 18 (!) long years until this game, when he revealed it to Estrin.

8	......	Q-B2
9	Q-N3!	B×Nch
10	Q×B	......

Already Black is on the brink of disaster.

10	......	N×P
11	N-N5	Q-B4
12	Q×P	......

Now the check on White's KB2, which clearly was the focus of Black's hopes, is seen to be merely a pin-prick, while White's threats are irresistible.

12	......	R-B1
13	B-R6	Q×Pch
14	K-Q1	N-Q2
15	R-K1	N/5-B3
16	B×P	Q×QNP
17	R-QB1!	Resigns

It is interesting that Estrin, the player on the receiving end of this innovation, is one of the advocates of a rather widespread attitude among opening experts, who limit their theoretical work to scrupulous study and memorization of opening novelties. Young players are particularly guilty of this, and it is understandable. For the relatively inexperienced player there is a great temptation to put his faith in theory as set forth by the experts, particularly since he is often rewarded initially with the dividend of won games. Moreover, most theoretical innovations bear the names of famous chess players and are imitated solely for that reason. But such thoughtless imitation can become a bad habit; not only can it slow the progress of the student, it can actually hinder the realization of his talent.

I speak from experience: in the Georgian Championship of 1944 I made this very mistake in my game against the experienced master Mikenas. I was then 15 years old; I had an excellent memory and I loved to read chess books, drinking in all that flowed before my eyes. In Tbilisi, where I was born and grew up, and where I was formed as a chess player, my knowledge of the game had not undergone serious trials.

Here is the game with Mikenas, who in those days was probably the only master who believed in Alekhine's Defense. But this did not disturb me: I had studied the late master Lisitsin's book on the 10th USSR Championship, in which the author's notes to the opening of the game Panov-Rabinovich sounded the death knell of this defense, it seemed.

ALEKHINE'S DEFENSE

	Petrosian	**Mikenas**
1	**P-K4**	**N-KB3**
2	**P-K5**	**N-Q4**
3	**P-Q4**	**P-Q3**
4	**N-KB3**	**B-N5**
5	**P-KR3**	......

White's last move was awarded an exclamation point in the book. Oh, those exclamation points! How they erode the innocent soul of the amateur, removing all hope of allowing him to examine another player's ideas critically!

5	......	**B×N**
6	**Q×B**	**P×P**
7	**P×P**	**P-K3**
8	**P-R3**	......

"Defending the Queenside from aggression by 8 ... N-N5. Bad is 8 P-B4 N-N5 9 Q×P N-B7ch 10 K-K2 N-Q2, and White has to resign." Rabinovich answered the text move with 8 ... P-QB3. "If 8 ... N-Q2 then 9 P-B4 N/4-N3 10 Q×P N×KP 11 Q-K4," said the book, and there the analysis ended.

Armed to the teeth with this opening wisdom, as I thought, and with complete faith in the recommendation of such a strong master as Lisitsin, I confidently followed his advice.

8	......	**N-Q2**
9	**P-B4**	**N-K2**

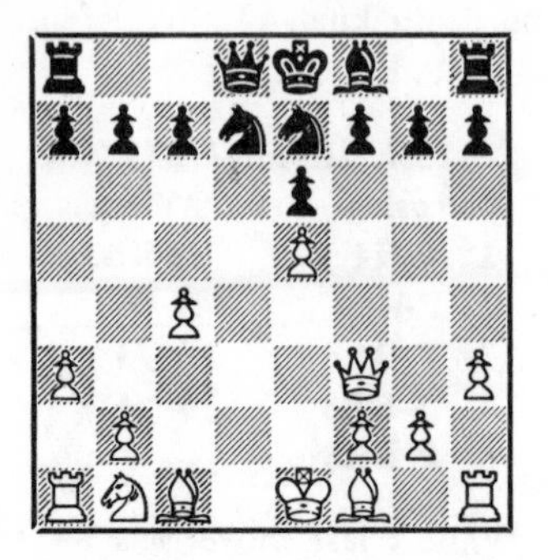

But with his last move Mikenas did not play by the book, and I realized that I was in unfamiliar terrain. Today, all this can be found in Bagirov's monograph on Alekhine's Defense, which says that in Moscow 1943 a game continued 10 Q×P P-QB3! 11 P-QN4 P-QR4 12 B-N2 N-QB4!, and Black had the advantage against the experienced candidate-master A. Khachaturov. Suffice it to add, as you may have guessed, that Mikenas played Black!

I did not know that game, of course. The effect of the surprise was so great that I was able to hold out for only another 20 moves.

Evidently I considered this entire episode merely an annoying accident, for exactly a year later, playing White against the same Mikenas, I again entered into a theoretical duel. This time the authority I followed blindly was P. Romanovsky.

GRUENFELD DEFENSE

	Petrosian	**Mikenas**
1	**P-Q4**	**N-KB3**
2	**P-QB4**	**P-KN3**
3	**N-QB3**	**P-Q4**
4	**N-B3**	**B-N2**
5	**Q-R4ch**	**B-Q2**
6	**Q-N3**	**P×P**
7	**Q×BP**	**O-O**
8	**P-K3**	......

During his analysis of master games with this then-fashionable variation, Romanovsky claimed that "8 . . . B-K3 is worth consideration and if 9 Q-R4 then perhaps the immediate . . . P-B4. However, White can play 9 Q-N4 attacking QN7." So:

8	......	**B-K3**
9	**Q-N4**	......

". . . and if 9 . . . N-B3 he can boldly take the pawn," continued Romanovsky. Having diligently examined the consequences of the capture on QN7, having convinced myself that this was actually favorable for White, and having consulted with friends, I was ready to "boldly take the pawn."

9	......	**Q-B1**

But again Mikenas outwitted me. His move prevented me from capturing his QNP and threw me into a turmoil. I will never forget how my poor Queen, after . . . N-QB3, had to roam over the entire board, ducking the blows of the Black pawns and pieces.

The last straw which finally destroyed my blind faith in the printed chess word was the game Petrosian-Averbakh, USSR Championship Semifinals, 1947. In those days the Marshall Attack in the Ruy Lopez was rarely seen in tournaments.

RUY LOPEZ

	Petrosian	**Averbakh**
1	**P-K4**	**P-K4**
2	**N-KB3**	**N-QB3**
3	**B-N5**	**P-QR3**
4	**B-R4**	**N-B3**
5	**O-O**	**B-K2**
6	**R-K1**	**P-QN4**
7	**B-N3**	**O-O**
8	**P-B3**	**P-Q4**
9	**P×P**	**N×P**
10	**N×P**	**N×N**
11	**R×N**	. . . . . .

Even I was a "theoretical expert" then, having recalled that in a magazine published in 1938 the game Alexander *vs.* Milner-Barry had been analyzed. The line beginning with 11 . . . P-QB3 was not well known then.

11	. . . . . .	**P-QB3**
12	**P-Q4**	**B-Q3**
13	**R-K1**	**Q-R5**
14	**P-N3**	**Q-R6**

Here the annotator of that game suggested that 15 R-K4 was strong, and he offered some analysis that seemed to prove that White could get the advantage. Needless to say, I tried it.

15 R-K4 . . . . . .

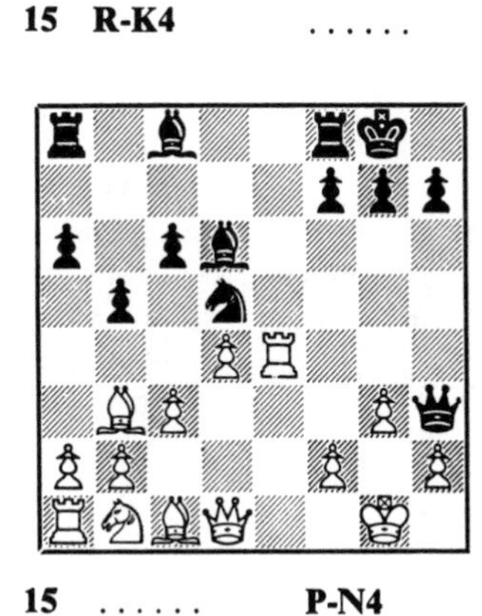

15 . . . . . . **P-N4**

Black's reply came as a great surprise, and I lost the game.

These incidents led me to believe that it can be dangerous even to know the recommendations of the theoreticians, and I became a believer in the Russian proverb: Measure the cloth seven times before cutting it once. Of course, you should not discard your chess books just because of an old proverb. No, I ask you only to use restraint in your admiration of book analysis and to examine it all thoughtfully, even if it comes from well-known players.

Myself included.

II: Famous Opening Catastrophes

The art of opening preparation is just one facet of chess mastery. It is possible, of course, to discuss the most important factors in the selection of an opening repertoire. It is equally important, however, to have dependable and complete information about games in which the openings under examination are used, as well as an open-minded investigative approach to the analysis of those games. Neglect of either of these principles could undermine the foundation on which your chess ambitions are being built.

I have already explained how I became cautious after disappointments when I was young and innocent and uncritically trusted the books, word for word. However, even years of experience cannot always shield one from misfortunes in the opening. Even the most distinguished players have in their careers experienced severe disappointments due to ignorance of the best lines or suspension of their own common sense.

In 1941 there was a tournament called "Match-Tournament for the Title of Absolute Champion of the USSR." This was the first and probably the last tournament with such a pretentious name, as if it were the title of a boxing match. Six of the strongest players in the Soviet Union took part: Botvinnik, Keres, Smyslov, Boleslavsky, Bondarevsky and Lilienthal.

There were no ratings then; nevertheless, a few players, because of their outstanding results, were felt to have the right to challenge Alekhine, then World Champion. Undoubtedly Botvinnik and Keres were among the most worthy candidates to achieve a match with Alekhine, so it was anticipated that an interesting race between them would develop in the 1941 tournament. Actually, they finished in the top two places (Botvinnik first, Keres second), but the tight race expected between them did not materialize, due in part to the following game in the third round:

NIMZO-INDIAN DEFENSE

	Keres	Botvinnik
1	P-Q4	N-KB3
2	P-QB4	P-K3
3	N-QB3	B-N5
4	Q-B2	P-Q4
5	P×P	P×P
6	B-N5	P-KR3
7	B-R4	P-B4
8	O-O-O	......

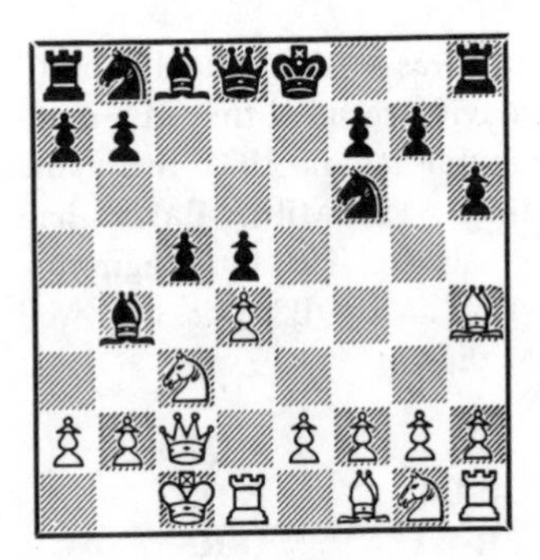

8	......	**B×N**
9	**Q×B**	**P-KN4**
10	**B-N3**	**P×P**
11	**Q×P**	**N-B3**
12	**Q-QR4**	**B-B4**
13	**P-K3**	**R-QB1**
14	**B-Q3**	**Q-Q2**
15	**K-N1**	**B×Bch**
16	**R×B**	**Q-B4**
17	**P-K4**	**N×P**
18	**K-R1**	**O-O**
19	**R-Q1**	**P-N4**
20	**Q×NP**	**N-Q5**
21	**Q-Q3**	**N-B7ch**
22	**K-N1**	**N-N5**
	Resigns	

Such a terrible rout at the beginning of a tournament could knock anybody out of action. Who was the guilty party? Perhaps Mikenas. The Lithuanian master, a long-time friend of Keres, had played Botvinnik several months earlier; he castled on the Queenside and won the game. But Botvinnik, in the position of the preceding diagram, played 8 . . . O-O 9 P×P B×N 10 Q×B P-KN4 11 B-N3 N-K5 12 Q-R3 B-K3 13 P-B3 N×B 14 P×N Q-B3, and after 15 P-K3 R-B1 16 K-N1 N-Q2 17 N-K2 R×P 18 N-Q4 P-R3 19 B-N5 QR-QB1 20 B×N B×B, Black had a difficult position. It would be naive to suggest that such a loss did not trouble Botvinnik, especially since at that time the Nimzo-Indian Defense occupied a very important place in his opening repertoire.

Another factor that contributed to Keres's misfortune was the fact that he was not familiar with the game between Belavenets and Simagin played in the 1941 Moscow Championship, while Botvinnik, in his own words, "had seen the Belavenets-Simagin game in which Simagin had played the first two moves of the correct plan."

The subtlety of Botvinnik's play is reflected primarily in three moves. The first of them, 8 . . . B×N, removes the Knight on White's QB3 which was blocking the QB file and which, together with the Bishop on KR4 and the Rook on Q1, was exerting pressure along the Queen file. The next move, 9 . . . P-KN4, breaks the pin on the Knight, while the third, 10 . . . P×P, wins a very important tempo for the development of Black's Queenside.

Not one of the currently successful masters has been able to equal Botvinnik in his ability to follow the development of a concept, to find in it something new and valuable, and to apply such great analytical skill. His reward has been the winning of many "opening games"—games that were in effect decided in the opening—against some of the strongest players of our time. Here is another example:

World Championship Match 1957
NIMZO-INDIAN DEFENSE

	Botvinnik	Smyslov
1	**P-Q4**	**N-KB3**

2	**P-QB4**	**P-K3**
3	**N-QB3**	**B-N5**
4	**P-K3**	**P-QN3**
5	**N-K2**	**B-R3**
6	**P-QR3**	**B-K2**
7	**N-B4**	**P-Q4**
8	**P×P**	**B×B**
9	**K×B**	**P×P**
10	**P-KN4**	**P-B3**
11	**P-N5**	**KN-Q2**
12	**P-KR4**	**B-Q3**
13	**P-K4**	**P×P**
14	**N×P**	**B×N**
15	**B×B**	**O-O**
16	**P-R5**	**R-K1**
17	**N-Q6**	......

White has a great advantage and won quite rapidly. Everyone was impressed by Botvinnik's idea beginning with his 10th move, but I found an antecedent without much difficulty. In the New York 1951 international tournament, the American master G. Shainswit already discovered this idea in his game against Grandmaster R. Fine, though he interpolated the somewhat inferior 10 Q-B3, forcing Black to play the useful 10 ... P-B3.

Certainly, a more refined method of preparation would be to study the preferences of your future opponent and attempt to penetrate his thoughts to understand how he will react in various situations. It is unclear why opening "theory" does not take into account the opening preferences of the most important group of players in the world—the leading grandmasters.

In 1971, before my match with Fischer, I was making my opening plans for that contest. At the time I rarely played the Rubinstein Variation of the French Defense, but in studying Fischer's games I noticed that as White he almost never had to meet this rather solid system. In one game, against Minev at the Havana Olympiad in 1966, the following occurred:

FRENCH DEFENSE

1	**P-K4**	**P-K3**
2	**P-Q4**	**P-Q4**
3	**N-QB3**	**N-KB3**
4	**B-N5**	**P×P**
5	**N×P**	**B-K2**
6	**B×N**	**P×B**
7	**P-KN3**	......

This is one of the rarer continuations. Now, after 7 ... B-Q2 8 N-KB3 B-B3 9 Q-K2 P-B4 10 N/4-Q2 B-B3 11 P-B3, Fischer had a splendid position.

Was it not reasonable to wonder, in view of White's success in the above game, why 7 P-KN3 was so rarely seen? Was it an innovation? No: in 1941, in the six-grandmaster tournament mentioned above, Smyslov played just that against Boleslavsky and won rather easily, due in particular to the advantage he obtained in the opening. Moreover, opening reference works will show instantly that the correct road to equality was demonstrated by Salo Flohr back in 1930, playing Black against Opocensky in a tournament in Sliak:

7 ...... P-KB4
8 N-QB3 P-QB3
9 B-N2 P-N3

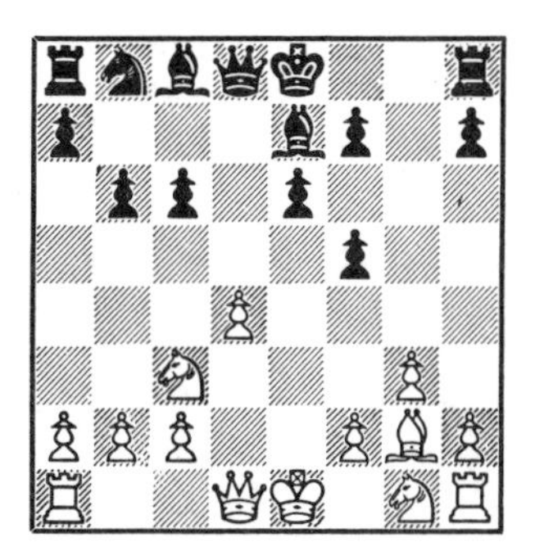

The Opocensky-Flohr game continued 10 KN-K2 B-N2 11 N-B4 Q-Q3 12 Q-K2 N-Q2 13 O-O-O O-O-O, with an equal game, clearly a correct evaluation. Could it be that when Fischer played 7 P-KN3 he was counting on the likelihood that his opponent would not be familiar with the rare variation? Would Fischer really harbor such a naive hope?

Once again, I set up the chess pieces and slowly, move by move, began to replay the moves of the game, as carefully as a field engineer with a mine detector who passes over and over again an area marked ALL LAND MINES HAVE BEEN CLEARED IN THIS AREA because his intuition warns him that it just may not be true.

I did not have to look long. I stared at this position for a few seconds and suddenly realized that White gets a clear advantage with 10 P-Q5! BP×P 11 N×P. But it turned out that I had "discovered America" a little late: in the 1957 Moscow Championship, the game Estrin-Nikitin developed in the same manner, and the game was published in the 1957 *Yearbook* in Moscow.

At the 1970 Interzonal in Palma de Majorca, a game was played that was truly cause for amazement (Fischer-Matulovic). It would be difficult to find another game in which Fischer, playing White, had such a deplorable position by only the 12th move.

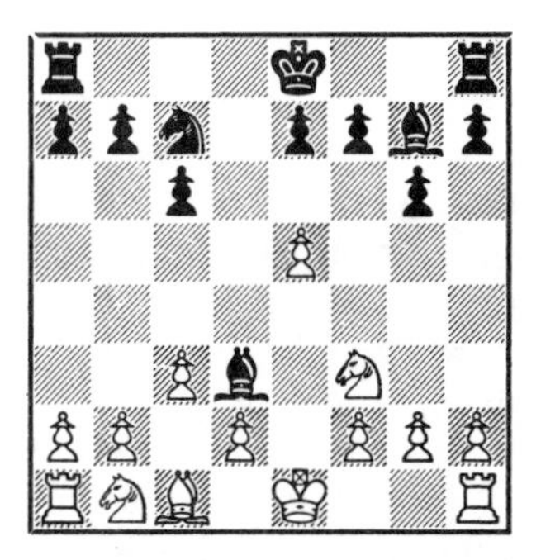

It is not difficult to see that the Black Bishop on Q6 cuts through White's position like a knife. White's game is extremely precarious; how could Fischer have gotten into such an unfavorable situation? Here are the opening moves of Fischer-Matulovic:

SICILIAN DEFENSE

1	**P-K4**	**P-QB4**
2	**N-KB3**	**N-QB3**
3	**B-N5**	......

Because this is uncharacteristic of Fischer, it may be assumed that he had something special in mind.

3	......	**P-KN3**
4	**P-B3**	**N-B3**
5	**Q-K2**	**B-N2**
6	**P-K5**	**N-Q4**
7	**Q-B4**	......

This is the point of White's idea: Black now has two men under attack, the Knight on Q4 and the QBP. The game continued 7 ... N-B2! 8 B×N (on 8 Q×P, the simple 8 ... P-N3 is good) 8 ... QP×B 9 Q×P Q-Q6! 10 Q-K3 B-B4 11 Q×Q B×Q, and we have reached the position of the diagram above.

Had Fischer been incautious enough simply to go running after a pawn? Did he know something that was not in the books? Well then, let us look in the books.

In Boleslavsky's *Caro-Kann bis Sizilianische,* published in 1968, we find this entire variation through the 5th move, and then 6 O-O is examined. The analysis breaks off after the 9th move with the verdict, "White stands freer but Black has a solid position." What if this is not to White's liking? Can he find a less-analyzed path to refute this "last word" of theory?

Yes, there is the recommendation 6 P-K5 N-Q4 7 Q-B4, as Fischer played, but Boleslavsky suggests that White should not attempt to win the pawn since he is not developed enough for such operations. He offers this as refutation:

7	......	**Q-N3**
8	**P-Q4**	**P-Q3**
9	**KP×P**	**KP×P**

Boleslavsky claims "a good game" for Black, continuing his analysis with 10 Q×N Q×B 11 Q×QP P×P 12 P×P B-K3 13 N-B3 Q-Q6 14 B-K3 B-KB1 15 Q-B7 B-QN5 16 R-QB1 O-O, with a strong attack for Black.

So now what? Is there a fly in the ointment? I tackled this problem with the Moscow master Igor Zaitsev. Fortunately, we were able to avoid the unimaginative type of analysis that is characteristic of very many strong grandmasters.

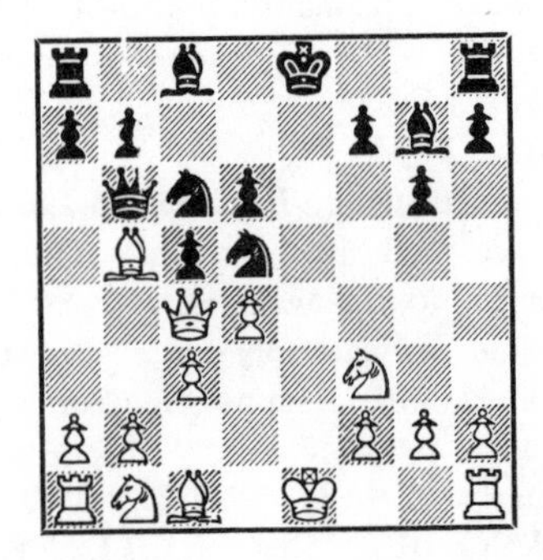

In this position White does not have to employ his strongest piece as a pawn-snatcher, but can play simply:

10 Q-K2ch ......

This move may seem absurd: the White Queen seems to be running back and forth without knowing where it is best placed. But if we reject this argument as abstract, and look instead for a concrete reply, it becomes clear that the poisonous check is not so easily answered. Any interposition on the King file leads to loss of a piece: if 10 ... B-K3? 11 P-B4, or if 10 ... N/4-K2? 11 P-Q5. Consequently, Black is forced to continue the fight with an uncastled King—not a very pleasant prospect in this situation. Perhaps this is what Fischer intended, but Matulovic's 7 ... N-B2 did not give him the chance.

The variations in your opening repertoire should be based on your own critical evaluation. We have already seen how again and again the road to the truth is littered with tactical subtleties. Dependence on general strategic concepts alone very often may cause you to miss what is actually the tactical basis of an opponent's idea, although positional understanding may lead to questioning the idea's strategic validity.

Several years ago, East German players discovered the following method of play for White in one of the most carefully studied variations of the Queen's Gambit Declined, the Makogonov-Bondarevsky system. No less than the distinguished Spassky had the opportunity to face White's new idea; the game was Malich-Spassky, Lugano Olympiad 1968.

QUEENS GAMBIT DECLINED

1	**P-Q4**	**N-KB3**
2	**P-QB4**	**P-K3**
3	**N-KB3**	**P-Q4**
4	**B-N5**	**B-K2**
5	**N-B3**	**P-KR3**
6	**B-R4**	**O-O**
7	**R-B1**	**P-QN3**
8	**P×P**	**N×P**
9	**B×B**	**Q×B**
10	**N×N**	**P×N**
11	**P-KN3**	......

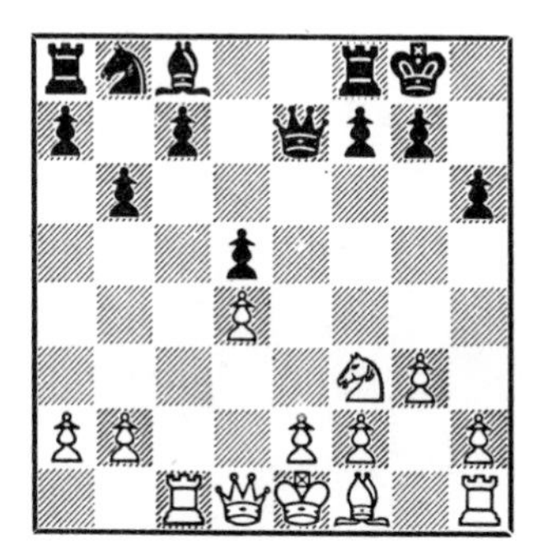

After this move White's idea becomes clear, while after 11 P-K3 the game would enter usual lines. The development of the Bishop on KN2 seems very promising. The KP can remain on K2, saving time. Also, if White were to fianchetto his Bishop *after* advancing the KP, Black could play ... B-R3 to impede White's castling. Note further that the exchange of Queens possible after . . . Q-N5ch would be favorable for White.

The Malich-Spassky game continued: 11 . . . B-K3 12 B-N2 P-QB4 13 N-K5 (preventing the normal development of the Black Knight, for after 13 . . . N-Q2 14 N×N Black loses a pawn without compensation) 13 . . . N-R3, and after 14 O-O QR-B1 15 P-B4 Spassky had to resort to tactical tricks to avoid falling into a difficult position with absolutely no prospects: 15 . . . B-B4 16 B×P, and White had the advantage.

If you study the position after 11 P-KN3 carefully (see diagram above), you will find a fairly good move.

11 . . . . . . R-K1

Black exerts pressure on the KP, hoping to induce White to advance it.

12 B-N2 B-R3

Black's last two moves look so natural that no one could doubt their merit. An experienced master encountering the diagramed position for the first time would surely make these moves, demanding hard proof that they are insufficient.

13 N-K5 . . . . . .

This move, however, seems to give White lasting pressure on Black's position, requiring him to bend every effort in the difficult task of completing the development of his Queenside. The variation 13 . . . N-Q2 14 R×P Q-N5ch 15 Q-Q2 N×N, intending 16 Q×Q N-Q6ch followed by . . . N×Q, is rather transparent and is refuted by the prosaic 16 P×N Q×Qch 17 K×Q R×P with a clear advantage for White. There is no time for even one preparatory move by Black, say 13 . . . Q-Q3, since then the apparently logical moves 11 . . . R-K1 and 12 . . . B-R3 would turn out to have been so much wasted time.

In other words, Black's problems in the Makogonov-Bondarevsky system seem to have increased.

This situation gave rise to some thinking about the basis of Black's entire strategy. Was it possible that finally a refutation of one of the most complicated systems for Black in the Queen's Gambit had been found? And why not? White has obviously committed no strategic errors: he did not neglect his development and his general strategy was not in conflict with the tactical possibilities in the position.

The only suspicious thing about White's position is that he has still not castled, but Black seems unable to take advantage of this circumstance. The White King is prepared to flee to safety, although in this case even on its original square, K1, it seems in no particular danger.

And what about Black? He has not been playing with his eyes closed, but has deliberately searched for his very best chances. His King is in a safe place and his pieces have not been developed haphazardly; on the contrary, those that are developed fulfil clearly defined functions.

So who was right? Perhaps—and this is true in similar situations—it could be concluded that the entire variation was undergoing a serious crisis; it is reasonable to expect that new ways would be found for White to deploy his forces.

In 1970, Grandmaster Uhlmann (White) and one of the oldest active Soviet masters, Gabriel Veresov, met over the board. To Uhlmann's misfortune—and the benefit of chess—Master Veresov belongs to the old guard. He is one of many who late in their careers seek not high places in the tournament tables necessarily, but rather victory in the search for truth.

Only that can explain the following continuation.

13 ...... **N-Q2**

Anyway!

14 R×P ......

The basis of White's entire plan.

14 ...... **QR-B1!!**

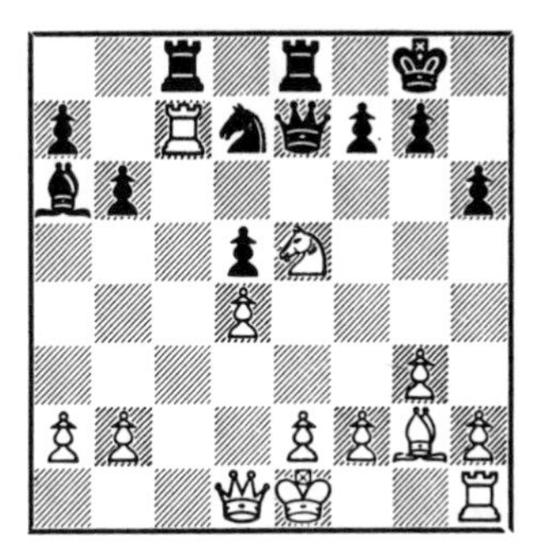

Let us tip our hat to the master who found the correct basis for Black's 13th move, which at first glance seems to be a rather bad mistake. When something like this is found, everyone seems surprised that it had not been discovered earlier since the whole idea is so logical.

It seems that White has a vast selection of replies here, but in fact his choices are almost nonexistent. After careful study you will see that on 15 R×N Q-N5ch White cannot play 16 Q-Q2 because of 16 ... R-B8 mate. On 16 K-B1, with the idea of answering 16 ... Q×NP with 17 B×P R-B8 18 Q×R Q×Qch 19 K-N2, winning, Black would answer 16 ... Q×QP!!

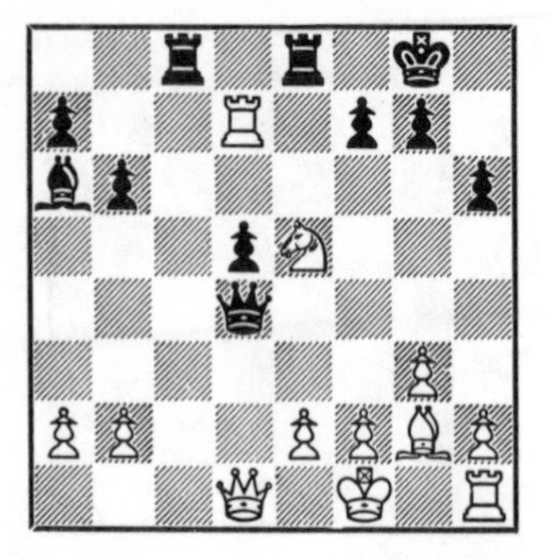

Position after 16 . . . Q×QP!!

Now 17 Q×Q is impossible because of 17 . . . R-B8ch. There is no future in 17 R×QP due to 17 . . . Q×Qch 18 R×Q R×N. And on 17 N-Q3, Black's pieces finally consummate their hopes, pouncing on K7: 17 . . . R×P!, and White may wonder whether Black will be satisfied with equality after 18 K×R B×Nch 19 Q×B Q-K4ch, or whether he will play for a win.

One question remains unanswered: Was all this a complete surprise for the German grandmaster? Or was he being adventurous, knowing about the refutation but assuming that there was little chance of having to come up against it? Probably, Uhlmann was really surprised, since he was unable even to draw.

15	**R×R**	**R×R**
16	**O-O**	**N×N**
17	**P×N**	**Q×P**
18	**R-K1**	**P-Q5**
19	**Q-Q2**	**R-K1**

And Black won, although the position is absolutely equal.

III: Some Notes on the Move B-KN5

Lives there a chess player who has not liked to pin the Black King Knight in the opening with B-KN5? Compared with the relatively harmless white-squared Bishop, which for long generations in the Ruy Lopez has given Black misgivings about his QN4 square, the black-squared Bishop on KN5 is far more insidious.

However, there is a game known to theory which could induce some pessimism about the miraculous strength of that move.

GIUOCO PIANO

1	**P-K4**	**P-K4**
2	**N-KB3**	**N-QB3**
3	**B-B4**	**B-B4**

I am convinced that every player in the world has played this at least once in his life.

4	**P-Q3**	......

A move consistent with White's idea of completing his development and attacking KB7 with the assistance of N-KN5.

4	......	**N-B3**
5	**O-O**	......

Of course, the immediate B-KN5 is possible also, but White assumes that this possibility will not disappear. After all, in the introductory pages of virtually every textbook the student is warned against making unnecessarily cautious moves like P-KR3 and P-QR3 in the opening.

5	......	**P-Q3**
6	**B-KN5**	**P-KR3**
7	**B-R4?**	......

It is easy to give a question mark to a move when you know the refutation. If White was not prepared to exchange his Bishop for Black's Knight, he should not have set up this pin.

7	......	**P-KN4**
8	**B-KN3**	**P-KR4!**

This looks pretty crude.

9	**N×NP**	......

The pawn is taken, but not with great enthusiasm. White hopes to gain time because of the threat of 10 N×P.

9	......	**P-R5**
10	**N×P**	**P×B!!**

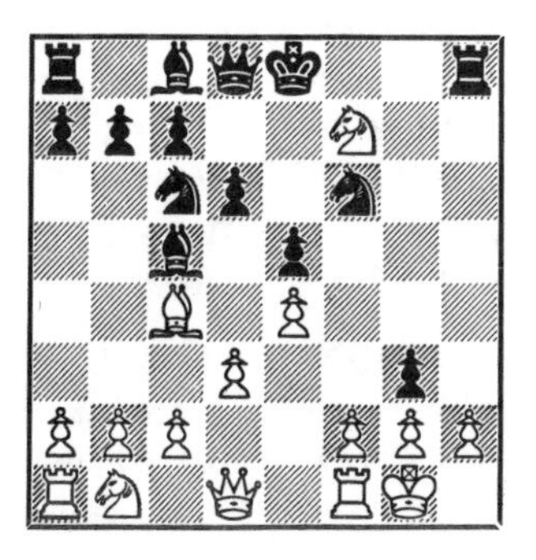

This variation is so colorful that each of the following moves deserves a diagram. And the finished product is a work of art.

11	**N×Q**	**B-KN5!!**

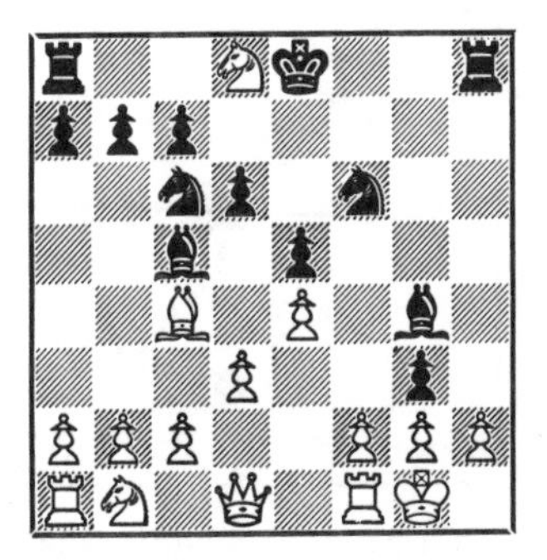

Moves that do not give check or capture material are called quiet moves. But everyone's heart begins to pound when his Queen is attacked. Clearly absurd is 11 ... B×Pch, praying for 12 K-R1 R×P mate, but obviously 12 R×B takes care of this matter.

12	**Q-Q2**	**N-Q5!!**

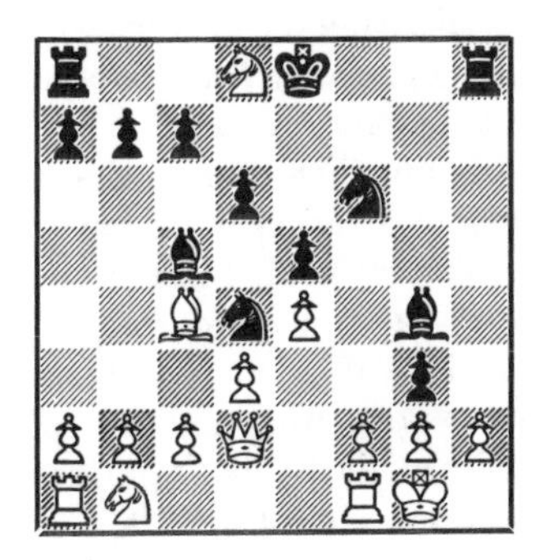

Now White can choose between

13 N-B3 N-B6ch 14 P×N B×P with inevitable mate, or the much prettier mate, in my opinion: 13 P-KR3 N-K7ch 14 K-R1 R×Pch 15 P×R B-B6 mate!

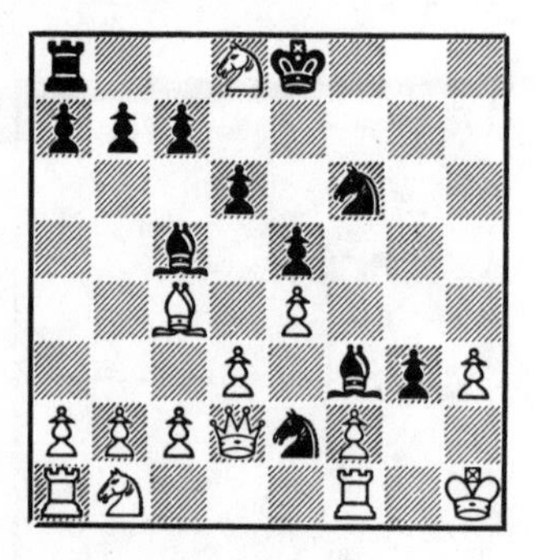

Such a game is bound to make a deep impression. But before abandoning the idea of B-KN5, it should be remembered that any method of development which can simultaneously cause trouble for your opponent and maintain a sound position for yourself is worth attention.

Today it is hard for me to recall which games of the old masters suggested to me the great significance of "His Majesty B-KN5" in the closed openings. When I began to meet masters regularly, in the late 1940s, my main concern was the planning of an opening repertoire. My games with Mikenas (given above) had proven to me that in a struggle with a more experienced master—one who not only knows published theory but who has the variations etched into his hide—my lack of experience put me at a disadvantage. What was to be done?

The answer came almost imperceptibly from my knowledge of some older games. While reflecting on how to avoid confronting the main theoretical lines of the Nimzo-Indian Defense, I decided that the half-forgotten order of moves 1 P-Q4 N-KB3 2 N-KB3 P-K3 3 B-N5 might be worth rehabilitating. The Nimzo-Indian proper has not yet been reached, while Black still has the possibility of playing the Queen's Indian Defense. I have always believed—and nothing has convinced me that my opinion should be re-examined—that after the normal order of moves in the Queen's Indian Defense (1 P-Q4 N-KB3 2 P-QB4 P-K3 3 N-KB3 P-QN3), White can obtain no advantage at all, not to speak of serious winning chances.

I believe my first chance to test my "innovation" against a strong opponent was my game with Viktor Lyublinsky, a master, in the 1949 USSR Championship.

INDIAN DEFENSE*

	Petrosian	Lyublinsky
1	P-Q4	N-KB3
2	N-KB3	P-K3
3	B-N5	P-B4
4	P-K3	B-K2

4 . . . P-QN3 is not bad, which is what Averbakh played against me in the 1950 Moscow Championship. I followed known paths by

*Also known as the Torre Attack.—Ed.

5 QN-Q2 B-N2 6 B-Q3 B-K2 7 P-B3 O-O 8 O-O N-B3 9 Q-K2, which led only to an equal game and a rather quick draw. However, while studying the position after 4 . . . P-QN3, I was struck by an idea. But I had to wait ten years for an opponent to fall into my outspread net.

In 1960, at the Olympiad in Leipzig, Czech master Kozma played the line against me. Finally I revealed my secret: **5 P-Q5!** The point is that after **5 . . . P×P 6 N-B3 B-N2 7 N×P B×N 8 B×N Q×B 9 Q×B** —as played in the game with Kozma —White has Q5 safely under control and can avail himself of a small tactical finesse: **9 . . . Q×P 10 R-Q1!**

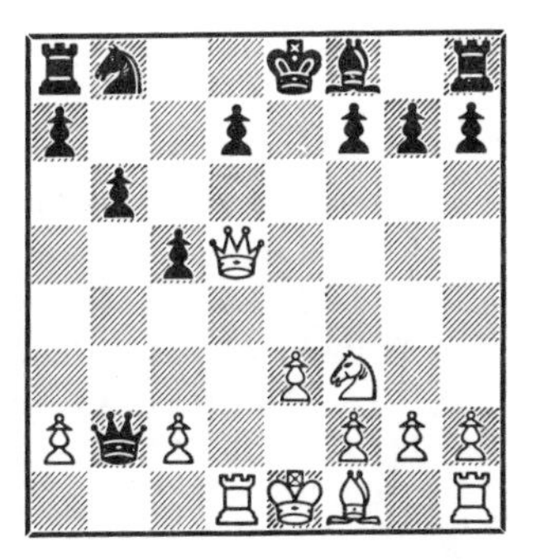

Position after 10 R-Q1! (analysis)

Doesn't this win a Rook? Black's Knight cannot move because of mate on Q7, and 10 . . . Q-B6ch is useless since after 11 R-Q2 Black has one check on QR8 and after 12 K-K2 White will win a Rook. The Black Queen could check from QN5 instead of QB6, to which White can also interpose the Rook. Then, after 11 . . . Q-N8ch it seems that White has gained nothing, for 12 K-K2 allows Black to defend his Rook by 12 . . . Q-N4ch and 13 . . . Q-B3. But have we forgotten that the check by the Black Queen on QB6 loses a Rook for Black? Therefore we must entice the Queen to QB6: 10 . . . Q-N5ch 11 P-B3! Q×Pch 12 R-Q2, and Black can no longer molest the White King.

The following setup has been considered satisfactory for Black: **1 P-Q4 N-KB3 2 N-KB3 P-K3 3 B-N5 P-B4 4 P-K3 N-B3 5 QN-Q2 P-QN3 6 P-B3 B-K2 7 B-Q3 O-O.** Through a different order of moves (including the substitution of . . . B-N2 for . . . O-O by Black), Frank Marshall, White against Capablanca in Kissingen 1928, unsuccessfully tried the idea of placing the Queen on K2, which gave Capablanca the opportunity to force an exchange by . . . N-Q4. After the exchange of black-squared Bishops it is clear that although the Black Knight on Q4 is far from impregnable—it can be attacked by a pawn from either side—the question of how to attack it is not so simple. If the QBP advances the Knight retreats to KB3; then, despite White's seeming advantage in the center, his central pawn formation is insecure. On the other hand, if the Knight is driven back by the KP, then it goes to KB5 with gain of tempo. This is where the somewhat misplaced Queen becomes problematical.

While studying the Marshall-Capablanca game I noticed that the White Queen does nothing on K2. So when I entered this variation in my game with Taimanov in the 1960 Soviet Championship I intended to omit Q-K2. Fortunately, my opponent was of great help to me in the opening. After **8 O-O** he played **8 ... P×P** and after **9 KP×P** continued **9 ... N-Q4 10 B×B N/3×B** (Taimanov noticed that if 10 ... Q×B, White's 11 R-K1 prepares the retreat KB1 for the Bishop while laughing quietly at the Black Queen) **11 R-K1 B-N2 12 B-B1 P-B4 13 N-K5 Q-B2 14 QR-B1 QR-K1 15 P-QB4 N-KB3 16 Q-N3,** and White had the better position.

Now let us return to my game with Lyublinsky.

5	**QN-Q2**	**P-Q4**
6	**P-B3**	**QN-Q2**
7	**B-Q3**	**O-O**

"An inaccuracy," I wrote in 1949, "giving White the chance to invade K5 with his Knight with an active game. Correct was 7 ... Q-B2."

8 N-K5! ......

The key move. If White cannot post his Knight on K5, then his entire system of play is to no purpose. Now it is obvious why 7 ... Q-B2 was recommended. The White Knight in that case could not have gone to K5, while the attempt to enlist the help of the Bishop to secure K5 by 8 B-KB4 would be parried by 8 ... B-Q3. Often I have been unable to establish a Knight outpost on K5 in this system and therefore could gain no advantage. But fortunately not all of my opponents in those days took the system with B-KN5 seriously, evidently considering it an invention as provincial as the horse and buggy.

8	......	**N×N**
9	**P×N**	**N-Q2**
10	**B-KB4!**	......

To exchange Bishops would be absurd. The KP cramps Black's position, and each exchange would ease his situation by reducing the number of pieces. Fewer pieces need less space in which to maneuver. Furthermore, after 10 B×B Q×B 11 P-B3 or N-B3, Black would begin to attack White's pawn center with 11 . . . P-B3.

But if now 10 . . . P-B3, then very unpleasant is 11 Q-R5, forcing 11 . . . P-B4 since 11 . . . P-KN3 is answered by the obvious sacrifice 12 B×P P×B 13 Q×Pch K-R1 14 P-KR4, and White's threats are irresistible; for example 14 . . . P×P 15 Q-R5ch K-N1 16 B-R6 R-B3 17 R-R3. It is natural, therefore, that Black wants to suppress the possible threats along White's QN1-KR7 diagonal at once.

10 . . . . . . P-B4

A very good move in this situation. It seems that now White will have difficulty working up an attack.

What plan should White choose? Should he prepare to castle on the Queenside? Black would then try to rapidly advance his Queenside pawns, and if he could establish a pawn on his QB5 it would neutralize the effect of White's cramping KP. And should a Black pawn reach QN5, Black's attack clearly would develop more quickly than White's.

Castling on the Kingside is immediately possible, but nonsensical: 11 O-O P-KN4 12 B-N3 P-KB5, and the Bishop is trapped. Kingside castling can be prepared by first withdrawing the Bishop to KN3. Until White has actually castled on the Kingside, Black does not intend to advance his KNP.

But have White's first 10 moves had no purpose other than determining which way to castle?

11 P-KR4! . . . . . .

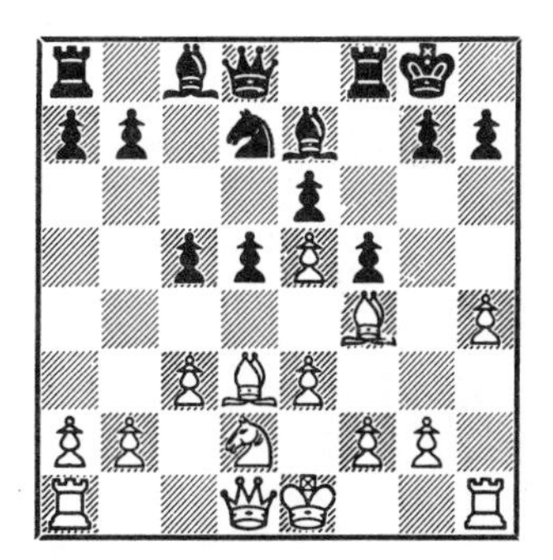

An important blockading move! Now the safety of the Queen Bishop has been guaranteed and another move is on the agenda: P-KN4. Note that now 11 . . . B×P? would be fatal for Black because of the obvious 12 Q-R5.

11 . . . . . . P-B5
12 B-B2 P-QN4

Better here is the immediate 12 . . . N-B4 so as to be able to close the White King Bishop's diagonal by . . . N-K5. See the next game.

13 N-B3 . . . . . .

Probably 13 P-KN4 would have been decisive. Today I would consider both these moves about equally good.

With 13 N-B3 White has created the concrete threat N-N5, which will be hard for Black to meet. Clearly, Black chose 12 . . . P-QN4 in order to start his Queenside pawn advance as quickly as possible, but now 13 . . . P-N5 14 N-N5 sets difficult problems before him. If 14 . . . N-B4 then 15 Q-R5 P-KR3 16 Q-N6. If 14 . . . B×N 15 P×B Q-K2, there follows the well-known sacrifice 16 R×P with a very strong attack, e.g. 16 . . . K×R 17 Q-R5ch K-N1 18 P-N6 N-B3 19 Q-R2! (stronger than 19 P×N P×KBP 20 B-Q6 Q-KN2). The threat of K-K2 and R-R1 would force Black to attack the KNP immediately with 19 . . . Q-K1, after which 20 P×N Q×P 21 P×KNP K×P 22 B-K5ch K-B2 23 B-Q1, and White wins.

13	**. . . . . .**	**N-B4**
14	**P-KN4**	**P-N5**
15	**P×BP**	. . . . . .

Too hasty. It seemed to me at the time that Black's attack was developing faster than my own. I obviously did not like 15 P×NP N-Q6ch 16 B×N B×Pch 17 K-B1 P×B 18 Q×P P×P, or 18 . . . P-QR4, and there seemed to be no way to continue White's attack. Strongest was 15 N-Q4, and White's excellently posted Knight would give him a superior position. White could then exchange on KB5 and Black would be forced to recapture with his KP, which would weaken his QP. The text move leads to a forced variation which I thought would win for me.

15	**. . . . . .**	**KP×P**
16	**N-N5**	**P-N3?**

Black does not want to allow the White Queen to get to KR5, but he overlooks White's obvious threat. After 16 . . . P-KR3 17 Q-R5 N-Q6ch (if 17 . . . Q-K1 White would still have his positional advantage) 18 B×N P×B 19 Q-N6 P×N 20 RP×P Q-K1 21 Q-R7ch K-B2 22 R-R6 R-KN1, the outcome of the game would be unclear.

17	**P-R5**	. . . . . .

Now the KR file will be opened, since after 17 . . . B×N 18 B×B Q×B 19 Q×Pch B-K3 20 Q×N White's advantage would be indisputable. And, after all this, White still has the option of castling on either side!

17	**......**	**N-Q6ch**
18	**B×N**	**P×B**
19	**RP×P**	**RP×P**

19 ... B×N is a little trap, for 20 Q-R5 would be answered by 20 ... P-KR3!, but White wins after 20 R×P!

20	**Q×P**	**P×P**
21	**P×P**	**B×N**
22	**B×B**	**Q-R4**
23	**B-B6**	**R-K1**
24	**Q-Q4**	**K-B2**
25	**P-K6ch**	**R×P**
26	**B-Q8**	**Resigns**

In 1951, Soviet master Bannik decided to imitate Lyublinsky's play up to the 12th move, playing the move I recommended in my annotations in 1949.

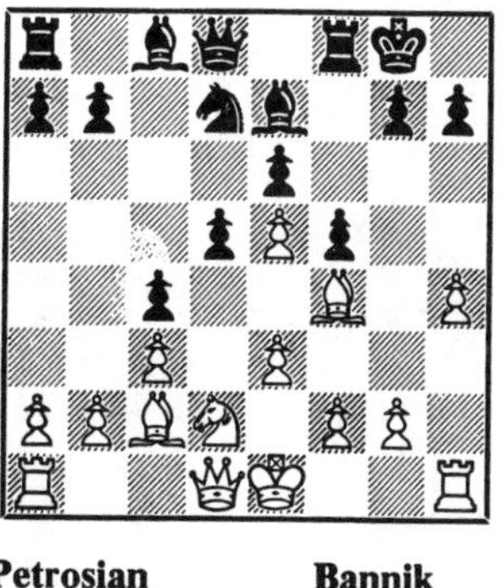

Petrosian **Bannik**

12	**......**	**N-B4**

The course of this game shows that White's chances are not limited to attacking on the Kingside.

13	**N-B3**	**B-Q2**
14	**N-Q4**	**Q-N3**
15	**B-N5!?**	**......**

The laudable idea of this move is to gain a lasting advantage based on the permanence of the Knight on Q4, which strikes in all directions. Some other piece on this square would not be nearly as effective. 14 B-N5, a move earlier, would have led to a protracted struggle.

As I remember, I was quite pleased with my rapid victory over Lyublinsky — certainly everyone likes to win quickly — and therefore I failed to calculate all the variations here to any great depth. I relied on the fact that if Black captured on his KN4 he would open the KR file for White, and I therefore considered this possibility extremely unlikely. Because of my inexperience, I did not spend time on the variation 15 ... B×B 16 P×B Q×P, which would give Black a playable game. After 17 R×P, Black has the satisfactory 17 ... N-Q6ch, and the variation 17 ... K×R 18 Q-R5ch K-N1 19 P-N6 Q×Rch 20 K-K2 KR-Q1 gives White no more than perpetual check. But evidently the experienced Bannik did not want to concede a draw to the young Petrosian.

15	**......**	**R-B2**
16	**B×B**	**R×B**
17	**Q-N1!**	**B-R5**
18	**P-QN3**	**......**

Of course, exchanging Bishops

is out of the question because of 18 . . . N-Q6ch.

18 . . . . . . P×P
19 P×P B-Q2
20 P-KB4! . . . . . .

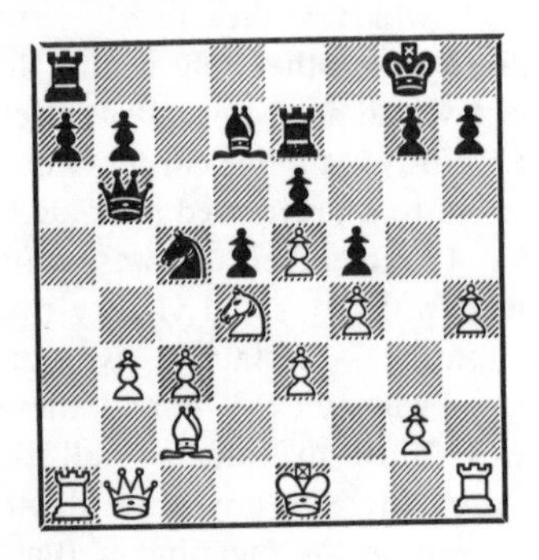

White cannot omit this move in view of the potential attack on his KP. Now the center—White's pawns on K3, KB4 and K5 against Black's on Q4, K3 and KB4—has frozen, and Black no longer has the possibility of . . . P-KB5. Of course, White also will not be able to conduct any pawn operations in the center. Nevertheless, White's position is better because his Bishop and Knight are clearly stronger than their Black counterparts.

White's problem is how to conduct the struggle so as to make use of his advantage. He wants to open a file for his King Rook; therefore, Black should have played 20 . . . P-KR4 to close the Kingside, and White would have had to look for play on the Queenside.

20 . . . . . . R-QB1

21 K-Q2! . . . . . .

The King moves to a safe position and frustrates Black's hopes of exerting pressure on the QBP.

21 . . . . . . P-QR3

Black misses his last chance to play . . . P-KR4.

22 P-KN4! . . . . . .

After this, Black's position is lost.

22 . . . . . . N-K5ch
23 B×N BP×B

White's powerful Knight on Q4 versus Black's almost immobile Bishop on Q2, combined with White's advanced Kingside pawns, will determine the outcome of this contest. White's major pieces will coordinate their activities with the Knight, and Black's positional weaknesses will lead to his collapse.

24 Q-R2 . . . . . .

The Queen looks for a target.

24 . . . . . . Q-B2
25 KR-QB1 B-N4
26 Q-R5 Q-Q2?

Better was the exchange of Queens followed by . . . B-Q6. Of course, one Bishop on Q6 cannot fight the entire battle. But when lines are opened, they will also be opened for Black's Rooks which could then obtain counterplay because of White's imprudence.

27 Q-N6 B-Q6
28 R-KN1! ......

Less good was the immediate 28 P-B5 P×P 29 P-K6 Q-K1 30 P×P Q-R4 31 R-KN1 Q×RP 32 R-N2 Q-B3, and it can be seen that White has rushed things a bit.

28 ...... Q-K1
29 QR-QB1 ......

This move is not without purpose. White prevents Black's counterplay after ... R/2-QB2.

29 ...... K-R1
30 P-R5 Q-B2
31 R-KR1 P-R3?

Black puts his own head in the noose. Now it is obvious that the advance of White's KNP will lead to the opening of the KN file and will present White with a fine square for his Rook on KN6. Instead of the text, it would have been better to resign the game.

32 R-R2 R/2-K1
33 R-KN1 Q-K2
34 Q-Q6! ......

After a series of unhurried moves, White proceeds energetically and quickly. The winning plan is no secret: the Knight on Q4 and the Rook that will land on KN6 will sweep through Black's position.

34 ...... Q×Q
35 P×Q R/B-Q1
36 P-N5 P-K4
37 P×KP R×KP
38 P×P P×P
39 R-N6 R-N4
40 R×Pch K-N2
41 R-K6 ......

Black resigned a few moves later.

Not only logical, objective maneuvering takes place on the chess board during a tournament. Many forms of subtle psychological warfare are also practiced. For example, occasionally an opening is used against an opponent who is known to favor it himself. The idea is to force him to fight against his own weapons, when he will have to face not only real dangers but very often imaginary ones as well.

Spassky made this "move" against me several times in our matches for the world championship. Naturally, I did not avoid the variations in question. But in one game I was surprised.

World Championship 1966
QUEEN'S PAWN GAME

Spassky Petrosian
1 P-Q4 N-KB3
2 N-KB3 P-K3
3 B-N5 ......

Noting the variation, someone remarked that Spassky "has invited Petrosian to play in the garden in which he grew up." Well said!

3 ...... P-Q4

4	**QN-Q2**	**B-K2**
5	**P-K3**	**QN-Q2**
6	**B-Q3**	**P-B4**
7	**P-B3**	**P-QN3**

This move does not contradict my comments in the game Petrosian-Lyublinsky. Black has no objection to a Knight incursion to K5 as long as he still has not castled. Besides, what better position is there for the Queen Bishop than QN2? With two good moves available, I decided to choose the one Spassky was probably not expecting.

8	**O-O**	**B-N2**
9	**N-K5**	**N×N**
10	**P×N**	**N-Q2**
11	**B-KB4**	......

White stays strictly within known lines. The QP has been transferred to K5, the black-squared Bishop has been preserved for future use, but—and it is a big "but"—because Black still has not castled, White's advanced pawn, if not put to good use, could become an object of attack. As commentators pointed out later, it was more reasonable for White to lead the game into quieter seas by 11 B×B and then P-KB4, refraining from overambitious plans.

11	......	**Q-B2**

More resolute was 11 ... P-KN4 12 B-N3 P-KR4 forcing 13 P-KR3, and Black has a very nice position.

12	**N-B3**	**P-KR3!**

Keeping in mind that the advance of the KNP and KRP has not been taken off the agenda.

13	**P-QN4!?**	......

A good sign, from Black's point of view. By offering to sacrifice a pawn, White says in effect that the present course of the game does not suit him. Black, however, has no intention of accepting the pawn sacrifice, which would let his opponent seize the initiative. After 13 ... P×P 14 P×P B×P 15 N-Q4 it is fairly obvious that Black's extra pawn will not play any significant role for a long time, while White's attacking chances after positioning the Queen on KN4 or KR5, occupying the QB file with the Rooks, and possibly advancing the KBP, would be extremely good. Of course, Black might have taken the pawn and tried to prove that he has a defensible position.

13	......	**P-KN4**
14	**B-N3**	**P-KR4**
15	**P-KR4**	......

After the natural 15 P-KR3, Black would advance his KNP and White could not maintain his KP. But now Black should not be tempted by 15 ... P-N5 because after 16 N-N5 N×P 17 B-N5ch he would be unable to castle in a position full of complications.

15	......	**P×RP!**
16	**B-KB4**	......

So White—for the moment!—has secured the KP.

16 ...... O-O-O!

A significant moment: the players are getting the maximum from the pieces that are in play, but the Rooks still have to be brought into the game. To find the best positions for the Rooks is the first priority for both sides. With this in mind, note that the capture on KR5 has opened the KN file for Black's Rooks. It is surprising, therefore, that Spassky does not exchange on QB5 to open the QN file for his Rooks. If Black were then to recapture with a piece, White could then throw his QRP into the fray.

17 P-QR4 P-B5!!

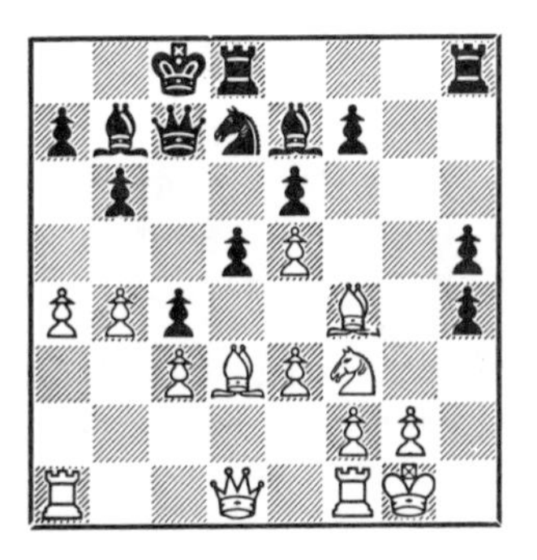

After the game I discovered that this move amazed the spectators. True, White's Q4 is now his for the taking, but under the prevailing conditions his Queen and Rooks can make no use whatever of this square. Even his Knight, which normally would work best on such a square, cannot get there because it is tied to the defense of the pawn on K5. Thus, while Black's Rooks have free rein on the KN file, White cannot similarly open the QN file.

Black is also threatening to transfer his King Bishop to KN2 to exert pressure against White's weakness, the advanced KP.

18 B-K2? ......

An interesting case of stereotyped chess thinking. White had the much better move 18 B-B5!, setting a little trap. If then 18 ... P×B 19 P-K6 B-Q3 20 B×B Q×B 21 P×Nch R×P, it seems Black is up two pawns, but now comes 22 N-Q4! and White would stand no worse. There would be a great difference in the strength of the White Knight compared with that of the Black Bishop, and Black's pawn weaknesses would be incurable. Curiously, Spassky saw this move and discussed it immediately after the game, but he did not like the retreat of the Bishop to KR3 should Black refrain from capturing it. Esthetically, it would look like only a big pawn, but it would fulfil an important function as defender of the KNP.

18 ...... P-R3!

An unprepossessing move, true, but it is the essence of Black's idea. Now Black can keep the Queenside closed no matter how White maneuvers his QRP and QNP; all the play will run through one gate —the Kingside.

19	**K-R1**	**QR-N1**
20	**R-KN1**	**R-N5**
21	**Q-Q2**	**KR-N1**
22	**P-R5**	**P-N4**
23	**QR-Q1**	**B-B1!**
24	**N-R2**	**N×P**
25	**N×R**	**P×N**
26	**P-K4**	......

The idea of 26 ... P×P 27 B×N Q×B 28 Q-Q8 mate is too obvious to be called a trap. White's last move should therefore be looked upon as an attempt finally to open lines for his Rook.

26	......	**B-Q3**
27	**Q-K3**	**N-Q2**
28	**B×B**	**Q×B**
29	**R-Q4**	......

It seems that White has raised some serious questions: Black's KNP has come under attack.

29	......	**P-K4**
30	**R-Q2**	**P-B4!**

31	**P×QP**	......

It looks as if 31 P×BP N-B3 32 Q-R6 would have been better; but after 32 ... Q-Q1 followed by ... R-R1 Black would maintain an excellent attacking position. Note that the threatened advance of the QP in conjunction with ... P-R6 hung over White like a black cloud. But now, at least, Black's Bishop on QN2 is locked out of play.

31	......	**P-B5**
32	**Q-K4**	**N-B3**
33	**Q-B5ch**	**K-N1**
34	**P-B3**	......

A piquant variation was 34 Q-K6 Q×Q 35 P×Q N-K5, threatening 36 ... N×Pch and 37 ... P-N6 mate!

34	......	**B-B1**
35	**Q-N1**	**P-N6**
36	**R-K1**	**P-R6**
37	**B-B1**	**R-R1**
38	**P×P**	**B×P**
39	**K-N1**	**B×B**
40	**K×B**	**P-K5**

41	**Q-Q1**	**N-N5**
42	**P×N**	**P-B6**
43	**R-KN2**	......

Too bad. Instead of staying with its army, the Rook desperately offers its own life. But it alters nothing.

43	......	**P×Rch**
	Resigns	

B-KN5 in the King's Indian Defense

It is usually assumed that the evolution of chess ideas comes about solely through the games of "important" players. But the fact is that significant new ideas, unaccompanied by glorious fanfare, occur also in the games of less-known players. If these ideas are repeated in the games of leading players, they then come under the scrutiny of theoreticians, make the rounds of the chess magazines, appear in chess books ... Finally there comes a time when it is difficult to discover who was the real source of Grandmaster A's system or Grandmaster B's variation.

If you look at an opening text you will discover that in the King's Indian Defense, there are two different systems which include the development of White's Bishop to KN5. One variation, 1 P-Q4 N-KB3 2 P-QB4 P-KN3 3 N-QB3 B-N2 4 P-K4 P-Q3 5 B-K2 O-O 6 B-N5, bears Yuri Averbakh's name. The other is 1 P-Q4 N-KB3 2 P-QB4 P-KN3 3 N-QB3 B-N2 4 P-K4 P-Q3 5 B-K2 O-O 6 N-B3 P-K4 7 P-Q5, and if either 7 ... QN-Q2, which is the older method, or 7 ... P-QR4, which is the newest, White continues 8 B-N5, which is known as the Petrosian Variation. I will not discuss the origins of the Averbakh system, but I would like to discuss how I, and others, came upon the idea of the move 8 B-N5.

Unfortunately, I cannot remember just why I began to pay any attention to this idea. In 1946, I believe it was Master Ratner who decided to pin the Knight on Black's KB3, and after the natural reaction, 8 ... P-KR3, the Bishop retreated along the QB1-KR6 diagonal having accomplished nothing. In the 1953 Zurich Candidates Tournament, the late Grandmaster Stahlberg, with White against me, played B-KN5. He then exchanged the Bishop for the King Knight, attempting to prove that White would have good prospects by saddling Black with a bad Bishop on KN2 with the center locked. That game made little impression on me at the time because I felt it was important for Black to have his King Bishop when its White counterpart was missing.

The first game in which I managed to show that the Bishop on KN5 contained its drop of poison was Petrosian-Suetin in the 1954 USSR Team Championship.

KING'S INDIAN DEFENSE

	Petrosian	**Suetin**
1	**P-QB4**	**N-KB3**
2	**N-QB3**	**P-KN3**
3	**P-K4**	**P-Q3**
4	**P-Q4**	**B-N2**
5	**B-K2**	**O-O**
6	**N-B3**	**P-K4**
7	**P-Q5**	**QN-Q2**
8	**O-O**	**N-B4**
9	**Q-B2**	**P-QR4**
10	**B-N5**	**P-R3**
11	**B-K3**	......

In this position Black had for many years continued 11 . . . N-N5 12 B×N P×B 13 P-KR3 N-B3 14 N×P N×QP 15 BP×N B×N 16 P-B4 B-Q5ch 17 K-R2 with sharp play. But Suetin continues rather unimaginatively.

11	......	**KN-Q2**
12	**N-Q2**	**P-B4**
13	**P×P**	**P×P**
14	**P-B4**	**P×P**
15	**B×P**	**N-K4**

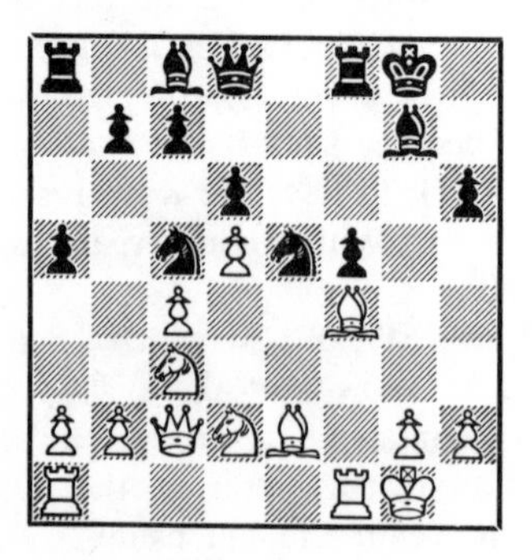

This kind of setup was considered satisfactory for Black. His pieces are harmoniously placed and it is not easy for White to find a plan offering any advantage in the middlegame.

16	**QR-K1**	**B-Q2**
17	**N-B3**	......

A significant point has been raised: if Black's KRP had not advanced, 17 . . . N-N3 would now be a good move, planning . . . P-B5 after White's Bishop retreats. With the KRP on R3, however, 17 . . . N-N3 18 B-K3 P-B5? 19 B×N and 20 Q×N loses a piece for Black. So there remains only the apparently quite normal text move.

17	......	**Q-B3**
18	**Q-Q2**	**QR-K1**
19	**N×N**	**P×N**
20	**B-K3**	......

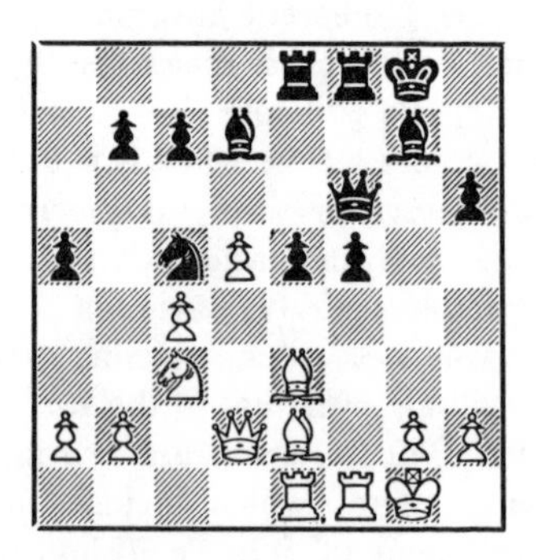

A strategically tense position has been reached.

One of the most complicated problems of strategy for a generation of chess players has been the question of "hanging pawns." (Two pawns on the fourth rank, isolated from other pawns of the same color, such as Black's KP and KBP in the diagram, are called "hanging.") Usually, hanging pawns arise (for either side) in the closed openings, particularly the Queen's Gambit. Some players purposely include hanging pawns in their arsenal and try to prove that their dynamic power in the middlegame gives them more bite than bark. Others consider such pawns merely weaknesses. And, of course, there are those specialists who have a precise feel for all the nuances of the positional struggle involving hanging pawns, and who can manage to play the role of advocate on either side of the controversy according to circumstances.

The next part of the game is rather boring, consisting mainly of positional maneuvering. If you do not fall asleep, keep in mind the following when you play over moves 21-32: Hanging pawns are good when they control important central squares, take an aggressive stance, and threaten to advance and disrupt the opponent's plans. It is therefore necessary to know that the most important way to fight against hanging pawns is by attacking them directly. Such attacks are often designed to provoke one of the pawns to advance, leaving a hole where the attacker may comfortably lodge his pieces. This game features a typical demonstration against hanging pawns.

20 ...... P-N3
21 B-R5 R-K2
22 B-Q1 Q-Q3
23 B-QB2 R/2-B2
24 K-R1 R-R1

Played to prevent P-QR3 and P-QN4. On 25 P-QR3 there follows 25 . . . P-R5.

25 R-K2 Q-B1
26 R/2-B2 N-N2

Black begins the transfer of the Knight to Q3, where it will protect the KBP when White's Queen is transferred to KR5.

27 Q-K2 N-Q3
28 P-B5 P×P
29 B×QBP R-N1
30 P-QN3 Q-B1
31 Q-R5 Q-R3

Black has clearly lost the strategic battle and now tries to save the KBP by tactical means: if 32 B×N P×B 33 B×P B×B 34 R×B Q×Rch.

32 P-KN4! P-B5

Forced. But now the passed pawns, which seemed so powerful, are easily blockaded. White, though in time pressure, quickly concludes the game by creating threats against the pawns as well as against the King.

33 R-K1 Q-B1

34	**B×N**	**P×B**
35	**B-N6**	**R-B1**
36	**N-K4**	**P-B6**
37	**P-N5**	**R-B5**
38	**R-KN1**	**B-B4**
39	**P×P**	**B×N**
40	**B×B**	**Resigns**

In spite of its success in this game, I still had the feeling that my invention was not very promising. But, except for the unnecessary 21 B-R5, no error could be found in White's play.

And no better continuation could be found for Black.

Several years elapsed. In the 1958 USSR Championship I again played White against Suetin.

KING'S INDIAN DEFENSE

	Petrosian	**Suetin**
1	**P-Q4**	**N-KB3**
2	**P-QB4**	**P-KN3**
3	**N-QB3**	**B-N2**
4	**P-K4**	**P-Q3**
5	**N-B3**	**O-O**
6	**B-K2**	**P-K4**
7	**P-Q5**	**QN-Q2**
8	**B-N5**	**P-KR3**
9	**B-R4**	......

Now it is not easy for Black to find a clear plan. His normal setup, which entails the posting of the Queen Knight on QB4, followed by the retreat of the King Knight and the advance of the KBP, is rather difficult to achieve here. On 9 ... N-B4 there would follow the very flexible 10 N-Q2 and Black would have to worry about the threat of P-QN4, driving his Knight back. It is not surprising, therefore, that after lengthy meditation Suetin makes a natural decision.

9	......	**P-KN4**
10	**B-N3**	**N-R4**

Practice has shown that similar plans have been quite satisfactory for Black.

11	**O-O**	**P-R4**
12	**N-K1**	**N-B5**
13	**N-B2**	**N-B4**
14	**N-K3**	**N×KP**
15	**N×N**	**N×Bch**
16	**Q×N**	**P-KB4**
17	**P-B3**	......

White is assured of a small but steady advantage. If 17 ... P×N 18 P×P, the prospect of a White Knight invading KB5 would give him the advantage.

17	......	**P-B5**
18	**P-B5**	**P×N**
19	**Q×P**	**B-B4**

20	QR-B1	Q-Q2
21	R-B4!	......

White intends to double the heavy pieces on the QB file, threatening P×P and eventually the win of Black's backward QP.

21	......	P×P
22	Q×BP	P-N3
23	Q-K3	Q×P
24	R×P	Q-Q5
25	B-B2	Q×Q

Probably better was 25 . . . Q×P so as to have some material compensation for White's attack. Now, although the position has been simplified, it becomes more and more difficult for Black to find a defense for each White move.

26	B×Q	B-K3
27	P-QR3	P-N4
28	B-Q2!	......

This Bishop is on its way to a better position at QB3 where it will secure the Queenside and train its sights on the Black QRP and KP. Black can move his QRP out of the Bishop's line of fire, but he will have to suffer with his weak KP.

28	......	KR-Q1
29	B-B3	P-R5
30	R-K1!	......

Very alert. If Black's KRP and KNP had stayed closer to their original positions, Black could try to save himself by the well-known method of abandoning one of his weaknesses for the sake of a greatly simplified position. But here, White's threat to bring his Knight to KB5 makes it clear that the Black King will himself come under attack.

30	......	QR-B1
31	R-N7	R-Q4
32	R-N6	B-B2
33	N-Q6	R-Q1
34	N-B5!	......

Now the weak Black pawns fall prey to White.

34	......	K-R2
35	R-N7	R/1-Q2
36	R×R	R×R
37	N×B	K×N
38	R×P	K-N3
39	R×P	R-Q8ch
40	K-B2	R-QB8

The rest of the game holds no further interest for us, though it continued until the 61st move.

Within a year I played another game (1959 Soviet Championship) in which the organic defects in Black's position as a result of the advance of his KRP and KNP were even more obvious.

KING'S INDIAN DEFENSE

	Petrosian	Yuchtman
1	P-Q4	N-KB3
2	P-QB4	P-KN3
3	N-QB3	B-N2
4	P-K4	P-Q3
5	B-K2	O-O

6	**N-B3**	**P-K4**
7	**P-Q5**	**N-R3**

This move has its good points: the Knight can go to QB4 without interfering with the diagonal of Black's Queen Bishop.

8	**B-N5**	**P-R3**
9	**B-R4**	**P-KN4**
10	**B-N3**	**N-R4**
11	**N-Q2**	**N-B5**
12	**O-O**	**N-B4**
13	**B-N4**	**P-QR4**

This move reveals that Black is placing his hopes in the strong position of his Knight on KB5. It seems very solid, for it would be bad for White to play B×N since the recapture by the KP would open the long diagonal for Black's King Bishop.

It was later shown that with 13 . . . B×B 14 Q×B P-KR4! 15 Q-B5 P-R5 16 B×N KP×B 17 N-B3 Q-B3! (not 17 . . . P-KB3?? or 17 . . . B-B3 because of 18 P-KN3 with advantage to White) Black had defensive possibilities.

14	**P-B3!**	. . . . . .

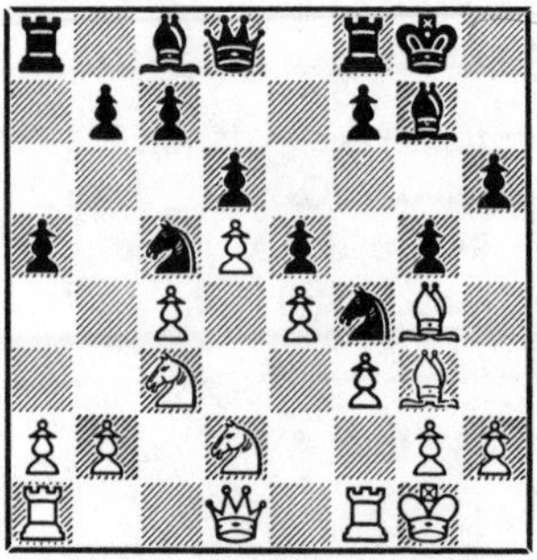

Now we see what White has in mind: he intends to replace his Bishop on KN3 with a pawn. The Black Knight will be unable to remain on KB5, and without it there Black's game will be lifeless. White would then maneuver a Knight to KB5 via K3.

As you continue playing over the game, you will notice that a White Knight never arrives at KB5. Do not be surprised; in an actual game, unrealized intentions play a greater role than the moves as played.

14	. . . . . .	**N/4-Q6**
15	**Q-B2**	**P-QB3**
16	**K-R1**	**P-R4**
17	**B×B**	**R×B**
18	**P-QR3!**	. . . . . .

A simple but important move. White wants to exchange his Bishop for the Knight without allowing Black's KP to recapture. But on the immediate 18 B×N there would have followed 18 . . . N-N5 19 Q-N3 KP×B, keeping White from exerting pressure on the QNP. If White wants to go after the QNP he will have to give up the idea of keeping Black's King Bishop imprisoned. The exchange of one type of advantage for another is quite common in chess, but in this case 20 P-QR3 N-R3 21 Q×P leaves the Queen trapped after 21 ... N-B4 22 Q-R7 R-R1.

18	......	**P×P**
19	**BP×P**	**N-B4**
20	**B-B2**	**P-N5**
21	**P-KN3**	**N-N3**

As we already know, a good answer to 21 ... N/5-Q6 is 22 B×N!, although the simple 22 B-K3 is also good.

22	**P×P**	**P×P**
23	**B-K3**	......

Black's position is lost. Few masters would suffer through such a bad position in the almost impossible hope of saving it.

23	......	**P-N4**
24	**N×P**	**Q-N3**
25	**P-QR4!**	......

White's position is overwhelming and he has an extra pawn as well. The curtain is quickly lowered.

25	......	**Q-R3**
26	**N-B4**	**P-B4**
27	**R×P**	**R×R**
28	**P×R**	**Q-N2**
29	**Q-N2**	**N-N6**
30	**N/5×P**	**Q-Q2**
31	**R-KB1**	**Resigns**

Despite these successes, one should not infer that this system leads automatically to a win for White. However, it was a rather long time before Black was able to find a way to obtain sufficient counterplay against it.

Another try for Black in this variation which at first seemed promising for Black was employed twice by Fischer against Tal in the 1959 Candidates Tournament, and again in Olafsson-Fischer at Zurich 1959.

KING'S INDIAN DEFENSE

1	**P-Q4**	**N-KB3**
2	**P-QB4**	**P-KN3**
3	**N-QB3**	**B-N2**
4	**P-K4**	**P-Q3**
5	**N-B3**	**O-O**
6	**B-K2**	**P-K4**
7	**P-Q5**	**QN-Q2**
8	**B-N5**	**P-KR3**
9	**B-R4**	......

This position, familiar from the

1958 Petrosian-Suetin game discussed above, was reached in three games with Fischer as Black in the 1959 Candidates Tournament. Each time, Fischer continued:

9 ...... P-R3

Black plans to play ... P-KB4, which could pose problems for White; a Kingside pawn storm is often a powerful weapon for Black in the King's Indian Defense. The position of the White Bishop on KN5, Black feels, should only help him win important tempos. But before Black can think of ... P-KB4 he must move his King Knight out of the way. And before he can do that he must unpin the Knight, which he intends to do by means of ... Q-K1. So, to avoid leaving his QBP unguarded he plays 9 ... P-R3 to prevent N-QN5.

10 N-Q2 Q-K1
11 O-O ......

This was the continuation of both Tal-Fischer games. Olafsson continued against Fischer 11 P-KN4!? N-R2 12 Q-B2.

11 ...... N-R2
12 P-QN4 ......

It becomes clear that it is still not easy for Black to advance his KBP: 12 ... P-KB4?? 13 P×P R×P allows a White Knight to occupy K4, and 13 ... P×P? loses material after 14 B-R5! So ... P-KB4 will have to await further preparation.

In the first of his two games with Tal in which this variation was discussed, Fischer played 12 ... N-N4, as did Olafsson against Gligoric in the same tournament (given below). This move costs Black a lot of time, as he will later have to move this Knight again in order to allow his KNP to advance. But time is often not of critical importance in closed positions.

Apparently satisfied with his opening play in that game (although he eventually lost), Fischer tried the variation against Tal in their second encounter with Fischer playing Black. But he tried a different 12th move.

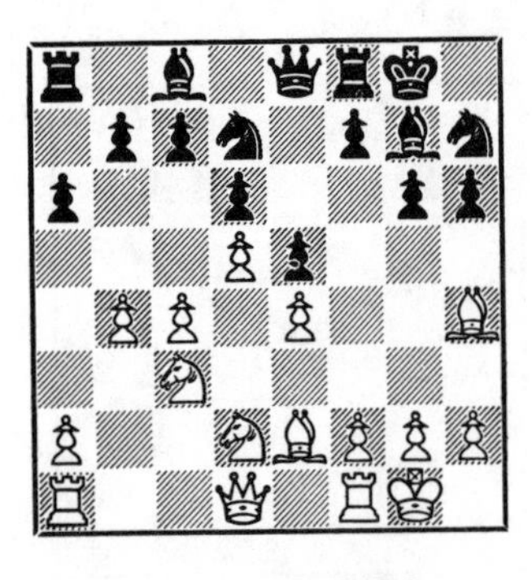

12 ...... B-B3

This is not as dangerous as some annotators claimed although, in principle, the exchange of black-squared Bishops should be advantageous for Black.

13 B×B N/R×B

14	**N-N3**	**Q-K2**
15	**Q×Q2**	**K-R2**
16	**Q-K3**	**N-KN1**

Black is now ready to play . . . P-KB4. Another plan was 16 . . . R-KN1 followed by . . . P-KN4 and . . . N-B1-N3.

17	**P-B5**	**P-B4**
18	**P×BP**	**NP×P**
19	**P-B4**	**KP×P**
20	**Q×P**	**P×P**
21	**B-Q3**	**P×P**
22	**QR-K1!**	**Q-B3**
23	**R-K6!**	. . . . . .

In positions where his opponent's pieces were uncoordinated or where the King's position had been weakened, Tal in 1959 felt like a fish in water. (Out of concern for the feelings of the present World Champion, I omit the rest of this game; the interested reader is referred to a collection of Fischer's games.)

By the end of the Candidates Tournament, the variation was well known to all devotees of the King's Indian Defense, and there were many in this tournament: Tal, Fischer, Gligoric, Petrosian, Olafsson. It was seen to be rich in dynamic possibilities for both sides.

Two rounds before the end, Gligoric, a confirmed King's Indian advocate, made a stand in this variation with Black against Olafsson. Although he lost the game he must have thought his middlegame chances were no worse than White's; otherwise, why would he have played the same thing against me in the final round?

In the position of the previous diagram, Olafsson-Gligoric and later Petrosian-Gligoric continued:

12	. . . . . .	**N-N4**
13	**P-B3**	**Q-K2**
14	**K-R1**	**P-KB4**
15	**R-B1**	**N-B3**
16	**P-B5**	**N-R4**

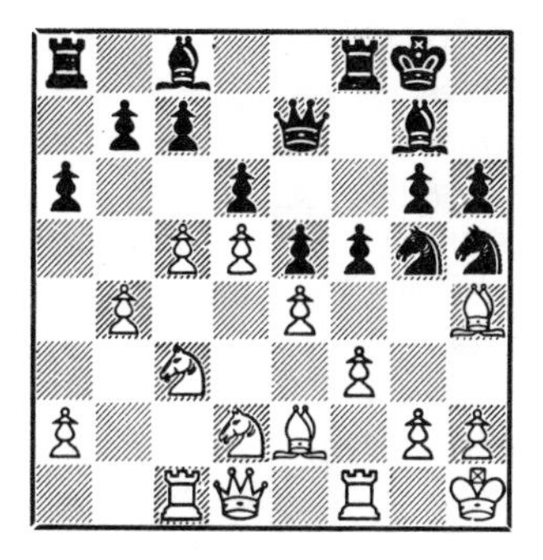

In this position Olafsson played 17 P×QP, and after 17 . . . P×QP 18 N-R4 N-B5 19 N-N6 R-N1 20 P-N5 P-QR4 21 N×B QR×N 22 R×R R×R 23 N-B4 B-B3 24 P×P P×P 25 N-K3 Q-R2 26 B-K1 B-Q1 27 Q-Q2 R-B4 an unclear and complicated position was reached. I would prefer to play White here, but Gligoric naturally found Black's position more to his liking. Perhaps he felt it was possible to improve his play at some point.

When I studied this game I noticed a rather amusing positional trap, and within 24 hours I had the chance to play it against Gligoric.

17 P-B6!! ......

Sheer madness? True, Black can hardly afford to capture on his QB3 because the center would be opened for White's pieces. White's plan would then be simple: he would exert pressure on Q5 and advance the QRP and QNP, eventually leading to the creation of an advanced passed pawn. If, on the other hand, Black allows White to capture on QN7, White will have easy targets to attack on the Queenside.

But Black can simply advance his QNP and permanently lock the Queenside. Then the action will take place only on the other half of the board, where Black is traditionally stronger in the King's Indian. Gligoric was therefore not overly concerned about the effectiveness of the new move.

17	......	**P-N3**
18	**P×P**	**P×P**

Now the King file and the KN file are half open, but it seems Black can operate along the KN file more effectively than White along the King file. Black's KP and KBP look very active.

19 P-N3! ......

This is the crux of White's idea. Black can parry White's threat to win a piece by 20 P-B4, but he will have to make positional concessions. The positions after 19 . . . P-B5 20 P-N4 N-B3, or 19 . . . N-B3 20 P-B4 P×P 21 P×P N/4-K5, have the same point: in both cases the Black Queen Bishop has been placed under house arrest along with his Queen Rook. For all practical purposes, White would have an advantage of two extra pieces.

Gligoric found another way to attempt to maintain a playable game.

19	......	**B-B3**
20	**P-B4**	**N-N2**
21	**N-B4**	......

Better was 21 P-R4, to guarantee the security of the Queenside.

21	......	**P×P**
22	**P×P**	**P-N4**
23	**N-Q2**	**N-K5**
24	**B×B**	**R×B**
25	**B-B3**	**P-QR4**
26	**P-QR3**	**P×P**
27	**P×P**	**R-N3**
28	**N/2×N**	......

White's advantage is indisputable.

CHAPTER 6

A Personal Approach to the Openings

by Bent Larsen

A Little Boy

"The King's Gambit is powerful like a storm; nobody can tame it. Nothing shows more clearly the lack of greatness in the chess professionals of today than the fact that none of them have the courage to play the King's Gambit." . . . I was nine and had found a chess book. My father had no idea how it got in the house (left by the former owner, perhaps). So I started playing the King's Gambit. The book was 20 years old, and the chess ideas of its author at least 60, but for a little boy they were not all that bad.

I learned the rules of the game before I was seven; my teacher was nine. He mated my naked King with his two Rooks and enjoyed it very much. His father was one of the best players in our town—I beat him seven years later. I joined the chess club when I was twelve, but by that time I was already studying chess more or less seriously. The public library had several chess books, including Bilguer's famous textbook, and bound volumes of the Danish chess magazine *Skakbladet* for ten years back.

I joined the chess club because I wanted to play stronger opponents than my father. Many winter evenings he and I played one or two games after supper. I began to keep score when I was eleven, which shows how serious I was by that age; but those games are not very interesting. In one or two I played an inferior kind of Pirc Defense, at that time an opening without a name. I guess I had seen some King's Indians and not understood them very well.

This was just after World War II, when international chess activities were slowly getting started again. It is not easy for a keen young chess player today to understand how slowly new opening ideas spread in those days. What the ordinary player knew was ten years out of date! International language-barrier-breaking publications on theory did not exist. Russian chess magazines were hard to get, and who could read them? By 1951, when I played in the first World Junior Championship in Birmingham, England, *Skakbladet* had published only one game using the Najdorf Variation of the Sicilian Defense. Yet I noticed that some of the strongest participants in this tournament were playing the Najdorf and Boleslavsky variations of the Sicilian with Black. Before the tournament ended I was playing them myself, and I liked them so much that I began playing the English Opening with White. I tried 1 P-QB4 P-K4 2 P-Q3 N-KB3 3 P-QR3, hoping Black would play P-Q4 so I could enter the Najdorf with colors reversed, and at that time many players did!

It has been said about the hypermoderns after World War I (led by Reti and Nimzovich) that, because of the great amount of hard work they did to develop their new ideas and gain recognition for them, they sometimes felt a little sad seeing players a few years younger understand and use these ideas as if they were just ordinary common sense. This happens all the time in chess, but it is easiest to follow in opening theory. Nowadays news travels at remarkable speed. A master plays a new move in a well-known position. It looks bad or goes against some accepted principle, or at least it does not repeat the famous master game everybody has been copying —and three months later young C-rated players on the other side of the globe are playing the new move.

Denmark was better off in chess literature than many small countries just after World War II. The war had not caused the same kind of chaos in our little butter country as in most of Europe. *Skakbladet* appeared early each month, and just when the war ended a translation of Euwe's works on opening theory was ready for publication. I bought it when I was 13; only three years later I realized how much had happened in chess since this book was written, at the beginning of the war. There had been one indication in *Skakbladet*, however: an inspiring article by Tartakower about the "Ultra-Catalan" (Barcza System).

Between 1951 and 1954 I changed my opening repertoire completely. My last King's Gambit in an international event was played in the World Junior Championship, Copenhagen 1953, and I used it then only because some of the other participants played the gambit so badly. My opponent that time was Jonathan Penrose, who played the Falkbeer Counter Gambit without knowing it well enough, and so lost in 20 moves. It was a nice good-bye, but it was good-bye. One year later, when I won the Danish Championship and made an international master result at the Olympiad, I played one Catalan after another. With Black the Najdorf was my favorite weapon against KP openings. Against 1 P-Q4 I had the Nimzo-Indian and Queen's Indian, which suited my style. Sometimes I played other defenses such as the Gruenfeld, King's Indian, Old Indian, and Dutch, but they were less natural for me. I shall try to explain this.

When I say an opening is natural for a player I mean that he *likes* it, and that he *believes* in it (which is not necessarily the same thing). I have never believed, or "felt," that the King's Indian is a correct defense for Black, but I have often liked playing it. I feel the same about the Dutch Defense, and in this case more masters will agree with me! When I throw the Modern Benoni into the basket marked "incorrect," Gligoric will probably agree, but he will not understand what his beloved King's Indian is doing there, and my "feeling" will not convince him. If general agreement is ever reached among experts it will not be in our time.

Some openings I consider absolutely correct, but I do not like to play them. There can be, for example, the problem of the isolated Queen Pawn. Take the Tarrasch Defense:

1	**P-Q4**	**P-Q4**
2	**P-QB4**	**P-K3**
3	**N-QB3**	**P-QB4**

But this is not a good example. I have played it a few times, but not only does Black get that isolated pawn in the center, which I do not like, but I am inclined to put the whole defense into the "incorrect" basket. Black's early sharp counterattack in the center, in an almost symmetrical position, has not been justified by any White error! When Spassky played the Tarrasch successfully against Petrosian, I shook my head and understood nothing—except that Petrosian was losing his title.

Better examples, positions I consider very good but don't like playing, can be found on the White side of many lines of the Queen's Gambit Accepted and the Nimzo-Indian. White gets more space and some unclear attacking possibilities on the Kingside, and evaluation of the position is really a matter of tempo: if White loses the initiative his isolated pawn will give him a headache. But look at this:

1	**P-Q4**	**P-Q4**
2	**P-QB4**	**P×P**
3	**N-KB3**	**N-KB3**
4	**P-K3**	**P-K3**
5	**B×P**	**P-B4**
6	**O-O**	**P-QR3**
7	**P-QR4**	**P×P**
8	**P×P**	......

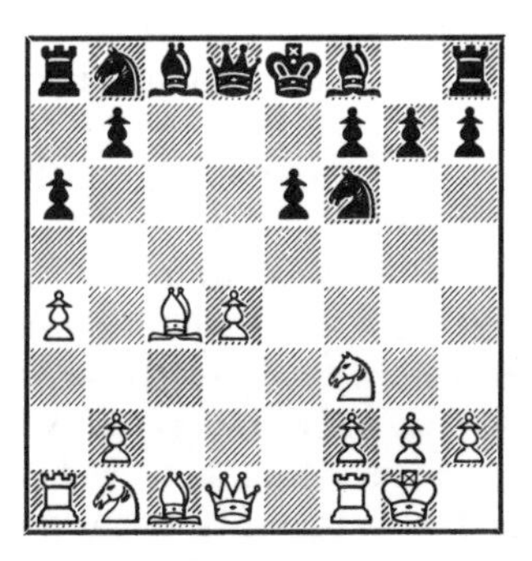

Gligoric likes it and plays it. So did Botvinnik, and Rubinstein! I see the isolated Queen Pawn and a hole in the White position on the Queenside. I see no initiative, but maybe White can draw with a quick P-Q5.

Now comes a shocker! Look at a Sicilian:

1	**P-K4**	**P-QB4**
2	**N-KB3**	**P-Q3**

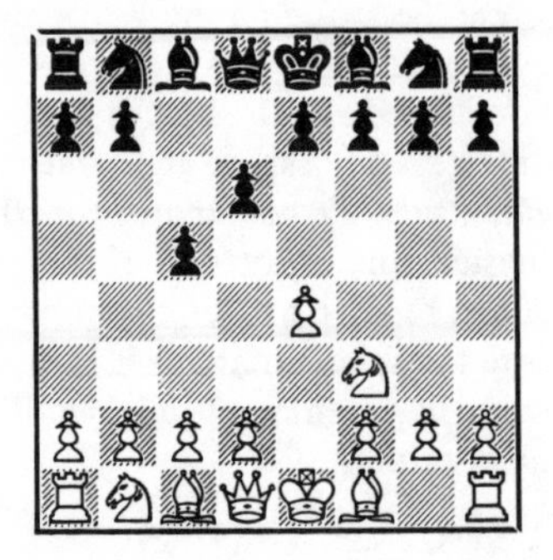

Almost everybody plays 3 P-Q4. But isn't this a positional error? I am not joking. I like my center pawns, and I like a QP better than a QBP! I know that sometimes White sacrifices a Knight on Q5 or K6 and smashes Black before he can castle, but in those games where this has been done, haven't improvements always been found for Black afterward? Well then, isn't 3 P-Q4 something like a cheap trap? I know it can be combined with purely strategical ideas, but I find it easier to discuss strategy when I have an extra center pawn! I cannot explain where I first got this idea, but I had it before I was Danish Champion and regularly playing 3 B-N5ch. Had I not played the Sicilian with Black I could have saved myself the trouble of studying for more than 20 years all the more popular lines of this opening, which comprise probably more than 25 percent of all published opening theory! This ought to start some amateurs thinking, instead of complaining that they haven't enough time to study theory. Is it the sum total of their ambition in chess to be two moves ahead of Fischer in the analysis of the Poisoned Pawn line of the Najdorf?

Experimenting

I became a grandmaster in 1956, at the Moscow Chess Olympiad. I beat Gligoric but drew with all the other grandmasters, making the best score on first board. But I wanted to beat grandmasters. Did this mean that I should choose sharper openings, or that I should continue playing the same openings, but better, more exactly? I began to experiment. Many of the experiments were successful, but some were "once and never again." For example, take Larsen-Olafsson, Hastings 1956/57:

1	**N-KB3**	**N-KB3**
2	**P-KN3**	**P-QN3**
3	**B-N2**	**B-N2**
4	**P-B4**	**P-K3**
5	**O-O**	**P-B4**
6	**N-B3**	**B-K2**
7	**P-Q4**	**P×P**
8	**N×P**	**B×B**
9	**K×B**	**Q-B1**

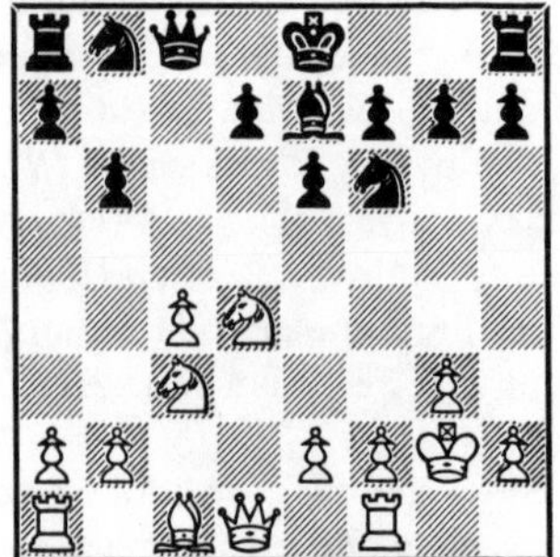

10 B-B4 ......

Instead of 10 P-N3 Q-N2ch 11 P-B3 P-Q4 (Botvinnik-Capablanca, Nottingham 1936).

10	**......**	**O-O**
11	**P-K4**	**Q×P**
12	**N/3-N5**	**......**

This is probably not good, though it is worth more analysis. This was my only loss at Hastings, in spite of some very experimental openings!

In Szabo-Larsen, Hastings 1956/57:

1	**P-K4**	**P-QB4**
2	**N-KB3**	**P-Q3**
3	**P-Q4**	**P×P**
4	**Q×P**	**N-KB3!?**

Instead of 4 ... N-QB3, or rather instead of P-QR3 or B-Q2; Black's idea is seen in the two continuations 5 N-B3 P-QR3 and 5 P-B4 N-B3.

5	**P-K5!**	**N-B3**
6	**B-QN5**	**Q-R4ch**
7	**N-B3**	**Q×B**
8	**N×Q**	**N×Q**
9	**N/3×N**	**P×P**
10	**N-B7ch**	**K-Q1**
11	**N×R**	**P×N**
12	**B-B4**	**P-K4!?**

12 ... N-Q4? 13 O-O-O is hopeless for Black.

13	**B×P**	**B-N5ch**

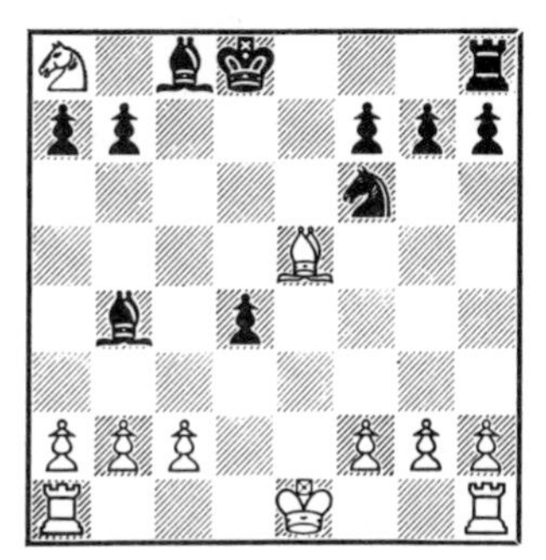

Szabo played 14 K-B1?; he feels uncomfortable when his opponent takes the initiative. Later he got Rook and three pawns against two minor pieces, but his King Rook could not get into play, and I won. Later analysis proved Black's idea unsound; the right move is 14 P-B3!

In Larsen-Gligoric, Hastings 1956/57:

1	**N-KB3**	**N-KB3**
2	**P-KN3**	**P-KN3**
3	**B-N2**	**B-N2**
4	**P-B4**	**O-O**
5	**P-Q4**	**P-Q3**
6	**O-O**	**P-B4**
7	**N-B3**	**N-B3**
8	**P×P**	**P×P**
9	**B-B4**	**N-Q5**

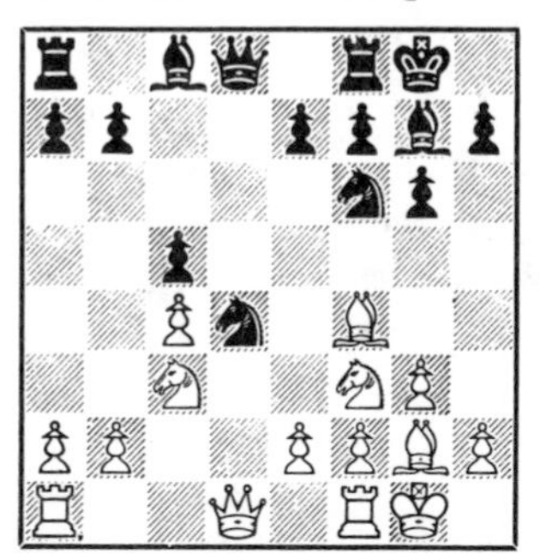

10	**P-K3?**	......

Sheer madness! Experiment for experiment's sake. After:

10	......	**N×Nch**
11	**B×N**	**N-Q2**

Black stood better. My only excuse is that Gligoric arrived quite late and I wanted to make him think. Well, each of us lost half a point (the game was drawn). Only later (Larsen-Evans, Dallas 1957) did I find the idea 10 B-K5 N-B3 11 Q×Q R×Q 12 B-B7!, which might have given Gligo a much harder time.

In Larsen-Teschner, Zonal Tournament, Wageningen 1957, last round:

1	**P-Q4**	**P-Q4**
2	**P-QB4**	**P-QB3**
3	**N-KB3**	**N-B3**
4	**N-B3**	**P×P**
5	**P-QR4**	**B-B4**
6	**N-R4!?**	**B-B1**
7	**P-K4!?**	**P-K4**
8	**B×P?**	**P×P**
9	**P-K5**	......

All this is an old recommendation by Alekhine!

9	......	**P×N!**
10	**B×Pch**	**K×B**
11	**Q×Q**	**P×P**
12	**Q-B7ch**	**K-K3!!**

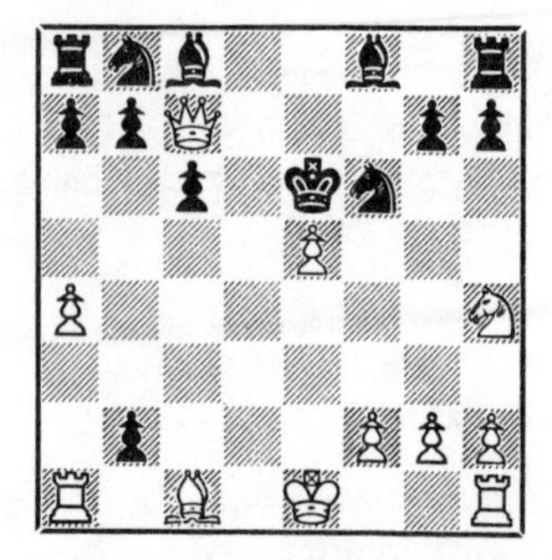

With decisive advantage for Black; see the analysis by Aitken in *British Chess Magazine,* 1940.

To play this in an important last-round game without deep study was crazy. It turned out that the Austrian theoretician Haberditz had sent Teschner an article about Aitken's analysis, one of the last things Haberditz did before he died — well, what can you call such luck in printable English? And Teschner had not published Haberditz's article in *Deutsche Schachzeitung,* the magazine he edits! He had not even studied it much, but he remembered 12 ... K-K3 and found the rest over the board. This story had a happy ending for me when I drew the game, a piece down:

13	**Q×Bch**	**N/1-Q2**
14	**Q×P!?**	**P×R=Q**
15	**Q×Pch**	**K-B2**
16	**P-K6ch**	**K-N1**
17	**O-O!**	**Q-K4!**

Better than Haberditz's 17 ... N-N3.

18	**Q×R**	**Q×P**

19	**Q×P**	......

Black ought to win, but later, in time pressure, allowed a draw by repetition of moves.

In Neikirch-Larsen, Interzonal, Portoroz 1958:

1	**P-Q4**	**P-KB4**
2	**P-KN3**	**N-KB3**
3	**B-N2**	**P-K3**
4	**P-QB4**	**P-Q3**
5	**N-KB3**	**B-K2**
6	**O-O**	**O-O**
7	**N-B3**	**Q-K1**
8	**R-K1**	**Q-N3**
9	**P-K4**	**N×P**
10	**N×N**	**P×N**
11	**R×P**	**N-B3**

If 11 ... Q×R 12 N-R4.

12	**R-K1**	**N-N5**
13	**P-QR3**	......

Theory now recommends 13 R-K2.

13	......	**N-B7**
14	**N-R4**	**B×N**
15	**B-K4**	**N×KR!**
16	**B×Q**	**N-B6ch**
17	**K-N2**	**P×B**
18	**P×B**	**N×Pch**
19	**K-N3**	**N-B4ch**
20	**K-N2**	**P-N3!?**

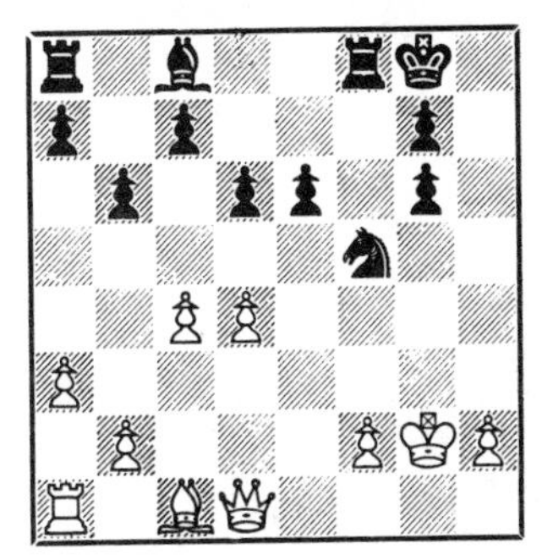

The year before, in the students' team tournament at Reykjavik, a game had been drawn after 20 ... N-R5ch. For theorists this was enough to start looking for improvements for White. That I won this game does not prove that Black stands better; but with Rook, Knight and pawn for the Queen Black has excellent chances, because his position is very solid. Compare van den Berg-Larsen, Beverwijk 1959:

1	**P-K4**	**P-QB4**
2	**N-KB3**	**P-Q3**
3	**P-Q4**	**P×P**
4	**N×P**	**N-KB3**
5	**N-QB3**	**P-KN3**
6	**B-K2**	**B-N2**
7	**O-O**	**O-O**
8	**N-N3**	**N-B3**
9	**K-R1**	**P-QR4**
10	**P-QR4**	**B-K3**
11	**P-B4**	**Q-N3**
12	**P-B5**	**B×N**
13	**P×B**	**Q-N5!?**
14	**B-K3**	**N-Q2**
15	**B-QB4**	**N-N3**

16 N-R2 N×B
17 N×Q N×B
18 Q-K2 N×R
19 N×N N-N6ch
20 P×N P×N

—with a difficult game for White! For the whole game and more comments, see my book *Larsen's Selected Games of Chess, 1948-69.*

In Gligoric-Larsen, Zurich 1959:

1 P-K4 P-QB4
2 N-KB3 N-KB3
3 P-K5 N-Q4
4 N-B3 P-K3
5 N×N P×N
6 P-Q4 N-B3!?
7 P×P B×P
8 Q×P Q-N3!

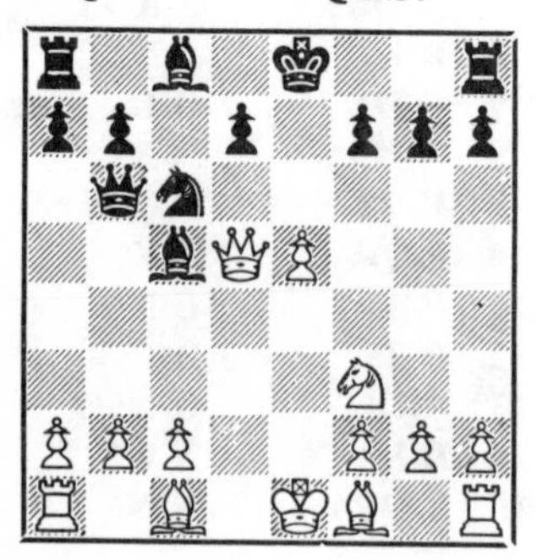

I got this idea from a comment by the old Danish theoretician Krause in *Skakbladet,* 1928! But I was not sure it was absolutely correct, and though I got good chances after:

9 B-QB4! B×Pch
10 K-K2 O-O
11 R-B1 B-B4
12 N-N5 N-Q5ch
13 K-Q3(?) Q-N3ch!
14 Q-K4 P-Q4!

I never played this line again. It became quite popular and was analyzed deeply, but for me it was a surprise weapon, to be used only once.

In Larsen-Donner, Zurich 1959:

1 P-KN3 P-K4
2 B-N2 P-Q4
3 N-KB3!? ......

3 ...... P-K5
4 N-Q4 P-QB4
5 N-N3 P-B5
6 N-Q4 B-QB4
7 P-QB3 N-QB3
8 N×N P×N
9 O-O N-K2

10 P-N3! ......

White has the initiative (see my book). At that time 1 P-KN3 was rare, and 3 N-KB3 was brand new! I liked it and played it quite a few times, obtaining very good results with these "Alekhine" and "Pirc" positions with colors reversed. In fact, in my first six tournament games with 3 N-KB3 I scored six points! Of course, this had something to do with my opponents' underestimation of White's chances with this "modest" opening.

These are examples of my experiments in my first three years as a grandmaster. Some were too wild, but they taught me a lot. Some were prepared at home, some were played on the spur of the moment—the wildest being against Olafsson, Beverwijk 1959. There, and in the Danish Championship the same year, I wanted to experiment in every game. Look what I discovered early one morning! (As in many tournaments, the last round at Beverwijk was played at an ungodly hour, when I wanted to sleep. In five Beverwijk tournaments I lost four last-round games!)

1	**P-KN3**	**P-K4**
2	**B-N2**	**P-Q4**
3	**P-QN4!?**	......

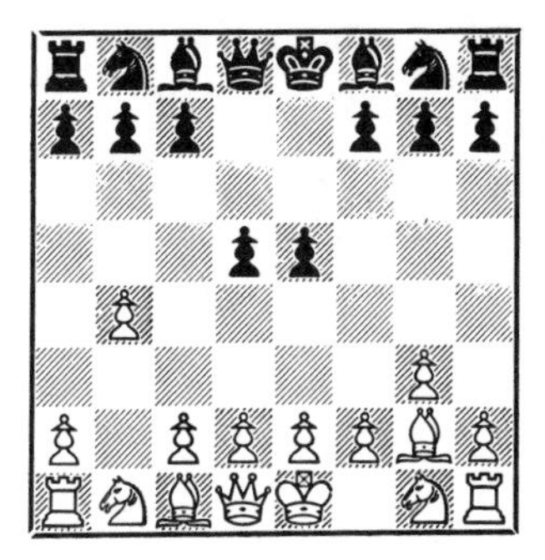

"Wonderful!" said Karel van den Berg. "The first example of dadaism in chess!"

3 ...... **B×P**

Probably not best. Donner recommended 3 ... P-QB3 4 B-N2 P-B3.

4	**P-QB4**	**B-K3**
5	**B-N2??**	**N-QB3**
6	**P-B4**	**N/1-K2**
7	**N-KB3**	**P-Q5**

and Black stood better. I didn't know what I was doing! But I think the fact that this was not a clear refutation of 3 P-QN4 shows the wide scope there still is for experiments in the opening. With 5 Q-N3! N-QB3 6 P-QR3! (vacating the QR2 square for the White Queen after P×P N-Q5), White would regain the pawn, and winning a center pawn for my QNP would have been just what I wanted. I played this once in a simultaneous exhibition in Switzerland; it is probably my only qualification as a dada artist.

My experiments and my desire to surprise my opponents gave me a very wide opening repertoire. Some experts may comment that I knew many openings but didn't know them well enough. That may be, but I want to stress that often my opponents did not know whether they were up against inspiration or preparation. Their uncertainty would use up a lot of time on their clocks!

I also like the story of Ivkov's preparations for our match in 1965. He studied 200 games with Bird's Opening! I didn't play it, and later Ivkov played it himself with White a few times—obviously, he didn't want all that work to go to waste.

With regard to White's first move, the latest addition to my repertoire has been 1 P-QN3. Internationally I played it for the first time in 1968. My success has been more limited than with 1 P-KN3, but 1 P-QN3 has become popular even among grandmasters, especially since I lost disastrously to Spassky in Belgrade 1970. It seems many players wanted something new; they were tired of all that theory which their opponents also knew. There was a brief time when I knew more about this opening than anybody else, but now there are several masters who have played it much more than I have.

Which openings don't I play? In 15 years I have played the main line of the closed Ruy only twice with White! That I do not like the commonest methods for White against the Sicilian has been mentioned already. I don't often play an ordinary Orthodox Queen's Gambit with Black. The Najdorf, as I mentioned, was my favorite defense against the KP opening when I was young; around 1955-56 I was really an expert on it and found important improvements for both White and Black. But soon afterward I almost stopped playing it, because it was being analyzed too much! Too many players knew some of the critical lines too well. I didn't like that and I turned to other variations of the Sicilian. Whether this was right or wrong is impossible to say, but if I had tried to follow all the ups and downs of the Poisoned Pawn Variation, the Polugaevsky Variation, and so on, there would have been much less time for me to study a lot of other interesting openings. And it would probably have bored me to play the same defense all the time.

It's Easy to Be an Expert

I have been called an expert on some openings where I am not. I played the Alekhine Defense now and then when it was not very popular, but that does not make me an expert. I have not added much new analysis, but there were some positions I liked to play with Black though most experts thought them slightly favorable for White. There was one move I was afraid of in the Four Pawn Variation, but people did not make a special study of this ambitious line because they were happy with the positions they got by simpler methods. Then suddenly everybody started playing the same move. I think Parma did it first, in Sarajevo 1970 against Mihaljcisin:

1	**P-K4**	**N-KB3**
2	**P-K5**	**N-Q4**
3	**P-Q4**	**P-Q3**
4	**P-QB4**	**N-N3**
5	**P-B4**	**P×P**
6	**BP×P**	**N-B3**
7	**B-K3**	**B-B4**
8	**N-QB3**	**P-K3**
9	**N-B3(!)**	**B-K2**
10	**P-Q5(!)**	**N-N5**
11	**R-B1!!**	......

White's choice of this move instead of the "natural" 11 N-Q4 faces Black with a new and difficult problem. Well, it was not new to me, but I had found it difficult for years. I had an emergency solution ready but never had to play it, since most opponents chose quiet lines like 4 N-KB3.

During the last four years more has happened in the Four Pawn Variation than in the preceding 25. I look at it now and then with interest, but I do little independent work on it. I am no expert on the Alekhine and I am not ready to do the necessary work to become one.

Around 1964 I became an "expert" on some museum openings such as the Vienna. That was easy; a grandmaster who played the Vienna Opening in three games was a leading expert! I played many more, with both the Vienna and the Bishop Opening (the latter often transposing into typical Vienna positions).

In October 1963 I finished my military service, during which I played little serious chess. But I had qualified for the Interzonal, Amsterdam 1964. I played in the Danish Championship in 1964, regarding it as a warm-up tournament for the Interzonal. And I played strange openings with great success. Look at Larsen-F. Petersen:

1	**P-K4**	**P-K4**
2	**B-B4**	**N-KB3**
3	**P-Q3**	**B-B4**
4	**N-QB3**	**P-Q3**
5	**Q-B3!?**	**N-B3**
6	**KN-K2**	**P-KR3**
7	**B-K3**	**B×B**
8	**P×B**	**N-QR4**
9	**B-N3**	**N×B**
10	**RP×N**	......

Two White pawns have captured toward the center!

10	......	**P-B3**

11	**O-O**	**O-O**
12	**N-N3**	**P-Q4**
13	**P×P**	**P×P**
14	**P-Q4**	**P×P**
15	**P×P**	......

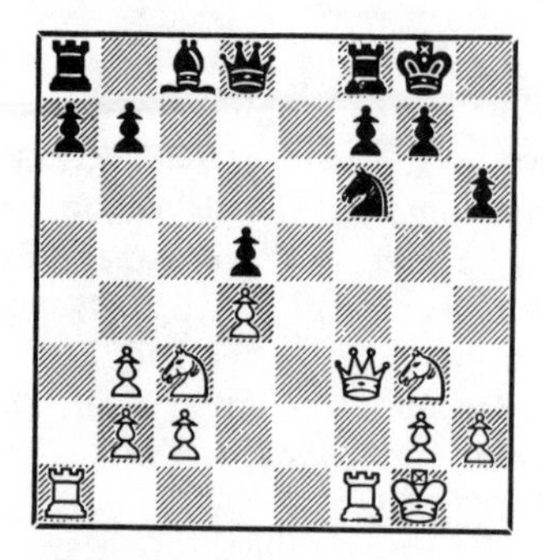

Note the isolated Black center pawn fixed on a square of the same color as his Bishop!

15	......	**B-K3**
16	**QR-K1**	**R-B1**
17	**R-K5**	......

White stands better. But what about 5 Q-B3? Well, it's not a bad move, and nobody knows what to do against it. Is White going to castle Queenside? Maybe. Is White going to advance his KNP? Could be.

For me, the Q-B3 idea began in Ostend in 1905! Very early in my chess career I became acquainted with the game Mieses-Tchigorin, which began:

1	**P-K4**	**P-K4**
2	**N-QB3**	**N-QB3**
3	**B-B4**	**B-B4**
4	**Q-N4!?**	**Q-B3??**
5	**N-Q5!**	......

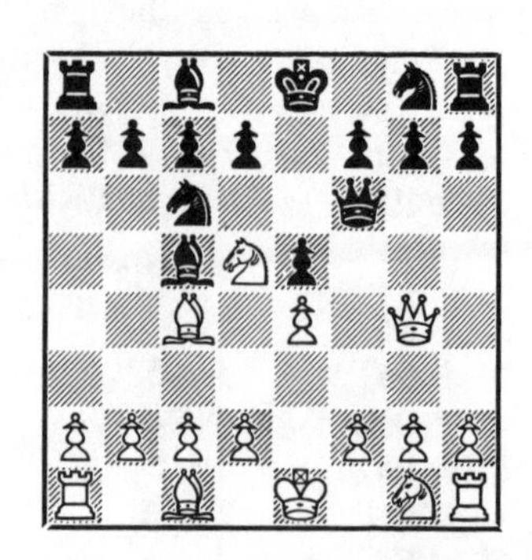

—and it's over, as detailed analysis reveals. This is a very nice trap. White's moves are correct, and the mistake 4 ... Q-B3 is very plausible. Among leading masters you cannot expect Black to fall into the trap, of course; most often he will play 4 ... P-KN3. Spielmann answered this with 5 Q-N3 several times, but 5 Q-B3 is probably stronger, for 5 ... Q-B3 6 N-Q5 Q×Q 7 N×Q obviously gives White the initiative, and after 5 ... N-B3 6 KN-K2 P-Q3 7 P-Q3 Black has weakened the black squares on his Kingside. (I didn't get the opportunity to play this against a grandmaster until Santa Monica 1966. Portisch did not find a completely satisfactory defense and lost.)

So I went to Amsterdam with a few new ideas in some very old openings, but I hadn't done much work on them. For instance, I didn't feel sure about this complicated variation:

1	**P-K4**	**P-K4**

2	N-QB3	N-KB3
3	B-B4	N×P
4	Q-R5	N-Q3
5	B-N3!?	N-B3!?
6	N-N5	P-KN3
7	Q-B3	P-B4
8	Q-Q5	Q-K2
9	N×Pch	K-Q1
10	N×R	P-N3

The Danish correspondence chess master Julius Nielsen believed Black's attacking chances to be insufficient (he later "proved" this several times), but I was not sure. What did I do? Against players who might go into this line I simply played 2 B-B4 N-KB3 3 P-Q3, normally transposing into a Vienna. But Berger played 3 ... P-Q4, which I considered an unjustified attempt by Black to seize the initiative. However, Lengyel is a peaceful man and would probably not play 3 ... N×P, so against him it was:

1	P-K4	P-K4
2	B-B4	N-KB3
3	N-QB3	N-B3
4	P-Q3	B-N5
5	N-B3	......

A Ruy Lopez reversed! White thinks the Black Bishop is misplaced.

5	......	P-Q3
6	O-O	B×N
7	P×B	N-QR4
8	B-N3	N×B
9	RP×N	......

Capturing toward the center!

9	......	O-O
10	P-B4	......

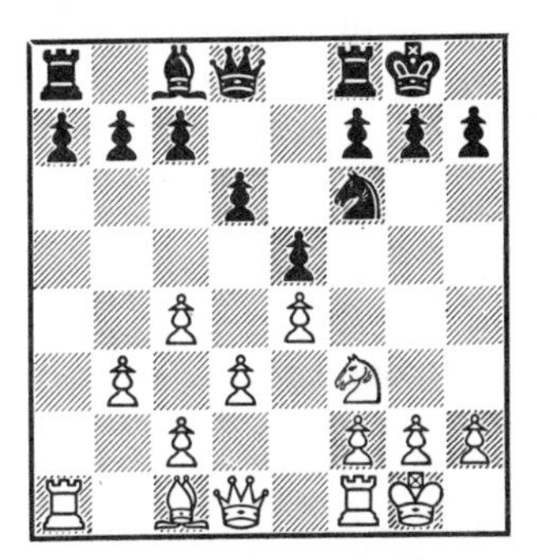

I do not believe that Black has equalized in this position, which I also got against Gligoric. Gligoric obtained a draw, Lengyel did not. (The games against Berger and Lengyel are in my book of *Selected Games.)*

It has been said that I added new ideas to these old openings by playing them in modern positional ways instead of with primitive attacking notions. This will be true every time a modern master handles an old opening. The Vienna and Bishop openings saved me a lot of work during my preparations for the Interzonal, and there and later they got me some valuable points. Because I have a reputation as an over-aggressive player it may have surprised some experts that I had the patience and the necessary technique to win a game like the one against Lengyel. Positionally I had a pleasant feeling of returning to my childhood darling, the King's Gambit. But the Vienna is slower, more subtle. In most modern variations of the Ruy Lopez White tries to get a space advantage by P-Q4. In the Vienna the Black KP is not so often attacked this way, and there are many opportunities to play a "King's Gambit without the P-KB4 pawn sacrifice." The King's Gambit Declined and the Vienna Opening have many positions, and even more ideas, in common. But no one has ever called the Vienna "powerful like a storm."

I experimented with another opening in the Danish Championship and won against three of the better players in 17, 21, and 26 moves, so I had to try it in the Interzonal!

1	**P-K4**	**P-QB4**
2	**P-KB4!?**	......

Not a move to occupy many pages in the books. Let me first show how the three games began. Round 3, Larsen-O. Jakobsen:

1	**P-K4**	**P-QB4**
2	**P-KB4**	**N-QB3**
3	**N-KB3**	**P-K3**
4	**B-N5**	**KN-K2**
5	**O-O**	......

Later 5 P-Q4 became popular in this position. Now Jakobsen should have played 5 ... P-Q4!

5	......	**P-QR3**
6	**B-K2**	**P-Q4**
7	**P-Q3**	**P×P?**

Very bad. Black's Q3 is weak, and his King Knight is misplaced. He underestimates the dangers in the position, either because he gets the Queens off the board or because White has played a "harmless" opening.

8	**P×P**	**Q×Q**
9	**R×Q**	**N-KN1**
10	**N-B3**	**B-Q2**

11	**B-K3**	**R-Q1**
12	**K-B1**	**P-QN4**
13	**P-K5**	**KN-K2**

Desperation, and rightly so.

14	**B×BP**	**N-Q4**
15	**N×N**	**B×B**

Without check, the reason for White's twelfth!

16	**N-B7ch**	....

—and White won. But that was the longest game!

Round 5, Larsen-B. Andersen:

1	**P-K4**	**P-QB4**
2	**P-KB4**	**N-QB3**
3	**N-KB3**	**N-B3!?**
4	**P-Q3**	**P-K3**
5	**P-B4!?**	**P-Q4**
6	**BP×P!?**	**P×P**
7	**P-K5**	**N-KN5**
8	**P-KR3**	**N-R3**
9	**P-KN4**	......

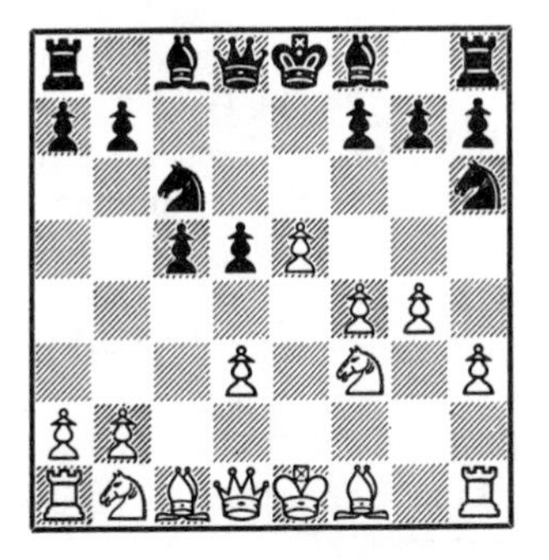

A very ambitious plan by White, in rather unexplored territory. Black has played aggressively; 7 ... N-KN1 would have been safer. But Black's next move is a mistake—much too optimistic!

9	......	**N-Q5?**
10	**B-N2**	**Q-R4ch**
11	**B-Q2**	**Q-N4**
12	**N-B3**	**Q×QP**
13	**N×N**	**P×N**
14	**N×P**	......

Winning, already.

14	......	**B-Q2**
15	**N-B7ch**	**K-Q1**
16	**N×R**	**B-N5**
17	**Q-K2**	......

Not 17 B×B Q-N6ch 18 K-B1 B-N4ch 19 K-N1 Q-K6ch 20 K-R2 Q×BPch, with perpetual check.

17	......	**Q-N6ch**
18	**K-B1**	**N×P**
19	**P×N**	**B×P**
20	**Q-B4**	**B×B**
21	**Q-B7ch**	**Resigns**

Round 9, Larsen *vs.* Brinck-Claussen:

1	**P-K4**	**P-QB4**
2	**P-KB4**	**P-K3**
3	**N-KB3**	**P-Q4**
4	**B-N5ch**	**B-Q2**
5	**B×Bch**	**Q×B**
6	**N-K5!**	......

6	......	**Q-B2**

If 6 ... Q-Q1 7 P×P P×P 8 Q-K2 winning a pawn, or 7 ... Q×P 8 Q-K2 with better development.

7	**P×P**	**P×P**
8	**N-QB3**	**N-KB3**
9	**Q-B3**	**Q-Q1(?)**

If 9 ... P-Q5 10 N-Q5 N×N 11 Q×N N-B3 12 N×N with a bad but not hopeless position for Black.

10	**Q-K2!**	**B-K2**
11	**Q-N5ch**	**QN-Q2**
12	**Q×NP**	**R-QN1**
13	**Q×RP**	**Q-B1**
14	**Q-R4**	**O-O**
15	**O-O**	**N-N3**
16	**Q-N5**	**N-B5(?)**
17	**N×QP!**	**Resigns**

Brinck-Claussen fell into something I had looked at. 5 ... Q×B is a mistake. After 5 ... N×B! I intended the quiet 6 P-Q3, trying to prove that it is bad for Black to obstruct his King Bishop on the first move! Also, White may try to prove an advantage in space on the Kingside, which is always helpful. But the Black position is solid. 4 ... N-Q2 may be playable, but after 5 P×P P×P 6 O-O Black has problems.

Some of these ideas came from a variation which in Holland is called the Vinken System: 1 P-K4 P-QB4 2 N-QB3 N-QB3 3 P-B4. In Denmark it was often played by C. Poulsen, a master of the attack without much knowledge of opening theory. White often plays his Bishop to QN5 and exchanges it for the Black Knight, and then starts something on the Kingside. It looks like a Nimzo-Indian Reversed if Black plays P-Q4, but White has played his pawn to K4 in one step instead of two and has one or two tempos more than Black in some quite satisfactory Nimzo-Indian lines. In recent years Zinn and other East German masters have had good results with this system. Similar ideas have been tried by Black against the English Opening, but after 1 P-QB4 P-K4 2 N-QB3 P-KB4 3 P-Q4 is considered strong.

I wanted to play something like the Vinken System, but in some lines the Queen Knight was wrong on QB3. So, 1 P-K4 P-QB4 2 P-KB4, and if Black played 2 ... P-Q4 3 P×P Q×P 4 N-QB3 Q-Q1 I would try to prove that my lead in development meant something. This was never played against me: most masters feel it may be good with a tempo more (3 P-Q4 in the English) but that Black must not lose so much time. So a nice positional idea is to prepare P-Q4 with P-K3, which was why I had analyzed Brinck-Claussen's continuation.

In Amsterdam, Peres played like Jakobsen (1 P-K4 P-QB4 2 P-KB4 N-QB3 3 N-KB3 P-K3 4 B-N5) but then 4 ... P-KN3 4 B×N QP×B. I like this kind of position very much. Black can do nothing on the Queenside and I am going to attack him on the Kingside (see my book). My willingness to give up the Bishop pair and double my opponent's pawns probably shows an indirect influence from Nimzovich, who lived his last twelve years in Denmark. Of course, we are looking at an opening which, like the Nimzo-Indian, you cannot dream of playing if you have a very hot relationship with your Bishops.

Even Larry Evans accepted the doubled pawn, but in a more tolerable form:

1	**P-K4**	**P-QB4**
2	**P-KB4**	**N-QB3**
3	**N-KB3**	**P-KN3**
4	**B-N5**	**B-N2**
5	**O-O**	**N-B3**
6	**B×N**	**NP×B!**
7	**Q-K2**	**O-O**
8	**P-Q3**	**P-Q3**

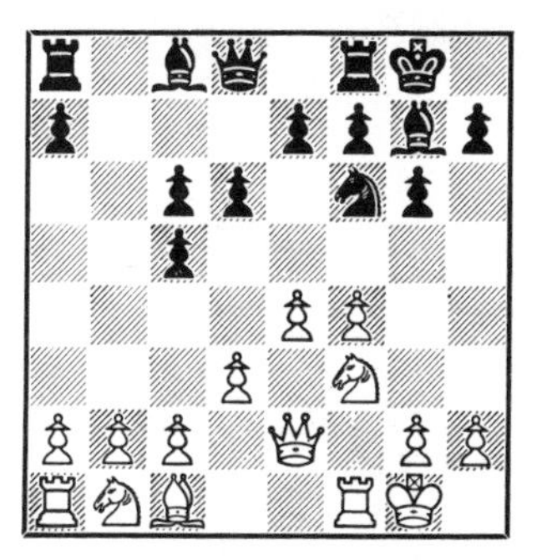

Though I like the White position, I would not feel unhappy with Black. Evans played well and drew. Of course, if Black prefers, he can avoid the doubled pawn, for example, 4 ... Q-B2 5 P-Q3 P-QR3 6 B×N Q×B, but White gets a lead in development and, consequently, attacking chances.

It is interesting to compare this with a variation of the English (Ree-Larsen, Teesside 1972):

1	**P-QB4**	**P-KB4**
2	**N-QB3**	**N-KB3**
3	**P-KN3**	**P-K4**
4	**B-N2**	**B-N5**
5	**Q-B2!**	......

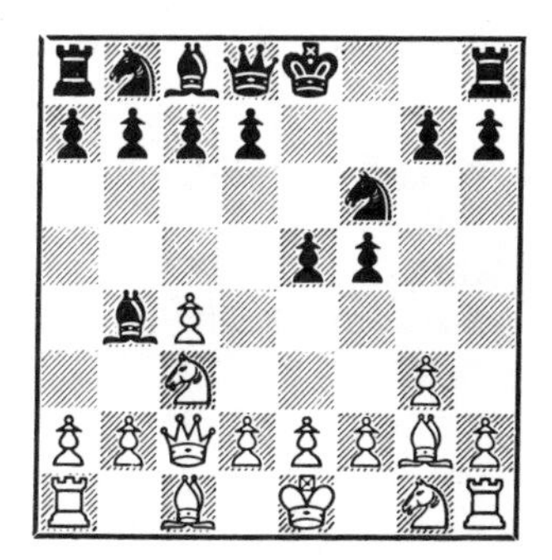

White's extra tempo becomes two tempos! Black cannot play 5 . . . P-Q3? because of 6 Q-R4ch.

5	......	**B×N**
6	**Q×B**	**P-Q3**
7	**P-K3**	**O-O**
8	**N-K2**	**Q-K1**
9	**P-N3**	**N-B3**
10	**B-N2**	......

Most masters would be reluctant to take the Black pieces now. I did not like it much myself, played badly, and was lucky to draw.

Tal, finally, played Pachman's recommendation:

1	**P-K4**	**P-QB4**
2	**P-KB4**	**N-KB3**
3	**P-Q3**	**P-Q4**
4	**P-K5**	**N-N1!**

Pachman now gave 5 N-KB3 B-N5, and a game he played in Bucharest 1949: 5 P-B3 N-QB3 6 B-K3 P-K3 7 N-B3 N-R3 8 P-KN3 N-B4 9 B-B2 P-KR4. The latter I did not like at all. But if I was not going to play P-Q4, was the first alternative so terrible? Of course, I could begin with 5 B-K2. But I played:

5	**N-KB3**	**B-N5**
6	**B-K2**	**P-K3**
7	**O-O**	**N-K2**
8	**P-B4!?**	**QN-B3**
9	**N-B3**	**P×P**
10	**P×P**	**N-B4**

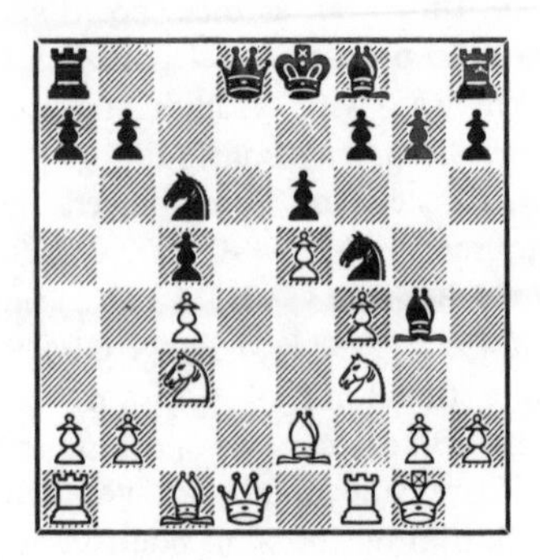

11	**Q-R4**	**N-Q5**
12	**N×N**	**Q×Nch**
13	**R-B2**	**B×B**
14	**N×B**	**Q-Q6**
15	**P-B5!**	**B-K2!**

This led to a short sharp struggle and then a peaceful draw. But wouldn't it be a little naive for another player to repeat these first ten moves against me? Bednarski did (Majorca 1967), and got punished. After 11 P-KR3! B×N 12 B×B the White KB is very strong, and 12 . . . Q-Q5ch 13 Q×Q P×Q? 14 N-K4 B-K2 15 P-B5 P-B3 16 N-Q6ch K-Q2 17 P-QN4! led to a winning position for White. 13 . . . N/4×Q would have been better, but after 14 B-K4 Black has a difficult game.

So I had a few ideas after 1 P-K4 P-QB4 2 P-KB4, but I didn't spend too much time on them. Without much work I had a repertoire to use against the many participants in that tournament who answered 1 P-K4 with P-K4 or P-QB4.

I didn't stick to it; against Ivkov

I played a normal Sicilian with 2 N-KB3 and 3 P-Q4—and lost!

Finding the Holes

What is this thing called theory? Partly it is just a collection of the first so-many moves of so-many games, followed by "with a slight edge for White" or "with good attacking chances" or "with compensation for the pawn." Or in modern computer style we have = and + − and such symbols. Some players learn a lot of variations by heart and repeat them in play whenever possible. But their opponents may be so ignorant or unkind that they step "out of the book" long before that wonderful advantage-for-me sign has been reached. I remember a young player who said he had lost three years of his life studying the Najdorf! He realized that he had learned variations, not chess.

On the other hand, it is perhaps overly simple to say that you must learn the ideas behind the openings. This kind of simplification can be continued until you reach the principle that the idea in playing chess is to win! But the trouble with chess is the opponent: if you know only the "ideas behind the openings," and he knows the ideas *and* a lot of variations, he is likely to beat you. So opening books will still be written and printed and read; and they will be misunderstood by some and understood by others.

How should you study opening theory? This can be as difficult to answer as the questions of theory themselves. I have described part of the development of my opening repertoire; maybe you can find useful hints there. If four examples leave you cold, the fifth one may teach you something. It is all study material, and that goes for those impressive theory books, too (they are incomplete and full of errors, but don't blame the authors too much, for their job is impossible).

In some very sharp variations the truth is found after a few games or a few years, especially when there are sacrificial attacks. Everyone is ready to sacrifice a lot of pieces if it leads to mate, but who wants to give up a Rook for nothing? Or even a pawn? So White wins two brilliant games and they get published everywhere: what a fine sacrifice! Ten or twenty masters find a defense and one of them uses this "secret" to win with Black, and suddenly nobody wants to play the fine sacrifice. Two or three lines in the books, problem solved, end of story. Many players have such secrets and are willing to reveal them for a very reasonable price: one point! Do not expect active grandmasters to write everything they know. It is good to be a writer, but who wants to reveal how he plans to beat Portisch next time?

To find "the only move" in a critical position does not always solve all problems. For example, the following variation is still under discussion:

1	**P-K4**	**P-QB4**
2	**N-KB3**	**P-K3**
3	**P-Q4**	**P×P**
4	**N×P**	**N-QB3**
5	**N-QB3**	**P-Q3**
6	**B-K3**	**N-B3**
7	**B-QB4**	**B-K2**
8	**Q-K2**	......

Many years ago Velimirovic recommended that the Yugoslav team play this system in the annual match against the Russians, but it was rejected as being too sharp!

8	......	**P-QR3**
9	**B-N3**	**Q-B2**
10	**O-O-O**	**N-QR4**
11	**P-N4**	**P-QN4**
12	**P-N5**	**N×Bch**
13	**RP×N**	**N-Q2**
14	**N-B5!?**	......

With this sacrifice Velimirovic won two games around 1965, so people started looking at other defenses for Black instead of 10 ... N-QR4. But in many variations of the Sicilian I like the idea of postponing O-O for Black in order to render an early White pawn storm harmless. So I didn't give up the variation.

14	......	**P×N**
15	**N-Q5**	**Q-Q1**
16	**P×P**	**B-N2**
17	**P-B6**	**P×P**
18	**KR-K1**	**B×N**
19	**R×B**	......

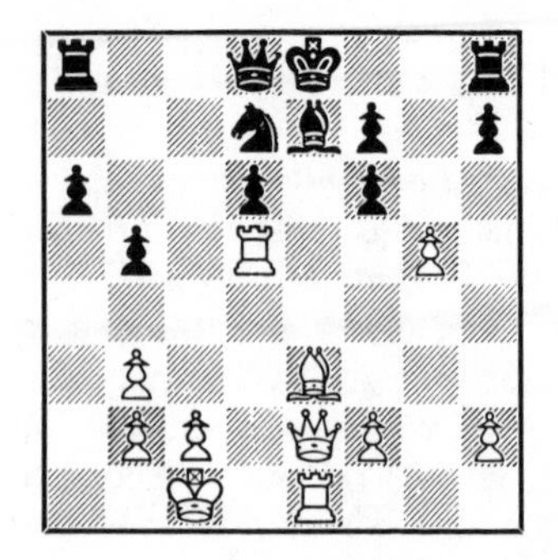

In this position, analysis by Velimirovic and others pretty much convinced me that White's attack was too strong after 19 ... O-O or 19 ... N-K4. Were there other moves for Black? Yes, plenty. Just to mention three: R-QB1, K-B1, and R-KN1. I looked at them and concluded that 19 ... R-KN1 was best and probably led to a decisive advantage for Black! I showed it to my teammates before the Havana Olympiad in 1966, but we did not get the opportunity to play it. Then I showed it to Hamann, and, at the Zonal Tournament, 1967, he beat Grandmaster Gheorghiu with it. Later many suggestions were made for White, but no clear continuation of the attack was found. Even so, such a respected theoretician as Boleslavsky wrote in an article that the Black position must be bad. But no analysis! He just explained that Bronstein felt that the White attack was more than enough compensation for the sacrificed Knight. Well, then it becomes a question of who is ready to sacrifice that Knight and rely on Bronstein's feelings. My readiness to take the Black position was shown in the last round of the Vinkovci tournament, 1970, against Minic. Minic sacrificed on move 14 —but offered a draw on move 16! At that moment my two closest rivals had just drawn and I was winner of the tournament by half a point, so across the board came my hand, though I was a little sad not to prove in practical play that 19 . . . R-KN1 is a good defense. The two rivals were Hort and—Bronstein! And up to the table rushed Velimirovic, trying to prove that after 19 . . . R-KN1 "White mates in a few moves." But there was something wrong with one of his variations.

But how did I find R-KN1, you ask. Is it such a strange move? The Rook moves to a half-open file which in many continuations will be opened by White's P×P. (Example: 20 B-Q2 K-B1 21 B-R5 Q×B 22 Q×Bch K-N2 23 R-K3 QR-K1!? 24 P×Pch? K-R1 25 Q×R N×P!) And apart from K-B1-N2-R1 there are possibilities of getting the King to KN1 after R-N2 or R-N3 or R×P. So I tried to find a win for White, and when I failed I thought that others might do the same, over the board especially. Seven years later they are probably still trying in Moscow, Belgrade, Budapest, and New York. Have fun!

Let me add that I did not find a White win against 19 . . . K-B1 either. But as the King had to return to its original square in many variations I found it more logical to look seriously at the Rook move first, and the more I looked the better I liked it. It is good to have two defenses, but in one game you can only play one of them. I did not expect to get the opportunity twice; if I won one game with this line it would quickly become known in all the important chess centers.

Maybe the most important part of my analysis was my first glance at the position. I refused to believe that Black was lost. Looking at the position I felt there must be a defense, and looking at the previous play I liked all of Black's moves! Not trying to find a defense for Black would have meant admitting that something was wrong with my concept of chess strategy.

The next example is different. Wade-Reshevsky, Buenos Aires 1960, was quoted in many theoretical articles:

1	**P-Q4**	**N-KB3**
2	**P-QB4**	**P-KN3**
3	**N-QB3**	**B-N2**
4	**P-K4**	**P-Q3**
5	**N-B3**	**O-O**
6	**B-K2**	**P-K4**
7	**O-O**	**N-B3**
8	**P-Q5**	**N-K2**
9	**N-K1**	**N-Q2**
10	**P-B3**	**P-KB4**
11	**P-KN4**	**......**

An interesting idea: after 11 . . . P-B5 12 P-KR4 White can keep the

Kingside completely closed (except for incorrect piece sacrifices by Black). White's space advantage on the other flank then offers some winning chances.

11 ...... P-KR4!?

Very sharp! Black doesn't care for a position without any play on the Kingside.

12 P-N5 P-R5
13 N-Q3 P-B5

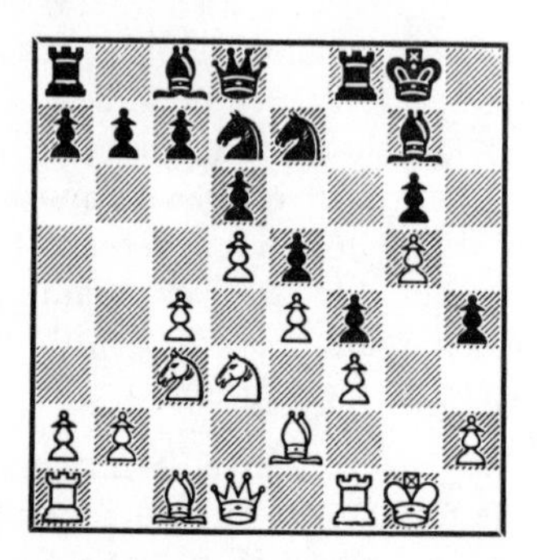

Black has isolated White's KNP. The game continuation was 14 Q-K1 K-B2, but White did not play 15 Q×P, because he saw that 15 . . . R-R1 would win the White KNP. This game was quoted by many theoreticians as showing a good method for Black, and nobody pointed out that 14 Q-K1 was a meaningless move if White was not going to play Q×P. White did not force Black to play K-B2; Black wanted to play that, planning to win that White pawn with R-R1-R4 and N-KN1, and if necessary B-KB1-K2. These maneuvers had to begin with K-B2!

But when you write an article about this variation of the King's Indian it is pleasant to have a good medicine against 11 P-KN4. Reshevsky beat Wade, so you give about eighteen moves of that game and write something about good prospects for Black and proceed to problems you consider more important. You go by the result of the game!

I don't believe I was the only player to discover this hole in existing theory in 1965. But I got the opportunity to play the line in my first match game against Tal. Less than a month before, 11 . . . P-KR4 got a "!" in an article in the Russian *Shakhmatny Biulletin.* After 13 . . . P-B5 I played

14 K-R1! ......

with great satisfaction. As expected Tal continued

14 ...... K-B2

and after

15 P-B5! ......

he probably felt almost lost already. 15 . . . P×P 16 Q-N3 K-K1 17 Q-B4 P-N3 18 P-N4 gives White a strong attack, and Black has no time to pick up that annoying White KNP. Tal did not play 15 . . . P×P, but his position was bad. White's action on the Queenside was well under way and it was impossible for Black to concentrate on winning a pawn on the other side. Since 1965 no grandmaster has played 11 . . .

P-KR4. Theory now gives it a "?".

I think I have already described the most important phase of this discovery. 14 Q-K1 was obviously wrong, so I had to find something better or abandon the whole variation! 14 K-R1 is a natural move, preparing R-KN1. Not only will the Rook protect the KNP, it also makes room for B-B1-R3. An exchange of the white-squared Bishops is obviously favorable for White in this position. All this looks like a good idea—and maybe Wade got it during the game! For when he decided not to play 15 Q×P he played 15 K-R1, but precious time had been wasted.

So you find 14 K-R1 but realize that after 14 ... K-B2 15 R-KN1 R-R1 16 B-B1 N-B1 White cannot exchange those Bishops: 17 N-B2 P-R6! and Black is ready to play R-R4 and N-R2, when White cannot hold the KNP. But after 14 ... K-B2, isn't the Black King a bit exposed? Then, the idea 15 P-B5 is not hard to find. In fact, even this happened later in the Wade-Reshevsky game. It looks fine. You go back and look at other moves for Black—maybe 14 ... P-N3 or 14 ... P-R4 to slow down the White Queenside action? Yes, but then 15 R-KN1 is strong, preparing B-B1-R3. Black has no time for K-B2, R-R1, and P-R6. His position is a mess, and White's action on the Queenside will come with great effect a little later.

This analysis was not very difficult: a master game with an obvious error, plus a little common sense and some ideas from that game. Maybe other masters had done this, but obviously not Tal. And how could he know that I would play a variation I had never played before? There was little time for preparations before the match. Maybe "Mischa" trusted that article; but maybe he had not seen it at all!

A special type of error is, of course, the misprint! Sometimes it's easy to detect; for example, when a move contains letters not normally used in English notation. But look at this analysis by Boleslavsky:

1	**P-Q4**	**N-KB3**
2	**P-QB4**	**P-KN3**
3	**N-QB3**	**P-Q4**
4	**P×P**	**N×P**
5	**P-K4**	**N×N**
6	**P×N**	**P-QB4**
7	**B-QB4**	**B-N2**
8	**N-K2**	**P×P**
9	**P×P**	**N-B3**
10	**B-K3**	**O-O**
11	**O-O**	**N-R4**
12	**B-Q3**	**P-N3**
13	**R-B1**	**P-K3**
14	**Q-Q2**	**B-N2**
15	**B-KR6**	......

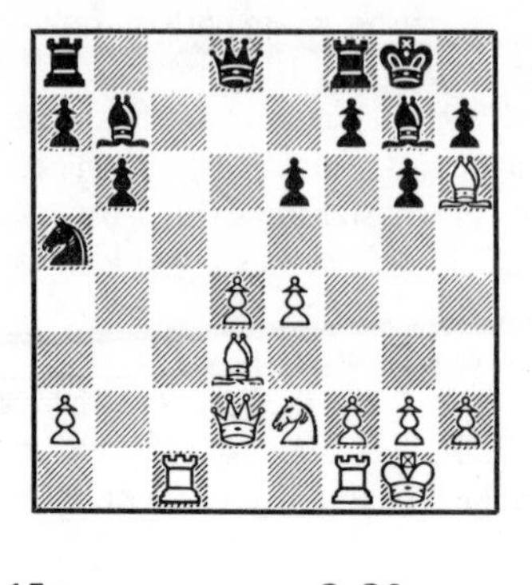

15	......	**Q-Q2**
16	**B×B**	**K×B**
17	**Q-B4**	**QR-B1**
18	**P-KR4**	**N-B3**
19	**P-R5**	**P-K4**

— "with sufficient counterplay." Chess magazines all over the world got letters from proud readers who had discovered that Boleslavsky had overlooked a mate in three (20 P-R6ch and 21 Q-B6, etc.).

Nonsense! The error is Black's fifteenth: the move is 15 ... Q-K2, of course. (In algebraic notation it said Qd7, where Qe7 was intended.) Maybe Boleslavsky mistyped or miswrote it and nobody caught the mistake; maybe the typesetter was guilty. But you can be sure that Boleslavsky did not analyze with 15 ... Q-Q2 in mind, for several reasons. First, it looks bad! White is attacking some black squares around the Black King; why shouldn't the Black Queen continue to protect them? Second, if the Black Queen is on Q2, why doesn't White play 17 P-KR4, why does he prepare it with Q-B4? Because the Black Queen is on K2!

I am not saying that the books never overlook mates in three. Mates in one have been overlooked in opening analysis in respected books, as have all kinds of simple combinations. If these misprints and oversights cost you valuable points it won't help you to sue the authors or printers or publishers. Just blame yourself and be a better reader next time! There are such mistakes in all books on the openings.

The Fight for the Initiative

Let us look at an opening like the Gruenfeld. Let's imagine that you know nothing about it, but a friend tells you what a wonderful opening it is, with sharp play from the start; that often Black gets the initiative; and that for a player like you it is just the right weapon against Queen Pawn openings. In an hour he shows you the most important lines. He concentrates on 4 P×P, and he also explains something about 4 B-N5: it's been popular for some time but is not dangerous, and he shows you a good continuation against it. About the other lines he says just a few words, and you have little time to study theory books. However, you like what the Austrian grandmaster invented just after World War I, and the day comes when you try it in a tournament for the first time. You don't know your opponent well, but your rating is a little better than his. He plays 1

P-Q4; now is the moment!

1	**P-Q4**	**N-KB3**
2	**P-QB4**	**P-KN3**
3	**N-QB3**	**P-Q4**

This is it, you're a Gruenfeld player now. He will probably play 4 P×P and 5 P-K4, and oh boy, are you going to attack that center! Yes, but the game continues:

4	**B-B4**	**B-N2**
5	**P-K3**	......

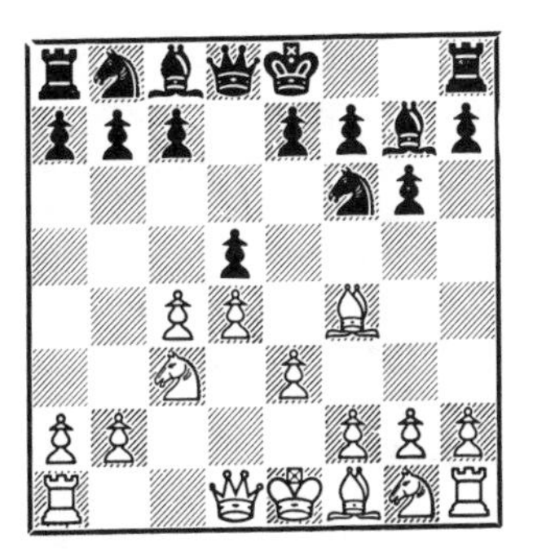

This is not dangerous for Black, you know that. Your friend said that after 5 ... O-O 6 P×P N×P 7 N×N Q×N 8 B×P Black gets a lot of compensation for the pawn. But are you sure? And how does Black continue? Maybe you should study this a bit before you give away that pawn. On the other hand, 5 ... P-B3 is not in the true aggressive spirit of the opening. You want to play the Gruenfeld, not the timid Schlechter Variation of the Slav—oh, now you remember, your friend said that if you don't want to sacrifice the pawn you can play 5 ... P-B4 at once, instead of 5... O-O with the idea of 6 ... P-B4. So you continue:

5	......	**P-B4**
6	**P×BP**	**Q-R4**
7	**P×P**	**N×P**
8	**Q×N**	**B×Nch**

You know that 5 ... P-B4 is playable, and you feel you have been playing forced moves since then. Must be OK.

9	**P×B**	**Q×Pch**
10	**K-K2**	**Q×R**
11	**B-K5**	......

Oh!

11	......	**Q-B8**
12	**B×R**	**B-K3**
13	**Q×P**	......

A primitive type who grabs everything! But you soon realize that you have to draw by perpetual check with 13 ... Q-B7ch. Against a player you thought you could beat you have lost half a point. If you had known that after 5 ... P-B4 White could force a draw, you would have played something else. In fact, you have played a variation that was used several times to draw in less than 30 moves during the years when FIDE tried to make peace-loving masters "work" with that special rule.*

*For a few years in the 1960's, there was a FIDE rule which "prohibited" a drawn game in less than 30 moves. The rule proved unworkable and was later dropped.

It is all true, what your friend told you about the Gruenfeld. It is a wonderful opening. But Black can fight so energetically for the initiative only if he knows a lot of variations thoroughly.

The Stonewall is entirely different. Nothing dramatic happens at first: you can play the first seven moves in your sleep, if White develops normally:

1	**P-Q4**	**P-KB4**
2	**P-KN3**	**N-KB3**
3	**B-N2**	**P-K3**
4	**N-KB3**	**B-K2**
5	**P-B4**	**P-Q4**
6	**O-O**	**O-O**
7	**N-B3**	**P-B3**

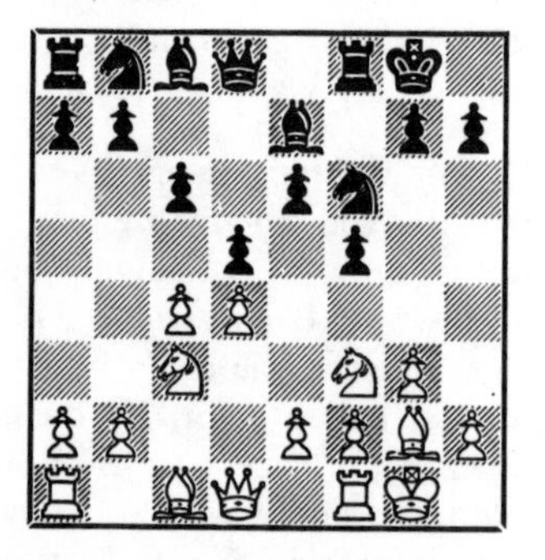

Solid, rock solid. Is this the answer to Black's dreams if he has little time for opening theory? For some players it may be, though it is a little discomforting that most experts think White has a small but clear positional advantage. Something about holes in the Black position, something about a nightmarish ending with a White Knight against Black's Queen Bishop. But tell the experts that when Botvinnik was young he got very good results with Black. Maybe the best players nowadays handle the White pieces a little better than Flohr, Capablanca and Reshevsky did. Maybe. But do your opponents? And isn't it true that Spassky, Ivkov and Larsen play the Stonewall now and then, and with good results?

The Stonewall can be played not only against 1 P-Q4 but against 1 N-KB3 and 1 P-QB4. Though some may call it primitive it is a fine solution to many of Black's problems. But some difficulties remain. First of all, the Stonewall is not so good if White does not fianchetto his KB! It is very much against this Bishop that Black's strategy is directed. So if White is not a fianchetto man you are probably wise to have another system ready. (Not all Stonewall fans will agree.) Second, in the move order given above Black must not fall off his chair if White plays the Staunton Gambit with 2 P-K4. And third, some experts think the Stonewall is a bad choice for ordinary players because it kills their imagination! There is some truth in this. Many Stonewall players automatically play Q-K1-KR4 and try to start some kind of attack against the White King. If their opponents are weak enough they succeed, but it all becomes routine. However, if you study some master games you will find that Black has other possibilities. Sometimes it is not the

Queen but the Queen Bishop that goes to KR4! Sometimes Black fianchettoes that problem child. Sometimes Black starts an action on the Queenside.

And so on. Chess is not an easy game. If you like the Stonewall, play it.

During the last three or four years the Benko Gambit has become quite popular. For some players this is almost the ideal defense against 1 P-Q4. But there is a problem here, similar to that with the Stonewall: If you play it very often, can you still get fresh ideas? For many moves Black has few opportunities for independent thinking. For example:

1	**P-Q4**	**N-KB3**
2	**P-QB4**	**P-B4**
3	**P-Q5**	**P-QN4!?**

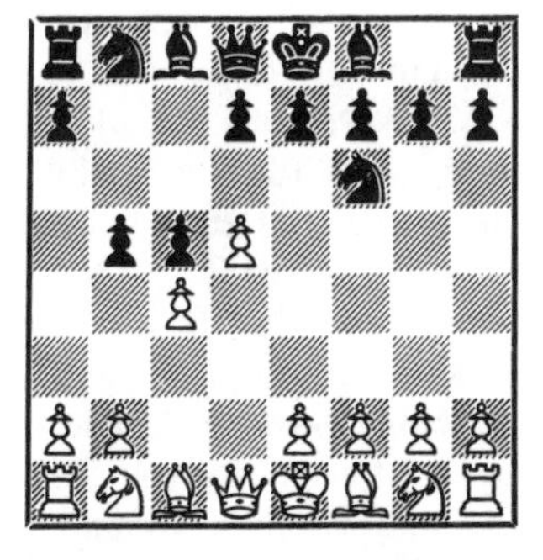

4	**P×P**	**P-QR3**
5	**P×P**	**B×P**
6	**N-QB3**	**P-Q3**
7	**N-B3**	**P-N3**
8	**P-KN3**	**......**

Many are more afraid of 8 N-Q2 B-KN2 9 P-K4, or 7 P-K4, but Black always gets some play for the pawn.

8	**......**	**B-KN2**
9	**B-N2**	**O-O**
10	**O-O**	**QN-Q2**
11	**Q-B2**	**......**

White has other moves at his disposal on his eleventh turn, such as 11 R-N1 and 11 R-K1, but Black has little choice. Depending on White's moves Black must now try to find out, for the hundredth time perhaps, if his Queen goes best to B2, N3, or R4. When he has solved this eternal problem he can return to routineland for a moment. His next move will probably be KR-N1; only then does the game really start. Some players find it boring to play the same first twelve moves over and over again; others don't mind. Some are even happy: if they can play these moves quickly there is less danger of serious time pressure. (The nasty part of me thinks this is why Benko likes the gambit—ten moves for a pawn!) Being a pawn down keeps many players awake. A gambit never becomes sheer routine as long as you fear you may lose the King and pawn ending!

I am not arguing against the Benko Gambit: I recommend it and sometimes play it. A couple of years ago a friend asked me about a variation of the King's Indian which he intended to play in a local tournament. His strength is probably that of a B player, but I soon found out that his understanding of the King's Indian was well below that. In half an hour I taught him the Benko Gambit, and he liked it and played it with great success. This is one of the openings I am thinking of when I say that if you are not afraid of unclear pawn sacrifices you should have no opening problems. (And this book is not about the endings.)

If you study modern opening theory you may well conclude that if Black does not want to have to defend carefully during the first part of the game he must give White something: more space, healthier pawn structure, the Bishop pair—or simply a pawn! In many variations of the King's Indian White has more space; in the Nimzo-Indian Black must be willing to give Bishop for Knight; in the Tarrasch Defense against the Queen's Gambit Black accepts an isolated center pawn; and so on. By playing openings with such a sharp struggle for initiative you slowly get an understanding of these problems. How much should you be ready to pay for the initiative? You cannot find the exact answer in the books, for your question is not "Who stands better?" or "Is this 100 percent correct?" You must know yourself, and you must study your own play and results. What type of play do you like? Are you patient? A good defender? Or are you only at home in the attack?

If you are a good defensive player, don't pay anything for the initiative! Your opponent will probably overreach himself if you defend well for a couple of hours. But are you sure you are such a good defender? Under master level they are rather scarce, as they were at the top level a hundred years ago, before Steinitz. But if you are one of those rare ones, just play a solid defense with Black. But don't do the same with White unless you know Black is ready to pay a high price for the initiative! For strange psychological reasons people are more careless with White than with Black. Do you remember the Candidates' Tournament, Yugoslavia 1959? It was a race between Tal and Keres, and Tal won. But Keres scored 12 points in 14 games playing Black, and only 7 points — 50 percent — playing White! This looks crazy. Had everyone prepared his Black openings better than his White ones? No, but with White everyone was a little too optimistic, a little too ambitious, and when they started sliding downhill they discovered it a bit too late.

If defensive play is your weakness, most of your opening problems are probably with Black. (But if it happens often that you play 1 P-QB4 and Black answers 1 ... P-K4 and wins with a Kingside attack—well, you should know one opening to avoid!) But don't get desperate! The Modern Benoni, the Gruenfeld, the Tarrasch, or the Benko Gambit may solve part of your problem. These openings can be recommended if you like them. But if you see yourself as a great romantic gambit player and are seduced by the charms of the Englund Gambit (1 P-Q4 P-K4?) or the Budapest Gambit (1 P-Q4 N-KB3 2 P-QB4 P-K4?!)—then I want to point out that these are only gambits if White wants them to be! If White clings to his extra pawn Black gets chances, but today it is not only the leading masters who know about giving back the pawn for better development or other advantages. The Budapest Gambit is much easier to play for White than for Black. If you make a special study of this opening you may now and then win a miniature against a weak opponent. Against even opposition you will get a little the worst of it. No minus pawn, no initiative; just a not-very-charming position where White is better placed in the center.

Better, but not very good, is the Albin Counter Gambit (1 P-Q4 P-Q4 2 P-QB4 P-K4?! 3 P×KP P-Q5), the opening Weaver Adams recommended for beating your neighbor. It is not quite correct, but it can lead to interesting play, often with O-O for White and O-O-O for Black, which can be dramatic. With good play White's attack comes first, but if you like the Black position and have studied theory and master games, go right ahead!

Against 1 P-K4, romantic or overaggressive players may feel tempted by openings like the Latvian Gambit, also called the Greco Counter Gambit (1 P-K4 P-K4 2 N-KB3 P-KB4?!), which is probably not 100 percent sound but can lead to interesting play—especially if White plays ambitiously. The trouble with this defense is that if White just makes normal moves he gets an advantage. Black is trying to give up a pawn for initiative, center, development, and so on, but if White refuses to win the pawn Black has to work hard to get a defensible position! I have some sympathy for this bold attempt to "refute" 2 N-KB3, but Black must know a lot of theory in order to get only a slightly inferior position, while White's job is comparatively easy even without deep knowledge of all the variations. As an occasional surprise weapon, the Latvian Gambit may be OK at under master level, but only for players who have studied it deeply. Few can spare that much time for an opening they only want to use two or three times a year.

Something similar can be said about the Schliemann Defense against the Ruy: 1 P-K4 P-K4 2 N-KB3 N-QB3 3 B-N5 P-B4?! Spassky and Tal played it in their youth and found a few new ideas. Matulovic has played it. So isn't this considered a correct defense by the grandmasters? No, not really. Black gives White a pleasant choice between some quiet lines which are good, and some very complicated lines which are probably even better. If White knows the complications thoroughly he goes into them; otherwise, he just plays a nice position with no problems. If he goes into 4 N-B3 P×P 5 QN×P P-Q4 6 N×P without knowing any analysis, then he would probably have lost no matter which opening Black played. White can get a position without complications with 4 P-Q3. This line is considered easy to play against the King's Gambit now, and with a tempo extra White should not be nervous.

At least the word "gambit" still has a romantic sound, a special attraction. There are other defenses or counterattacks that suffer from the same defects as the gambits above: it is too easy for White to play against them. For the average amateur it should not be significant if a variation is only 95 percent correct. The vital question is: Will the opponent be able to find the refutation over the board? Here is an example, an ambitious line for Black against the Ruy. (Alekhine once played it, so it *must* be good, right? Wrong!)

1	**P-K4**	**P-K4**
2	**N-KB3**	**N-QB3**
3	**B-N5**	**B-B4**
4	**P-B3**	**Q-B3?!**

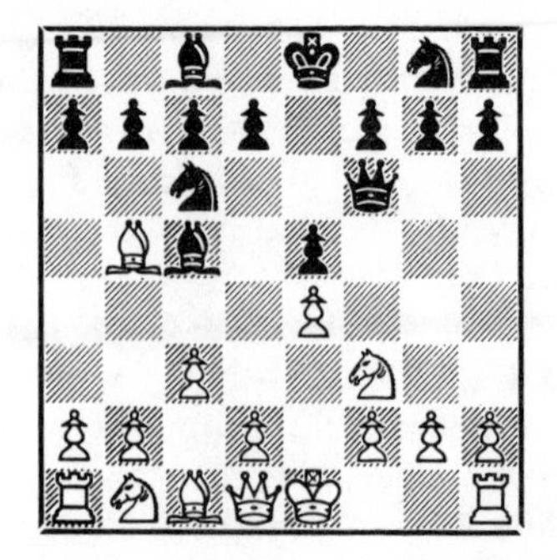

I like it, as you will understand when you have seen some of my strange Queen moves for White in the Vienna. Some of those positions look like a Ruy with colors reversed. There is just the difference of one tempo, but it is a decisive difference! Sometimes a tempo means only the difference between good and merely playable, but here it means the difference between good and unplayable. Alekhine's opponent did not play 5 P-Q4! But what White should do is think: If I cannot play P-Q4, my P-B3 was a stupid move—but P-B3 is a good book move, and Q-B3 is not even mentioned! If it stopped P-Q4 it would be the main line. Then White has to see one simple trick: 5 P-Q4 P×P 6 P-K5 N×P? 7 Q-K2! winning a piece. Maybe he sees no more than this: he plays P-Q4 and feels good; he is refuting an unsound opening and building a strong center. Black does not lose a piece but plays:

5	**P-Q4**	**P×P**
6	**P-K5**	**Q-N3**
7	**P×P**	**N×QP!?**

White had not seen this, but if he keeps his head he will still feel he is on the right track, because if Black's play were correct this would be a well-known and popular variation.

8 N×N **Q-N3**

This is Black's third Queen move, and he still cannot castle, and what about his Queenside development? White looks at 9 P-K6 and 9 N-B5, but both are unclear. What about some more development? He finds:

9 B-K3 **B×N**
10 Q×B **Q×B**
11 N-B3 ......

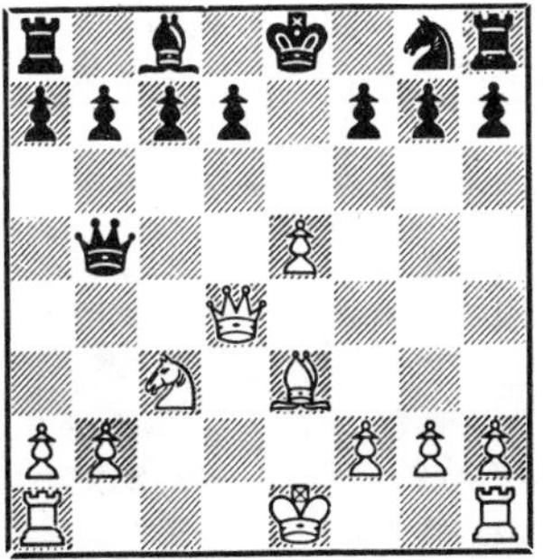

Black is a pawn up, but he's in trouble. If you think Black's position is tenable, play it and you'll learn something! It is not necessary for White to be a genius to reach this position after 4 . . . Q-B3.

I still like 4 . . . Q-B3, or the idea at least, but I don't play it. I don't often play a move I know how to refute. Twice a year maybe, and even then a move which I think my opponent would be able to refute only in correspondence chess.

Of course, 4 . . . Q-B3 violates a well-known rule: Do not bring your Queen into play too early. A very good rule indeed, but how early is too early? Was White's P-B3 such a wonderful developing move? No, but it planned P-Q4, and the Queen move deserves to be looked at because it's an attempt to stop P-Q4 and refute P-B3. It just doesn't work.

This reminds me of a rule I know very well because I made it up: When you are caught in an opening you don't know, play healthy developing moves!

Normally, early Queen moves are not "healthy developing moves." I am tempted to say about such moves what Gligoric has said about taking one of those "poisoned" pawns: Even when it's good, don't do it! But let me repeat, I am talking about positions where you do not know what theory says.

As everyone knows, there are many variations of the Sicilian where Black makes a Queen move very early—usually Q-B2. But this must not become automatic: there is one variation where I have seen early Black Queen moves lead to disaster many, many times. Two of the classics are Nimzovich-Gilg, Kecskemet 1927 (1 P-K4 P-QB4 2 N-KB3 N-QB3 3 B-N5 Q-B2, and White won in 20 moves), and Bronstein-Geller, Gothenburg 1955

(1 P-K4 P-QB4 2 N-KB3 N-QB3 3 B-N5 P-KN3 4 P-B3 B-N2 5 P-Q4 Q-N3, 23 moves). I was there to witness the latter game, and I have won similar games myself. Here are three more recent examples which I saw when they happened.

Ciocaltea-F. Petersen, Siegen 1970:

1	**P-K4**	**P-QB4**
2	**N-KB3**	**N-QB3**
3	**B-N5**	**P-KN3**
4	**O-O**	**B-N2**
5	**P-B3**	**Q-N3**
6	**N-R3**	**P-QR3**
7	**B-R4**	**N-B3**
8	**P-K5**	**N-KN5?**
9	**P-Q4**	**P×P**
10	**P×P**	**O-O**
11	**P-R3**	**N-R3**
12	**P-Q5**	**N-QN5**
13	**B-K3**	**Q-R4**
14	**B-N3**	**N-B4**
15	**B-Q2**	**Q-N3**
16	**N-B4**	**Q-B4**
17	**P-N4**	**P-QN4**
18	**B×N**	**Q×B**
19	**N-N6**	**Resigns**

Bronstein-Tomic, Vinkovci 1970:

1	**P-K4**	**P-QB4**
2	**N-KB3**	**N-QB3**
3	**B-N5**	**P-KN3**
4	**P-B3**	**Q-N3**
5	**B-R4**	**B-N2**
6	**O-O**	**P-K4**
7	**N-R3**	**KN-K2**

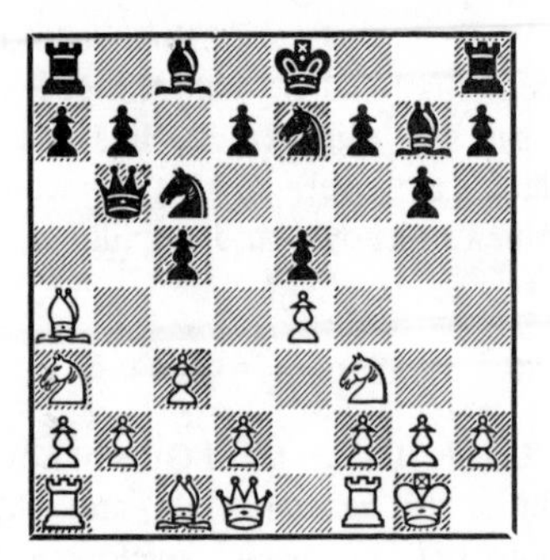

8	**P-QN4!?**	**P×P**
9	**N-B4**	**Q-B4**
10	**P-Q3**	**P×P?**
11	**R-N1!!**	**P-B7**
12	**Q×P**	**N-Q5**

and Black resigned, seeing 13 N×N Q×N/Q 14 B-K3 or 13 ... P×N 14 B-R3, which are hopeless.

Asmundsson- Bjerring, Ribe 1973:

1	**P-K4**	**P-QB4**
2	**N-KB3**	**P-Q3**
3	**B-N5ch**	**B-Q2**
4	**P-QR4**	**N-QB3**
5	**O-O**	**P-KN3**
6	**R-K1**	**B-N2**
7	**P-B3**	**P-K4**
8	**N-R3**	**Q-B2?**
9	**P-Q4**	**P-QR3**
10	**P×BP!**	**P×P**
11	**B-B1**	**KN-K2**
12	**N-B4**	**N-B1**
13	**P-R5**	**B-K3**
14	**B-K3**	**B×N**
15	**B×B**	**N×P?**

16	**R×N!**	**Q×R**
17	**B×Pch!**	**K-B1**
18	**N-N5**	**B-B3**
19	**Q-Q7**	**N-K2**
20	**B-N3**	**Resigns**

In the first two games Black's early Queen move was not a mistake in itself. Later, though, he had to play exactly, but he didn't because he underestimated White's chances in this "harmless" variation.

The Sicilian, of course, is an excellent fighting defense. But there are two things wrong with it. First, it is too popular; there is a lot of theory to learn and White may know it too. Second, Black does not often get a chance to start an early attack against the White King. (If you dream every night of attacking the enemy King you have a problem with Black after 1 P-K4.)

Some players reject the Sicilian in favor of Marshall's idea in the closed Ruy, really one of the better gambits:

1	**P-K4**	**P-K4**
2	**N-KB3**	**N-QB3**
3	**B-N5**	**P-QR3**
4	**B-R4**	**N-B3**
5	**O-O**	**B-K2**
6	**R-K1**	**P-QN4**
7	**B-N3**	**O-O**
8	**P-B3**	**P-Q4!?**

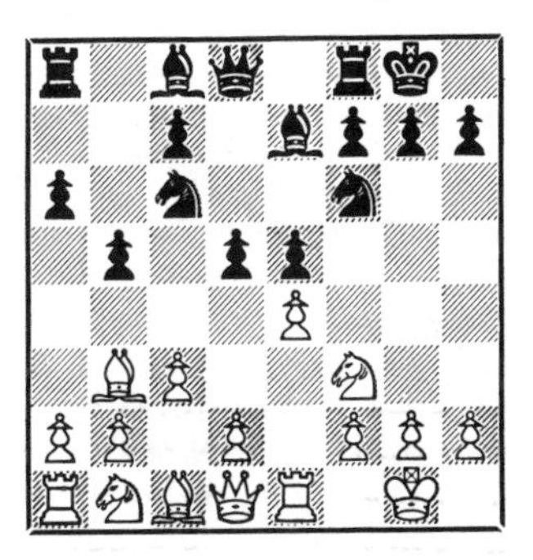

This is almost correct and leads to interesting play. But if White is afraid of it he can easily avoid it with 8 P-QR4, or with 5 P-Q3, or with 4 B×N, so it is not enough for Black to know the gambit lines.

Another possibility is the Open Variation with 5 . . . N×P, but White's alternatives on moves 4 and 5 avoid that too, of course. However, it must be admitted that with correct play these alternatives probably offer White less initiative than the main lines.

A good variation in which Black often gets play on the Kingside is:

1	**P-K4**	**P-K4**
2	**N-KB3**	**N-QB3**
3	**B-N5**	**P-QR3**
4	**B-R4**	**P-Q3**
5	**P-B3**	**N-K2**
6	**P-Q4**	**B-Q2**

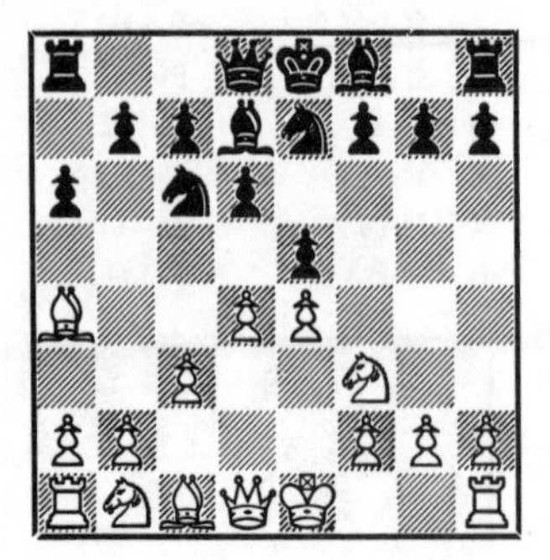

For example:

7	**B-N3**	**P-R3**
8	**QN-Q2**	**N-N3**
9	**N-B4**	**B-K2**

Black will follow with B-KN4. However, it is difficult for Black to get this position now, because 5 O-O has become more popular than 5 P-B3. But then Black may make a special study of the complications after 5 O-O B-N5 6 P-KR3 P-KR4!?, though most experts now consider them favorable for White.

I have sometimes played 3 . . . KN-K2 against the Ruy, avoiding the Exchange Variation. After 4 P-B3 P-QR3 5 B-R4 P-Q3 I get what I want, but I cannot recommend this old Cozio Defense because it is hard for Black to get a satisfactory position after 4 O-O or 4 P-Q4. However, this is an interesting example of transposition to avoid certain continuations.

I find it hard to understand what makes certain openings so popular and why other lines are not played just as often. One example: Why do so many play the King's Indian and so few the Leningrad System in the Dutch? If you check the books you will find very little about the Leningrad and there is obviously a lot of room for new ideas. For example, one of the main lines goes:

1	**P-Q4**	**P-KB4**
2	**P-KN3**	**N-KB3**
3	**B-N2**	**P-KN3**
4	**N-KB3**	**B-N2**
5	**O-O**	**O-O**
6	**P-B4**	**P-Q3**
7	**N-B3**	**P-B3**
8	**P-Q5**	. . . . . .

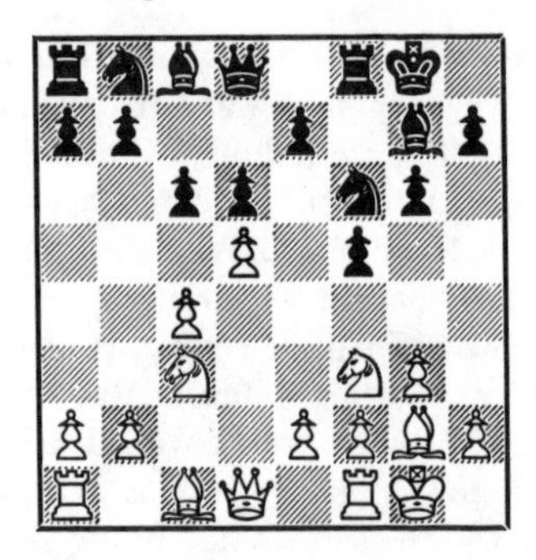

This looks almost like a King's Indian. The only difference is that . . . P-KB4 move which is directed against an early White P-K4 but which, on the other hand, weakens Black's K3. Nobody in the world can say for sure if this is better for Black than the King's Indian. The theoretical continuation is 8 . . . P-K4, but I don't like it! Black accepts a weak Queen pawn and his Kingside is weaker than in normal King's Indians. Also, it is rather easy to play White in that position: most players have seen a weak Black Queen pawn before and know how to handle it. I am not saying that the interesting Exchange sacrifice 8 . . . P-K4 9 P×P e.p. B×P 10 P-N3!? is correct or incorrect. If White does not want to play it, both 10 B-B4 and 10 Q-Q3 are excellent moves—and after these moves I would like to have the Black KBP on its original square!

Why not look for other possibilities? If a broad White advance in the center is impossible, why not start some play on one of the flanks? One idea is 8 . . . Q-K1 followed by . . . P-KR3, . . . P-KN4, etc., but it seems wrong because Black's King Bishop is not looking that way. So try the Queenside, where you can borrow many ideas from the King's Indian! For example, 8 . . . Q-N3 followed by . . . P-QR4 and . . . N-R3, and maybe . . . B-Q2 will be necessary to protect the QBP.

8 P-N3 (instead of P-Q5) P-QR4 9 B-N2 N-R3 transposes into Ogaard-Larsen, Ribe 1973, where after 10 P-Q5 B-Q2 11 N-Q4 Q-N3 12 P-K3 N-B4 Black got a promising position. But this does not solve the problem after 8 P-Q5. Black can choose from several possible moves here: B-Q2, Q-B2, Q-N3, Q-R4, P-QR4 are five already. At the moment I have tried only one: 8 . . . B-Q2 9 Q-N3 Q-N3 went very well in a game against the young English master Sidney Webb.

The position after 8 P-Q5 is difficult for both sides and therefore satisfactory for Black! Many White players are expecting the book move 8 . . . P-K4, and if Black does not play it they feel they are suddenly in an unclear and uncomfortable position. To study Black's possibilities in this position it may be a good idea to play it a few times with White! Beginning with 1 P-KN3 or 1 P-KB4 you will often be able to get the Leningrad System with an extra tempo.

In this chapter my intention has been to inspire, to present ideas. The average amateur cannot study the openings exactly like a grandmaster, for many reasons. (His job and his family are often the two most important ones.) Also, not being a master he probably has less understanding of the logic of the game, and probably cannot quickly assess a position that the expert pushes aside after a few seconds as unplayable, losing or too drawish. In most cases our amateur knows fewer recent master games and finds it hard to pick out the theoretically important ones. The detailed analysis of even a minor sub-subvariation can be very complicated, and not even a grandmaster can know everything about every opening.

One solution is to specialize in openings not often played in top-level chess. There is not as much theory to learn then, and important novelties do not appear often. But the amateurs want to play what the masters play, and it is an understandable feeling—but it costs a lot of work!

However, even grandmasters specialize. You must have a repertoire. It is good to own one of those big tomes with all the openings, but don't read it all! And when you get especially interested in one opening you will find there is not enough about it in that heavy book, but probably you can find a book about that opening alone. From then on, if you keep your interest in it, you will notice master games where it is played. When a new move is played, add it in the margin of the book or on loose sheets of paper or in a little notebook. And in your own games, when something goes completely wrong you must find your error!

Here is a proposed repertoire for a reasonably aggressive player. For Black against Queen pawn openings, study two of these five: Gruenfeld, Modern Benoni, Benko Gambit, Queen's Gambit Accepted, and Dutch (Leningrad and Stonewall). For Black against 1 P-K4: learn a rare variation of the Ruy Lopez (example: 3 . . . B-B4), and the Sicilian Dragon. For White: again study a rare variation of the Ruy (examples: 3 . . . P-QR3 4 B-R4 N-B3 5 O-O B-K2 6 P-Q4!?, or 5 N-B3!?) plus the Scotch (maybe even the Goring Gambit: 1 P-K4 P-K4 2 N-KB3 N-QB3 3 P-Q4 P×P 4 P-B3!?). In the beginning make just a rather superficial study of the Panov Variation against the Caro-Kann, 3 N-Q2 against the French (3 N-QB3 B-N5 is too much work!), and some strange line against the Sicilian. (I can recommend 2 P-KB4 or 2 N-KB3 N-QB3 3 B-N5, but here 2 . . . P-K3 requires special treatment, as does 2 . . . P-KN3. If you know the Dragon with Black, maybe you can play it with White also. I do not recommend the Morra Gambit, 2 P-Q4 P×P 3 P-QB3, which is popular in some circles. I don't like to give away a center pawn like that!)

Later you can widen your repertoire and sharpen your weapons against some rare openings and variations. But in the beginning it will probably be wise to study the Black openings more carefully than the White ones.

As you read the other chapters in this book, which were written by different authors, you will probably get an impression of many different attitudes toward opening problems in chess. This has something to do with differences in "style." It is hard to explain what this word means. But as you gain experience it will probably become important to find your own style and an opening repertoire in agreement with it.

CHAPTER 7

The Secret Workshop of a Grandmaster

by Paul Keres

"How should you open a chess game?" This question, though apparently simple, has caused many an expert of the royal game to rack his brains. There are, of course, many principles to guide a player in the opening, but it is obviously not enough to speak only of principles if you want to handle the openings well. It is well known, for example, that you must strive for rapid development of the pieces, that you should not move the same piece repeatedly, that pawn weaknesses are to be avoided, and so on. But it is just as well known that such principles are valid only in a general way and often allow exceptions which at first glance may seem incomprehensible.

This leads us to the next question: How can you tell when a violation of principle is acceptable and when it is incorrect? This is a much more difficult question, and to answer it requires not only extensive analysis of the specific position but a certain minimum playing strength. The player will have to be able to determine, independently, which side the position favors.

The chess fan has numerous resources at his disposal to make this task easier. First of all, there are the many books on opening theory which offer extensive analytical material on every opening. You need only refer to the page on which the variation in question is discussed and you will, it seems, gain a clear understanding of all the problems. This procedure, however, only works up to a certain point and depends again on your own practical playing strength. It is necessary to remember that books on opening theory are not really the result of careful theoretical study but are merely collections of practical experiences, i.e. actual games. It is rare, though, for a practical chess game to be played perfectly by both sides; consequently you can often find improvements on the moves played and then published.

This is easy to understand. Current opening theory is comprised principally of master games of the last hundred years, thousands and thousands of which were played in this period, and the number grows annually. Despite the analytical work of numerous theoreticians, it is practically impossible to undertake a critical study of this vast quantity of material; and this goes even for the reference books on opening theory written by leading grandmasters. The physical task alone of a conscientious examination of the material is necessarily impractical.

We must therefore conclude that so-called opening "theory" must be viewed with a critical eye if unpleasant surprises in practical play are to be avoided. General principles are helpful, but blind faith in the correctness of cited variations or analysis certainly is not. To learn an opening well and grasp its fine points more or less exhaustively, you must, besides studying the books, do much independent work and extend yourself in the search for new ideas and variations.

So we return to the question: How should you open a chess game? There is no one correct method, no single course which all students must follow. A great deal depends on individual inclination, on your own feelings for the structures of various openings, and, without a doubt, on your ability to analyze positions well and evaluate the various possibilities correctly. All this means that, as stated above, a certain minimum strength is needed.

In what follows I will not give detailed guidelines on the treatment of the openings. Many writers have already done this and there is an abundance of material of that kind. Besides, such advice would be merely theoretical, and theory often runs into difficulties when applied in actual practice. And chess is a practical game.

Therefore, I have limited myself to telling the chess fan something of how a grandmaster prepares at home for tournament play. I will try to show how a well-known variation is taken apart, subjected to a thorough examination of its principles, and, as far as possible, enriched with new ideas. Of course, it is easiest for me to do this by using my own games and analysis, since one knows oneself best of all.

In order to give this discussion the greatest practical value, I shall explain the following method. First, a well-known variation is chosen. Then the reader is offered analysis and other considerations, leading to certain conclusions. The result is a thorough examination of the resources available in the variation, subject to the addition of new ideas. I will then show the results of such prepared variations in practical play. Thus, the reader will see not only how a given variation is prepared, but also, through practical examples, the need for particularly careful attention in work of this kind. I believe such practical illustrations are of great value and contribute to facilitating the learning of complicated opening theory.

Variations can be prepared for general use. It is usually simpler, however, to prepare for a specific opponent. Every player has his favorite openings which he plays more than any others. It will be your job, then, to select one of these openings that also suits your own playing style, analyze it thoroughly, test it for inaccuracies, and develop new moves. On the basis of your opponent's previous games, it may be discovered which systems he uses most frequently and which ones may be examined for possible improvements. The field of study is relatively limited here.

The situation is somewhat different if your preparation is not directed at a specific opponent. Usually, when the new continuation is discovered it must be analyzed in detail to determine what practical value it possesses. It must be remembered that analysis may sometimes be too long; because of the resulting increase in the possibility of inaccuracies it may lose much of its practical value. On the other hand, it is possible to do without individual variations and explore entire new systems instead. In this case you may reach conclusions based on general considerations and according to your own feelings about the position. This type of preparation is naturally much harder; besides, amid the vast quantity of detailed analysis nowadays, it is difficult to find an area where one could discover an entire new system of development.

Opening theory develops further with each tournament. New variations are constantly being discovered and given practical trials. Analytic skill increases. With the aid of examples from my own over-the-board play, we will now take a look into the workshop of a grandmaster.

A New System

In the Ruy Lopez, the main variation is as follows:

1	**P-K4**	**P-K4**
2	**N-KB3**	**N-QB3**
3	**B-N5**	**P-QR3**
4	**B-R4**	**N-B3**
5	**O-O**	**B-K2**
6	**R-K1**	**P-QN4**
7	**B-N3**	**P-Q3**
8	**P-B3**	**O-O**
9	**P-KR3**	**N-QR4**
10	**B-B2**	**P-B4**
11	**P-Q4**	......

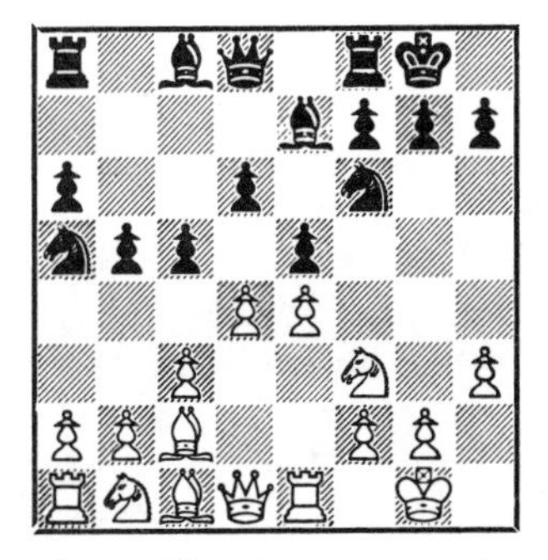

This position has occurred tens of thousands of times, perhaps hundreds of thousands. Black usually plays 11 ... Q-B2, but also 11 ... BP×P, 11 ... N-B3 and 11 ... B-N2 have been played, though without displaying any advantage over the usual move. It seemed unlikely that anything new could be discovered here.

While preparing for the Candidates' Tournament in Curacao 1962, I gave further thought to this position. I had been a long-time follower of this defense and wished to remain faithful to it in this tournament. It was therefore necessary to look for possible new systems and examine the latest experiences of the other masters. That the position of the diagram could be easily reached caused me to examine it thoroughly under a magnifying glass.

Clearly, Black must think strategically; he cannot solve his problems tactically. Question: What are Black's strategic possibilities?

Anyone who has played the Tchigorin Defense to the Ruy Lopez (which is what this system is most often called) knows that Black's only chance is counterplay against the center square Q5. He has two ways of approaching this. First, Black can increase the pressure on Q5 move by move, eventually forcing White either to exchange center pawns or to close the center with P-Q5. Second, Black can open the center by a double exchange on Q5 and look for counterplay through the harmonious cooperation of his pieces. But he must see to it that the initiative he attains by good piece play is not just temporary, else White will obtain a definite positional advantage because of his good pawn on K4 against the weak Black pawn on Q3.

Therefore, Black usually rejects that double exchange and tries to increase the pressure on Q5 by 11 ... Q-B2 followed by 12 ... N-B3. But is 11 ... Q-B2 necessary? Black protects the attacked KP, but does little to increase the pressure on Q5. Perhaps he can protect the KP in a different way, while initiating pressure on Q5 without loss of time.

This train of thought led me to test the move

11 ...... N-Q2!

This move has some advantages in comparison with 11 ... Q-B2. First, it frees the KB3 square for the Bishop, which will put pressure on Q5 supported by the subsequent ... N-QB3. Second, the Queen is not committed too soon and may also help in the siege of Q5 by moving to QN3. Third, Black's KBP is free to move to KB4 if White should decide to play P-Q5.

But 11 ... N-Q2 also has its disadvantages. On Q2, the Knight stands to a certain extent in the way of the other pieces. If White plays QN-Q2-B1-K3, Black's Q4 and KB4 will be inadequately guarded, and in some variations Black's useful pressure on his K5 is lacking. Nevertheless, I decided to examine the move more closely and to work out some strategic plans.

Although, as has already been said, the position requires a strategic approach and therefore forced continuations are not to be expected, you must still watch out for tactical tricks, for example 12 P×KP (or P×BP) P×P 13 Q-Q5, which is refuted by 13 ... B-N2. Strategically, you must consider the consequences of an exchange in the center: 12 P×KP P×P 13 QN-Q2. I dispensed with further examination of the position after 13 QN-Q2, assuming that the Black Knight on Q2, instead of the Queen on B2, was no disadvantage for Black. This judgment is essentially correct, but for practical reasons it would have been advisable to prepare plans of development to deal with this position in order to save thinking time during the game. The importance of this was proved in my first game against Bobby Fischer in this tournament.

I also rejected the immediate advance 12 P-Q5 as harmless for Black on account of 12 ... N-N3. With this Black sets up the positional threat of ... P-B4, and if 13 P-KN4 Black can seize control of the dark squares on the Kingside with 13 ... P-R4 14 N-R2 P×P 15 P×P B-N4. And if Black has doubts about 12 P×KP or 12 P-Q5, he can delay moving his KN with 11 ... BP×P 12 P×P N-Q2. Either way, White has accomplished nothing.

Thus, I finally decided on

12 QN-Q2 ......

This is White's most natural continuation. Now Black has several choices. First, 12 ... N-QB3, but then 12 P-Q5 is quite annoying since the Knight has no good retreat. After 13 ... N-R4 14 P-QN4, White has the better position. Second, 12 ... B-B3 has some drawbacks: after 13 P×BP P×P 14 N-B1, the Bishop on KB3 does not stand particularly well and Black will have difficulty equalizing. Third, a developing move like 12 ... B-N2 is also not without its problems: after 13 P-Q5 the Black pieces on the Queenside are in each other's way, and the Knight on QR4 is nothing for Black to be proud of.

I concluded that Black is better off interpolating a single exchange in the center.

12 ...... **BP×P**
13 P×P ......

Now Black may continue his plan of exerting pressure against Q5. But how should he begin? There is no reason for an immediate exchange 13 ... P×P 14 N×P, so Black has to choose between 13 ... B-B3 and 13 ... N-QB3.

Both moves are positionally motivated and both are good. 13 ... B-B3 keeps White from protecting his QP by 14 N-N3, since Black's position would be satisfactory after 14 . . . N×N 15 B×N B-N2. But if 14 P-Q5, Black's Queenside pieces stand somewhat awkwardly (14 . . . N-N3 15 N-B1 B-Q2 16 R-N1!, etc.). Although this would not be a lasting disadvantage, I preferred not to give White even that much, so I chose

13 . . . . . . N-QB3

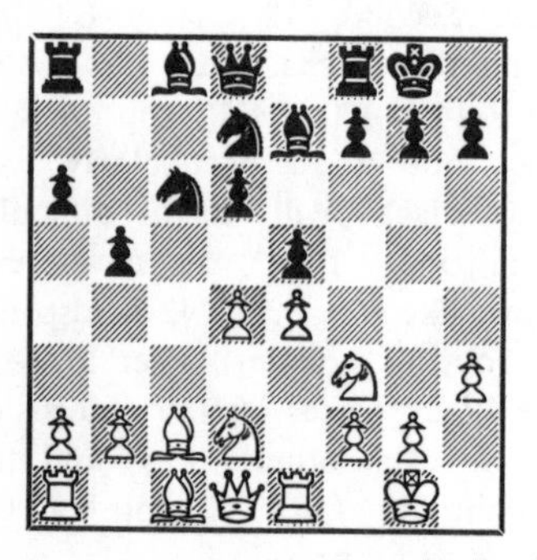

I was satisfied with this position and gave it only a superficial analysis. In my notebook I find the following possible variations:

(1) 14 P-Q5 N-N5 15 B-N1 P-QR4 16 P-R3 N-R3 17 P-QN4 P×P 18 P×P N-N3 19 Q-N3 B-Q2 with approximately even chances. (This position occurred later in Spassky-Tringov, Amsterdam 1964: 20 B-Q3 Q-N1 21 N-B1 N-B5 22 R-N1! with some initiative, made possible, however, by an absence of methodical Queenside action by Black. With 20 . . . N-B2 Black could have either simplified on the QR file or occupied the strong-point on QR5, after which it is not possible to speak of an advantage for White.)

(2) 14 N-B1 B-B3 (if 14 . . . N-N3 15 N-K3 B-B3 16 P-Q5 N-Q5 17 N×N P×N, where if 16 P×P P×P 17 N-Q5 N×N 18 P×N N-Q5, in both cases with an even game. To be considered, however, is 15 P-QN3!, and if 15 . . . P×P 16 B-N2, and White wins back the pawn with a good game; but with 15 . . . P-QR4 Black can maintain the tension in the center and initiate counterplay on the Queenside) 15 P-Q5 (as later games have demonstrated, White does best to maintain the tension in the center with 15 B-K3) 15 . . . N-N5 (there is also the double-edged 15 . . . N-Q5!? 16 N×N P×N, and it is not certain if White can take advantage of Black's weak Q5, e.g. 17 R-N1 B-N2 18 P-QN4 R-B1 with good counterplay) 16 B-N1 P-QR4 17 P-R3 N-R3 18 P-QN4 P×P 19 P×P N-N3, and Black has little to fear.

This analysis certainly provides a foundation for trying the new variation in serious play, but it is not enough to count on success merely by obtaining good general counterplay, which I learned by painful experience several times in Curacao. Further immersion in the position would be necessary to devise promising plans for specific opponents.

All the same, my playing experience, and that of most of my colleagues, shows that a new system in the opening almost always gains some immediate success if it has a solid positional base. In Curacao I played 11 ... N-Q2 in four games, and I won three of them. This is the kind of success you don't see every day with Black in the Ruy Lopez, an opening in which White, as is well known, usually has a lasting initiative. Below I will comment briefly on these four games, showing how my preparatory work proved its practical value.

First Try: a Qualified Success

The first chance to play the new system was in the second round against Tal. I did not feel quite secure about the fine points of the system and delayed ... N-Q2 in order to leave my opponent less of a choice.

11	......	**N-B3**
12	**QN-Q2**	**BP×P**
13	**P×P**	**N-Q2**

By transposition of moves, we are again at the position of the last diagram. To my surprise, Tal found a continuation which I had rejected as quite harmless, but which is now considered one of the best for White.

14	**N-N3**	......

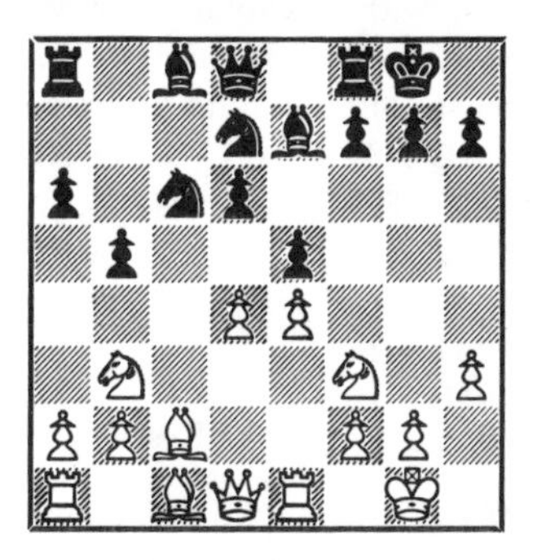

The move is logical: White sufficiently protects his pawn on Q4 and opens the diagonal for the QB. To be sure, White's QN is not safe, for it can be driven away easily by the routine P-QR4-5. But in the meantime White can develop his Bishop and further protect the strongpoint on Q4, while Black has to be careful that his pawn advance will not prove to be a weakening of his Queenside. Thus White has set Black a positional problem which is not to be solved at first glance and which certainly should have been prepared for at home.

Be that as it may, Black has no choice but to advance his QRP if he wants to justify his opening strategy.

14	......	**P-QR4**
15	**B-K3**	......

Suetin later tried the interesting attack 15 B-Q3, with the idea of 15 ... P-R5 16 B×P P×N 17 B×N R×P 18 R×R P×R 19

Q-R4, with advantage for White. If Black does not want to give up a pawn for the initiative with 16 ... Q-N3 17 B×N Q×B 18 QN-Q2 B-R3, he has the satisfactory answer 15 ... B-B3, as analysis and practical experience have shown.

15 ...... P-R5

White can retreat his Knight to Q2 or QB1; it is not easy to decide which is better. If 16 QN-Q2 Black usually continues with 16 ... B-B3 17 N-B1 P×P 18 N×P N×N 19 B×N N-K4 20 N-K3 (Gligoric-Tal, Amsterdam 1964), after which White supposedly stands slightly better. But Black could try to maintain the tension in the center with 17 ... N-N3, for the consequences of 18 P-QN3 N-N5 are apparently acceptable (19 B-N1 P×NP 20 Q×P N-B3!, etc.).

16 N-B1 ......

This also gives Black problems. If Black plays passively, White threatens to secure the strong square QN4 for his Knight by 17 P-Q5 followed by P-R3. Or White may prepare this by 17 N-Q3 or 17 P-R3. Black must therefore undertake something. And to find the correct plan during play is not so simple.

After long thought I decided to give up the center by exchanging on Q5, followed by good piece play. This plan, however, is double-edged. Only more accurate analysis later would reveal whether Black's counterplay is valid or just a temporary initiative. One Black alternative is 16 ... N-N3, whereby Black takes advantage of the fact that White cannot contest his QB4 by 17 P-QN3 (because of 16 N-B1 White's QR is unprotected). White can simplify the position with 17 P×P P×P 18 Q×Q B×Q, but he gains no advantage (telegraph game, Johansson-Keres, 1963). 16 ... P-R6 is worse, for after 17 P×RP R×P 18 N-N3 Black has difficulty finding an active plan (18 ... N-N3? 19 P×P P×P 20 Q×Q B×Q 21 B-B5!).

16 ...... P×P
17 N×P N×N
18 B×N B-B3

Clearly, Black cannot tolerate White's strong Bishop on Q4 forever, so 18 ... N-K4 would be logical, especially since 19 N-K2 N-B3 20 B-B3 P-N5 does not give the desired result on account of 21 N-Q4! With the next move White's QB will definitely be eliminated, but Black must still demonstrate that his pawn weaknesses have no practical significance.

19 N-K2 ......

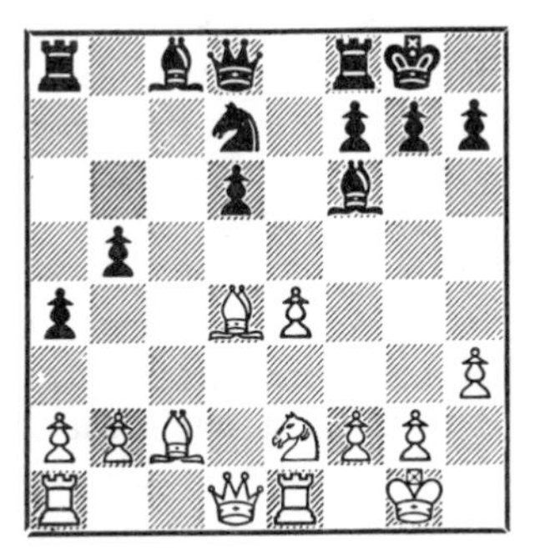

Tal aims at playing the Knight to Q5 or KB5. The position of the diagram is, in my opinion, critical for the entire variation.

Black must think out his plans precisely or he will run into difficulty. For example, the plausible 19 ... N-B4 gives White an advantage after 20 N-B3, which is also a strong answer to 19 ... N-K4.

19 ...... B-N2

Black has completed his development and apparently will be able to hold the balance. If 20 N-B3 B-B3, and it is not clear how White can obtain any advantage. Tal recommends the exchange 20 B×B N×B 21 N-Q4 in order to seize the initiative after 21 ... Q-N3 22 N-B5. But this is not convincing: it is not clear whether White's initiative yields anything tangible after 22 ... KR-Q1; furthermore, Black can more simply play 20 ... Q×B (21 N-Q4 Q-K4, or even 21 ... KR-B1!?).

20 Q-Q3 ......

This allows a favorable exchange.

20 ...... N-B4
21 Q×P B×P
22 B×B/4 N×B

Now the chances for both sides are equal and we can end our analysis of the opening phase. The game concluded 23 QR-Q1 P-Q4 24 N-B4? B×B 25 R×B Q-B3 26 Q×QP QR-Q1 27 KR×N R×Q 28 N×R Q-N4 29 P-B4 Q-R3 30 R×P Q-Q3 31 R-R5 P-R3 32 P-QN4 K-R2 33 R-B5 Q-R3 34 N-B3 R-Q1 35 P-B5 R-Q7 36 R-K8 Q-Q6 37 R-K4 R-QB7 38 P-QR4 R-B8ch 39 K-R2 Q-Q3ch 40 R/4-K5 R×N and White resigned. It was not necessary for White to lose this game; but if one wants absolutely to win . . .

Second Try: An Unqualified Setback

The next opportunity for use of my prepared variation was several rounds later, against Fischer. In the position of the first diagram, I proceeded immediately to the key move.

11 ...... N-Q2

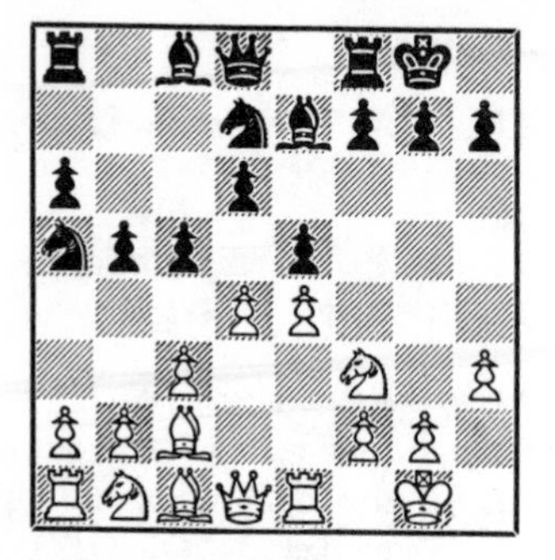

Fischer, confronted with this new move, apparently wanted to avoid possible home preparation and chose a tension-releasing exchange.

12 P×BP **P×P**
13 QN-Q2 ......

I have already mentioned how I considered this possibility and set it aside as not dangerous for Black. My reason for that judgment was: in the main variation of the Tchigorin Defense Black continues with 11 ... Q-B2, after which White can play the same 12 P×BP P×P 13 QN-Q2. The only difference in the game with Fischer is that Black's Knight is on Q2 instead of his Queen on B2. Is this difference so great that Black should fear the exchange on QB4?

Merely on general considerations I decided that this cannot be the case. The Knight does not stand badly on Q2 and has cleared the way for the KBP to make the good defensive move ... P-B3; the Knight aims at QN3 to support eventual counteraction on the Queenside. Although the important squares Q4 and KB4 are temporarily uncontrolled, Black need not worry for after ... N-N3 everything will be all right again.

The only drawback of 11 ... N-Q2 is that an important piece has been moved from the defense of the Black King. The question is: Can White take advantage of this fact for a successful attack on the King? This is a very difficult question, and perhaps it is impossible to answer considering the almost limitless number of variations. This is not so different from the variation with 11 ... Q-B2 12 P×BP P×P 13 QN-Q2: White has some initiative, which forces Black to worry for the time being about the safety of his King. If Black can defend against White's tactical threats, he will usually get a good position. Experience teaches us that Black, given well-considered counterplay, need not fear this simplifying variation. It is mostly a question of style; whether, in the end, you would rather play White and attack in this position, or defend with Black.

My devoting so little time to this line was irresponsible. Instead of having looked at the position quietly at home and prepared effective piece play for Black, I had to rack my brains during the game to decide how to develop further.

And, as the game shows, I did not carry out this task successfully.

13 ...... Q-B2

This is not the best method to reinforce Black's KP. The Queen is exposed to a possible Knight attack on Q5, and Black loses the chance of threatening the exchange of Queens later with ... N-N3, thereby winning an important tempo.

How should Black develop? It is practically impossible to say which of the many possible plans is best, for the position has been too little tested in practice. But on the basis of the few games played, and later analysis, I have come to agree that Black should play 13 ... P-B3!, firmly protecting the KP and freeing the Knight. If 14 N-B1, N-N3 wins an important tempo by threatening the exchange of Queens, and after 15 Q-K2 B-K3 or 15 ... R-R2 Black has little to fear. White achieves just as little with 14 N-R2 N-N3 15 Q-B3 B-K3, etc.

Apparently, White must accept Fischer's recommendation of 14 N-R4! if he wishes to achieve anything. After 14 ... N-N3 15 N-B5 R-B2, Fischer recommends (instead of 16 N×Bch in Fischer-Ivkov, Havana 1965) 16 Q-N4 K-R1 17 P-KR4!, with the idea of P-R5 and N-B3-R4. Since 17 ... P-N3 18 N-R6 R-N2 19 Q-B3 is favorable for White, acording to Fischer, Black will have to resolve on a difficult defense in which there is, however, some chance of success. And Black could have played more accurately with 15 ... K-R1 instead of 15 ... R-B2, temporarily preventing the White Queen's sortie to KN4 and allowing Black to think of such counterthreats as 16 ... N/4-B5 and 16 ... P-N5. Detailed analysis of the possibilities here would take us beyond the scope and purpose of this book, but I do advise readers to work out their own independent analysis, which will be found rewarding.

14 N-B1 ......

Now can Black nullify the threat of N-K3-Q5? During the game I could not find a satisfactory answer; perhaps, after the faulty 13 ... Q-B2?, the answer does not exist.

14 ...... N-N3
15 N-K3 R-Q1

To be considered is 15 ... N/4-B5.

16 Q-K2 B-K3

I was stunned by Fischer's following super-move.

17 N-Q5! ......

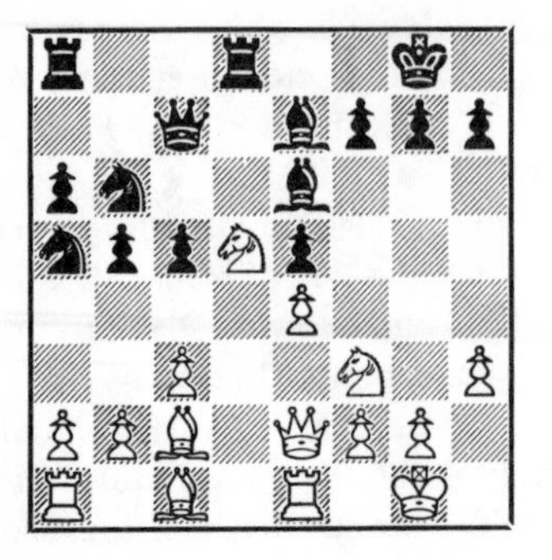

This leads only to the exchange of center pawns and thus to the opening up of the game, but that is just what most clearly reveals White's opening advantage. The point is that after the disappearance of the pawns on K4 and K5, Black's King will be suddenly exposed to an attack against which a good defense is difficult to find. As already stated, this is the disadvantage of the Knight maneuver N-Q2-N3—Black loses time and deprives his King of an important defensive piece.

Black must exchange on Q4, or he loses his KP without compensation. The question is: Should he keep the Bishop or the Knight? After 17 . . . B×N 18 P×B N×P 19 N×P White undoubtedly stands better with his two Bishops, and if 18 . . . P-B3 Fischer's 19 P-KR4!, with dangerous threats on the QN1-KR7 diagonal, is very strong. Therefore, Black decides to keep the Bishop.

17 . . . . . . N×N

18 P×N B×QP

Perhaps it is worthwhile giving up the Exchange for a pawn with 18 . . . R×P 19 B-K4 P-B3.

19 N×P . . . . . .

With this we may conclude our examination of the opening of this game. White clearly has the advantage and Black will hardly be able to get out of his difficulties without damage. For those interested in the fine points of this position, we recommend the notes by Fischer in his excellent book *My 60 Memorable Games*. For the sake of completeness, here are the concluding moves of the game: 19 . . . R-R2 20 B-B4 Q-N3 21 QR-Q1 P-N3 22 N-N4 N-B5 23 B-R6 B-K3 24 B-N3 Q-N1 25 R×Rch B×R 26 B×N P×B 27 Q×P Q-Q3 28 Q-R4 Q-K2 29 N-B6ch K-R1 30 N-Q5 Q-Q2 31 Q-K4 Q-Q3 32 N-B4 R-K2 33 B-N5 R-K1 34 B×B R×B 35 N×B Q×N 36 Q×Q P×Q 37 R×P R-Q8ch 38 K-R2 R-Q7 39 R-N6 R×BP 40 R-N7 R-B3 41 K-N3 and Black resigned. A fine performance by Fischer.

Third Try: Encouragement

Despite this defeat I did not lose confidence in the defensive system and used it again with Black in my second game against Tal. We refer the reader to the first diagram.

11 . . . . . . N-Q2
12 QN-Q2 BP×P

13 P×P N-QB3

We have reached the position of the diagram on page 202.

Now that I had used my defense in two games of the tournament, I had to assume that Tal was by this time prepared for it and that he would show me the results of his home analysis. Sure enough, I was confronted with a new move.

14 P-R3 ......

I had not considered this in my analysis, and again I had to try solving a complicated positional problem during the game.

White's plan is clear. After denying QN4 to Black's Knight, he wants to play 15 P-Q5 (for example, after 14 ... B-B3), which would give him a significant spatial advantage. Black cannot undertake much if he doesn't want to allow White this advantage; he must exchange.

14 ...... P×P
15 N-N3 ......

It is clear that Black cannot hold his extra pawn and must seek counterchances in active piece play.

15 ...... N/2-K4
16 KN×P ......

16 QN×P N×Nch 17 N×N B-B3 looks very good for Black.

16 ...... B-B3

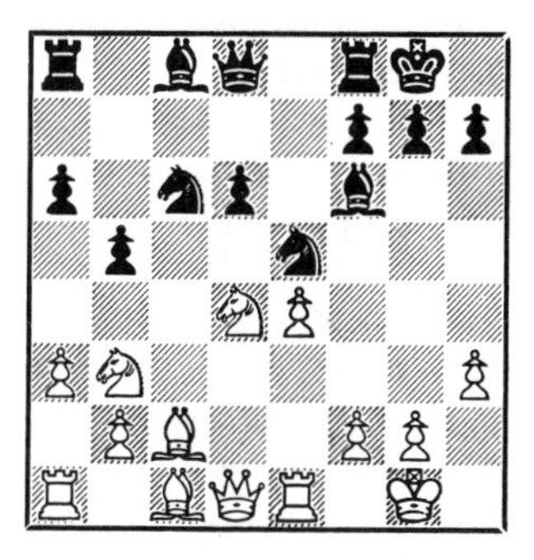

The critical position of the line that began with 14 P-R3. It seems to me that Black is proving his strategy to be correct, for his pieces are active and permit White few prospects for the initiative. For example, the violent 17 P-B4 N×N 18 N×N N-B5 would only weaken White's position, and Black certainly has no objection to 17 N-KB5 N-B5. But if White wishes simply to complete his development with 17 B-K3, then, in addition to other possibilities, 17 ... N×N 18 B×N N-B5 19 R-N1 B-K4 is acceptable for Black. And Black need not fear 17 N×N N×N 18 R-N1 N-K4 or 18 ... B-K3.

To get something out of the opening, Tal decided on a move to reinforce his strongpoint on Q4.

17 B-Q2!? ......

Obviously, White wants to play this Bishop to QB3, where it will stand well, assuring him some hopes of an advantage. But a tactical finesse exists, whereby Black frees himself of all his opening problems at one stroke. White has cut off his Queen's connection with Q4, thus depriving his Knight there of reinforcement; this offers Black the opportunity for tactical complications. Black must enter these hair-raising complications whether he wants to or not, though the consequences can hardly be calculated.

17 ...... **N×N**
18 N×N ......

The zwischenzug 18 B-R5 is no good on account of 18 ... N/5-B6ch!

18 ...... **N-Q6!**

This practically forces White to go into the following complications. If 19 B×N B×N (with the threat of 20 ... Q-B3), or even 19 B-R5 Q×B 20 Q×N P-N3, Black's position is excellent and it is White's turn to worry about equality. Tal's continuation is therefore understandable.

19 N-B6?! ......

This move was later labeled as a mistake, with 19 B×N or 19 B-R5 recommended instead. To be sure, either move would have been objectively better for White, but the critics forget that 19 N-B6 is part of White's plan. Tal would never have played 17 B-Q2 in order to fight now merely for laborious equality.

My counterblow was planned.

19 ...... **N×BP!**

The quiet continuation 19 ... Q-N3 20 B×N Q×N would not be pleasant for Black after 21 R-QB1, to say nothing of the possible complications after 21 P-K5.

Here we could end our analysis of the opening in this game, since its further course, as well as later analysis, proves that Black obtains an advantage by force. The position is so complicated and interesting, however, that I would like to present the results of the later analysis, as well as the game conclusion.

White has only a choice between 20 Q-B3 and 20 Q-R5, for 20 N×Q N×Q or 20 K×N Q-N3ch have no practical value. Tal took a long time to decide on his move.

20 Q-B3 ......

He had in mind the plausible 20 ... Q-N3 21 P-K5! N-N5ch 22 B-K3! (if 22 K-R1 N×P 23 N×N B×N 24 R×B P×R 25 Q×R B-N2 26 B×Pch K×B 27 Q×R, Black wins with 27 ... Q-B7 28 R-KN1 Q-N6, etc.) 22 ... N×B 23 P×B! N×Bch 24 K-R2 N×KR 25 R×N and, despite being down a whole Rook, White has an extremely dangerous attack.

Subsequent analysis has shown that White could have presented his opponent more difficult problems with 20 Q-R5. Now 20 ... P-N3 won't do because of 21 Q-B3, and after 20 ... Q-N3 21 P-K5! complications result which cannot be calculated correctly over the board. Here is one possibility: 21 ... N-K5ch (after 21 ... N-Q6ch 22 B-K3 Q×N 23 P×B! Black loses material on account of the mate threat with 24 Q-N5) 22 K-R2 (22 B-K3 is now answered simply by 22 ... Q×N) 22 ... B×Pch (after 22 ... P-N3 White does not withdraw his Queen by 23 Q-K2 Q×N 24 B×N B×Pch 25 K-R1 P-Q4, etc., but sacrifices it with 23 P×B! P×Q 24 B×N and, although White has only two pieces for the Queen, his many threats are not to be underestimated) 23 N×B N-B3! followed by ... P×N and Black has nothing to fear.

Black has a stronger move after 20 Q-R5, namely 20 ... N×Pch! If White now takes with 21 P×N or 21 Q×N, he loses back the Knight after 21 ... Q-N3ch. And after 21 K-R2 P-N3! (not, however, 21 ... B-K4ch 22 Q×B! P×Q 23 N×Q R×N 24 B-R5, etc.), he is in trouble. The endgame after 22 N×Q P×Q offers White little joy, and 22 Q×N B-K4ch! followed by 23 ... Q-B2, and 22 Q-Q5 Q-Q2, are insufficient. White probably has to play 22 Q-B3, but 22 ... B-K4ch! leads to about the same position as in the game (23 N×B P×N 24 B-R6 Q-R5!).

20 ...... N×Pch!

Looking forward to 21 P×N (or 21 Q×N) 21 ... Q-N3ch, etc. Tal planned 21 K-B1, but there follows 21 ... Q-N3 22 P-K5 B-N5! 23 Q-K3 (or 23 B-K3 B×Q 24 B×Q B×N, etc.) 23 ... Q×N 24 QR-B1 Q-B5ch 25 B-Q3 Q-B5ch with enough superiority to win. If 21 K-R1 Q-N3 22 P-K5 B-N5! Therefore, Tal has only one choice.

21 K-R2 B-K4ch!

Black's advantage is evident. White must exchange on K5, for after 22 K-R1 Black can simply continue with 22 ... Q-B2 and maintain his material advantage.

22 N×B P×N

If 23 B-N4, Black has the saving 23 ... N-N4, maintaining his two plus pawns.

The game is lost for White; there followed: 23 KR-Q1 N-B5 24 P-KN3 N-K3 25 B-B3 Q-N4 26 R-Q6 Q-R3ch 27 K-N1 N-Q5 28 R×Q N×Qch 29 K-B2 P×R 30 K×N R-K1 31 R-R1 K-N2 32 B-N3 B-N2 33 B-Q2 P-B4 34 R×P QR-Q1 35 R-N6 B×Pch 36 K-K2 B-B6ch 37 K-K1 P-B5 38 B-B3 P×P 39 R×RP R-Q5 40 R-R7ch K-R3 41 R-KB7 and White resigned without waiting for Black's reply.

Fourth Try: Success

Experienced grandmasters maintain that you should not give up a variation as long as it succeeds. Adhering to this wisdom, I tried it once again in my second game as Black against Fischer. The reader is referred to the first diagram.

11 ...... N-Q2

This time I had prepared, on 12 P×BP P×P 13 QN-Q2, the defense 13 ... P-B3. But perhaps Fischer was not completely convinced of the soundness of his method, or he wanted to play a sharper variation on account of his unsatisfactory standing in the tournament.

12 P-Q5 ......

This advance, in my opinion, is premature.

12 ...... N-N3

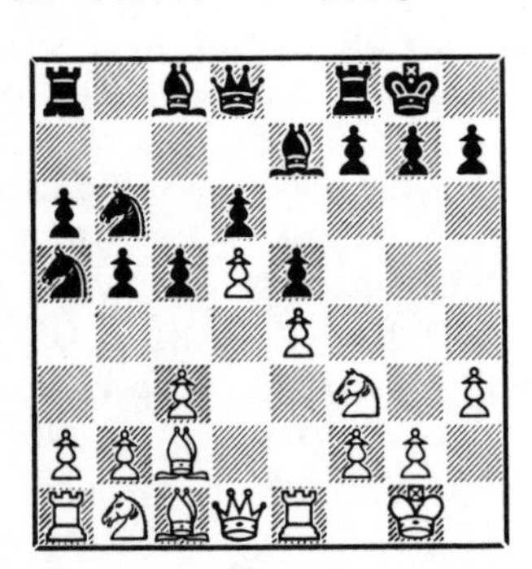

White is in somewhat of a predicament. Should he allow ... P-B4 or prevent it with 13 P-KN4? There are drawbacks either way. If White continues his development with 13 QN-Q2, then after 13 ... P-B4 14 P×P B×P 15 B×B R×B 16 N-K4 Q-Q2, Black has the very annoying threat 17 ... Q-N2. If Black can eliminate White's KP, White will have trouble protecting Q5. So Fischer chooses to prevent ... P-B4.

13 P-KN4 ......

This advance is very often played in the closed variations of the Ruy Lopez, aiming for aggressive action on the Kingside. Here, however, the move is premature and leads to Black winning absolute control of the dark squares on the Kingside. White is not sufficiently developed to begin an active operation.

13 ...... P-R4!

This presents White with an unpleasant choice. His KNP needs protection, so the Knight will have to move into a passive defensive position on KR2. Equally unsatisfactory is 14 P×P B×P, since to forestall 15 ... B-N5 White must play 15 N-R2, and then 15 ... B-N4! clearly yields Black the better game.

14 N-R2 ......

By advancing his KNP White has significantly weakened the dark squares on the Kingside. Naturally, Black takes immediate advantage of this weakness.

14 ...... P×P
15 P×P B-N4!

Black obtains many advantages by this maneuver. First, he can exchange his rather inactive Bishop; second, he further weakens the dark squares on White's Kingside; third, he is first to occupy the open KR file and can initiate an attack there. Black should be completely satisfied with the results of the opening.

16 N-Q2 P-N3
17 QN-B3 B×B

17 . . . B-B5 also deserved attention here. To forestall an attack along the KR file, Fischer offers to exchange Queens.

18 Q×B K-N2
19 Q-N5 ......

Black now has the pleasant choice between trading Queens with a good endgame, and avoiding the exchange by 19 . . . P-B3. I preferred the endgame, perhaps wrongly.

19 ...... N-N2

My move is somewhat inaccurate and allows White some counterplay on the Queenside. Best is 19 . . . B-Q2, necessary sooner or later, preventing P-QR4 and maintaining the initiative on both flanks.

20 Q×Q R×Q
21 P-R4! ......

The threat is 22 P-R5 followed by P-N4. In order not to let the Queenside be closed, I exchanged.

21 ...... P×P
22 B×P N×B
23 R×N B-Q2
24 R-R2 ......

But by now White has obtained some counterchances on the Queenside, which makes Black's task more difficult.

The rest of the game saw the chances switch back and forth, but it was surely not played by me in the best way. Fischer, though, superbly made the most of his chances and almost succeeded in getting out safe and sound: 24 . . . P-B5 25 N-Q2 B-N4 26 KN-B1 R-R1 27 N-K3 R-R5 28 K-N2 QR-R1 29 N-B3 R-R6 30 N-B1 N-B4 31 N-N3 B-Q2 32 P-N5 P-B3 33 P×Pch K×P 34 R-K3 K-K2 35 N-Q2 R-R7ch 36 K-N1 B-N4 37 R-R1 R/7-R5 38 K-N2 R-KB1 39 R-B3 R-QN1 40 K-N1 R-QR1 41 R-R5 R-QB1 42 R-R3 R-QR1 43 R-R5 R/1-R2 44 K-N2 N-N2 45 R-R1 P-R4 46 N/3-B1 N-B4 47 N-K3 P-R5 48 R-KR3 R×R 49 K×R N-Q6 50 R-R2 N×Pch 51 K-N3 N-Q6 52 N/3×P R-R1 53 N-N6 R-R3 54 N/6-B4 N-B4 55 K-B3 R-R1 56 P-N4 N-N6 57 N-R3 B-Q2 58 K-N2 B-N5 59 N/3-B4 R-QB1 60 N-K3 B-Q2 61 P-B4 R-QN1 62 P-N5 N-B4 63 N-Q1 K-Q1 64 N-QB3 R-R1 65 N-B3 K-B2 66 N-N5 K-N3 67 N-B7 R-KB1 68 R-KB2 P-R6 69 R-B3 B-N5 70 R-B2 P-R7 71 N×RP N×P 72 R-B1 B-B4 73 P-B5ch P×P and White resigned.

Of four games played with Black, three were won and one was lost — an excellent result. Of course, you should not jump to conclusions about the new defensive system; note that, as usual in the Ruy Lopez, Black starts out on the defensive. But if a defensive position has possibilities for active counterplay it always offers prospects of success, particularly when you consider that it is White who expects to achieve something.

An innovation always has a chance of early success. The theory of openings has advanced broadly, and players know the commonest variations by heart. In many variations exhaustive analyses extend deep into the middle game, but the player who knows "everything" runs into the danger of losing the capability for creative thought in the opening. To an extent it becomes a habit to play everything by the book.

A player who is presented suddenly with a new line must switch his train of thought — easier said than done. He tends to become unsure, even to lose the thread; rarely does he find the best countermove. And even if he does, he is still in an unequal position: his opponent knows the fine points of the system because of his home analysis, while the player facing the new variation for the first time must figure everything out over the board. It is this advantage that promises success to the player who can present his opponent new problems.

Unfortunately, in three of the four games above, after a few moves I faced the same problem as my opponents and did not know what to play next. This is because my preparation of the new line was inadequate, and therefore the advantage discussed above was nonexistent. In fact, an innovation need not be especially ingenious, but it *must* be well worked out.

To be sure, my new line against the Ruy Lopez could be called an entire system of development, rather than a tactical surprise. It would have been difficult, even with further prepared analysis, to foresee all the possible choices an opponent would make. Now, however, I will deal with an innovation in a specific variation where the game often develops in a forced tactical manner, so that home analysis can determine the consequences of a new move with a high degree of accuracy. If the homework is thorough and free of error, and if the innovation itself is not unsound, you can have high hopes for complete success.

A Sharp Variation

In the 1950s I spent some time on the Siesta Variation of the Ruy Lopez:

1	**P-K4**	**P-K4**
2	**N-KB3**	**N-QB3**
3	**B-N5**	**P-QR3**
4	**B-R4**	**P-Q3**
5	**P-B3**	**P-B4**

Black's sharp pawn advance was introduced into tournament play by Capablanca in 1928. Frequently played after that, it was thoroughly analyzed; the results of the games, supported by the analysis, led to the evaluation that White had somewhat better prospects. Therefore, this move lost most of its early popularity.

Favorable or not for Black, 5 ... P-B4 is very complicated. And where there are complications there is always the chance that a hole will be found somewhere in the analysis, or a possibility that had not been noticed before. I knew that Capablanca had an especially fine feeling for the openings, and therefore one must seriously consider his recommendations. Thus it is not surprising that I wanted to investigate this interesting variation further.

6 P×P B×P

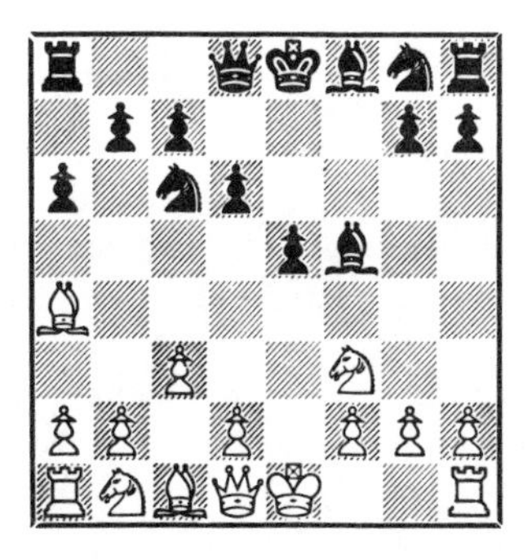

There are two ways for White to continue fighting for the initiative. In the early years 7 P-Q4 was played exclusively; this led after 7 ... P-K5 8 N-N5 P-Q4 9 P-B3 to a sharp position where practical play has shown that Black can develop an annoying initiative with 9 ... P-R3 10 P×P P×N 11 P×B B-Q3, or with the pawn sacrifice 9 ... P-K6 10 P-KB4 B-Q3. I will not analyze this further here, but I refer the interested reader to any good book on the openings.

In 1948, Panov came up with the bizarre idea of allowing the blockade ... B-Q6.

7 O-O B-Q6
8 R-K1 ......

If 8 Q-N3, theory gives 8 ... P-QN4 9 Q-Q5 N-Q5! 10 N×N N-K2 11 Q-B3 P-K5, or 10 P×N N-K2 11 Q-K6 B×R 12 K×B P×B 13 N-N5, after which White is supposed to take a perpetual check. For the time being, let us merely accept this judgment!

8 ...... P-K5
9 R-K3 ......

Now White threatens to break up the opponent's blockade by 10 N-K1 with an advantage.

This is the position that interested me. It is clear that Black cannot maintain his hold on Q6 and will have to sacrifice a pawn there. But it will cost White two moves to win that pawn and then his Rook will stand very awkwardly on Q3. I had the idea that Black could take advantage of this gain of time to develop a sufficient initiative. The question is: How should Black develop his pieces while White occupies himself with conquering Q3?

One plausible idea is 9 . . . N-K2 10 N-K1 N-B4, forcing 11 R-R3. Black has won several tempos, but his initiative is not easy to develop further. After 11 . . . B-K2 12 N×B P×N 13 B-N3!, the position may be judged as favorable for White. (Even here one need not follow blindly the opinion of the wise men; the variation has not been tested often enough in actual play and the position of White's pieces, scattered by bad development, challenges the analyst to seek stronger continuations for Black.)

I concentrated my attention on another possibility.

9 . . . . . . **B-K2**
10 N-K1 . . . . . .

In published works on opening theory I found only one game: 10 . . . B×N 11 R×B N-B3 12 P-Q3 P-Q4 13 R-R3 with advantage for White (Boleslavsky-Ragozin, Moscow 1949). But why capture on QN8? Surely the idea of Black's blockade was not this inglorious exchange, but a pawn sacrifice on Q6 followed by a considerable lead in development which should compensate for the material deficit. First, Black needs to interpolate a move.

10 . . . . . . **B-KN4**

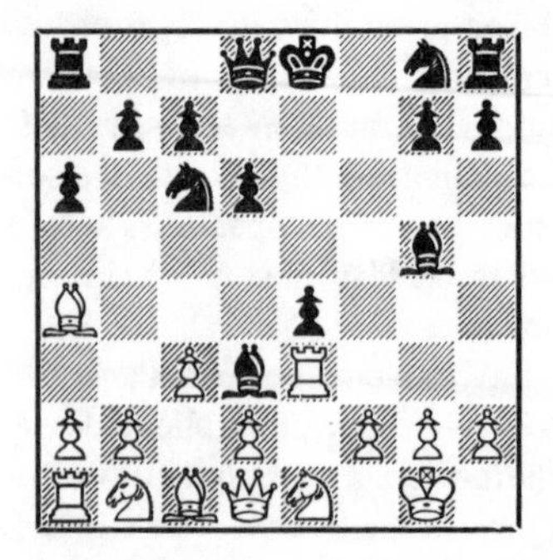

It is evident that this position contains forcing moves and direct threats; it can therefore be analyzed with accuracy. Only three moves by White need be considered, namely 11 R-R3, 11 R-N3 and 11 N×B. Here is the substance of the notes I made on these moves at the time.

(1) 11 R-R3! (this I considered, probably correctly, to be the best continuation for White) 11 . . . N-R3 (in practice 11 . . . N-B3 has been played instead; after 12 N×B P×N 13 R×QP O-O, Black's lead in development is sufficient for equality, as Smyslov-Lutikov, Moscow 1961, showed) 12 N×B P×N 13 R×P (13 Q-R5ch makes less sense on account of 13 . . . P-N3 or 13 . . . N-B2) 13 . . . O-O and I would say Black's lead in development offers adequate compensation for the pawn.

(2) 11 R-N3 (a plausible move which nevertheless leads, according to my analysis, to an advantage for Black) 11 . . . B-R5 12 R-R3 (if 12 R×P, naturally 12 . . . B×Pch, and

if 12 N×B B×R 13 N-N4 B×Pch! leads to the variation below. After 12 Q-R5ch, however, then 12 ... P-N3 13 R×P P×R 14 Q×R K-B1, and with his blocked Queenside White cannot hope for much) 12 ... B×Pch 13 K×B Q-B3ch 14 N-B3 (or 14 R-B3 P×R 15 N×B P×Pch 16 K-N1 N-K2, with an advantage for Black) 14 ... P-KN4! 15 P-KN4 N-R3, and Black's attack is more than enough compensation for the sacrificed pawn.

(3) 11 N×B. Against this move I succeeded in discovering an effective continuation of Black's attack: 11 ... B×R 12 N-N4 (apparently White obtains the advantage with this, since on retreats by the Bishop, White wins back the lost material with interest by 13 N×N. But it is again not so simple) 12 ... B×Pch! 13 K×B Q-R5ch 14 K-N1 N-R3! On this interesting position, to which the last more or less forced moves have led, the merit of the whole variation depends. White has two minor pieces for Rook and pawn and can win further material by capturing on QB6. The material seems, however, to be of less importance than the unprotected position of White's King, against which Black initiates a strong attack. 15 ... N-N5 is threatened, and 15 P-KN3 Q-R6 changes little.

After 15 N×N O-O! I left off analysis, holding the opinion that Black has a decisive attack on White's King. For example, 16 N-K7ch K-R1! 17 Q-K2 N-N5 18 P-KR3 N-K4!, or 18 ... N-B7; again, 16 P-KN3 Q-R6 17 N-K7ch K-R1 18 Q-K2 N-N5 19 Q-N2 Q-R4 with the inescapable threat of 20 ... R-B7; finally, 16 Q-K2 P×N (16 ... N-N5 also deserves attention) 17 B×P QR-Q1, and if 18 B×P P-Q4, etc.

Later analysis has proved most of these judgments valid, but in the earlier moves a correction was found to be needed. The advance 8 ... P-K5 is perhaps premature, since White does not have to play 9 R-K3, but can try with 9 B-B2! to break the blockade immediately. After 9 ... K-Q2 10 B×B P×B 11 N-Q4 (11 Q-R4 also deserves attention) 11 ... Q-R5 12 N×N P×N 13 Q-B3, White wins the pawn on Q3 with the better game (Gurgenidze-Sakharov, Leningrad 1960).

Therefore, Black must play the more accurate 8 ... B-K2, only after 9 R-K3 reverting to the main line with 9 ... P-K5. Here 9 B-B2 B×B 10 Q×B N-B3 is not dangerous for Black. 9 Q-N3 can lead to complications, but even this does not seem dangerous for Black, for example, 9 ... P-QN4 10 Q-Q5 Q-Q2 11 Q×B P×B 12 Q-B2 N-B3 13 Q×QRP O-O 14 P-Q3 N-Q5 15 Q-Q1 N×Nch 16 Q×N N-N5, and Black has adequate compensation for the pawn (Geller-Lutikov, Moscow 1961).

Despite the venerable age of this

analysis I have had no opportunity to test it in practice. But my training partner at that time, Master V. Mikenas, whom I had consulted to test my analysis, played the variation (against Klavin, Riga 1959) with the more accurate sequence 8 ... B-K2, and soon reached the position of the last diagram.

It was again confirmed that a well-prepared innovation has excellent chances for success. Klavin was not able to correctly calculate the complications and missed the best continuation 11 R-R3.

11	**N×B?!**	**B×R**
12	**N-N4**	......

With the erroneous notion that he was winning material.

12	......	**B×Pch!**
13	**K×B**	**Q-R5ch**
14	**K-N1**	**N-R3**

Klavin, taken by surprise, did not always take advantage of the defensive resources at his disposal, but he did succeed in finding a defense we had examined only slightly. It is no small gain to have recognized that the plausible 15 N×N O-O 16 N-K7ch K-R1! only loses time for White and should lead to a decisive attack by Black.

15	**P-KN3**	**Q-R6**
16	**P-Q4!?**	......

White finally does something for the development of his Queenside and having now the possibility of B-B4, he does something against the threat of a mating attack. However, the idea is not completely satisfactory because Black still maintains the initiative, and almost without material loss. He has a Rook and a strong passed pawn for two pieces, and his attack is by no means over. If White cannot get any material advantage from this variation, then his opening strategy is wrong. And his undeveloped Queenside is no credit to White's position!

As the continuation shows, White has hardly any prospects to equalize after the text. Is the variation really so bad for White, or can he defend better? This is not easy to answer, but I have the impression that the whole variation is favorable for Black. Perhaps 16 Q-B1!? offers the best practical chances. 16 ... O-O is prevented, and if 16 ... Q-R4 17 N×N. Black apparently has to be satisfied with 16...Q×Qch 17 K×Q O-Och, yielding him the more promising position after 18 K-K2 N-K4.

Thus it is seen again that innovations are rarely answered the best way over the board.

16	......	**N-N5**
17	**Q-K2**	**O-O**

This threatens mate in two starting with 18 ... R-B8ch. The reply is practically forced.

18	**B-B4**	......

18 Q-N2 can hardly be considered on account of 18 . . . Q×Qch 19 K×Q R-B7ch or 19 . . . P-K6. And instead of 18 . . . Q×Qch Black can play on for the attack with 18 . . . Q-R4. The pretty variation 19 B-Q1 R-B8ch! 20 K×R N-K6ch 21 B×N Q×Bch 22 K-B2 R-B1ch 23 B-B4 P-K6ch! 24 K×P R-K1ch 25 B-K5 N×B 26 P×N R×Pch 27 K-B4 P-N4 mate is certainly wonderful, but it is unfortunately not forced. Instead of 19 B-Q1, White plays the stronger 19 B-B4, after which Black comes out hardly better than after the simple Queen exchange, e.g. 19 . . . N×N 20 P×N P-KN4 21 P-KR3 P×B 22 P×N Q×P 23 P×P, and although Black does stand better, White has prospects of saving himself.

18 ...... P-KN4!

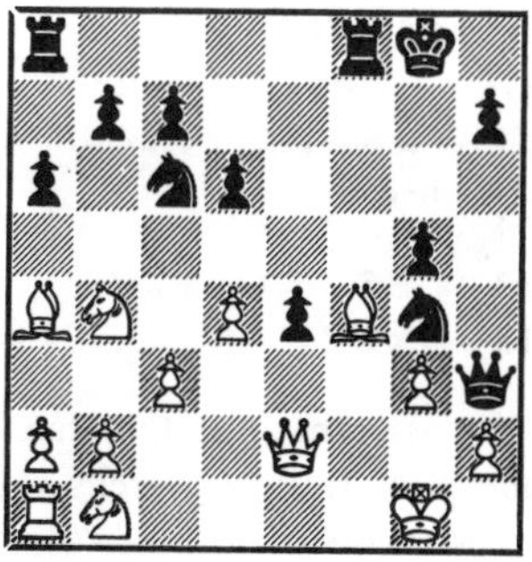

This is practically the deathblow; White cannot avoid further material loss. The effectiveness of the innovation is therefore proven. From the point of view of opening theory, the discussion could be broken off here, but since the position still has a wealth of tactical possibilities, let us analyze a little further.

White's QB obviously must not move, and to save the piece White must counterattack the Knight on White's KN4. 19 B-Q1 would obviously be inadequate on account of 19 . . . P-KR4, and after 19 N-Q5 P×B 20 N×KBP R×N 21 P×R R-KB1 Black is at least a pawn up.

19 B-N3ch K-R1
20 B-K6 ......

This is almost forced, as is Black's reply (after 20 . . . P-KR4 21 B×N P×B 22 B×NP, White would be all right).

20 ...... P×B
21 B×N ......

If 21 Q×N Q-R3! with decisive threats (22 N-Q2 P×P).

21 ...... Q-R3

White's situation is desperate, since Black's passed pawns are extremely strong and neither of them may be captured: 22 Q×KP QR-K1, or 22 P×P R×P 23 P-KR3 QR-KB1, in both instances with a decisive attack.

22 N-Q2 P-B6

This brings a quick decision. After 23 Q-Q1 N×N 24 P×N Q-K6ch 25 K-R1 Q-B7 26 B-R3 QR-K1 27 R-B1 P-K6 White resigned.

Despite this victory, the variation was not satisfactorily prepared. If you look at the notes on page 216, the inadequacy of the preparation against White's best reply 11 R-R3! is at once apparent. And even the position of the previous diagram was not analyzed well enough, as the game clearly demonstrated. Only the general evaluation was correct and this, to be sure, protected Black from unpleasant surprises. It would be good practice to play some training games starting from both diagrams, uncovering the possibilities hidden in the positions and working them out.

A Specific Opponent

The next example is an opening variation that was prepared for a specific opponent. Every player has his favorite openings and variations; what is needed is something to play against his pet opening. Everyone knows that no matter how often a variation may be used, no player can be said to handle it flawlessly every time. Looking for errors, even small ones, in the favorite variation of a future opponent is a well-known and often successful way of preparing opening theory.

Only rarely, however, can you succeed in refuting the whole variation. You have to look for ways to lead the opponent away from his known paths, and force positions on him that are less suited to his style, positions he will not feel comfortable in. If this is done, the prepared variation has, more often than not, chances of fulfilling its purpose.

When I was preparing for a game against Grandmaster Boleslavsky in the USSR Championship of 1957, the following variation of the Sicilian Defense was in vogue.

1	**P-K4**	**P-QB4**
2	**N-KB3**	**N-QB3**
3	**P-Q4**	**P×P**
4	**N×P**	**N-B3**
5	**N-QB3**	**P-Q3**
6	**B-KN5**	**P-K3**
7	**Q-Q2**	**B-K2**
8	**O-O-O**	**O-O**
9	**P-B4**	**N×N**
10	**Q×N**	**P-KR3**
11	**B-R4**	**Q-R4**

Here everything had been tried, from 12 B-B4, 12 Q-Q2 and 12 Q-Q3, to such bizarre moves as 12 Q-N1 and 12 R-N1, without shaking Black's formation substantially. Finally, a simplifying continuation was turned to.

12	**P-K5**	**P×P**
13	**Q×KP**	......

The assumption is that the endgame after trading Queens will be somewhat favorable for White.

Black has nothing better than exchanging on K4, for 13 ... Q-N3? is refuted by 14 N-R4! Boleslavsky's try against Gligoric in Zurich 1953 (13 ... P-QN3) is also not quite satisfactory. After 14 B-K2! Black is practically forced to exchange Queens, and 14 ... Q×Q 15 P×Q N-Q4 16 B×B N×B 17 B-B3 R-N1 18 N-N5 gives White a noticeable advantage.

13	......	**Q×Q**
14	**P×Q**	**N-Q4**
15	**B×B**	**N×B**

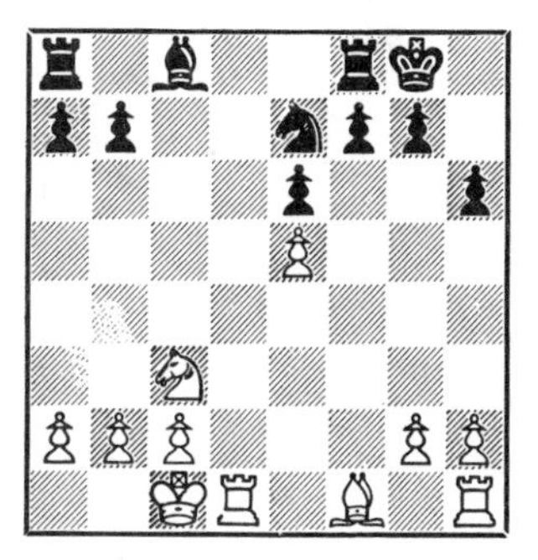

In the 1950s this position, critical to the variation, occured frequently in tournaments and was thoroughly analyzed. Usually White played 16 B-Q3. Grandmaster Boleslavsky liked to play this position with Black and usually defended with 16 ... N-B3 17 KR-K1 R-Q1. Later he developed his Bishop to Q2 and successfully repelled all attempts to refute his system of development.

I asked myself if there was any sense playing this variation against Boleslavsky, who liked to play the position and knew all its fine points. Obviously not, unless I could think up something new. But what if I could force him into another piece formation instead of Knight on QB3, Rook on Q1, and Bishop on Q2? That would be worth considering, since it is known Black has to play very accurately in this variation so as not to get a decisive disadvantage. And it would be difficult to find a very accurate defense over the board against a new line.

I began to search for a continuation where the usual piece formation would not be favorable to Black. Finally I arrived at the unusual 16 B-N5!?, after which 16 ... N-B3 is surely bad because of 17 B×N P×B 18 R-Q6, etc. But what is the point of the move if Black can drive the Bishop away immediately with 16 ... P-R3?

It was just that move I wanted to provoke; then I would play 17 B-Q3. If Black then chooses his usual means of development with 17 ... N-B3 18 KR-K1 R-Q1, there follows 19 N-R4!, and Black runs into serious difficulties on account of his weakness at QN3. If Black does not play 17 ... N-B3 and 18 ... R-Q1, and plays, for example, 17 ... P-QN4, I could find no way for White to obtain any tangible advantage. But White risks nothing with his Bishop maneuver and after 18 KR-K1 has the more active position. Why not try a new move, then, if nothing is risked by it? Black may fall into the positional trap and at least he will be steered away from his favorite and familiar continuation.

No sooner said than done! In our game the position of the diagram was soon reached, for Boleslavsky had been given no reason not to trust in the soundness of the variation. Then I confronted him with the new move.

16 B-N5!? ......

Boleslavsky sank into deep meditation and soon comprehended the idea of the move (19 N-R4!), but how was he supposed to develop?

He could not solve the new problems on the board in a satisfactory manner. Later analysis established that Black attains full equality with 16 . . . P-R3 17 B-Q3 P-QN4!, since 18 B-K4 R-N1 gives Black the annoying threat of . . . P-N5 followed by . . . R-N4. However, with 18 KR-K1 White might retain a promising position.

In the game Boleslavsky did not decide on 16 . . . P-R3 and chose a passive move.

16 ...... R-N1

This is already a success for White: first, Black is worse off than in the usual variations of this system; second, Boleslavsky has left his usual path of development.

17 KR-K1 P-QN3
18 P-KN3 ......

Black already has problems with the development of his Queenside, for the plausible 18 . . . B-N2 19 R-Q7 N-N3 20 B-Q3 gets him into difficulties. He tried leaving his Bishop on QB1, where among other things it controls the invasion square Q2.

18 ...... R-N2
19 N-K4 R-B2
20 N-Q6 ......

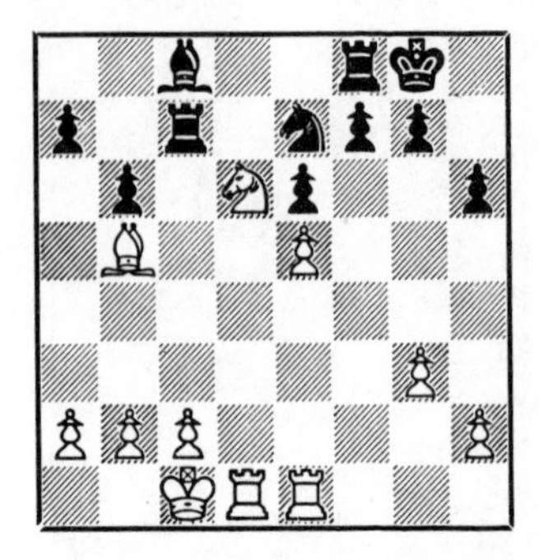

Naturally, White fixes his Knight on this strong foothold, and has attained a significantly better position.

We may cut the analysis short here as far as opening theory goes. White has achieved his objectives: his pieces are on effective posts, and he has nearly tied up his opponent. After Black's best reply, 20 . . . B-Q2, White can gradually advance his pawns on the Queenside and get a passed pawn there. Actually, Black makes it easier for him by losing two tempos and finally leaving the Exchange en prise: 20 . . . R-B4 21 P-QN4 R-B2 22 K-N2 B-Q2 23 K-N3 B×B 24 N×B R-N2 25 P-B4 KR-N1 26 R-Q6 P-R3 27 N-Q4 R-QB1 28 R-Q1 K-B1 29 P-QR4 R/2-B2 30 N-N5 and Black resigned.

The Stubborn Opponent

You should now have some idea of how a grandmaster prepares variations at home and uses them in play. Among grandmasters, there are of course different ways of preparing for tournaments, and I have limited myself to my own experiences.

To complete this discussion, I would like to mention one more type of game preparation, one that has purely practical applications and often leads to excellent results.

As I have mentioned before, all players have certain favorite variations or opening systems. But there are some players who for long periods like to play the same opening at every opportunity and against almost every opponent, even if the variation has been practically refuted. (This is not the same as the player who prefers certain specific lines; that player will choose different opening systems according to his opponents.)

The tactic has advantages: in particular, he knows the chosen opening or variation by heart, and he saves the time and energy he would otherwise have to spend in the opening. The trouble is that, since you know in advance what he will play, your opening preparation is significantly easier.

During the tournament, take a good look at the games of this opponent, noting which variation he is currently using. Then look for improvements in this variation, without paying attention to whether or not the variation is producing objective successes. If you find a flaw in one of the opponent's favorite variations, it is worth analyzing the position exhaustively. If you conclude that the now improved variation is to your advantage, there is every reason to try it in your game. Based on practical experience, the chances are good that the unsuspecting opponent will enter the studied variation. And if he doesn't, nothing has been lost. The attempt involves no risk.

An appropriate example is from the 1959 Candidates' Tournament in Yugoslavia, where Grandmaster Benko defended several times with the Breyer Defense in the Ruy Lopez:

1	**P-K4**	**P-K4**
2	**N-KB3**	**N-QB3**
3	**B-N5**	**P-QR3**
4	**B-R4**	**N-B3**
5	**O-O**	**B-K2**
6	**R-K1**	**P-QN4**
7	**B-N3**	**P-Q3**
8	**P-B3**	**O-O**
9	**P-KR3**	**N-N1**
10	**P-Q4**	**B-N2**

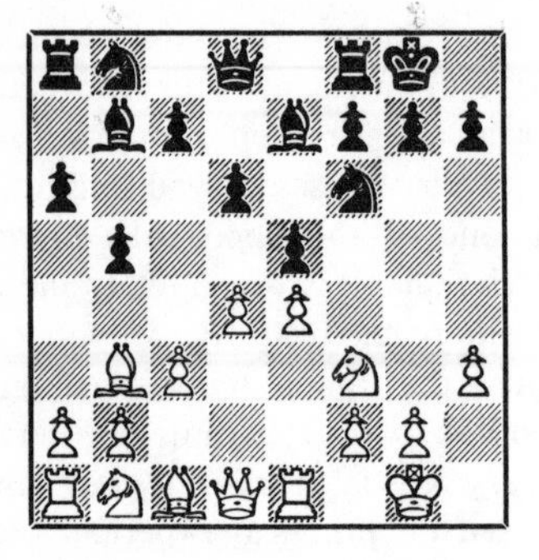

The idea of 10 ... B-N2, rather than the usual 10 ... QN-Q2, is clear. Black wants a compensatory attack on White's KP in case of 11 P×P. Olafsson, the first against whom Benko tried this defense, let himself be persuaded and refrained from 11 P×P. But 11 QN-Q2 QN-Q2 12 B-B2 R-K1 13 N-B1 B-KB1 led to a well-known position in the Breyer Variation where Black soon attained equality—and, in this game, Black finally obtained a decisive advantage. After such a win under his belt, Benko could be expected to use the system again.

Evidently Gligoric thought so, for when he encountered Benko several rounds later he opened with the Ruy Lopez. And Gligoric was right, for the position of the diagram quickly appeared on the board. Gligoric had realized that the exchange on K5 makes it ticklish for Black and he prepared the variation at home. After 11 P×P N×P he played 12 P-K6! Probably correctly assuming that after 12 ... P-KB4 13 QN-Q2 the advanced pawn on K6 represents more a strength than a weakness (later analysis turned up the pretty variation 13 ... P-Q4 14 N-B1 Q-Q3 15 N-K3 P-B3 16 N×BP! R×N 17 R×N P×R 18 Q×Q B×Q 19 P-K7ch and wins), Benko played 12 ... P×P, but he got the worst of it after 13 B×Pch K-R1 14 B-Q5 N-B4 15 B×B N×B 16 P-QR4, finally losing in the endgame.

After a few rounds it was my turn to play Benko. After he lost to Gligoric, it seemed to me he would not use the variation again, especially since immediate analysis confirmed that White has the advantage after 12 P-K6. But perhaps Benko would decide the variation is still good if he replaced 11 ... N×P with 11 ... P×P.

That certainly had to be checked. It seems Black has little to fear after 11 ... P×P, since the Queen exchange leads to simplifications with material equality, and if White doesn't exchange Black protects his KP with 12 ... QN-Q2 and has a good game. But it only seems so, for the Queen exchange actually exposes substantial weaknesses in Black's position. After 12 Q×Q Black cannot play 12 ... R×Q, since after 13 N×P Black's KBP is hanging and he loses a pawn without compensation. And after 12 ... B×Q White opens up the position further by the exchange of pawns in the center and will maintain strong pressure because of the weakness of Black's Queenside. Black may be able to equalize in time by prudent defense, but his task will certainly not be easy.

A candidates' tournament does not offer a favorable atmosphere for deep analysis. I contented myself with the above brief review and decided to try the variation, given the chance. And sure enough, Benko remained true to it, playing 11 ... P×P as I had hoped. (See the previous diagram.)

11	**P×P**	**P×P**
12	**Q×Q**	**B×Q**
13	**N×P**	**N×P**

Now I began to think about how to develop my pieces. 14 N-Q2 looked tempting, for after 14 ... N×N 15 B×N I could see no good way to parry the threat of 16 N×P. But 14 ... N-B4 is stronger; Black proceeds to develop his Queenside. I wanted to prevent that, at least for now, so I played a natural developing move.

14 B-K3 ......

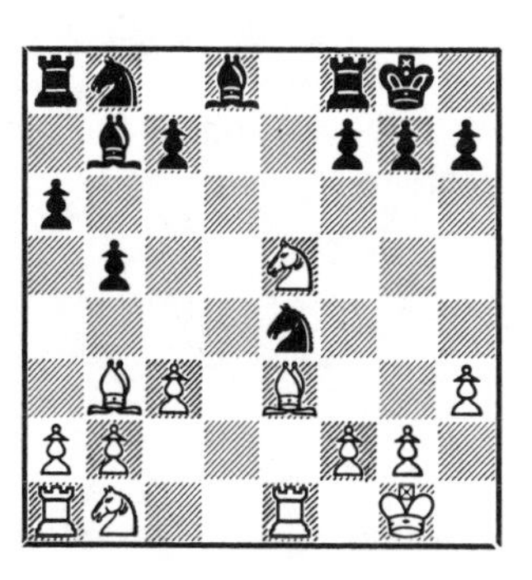

This move takes control of the important QB5 (14 ... P-B4! 15 P-B3!).

My evaluation of this position was correct. Black has to struggle with great difficulties. The immediate 14 ... N-QB3 is no good because of 15 B-Q5 N-R4 16 B×N B×B 17 B-B5 R-K1 18 R×B P-KB3 19 P-QN4! and White wins a pawn after 19 ... N-N2 20 B-Q4. Therefore, Black must move the Bishop on Q1, but where?

14	......	**B-KB3**
15	**N-N4**	......

Immediately attacking the Bishop. 14 ... B-K2 also had its drawbacks (15 N-Q2).

Black should probably now play the Bishop back by 15 ... B-K2 in order to avoid the exchange and fight for Black's QB4. Even then, White is better, for example after 16 B-KB4, but with prudent defense Black may be able to hold.

But you rarely find the best defensive moves in an inferior position without active counterplay. Black did not find 15 ... B-K2.

15 ...... **N-Q2**

Black is finally able to develop his Queenside, but his pieces, especially the KB, are precariously posted.

16	**N-Q2**	**N×N**
17	**B×N**	......

White has completed his development and now threatens, after the exchange on KB6, to penetrate with the Rook to K7.

17 ...... KR-K1
18 B-KB4 ......

This poses new problems for Black. How should he protect his QBP? The natural 18 ... P-B4, though it allows a very unpleasant attack with 19 KR-Q1!, after which 19 ... N-B1 20 N×Bch P×N 21 K-B1 clearly leads to a better endgame for White, is still probably the best Black has. But who would enter such an endgame willingly?

18 ...... R×Rch?
19 R×R R-QB1

It is understandable that Benko tries to protect the pawn, in order to safeguard himself more or less with 20 ... K-B1. Possible loss of a pawn by 20 N×Bch N×N 21 R-K7 can be avoided with 21 ... N-Q4! But such an attempt is usually connected with great danger. White finds a crushing move.

20 B-B2! ......

Black's problems are insoluble. 21 B-B5 is threatened, and no satisfactory answer is to be found. If 20 ... P-KR4 21 B-B5 anyway, and after 21 ... P×N 22 B×N followed by 23 B×KNP, White has one more healthy pawn and a good position. If 20 ... B-Q4 21 B-B5 B-K3 there follows 22 R×B! On other 20th moves Black must lose at least the QBP. In this difficult position Benko committed a blunder.

20 ...... P-N3?
21 R-Q1 ......

This wins a piece outright. Black resigned.

I could cite prepared variations and their practical application almost without end, and other tournament players no doubt have their experiences too. The examples cited should contribute something to making chess players more familiar with the art of preparation and convincing them of its importance. There are many grandmasters with different opening repertoires and methods of game preparation, but they will all agree that in today's master tournaments you can hardly count on success without good preparation.

INDEX OF OPENINGS

(continued on next page)

List of Openings

(Covering all Important Variations in each Opening)

- Sicilian
- King's Indian
- Grünfeld
- Nimzo-Indian
- English
- Reti
- Pirc
- Alekhine
- Ruy Lopez
- Benoni
- French
- Caro-Kann
- Dutch
- Larsen's
- Queen's Gambit
- King's Gambit
- Queen's Indian
- Benko Gambit

(additions will be made)

All "Chess Opening" theory is in a perpetual stage of change, some lines being successfully challenged and discarded, other lines improved, new and promising lines being continually discovered as thousands of games are played in current grandmaster tournaments.

Not only can your own game in your favorite Openings be greatly improved by study of the 100 current games in the Openings section selected by you, but you will gain new and valuable insights into the middle game play and end game play flowing naturally from each line through the individual game annotation and analysis-in-depth by the many world-famed grandmasters who will be serving on our Board of Contributing Editors.

The average cost of each full-size section containing all we have just described should be modest, but **send no money**—only your name and address on a postcard—so that you will be entered as a subscriber to receive announcements and full descriptions of each Openings section as they become ready for shipment. There is no charge for entering this subscription, and it puts you under no obligation. You later order only what you wish to order.

But you can help us (and yourself) by listing on the postcard the **5 top choices of Openings** you would like to see covered. This informal "straw poll" will guide us in the order of publication of individual Openings sections.

We are now preparing publication of sections covering some of the most popular Openings and commencing work on all the rest, and to receive announcements of each section as it becomes available, merely send your full name and address on a postcard to:

U.S., Canada, Mexico, Puerto Rico

R.H.M. Press
417 Northern Boulevard
Great Neck, New York 11021

Europe and elsewhere

R.H.M. Europe
110 Strand
London WC2R OAA, England